REMARKABLE, UNSPEAKABLE

NEW YORK

REMARKABLE, UNSPEAKABLE

NEW YORK

A LITERARY HISTORY

SHAUN O'CONNELL

BEACON PRESS

BOSTON

Beacon Press
25 Beacon Street
Boston, Massachusetts 02108-2892

Beacon Press books
are published under the auspices of
the Unitarian Universalist Association of Congregations.

Grateful acknowledgment is made for permission to reprint the following:
Excerpt from "The Bridge," from *The Poems of Hart Crane*, edited by Marc
Simon, copyright © 1933, 1958, 1966 by Liveright Publishing Corporation,
copyright © 1986 by Marc Simon, reprinted by permission of Liveright Publishing
Corporation; excerpt from "I Love Old Whitman So," from *White Shroud Poems,
1980–1985*, by Allen Ginsberg (New York: Harper & Row), copyright © 1986 by
Allen Ginsberg, reprinted by permission of the author.

99 98 97 96 95   8 7 6 5 4 3 2 1

Text design by John Kane
Composition by Wilsted & Taylor

Library of Congress Cataloging-in-Publication Data

O'Connell, Shaun.
Remarkable, unspeakable New York : a literary history / Shaun
O'Connell.
p.   cm.
Includes bibliographical references (p.) and index.
ISBN 0-8070-5002-4
1. New York (N.Y.)   2. American literature—New York (N.Y.)—
History and criticism.   3. Authors, American—Homes and haunts—New
York (N.Y.)   4. Literary landmarks—New York (N.Y.)   5. New York
(N.Y.)—Intellectual life.   6. New York (N.Y.)—In literature.
I. Title.
PS255.N5036   1995
810.9′327471—dc20   94-36415
CIP

C O N T E N T S

ACKNOWLEDGMENTS

ix

PREFACE

xi

FROM MANNAHATTA TO GOTHAM

New York as City and Image   1

OLD NEW YORK FADES

New New York after the Civil War   34

FIN DE SIÈCLE NEW YORK CITY

New York's "New People" and New Era   83

FLAPPERS AND PHILOSOPHERS

New York in the Twenties   121

BLACK METROPOLIS

Harlem from the Renaissance to the 1990s   163

NEW YORK CITY IN THE THIRTIES

New York's Hard Times   206

NEW YORK CITY'S GOLDEN AGE

New York After World War II   231

BRIGHTNESS FALLS

Contemporary New York   281

NOTES

309

INDEX

355

ACKNOWLEDGMENTS

I THANK WENDY STROTHMAN, THE DIRECTOR OF BEACON Press, for urging me to write this book. I thank the following colleagues at the University of Massachusetts, Boston, for their encouragement in this project: Sherry Penny, Chancellor; Fuad Safwat, Provost; Richard Freeland and Louis Esposito, deans of the College of Arts and Sciences; Susan Horton, Martha Collins, and Al Divver, chairs of the English Department; Professors Chet Frederick, Lee Grove, Duncan Nelson, and elsewhere, Professors William Barker, Arnold Gordenstein, William Keough, John McGrail, and Erwin Pally. I thank my students at the University of Massachusetts, Boston, and the Harvard Extension School for helping me to think about the writers and issues examined in this book. I thank the various audiences who have listened to me talk on "The Sense of Place." I thank Padraig O'Malley, the editor of the *New England Journal of Public Policy*, for publishing my essay "New York Revised" in 1992. I thank David Mehegan of the *Boston Globe* for inviting me to review books that contributed to my understanding of New York City's literature. I thank Dan Wakefield, author of *New York in the Fifties*, for providing me with an example of literary dedication and for encouraging me to complete the project. I thank Professor Carol Singley of Rutgers University for her sensitive and supportive reading of the first draft. Finally, I thank Susan G. Worst, associate editor of Beacon Press, for her attentive and intelligent editorial suggestions throughout the writing of this book, and Carlisle Rex-Waller for her careful editing of the manuscript.

PREFACE

New York City lies two hundred miles from Boston, the center of my universe. Long before I traveled to the City, I knew that New York was out there, somewhere over the horizon—that place, people said, so exciting to visit, but where you wouldn't want to live; that city where everyone lived next door to strangers; that metropolis in which *anything* could happen to you. When I read Yeats on Byzantium, I thought of New York City, for it too is no country for old men; it too is a land where lords and ladies hear songs of what is past, or passing, or to come.

If Boston took shape around circuitous by-ways, paved-over cow paths, then New York City rose over cross-hatched streets and straight, roaring avenues. If Boston treasured the burden of history and resisted change, New York City willingly razed its past and promised a bright future. If Boston is, or was, the Hub of the solar system, drawing cultural energies to its center, then New York City has become the Dynamo whose centrifugal force spreads its cultural influence far and wide. If Boston "is a grown-up city," a city that insists that its citizens take responsibility and prepare a moral accounting for the next world, New York City "makes one think of the collapse of civilization, about Sodom and Gomorrah, the end of the world."[1] Paradoxically, if Boston has been the also-ran Red Sox, New York has been the perennially victorious Yankees.

For me, Boston is Ted Williams, the Splendid Splinter: that savage, some-times surly, supremely confident and unmatched talent, that man whose every move on the baseball field, from his shoulder twitch in the on-deck circle to his long, loping stride around the bases, is still vivid in my mind's eye, though he hit his last home run in 1960. New York, of course, is Joe DiMaggio, the Yankee Clipper, the player we could not hate, no matter how many times he broke Bos-ton's hearts with crucial hits, for he was the most elegant athlete—with that per-fect, sweeping swing—we had ever seen. Williams personified individual per-fectibility and transcended the known limits of the game; DiMaggio chose his moments of excellence and suited his talents to his team's needs with devasta-ting effects. Ted shot off his mouth, while Joe kept his counsel. In many ways, DiMaggio's self-effacing style might have suited him better in stoic Boston—his bespectacled brother, Dom, patrolled center field and batted with colorless re-liability for the Red Sox—where Joe's line drives would have hammered Fen-way Park's short left-field wall. Ted's boastful, self-aggrandizing style—as a young player he was sometimes too bored to run down fly balls in left field, while Joe was always a supreme center fielder—might have better suited the Bronx, where his high-arcing hits, which were so often caught in the deep right field of Fenway, would have been home runs in the Ruth-shortened right field of Yan-kee Stadium. But the world is full of ironies and disappointments, my friends and I learned as lads growing up in and around Boston, our ears pressed against radios for crackling sounds of painful, late-season defeats suffered by the Sox at the hands of the merciless Yankees.[2] To be a Bostonian is to learn that true glory is not likely to be found in this world. To be a New Yorker is to learn that the world is there for those who seize the day.

Moments of high intensity flash in my memories of decades of visits to the City—Pee Wee Russell rip-roaring a clarinet solo through "China Boy" in some Fifty-second Street jazz joint; an evening in an Upper East Side lounge spent drinking and listening to a light-fingered pianist play Irving Berlin nonstop; Broadway and off-Broadway performances, from Paul Newman and Geraldine Page in *Sweet Bird of Youth* in the late 1950s to Jack Lemmon in *Long Day's Journey into Night* in the late 1980s; drinks in dozens of bars I could no longer find, even if they are still there; the reassuring quiet, but for the plash of the fountain, in-side the Frick; that white polar bear named Gus swimming laps in his pool at the splendidly refurbished zoo in Central Park; the rush of the Upper West Side; the delight of rummaging through the book-packed shelves of the Strand or shop-ping at Zabar's; the slow pleasures of wandering through the Village, trying to decide which Italian restaurant to enter, knowing they all would be wonderful.

New York City has been the site for some of my best and my worst times; I can never take the City casually. For years I expected too much of my visits, drank too much while I was there, and dashed about with feverish intensity in search of I know not what. These days, sober and slower, when I visit the City I stay with my friends, Marguerite and L. G. Smith. Their Central Park West co-op looks out over the Reservoir, where I run in slow, long circles, letting the wonder of the City—the extraordinary Park, festooned by colorful and some-times predatory New Yorkers, watched over by those dreamy, expensive spires—sink into my mind. Or, with Dan Wakefield, who has so vividly evoked the City in *New York in the Fifties*, I stroll Village streets where the presence of the past is palpable. The City teases, challenges, mocks, entices, and flashes with epiphanies that dissolve when I try to grasp them. Dangers and delights lurk around any corner. New York City turns me inside out; it works its way under my skin and demands constant attention; it breathes in my face like its panhandlers, and it yells in my ears like those angry men with squeegees who used to rush your car when you drove into the City. New York throws you around, like its cabs and subway trains. Its crowds of know-it-alls push past you as though you were not there. "Who the hell *are* you, anyway, and what do you want here?" the City seems to say.

This book—a visitor's view of the City, a constant reader's vicarious appreci-ation of what a number of American writers have made of the City—sets out to answer that and other questions, to portray what the City has meant in our imagi-nations, to show how those meanings have changed, and to understand what we now think of the City.

New York's literary image reveals that, more than any other city, it has embodied the American dream, the promise of life, liberty, and the pursuit of happiness. "The old island here that flowered once for Dutch sailors' eyes" constituted, in the words of F. Scott Fitzgerald, "a fresh, green breast of the new world," a place that pandered "to the last and greatest of all hu-man dreams"—inchoate, elusive dreams of transformation, perfectibility, and community.[3]

As we come to terms with New York City, with both what it has been and what it has meant to its most observant citizens, we better understand ourselves as Americans. While some would agree with Thomas Bender that "New York stands semi-detached, shunned but indispensable," most see New York as America's quintessential city.[4] "Other Americans insist that New York is not

America," says historian Oliver E. Allen, "but, like it or not, it is."[5] Indeed, because it contains American multitudes and contradictions, illustrating the nation's best and worst versions of itself, New York is the representative American city—heterogeneous, transient, energized by the dream of success, haunted by examples of failure. Though citizens from the provinces often recoil from New York City (at the same time tales from Sodom on the Hudson titillate them), the rest of the world has long equated Gotham with America.

As we read the text of the City—so extravagant in its tropes, so intense and varied in its rhythms, so bold in its presence, so encompassing in its reach, so firm in its grasp—it also reads us, or rather, shows us how to read ourselves. New York City is both fact and symbol. Its significance is delineated in a vast body of literature—testimonies, myths, fables, stories, plays, and poems that affirm its central symbolic importance. Writers' views of the City range from suspicion and hostility to celebration and wonder; the over- and-undertones of their styles, the reverberations of meanings between their story lines, the implications of their structural arrangements are important to a true understanding of how American cities have been known and judged. The City has taught writers, who in turn teach us, how to see ourselves, our nation, and its art anew. In the judgment of Alan Trachtenberg, "the presentational forms through which our writers have projected the city's disordered mind are thus of incalculable value as history and as art."[6] It is just those "presentational forms" that concern this study of New York City, the multiple acts of imagination that have given the City coherence in an impressive range of literary structures. "A city is experienced all of a piece," writes architect Witold Rybezynski.[7] Some writers, for whom New York City matters, agree, while others see the City as fractured and fragmented. It is the goal of this study to trace the contours and implications—from fragmentation to coherence, from celebration to denunciation—of the various experiences of urban place reflected by New York writers, writers who possess an acute sense of the City's symbolic importance, writers for whom the City is no mere backdrop but, instead, a living thing.

Above all, New York has been America's most important city because it reflects our nation's historical commitment to the democratic ideal that each of us holds the potential for excellence, that the free expression of many individual wills can compose a great and unified nation. Mario

Cuomo called this "the New York idea." Speaking for the city in which he was born and the state he then governed, Cuomo writes, "In the end, like much of America, New York is the place where people have overcome great odds to pursue the American Dream by earning their own bread, and more, in a free enterprise economy."[8] Emma Lazarus's famous words, which are inscribed on the Statue of Liberty in New York Harbor, evoke the idea of America as the last best hope of mankind. For many immigrants, New York City stands as their first sight and final idea of democracy.

> *Give me your tired, your poor,*
> *Your huddled masses yearning to breathe free,*
> *The wretched refuse of your teeming shore,*
> *Send these, the homeless, tempest-tost to me:*
> *I lift my lamp beside the golden door.*[9]

It is fitting that this articulation of the democratic ideal was expressed in a poem, for New York City became the nation's center of literary consciousness around the time Lazarus's words were inscribed. Walt Whitman, New York City's most ardent celebrator, welcomed foreign immigrants and aspiring poets through the golden door, for Whitman believed that a nation's culture should be measured both by its diversity and by its ability to produce great expressions. It is important, then, to know the American city—to understand New York City in particular—as a way to realize who we have been as a people, to learn where we now stand, and to imagine what may become of us. If the American democratic ideal cannot be persuasively articulated and plausibly lived out in New York City, for so long our largest and most culturally various city, then where in the nation—indeed, where in the world—can it be located? The literary record provides a way, perhaps the best way, to measure these questions, to know New York and, by extension, the nation.

Though, as we shall see, more writers have been pessimistic than optimistic about the possibilities of finding fulfilled lives in New York City—literature about the City has grown increasingly dystopian—all the writers here discussed have responded to its energy. All of these writers have seen the City as a challenge, an opportunity, a provocation, a compelling presence, to their literary imaginations. Often the City has brought out the best from those writers who most vigorously denounce it. New York City is constantly portrayed as a source of realization, for better or for worse. Its extravagance elicits equally extravagant literary responses. Surely no other American place has so inspired writers to rhetorical flights of praise and denunciation. In the words of Alfred Kazin, "This is where American writing came of age, if you like; or ceased to find the New World new."[10] New York City, taken as image and symbol, has long stood as a revealing paradigm of the American character; as New York City is seen, so too is registered each era's degree of faith in the promise of American life.

FROM MANNAHATTA

TO GOTHAM

New York as City and Image

THE ESTABLISHMENT AND DEVELOPMENT OF NEW YORK City, from its seventeenth-century settlement to the Civil War, was paralleled by an array of striking literary responses by authors who strove to account for the City's significance. The City came to illustrate, for better and for worse, the essential idea of the American experiment in democracy and culture. In the nineteenth century, the City was read, like a living text, by several eloquent foreign visitors and resident writers. In the eyes of its beholders, New York both was and was not America. The City has long been seen by some observers as a site and a spirit separate from and far ahead of the American heartland, but for most it has served as the source of values, styles, and habits that eventually took hold in the Republic. New York City, then, stands as an intensified model of America, a model defined in a series of compelling literary images, embodying the long reach and more limited grasp of the American dream of success and ideal of culture.

The expanding presence of the City and its developing significance in the minds of its most articulate observers engendered debate over its symbolic implications. In a variety of charged literary responses to the City, optimism and pessimism vied, sometimes within the same writer, often between literary factions. Conservative Whigs saw the City from one perspective in Washington Irving's day; liberal Young Americans saw it from another in the era of Herman Melville and Walt Whitman. Each side not only expressed its social values but also composed its literary visions in strikingly different ways. As New York's businessmen competed with each other, expanding the City uptown and extending its influence, at home and abroad, as America's center of trade and culture, so those who built cities of words vied for the authority to define New York. Out of the complex interplay of these forces, values, and visions emerges America's most resonant and impressive city.

NEW YORK CITY DID NOT BECOME AMERICA'S COMMERCIAL and cultural center until the time of Walt Whitman, the poet who extolled New York City as the soul of American democracy before the Civil War. "He who touches the soil of Manhattan and the pavement of New York," wrote Lewis Mumford, "touches, whether he knows it or not, Walt Whitman."[1] Before Whitman the literary idea of the City was coming into being; after Whitman the literary vision of the City as the embodiment of the democratic ideal of America, a conceit he established most persuasively, came under revision.

From its beginnings as a Dutch trading post early in the seventeenth century to its assumption of the role of America's most important city at the close of the Civil War, New York teased the imaginations of generations of observers, American and foreign, who saw in the City something new under the sun. For them New York, more than Boston or Philadelphia, meant America: where the wealthy and the poor were pressed together on a narrow isle, where the "pursuit of happiness" was dramatically evident, where newcomers in amazing numbers were transformed from foreigners to citizens, where American commerce and culture were increasingly centered. Social commentators and historians from abroad—Alexis de Tocqueville, Charles Dickens, Anthony Trollope, most prominently—helped to articulate the contours of the myth of the City and to define the terms by which its significance was debated. New York, a city of extremes, has seldom elicited temperate responses. Observers have imagined it in fittingly hyperbolic and often contradictory terms—as democracy's shining future or as America's doom. Such discusions were artfully amplified in the works of New York's major literary voices of this period: Washington Irving, James Fenimore Cooper, Herman Melville, and, most important, Walt Whitman.

New York's history during this period chronicles the City's developing character and hints at its defining themes. "Before it was anything else," wrote A. J. Liebling, "New York was a seaport, and before anything else it still is."[2] Built at the mouth of an extraordinary harbor, set at the confluence of two rivers, and located near the center of the colonies, New York predictably took on a commercial role. To paraphrase Heraclitus, the City's location became its fate. While English Puritanism gave rise to Boston, a city located two hundred miles to the north at the confluence of smaller rivers, and Quaker piety inspired Philadelphia, a city that lies one hundred miles inland on the bank of a modest river, no similar high-mindedness shaped the character and purpose of the Manhattan Island colony: "New York from the beginning was all business, a wide open trading town."[3] Because of the primary commercial occupations of its residents, New York developed an open-ended, heterogeneous, and cosmopolitan society, focused on this world rather than the next. In this regard, "New York was or was always becoming what the rest of the nation turned out to be."[4] From the first, money and entertainment defined the City, as Elihu Hubbard Smith, a seventeenth-century diarist, made clear: "Commerce, News, & pleasure are the giddy vortices which absorb the whole attention of our people." In New York, he decided, "the mass of inhabitants are too ignorant; & all, are too busy" for culture.[5] New Yorkers were not, then or later, noticeably shaken by such frequently expressed criticisms.

Manhattan Island was occupied by tribes of Algonquins when, in 1524, it was "discovered" by Giovanni da Verrazano, an Italian explorer. Verrazano's brief visit was followed in 1525 by Esteban Gomez, a Portuguese navigator who was representing the Holy Roman Emperor, Charles V of Spain. Thus, from the first, Manhattan attracted voyagers from many nations. However, it was the Dutch who came, conquered, and remained. In 1609 Henry Hudson, an English explorer working for the Dutch East India Company who was seeking a northwest route to the Indies, landed at a low peninsula at the entrance to New York Bay. A series of settlements that became trading posts were soon established in the territory, encompassing the island, which came to be known as New Netherland, with the city of New Amsterdam occupying its lower tip.

Peter Minuit, third governor-general of the Dutch West India Company, bought the island for sixty guilders in 1626, after which relations between the Dutch and the Algonquins rapidly deteriorated. William Kief's governorship included the Indian War of 1643–45, a period characterized by Dutch brutality. Peter Stuyvesant, seventh governor-general, took over in 1647 and supervised the small colony for its final seventeen years.

The Dutch left no noteworthy literary record, though Jacob Steendam, a Dutch poet, paid tribute to "New Netherland, thou noblest spot of earth."[6] Despite such praise, New Amsterdam failed as a commercial enterprise and was bankrupt by 1661. It also failed to sustain itself as a coherent society. In Manhattan public disorder (created by a populace that ignored health and safety ordinances) and official corruption (exemplified by embezzlement in high offices) began, not in the nineteenth-century era of the Tammany Hall Irish, but in the seventeenth-century reign of the Dutch.

In 1664 England's Charles II granted his brother, the duke of York, territory that included New Amsterdam. Within six months of this grant, the English were in control, immediately renaming the colony New York. A free press was established; the *New-York Gazette* (1725) and the *New-York Weekly Journal* (1733), under the editorship of Peter Zenger, began as newspapers in opposition to the government. A municipal structure of governance was instituted. Religious freedom, free schools, and a public library (1731) set a tone of openness and tolerance for the City's future. However, other events suggested more ominous prospects, particularly the 1741 "Negro plot." Blamed for setting fires, one hundred African-Americans were arrested, twenty-nine were burned at the stake, and eighty-eight were transported.

Under the Dutch many churches were established, though the Dutch Reformed Church dominated. Under the British the Anglican Church became central, though Quakers, Anabaptists, Catholics, and Jews also worshiped openly in the City. In 1685 William Byrd, visiting from Virginia, noted the City's many sects, "all being tolerated, yet the people seem not concerned what religion their neighbor is of, or whether hee hath any or none."[7] Taverns, gaming places, and houses of prostitution also flourished.

Sarah Kemble Knight, a Boston boardinghouse manager and a schoolteacher, visited New York during the winter of 1704–5. Her journals provide a valuable glimpse of the City at the beginning of the eighteenth century. "The city of New York is a pleasant, well-compacted place, situated on a commodious river which is a fine harbor for shipping. The buildings brick generally, very stately and high, though not altogether like ours in Boston," she wrote. "They are not strict in keeping the sabbath as in Boston and other places where I have been, but seem to deal with great exactness as far as I see or deal with." "They" also dressed in a gaudy fashion and drank "liberally" in New York City. She was also impressed by their fondness for sleigh rides. Indeed, New Yorkers "do not spare for any diversion the place affords, and sociable to a degree, they're [*sic*] tables being as free to their neighbors as to themselves." Though she looked upon New York as a place inferior to Boston, Madame Knight had to admit that the City was fun. "Having here transacted the affair I went upon and some other that fell in the way, after about a fortnight's stay there I left New York with no little regret."[8]

The City continued to evolve a sense of itself and a cultural presence. In 1754 King's College (renamed Columbia College in 1784) and the New York Society Library were founded.[9] However, Van Wyck Brooks suggests that "in its intellectual interests, the little brick town at the foot of the island was less advanced than Philadelphia. The Dutch, as compared with the Yankees and even the Quakers, had small regard for education, and, while Columbia College ranked with the best, the atmosphere of New York was distinctly commercial."[10] New York City did not begin to rival Boston as the moral, cultural, and political center of the colonies before the Revolutionary War.

In 1763 the Treaty of Paris resulted in peace with the French and the Indians, allowing New Yorkers to devote their energies to business and to urban expansion. Despite colonial unrest and anti-British sentiment, the population of the City increased from 12,000 to 21,800 between 1763 and 1771. In 1776 war came to New York City when George Washington's troops fought the Battle of Brooklyn Heights, then defeated the British at the Battle of Harlem Heights, though the British continued to occupy the City until 1783.

In 1774 Boston patriot John Adams anticipated the frequently expressed charge that New York was fast becoming too democratic and vulgar. Attending the Continental Congress, Adams complained, "with all the opulence and splendor of this city, there is very little good breeding to be found." Adams granted, "We have been treated with an assiduous respect; but I have not seen one real gentleman, one well-bred man, since I came to town. At their entertainments there is no conversation that is agreeable; there is no modesty, no attention to one another. Their talk is very loud, very fast, and altogether. If they ask you a question, before you can utter three words of your answer, they will break out upon you again, and talk away."[11]

That same year, a Scottish visitor also found New York to be a place where high and low cultures converged. When Patrick M'Robert visited the City, he noted that the entrance to King's College "is thro' one of the streets where the most noted prostitutes live." Also, he observed, "above 500 ladies of pleasure keep lodgings contiguous within the consecrated liberties of St. Paul's."[12] Indeed, New York was a city at odds with itself during the Revolution, for it housed both rebel Patriots and Tory Loyalists.

At the close of this near civil war, New York City became the capital of the new nation for fifteen months in 1789 and 1790. Had the City remained the nation's political center, the United States may have been influenced by New York to become more urban in its identity. Thomas Jefferson, the first president to serve his full term in Washington, feared just that: that American cities might grow to resemble European cities and become centers of inequity, vulgarity, and crime.[13]

Along with Alexander Hamilton, a pragmatic New Yorker, Jefferson worked out "the deal" that removed the capital, first to Philadelphia for ten years and finally to the Potomac, in exchange for the support of southern states in bearing a share of the national debt.[14] When New York's state capital moved to Albany in 1797, the City's residents were left free to concentrate on trade. New York City thus gained financial and cultural power in the new nation, but lost its political dominance. Thomas Bender suggests that these events led to New York's problematic relationship with the rest of America. "It was as if, having been shunned as being unsuitable for the nation's capital, New York decided to go it alone. New York would not be America."[15] Yet the City would become American by exerting its powerful influence over the nation as an image of urban democracy and as a center of cultural consciousness.

Throughout this period, indeed throughout its history, New York City remained a vital center of trade, as Tallyrand, the French diplomat who visited in 1790, noted. "Its good and convenient harbor, which is never closed by ice [and] its central position to which large rivers bring the products of the whole country, appear to me to be decisive advantages" over Philadelphia, which "is too buried in the land and especially too inaccessible to wood of all sorts," and Boston, which "is too much at the extremity of the country, does not have enough flour, and has not a large enough outlet for the commodities of the West Indies, except molasses."[16] New York City was the American marketplace.

In his sweeping social history, *The United States in 1800*, which comprises the first six chapters of *History of the United States during the First Administration of Thomas Jefferson* (1889), Henry Adams characterized New York City as a site of "innovation," a necessary counterpoint to the conservatism of Massachusetts and Virginia, among the states composing the young Republic. At the start of the nineteenth century, New York City was a small urban center, where some 60,000 citizens lived, fewer than those who dwelled in Philadelphia, though more than the relatively static population of Boston. For Adams, Boston was our Bristol, New York our Liverpool, and Philadelphia our London. New York City still lacked the essential ingredients of a metropolis—factories, stores, a public transportation system—and its citizens were huddled on the southern tip of the island, within a mile of the Battery, site of early Dutch and British fortifications and, in 1808, the erection of Castle Clinton. In 1800 it was a mere "walking city," crossed in twenty minutes, little more than an expanded village.[17]

In Henry Adams's view, young New York was indifferent to "the metaphysical subtleties" of discourse that preoccupied other states. "New York remained constant to no political theory. There society, in spite of its aristocratic mixture, was democratic by instinct."[18] Living at the end of the nineteenth century, in an era when he believed the old American families had been ignored, a time when massive immigration was transforming the nation he had known into a threatening mystery, Adams reviled New York for its lust for innovation and its leveling democratization. Although Adams treated New York with an even hand in his *History*, he was clearly out of sympathy with a city whose principal trait was a Hamiltonian readiness to strike political compromises and conduct business: "The political partnership between New York Republicans and Virginians was from the first that of a business firm; and no more curious speculation could have been suggested to the politicians of 1800 than the question whether New York would corrupt Virginia, or Virginia would check the prosperity of New York."[19] Either way, for Henry Adams New York in 1800 meant the corruptions of commerce—not the occupation preferred for the nation by the high-minded, Boston-based Adams family.

By 1815, after another war with Britain, New York City held 100,000 citizens, enough to supplant Philadelphia as the nation's largest city. Broadway extended for two miles up the island, and the City was ruled from an opulent City Hall, opened in 1811. Other signs of increasing civility were registered when the New York Academy of Fine Arts was opened in 1802 and the New York Historical Society was founded in 1804. However, in 1825 De Witt Clinton's Erie Canal opened a northwest passage of trade from the Atlantic to Lake Erie—at the cost of some eight million dollars and the lives of many immigrant laborers—which secured the City's commercial eminence in the new nation and overshadowed any other development of the period.

The first half of the nineteenth century in New York City was marked by a series of extreme conditions. (As a result, not only hyperbole, but dislocation and juxtaposition became standard rhetorical devices for describing the fluctuating and fragmenting life of the City.) The postwar economic boom of 1812 was soon followed by the bust of 1815–16, when soup kitchens were established. Another economic depression, in 1837, resulted in riots. In 1857, work on Central Park began, though some 40,000 laborers lost their jobs because of economic reversals the same year. New York suffered four epidemics between 1818 and 1834. Street gangs like the Dead Rabbits and the Bowery Boys preyed on the

City and tested the strength of its weak police force. On the other hand, in 1853–54 an "Exhibition of the Industry of All Nations," inspired by London's Crystal Palace Exposition of 1851, displayed the City as a world center of commerce.[20] Between the lines of the story of New York's growth struggles another tale was being written: the City's developing sense of itself as a resonant American symbol.

NEW YORK CITY BECAME A METROPOLIS IN AN AMERICA committed to a pastoral ideal. J. Hector St. John de Crèvecoeur, who emigrated to the American colonies in 1759 at age twenty-four, posed the crucial question: "What then is the American, this new man?" For Crèvecoeur, who lived on a farm in Orange County, New York, the American was one "who leaving behind him all his ancient prejudices and manners, receives new ones from the new mode of life he has embraced, the new government he obeys, and the new rank he holds. . . . *Here individuals of all nations are melted into a new race of men.*"[21] But Crèvecoeur, whose *Letters from an American Farmer* was published in 1782, could not envision the future of the American city. His "new man" was a farmer—a simple, dignified, honest, rural man. Ralph Waldo Emerson, who also saw in America an "asylum of all nations, . . . as vigorous as the new Europe which came out of the smelting pot of the Dark Ages," nevertheless said that he shuddered every time he approached the exploding metropolis of New York.[22] Crèvecoeur and Emerson, then, saw "America" fulfilling a manifestly pastoral destiny, becoming a democracy into which strangers from strange lands would "melt" into unity through their paradoxical dispersal to open lands, from sea to shining sea. However, despite the persistent mythology of rural America, the real test of American democracy would occur in the cities, in particular, in New York City, which attracted, in the words of Herman Melville, "all tribes and people" and blended them "into one federated whole."[23] Would citizens who had chosen the City as their destiny, then, have to melt down their distinctions into an undifferentiated whole to be fully accepted as Americans, or could they retain their group identities and live in harmony? New York City would hold the answer to this and to other questions about the fate of the nation.[24]

IN 1859, AT THE CLOSE OF THIS PERIOD OF ACTUAL AND symbolic development, the aristocrat diarist George Templeton Strong, contemplating the muddy beginnings of Central Park, that pastoral retreat at the heart of the City, wondered if New York, suffering from crime and poverty then as now, would survive by the time the trees in the Park matured: "Perhaps the city itself will perish before then, by growing too big to live under faulty institutions, corruptly administered."[25]

A series of nineteenth-century witnesses to the phenomenon of the "new man" in the new American metropolis helped to give lasting power to Strong's dire predictions for New York. Alexis de Tocqueville, Charles Dickens, and Anthony Trollope came from Europe to New York at different times, saw the City from different angles, with different prejudices and purposes; however, they all agreed that the City exemplified the problems of American democracy, a system of government in which, as they saw it, mob opinion ruled. The City, for them, held many wonders of the modern world, but it also illustrated the dangers of unchecked ambition for wealth in a people unrestrained by any faith in a class system. Their New York lacked ameliorating cultural institutions or arts; it revealed the absence of beauty in the gridlike arrangement of its streets, as Manhattan spread northward; sordid actions occurred on those streets and the frighteningly tall buildings turned them into dark and dangerous caverns. New York City, in differing degrees for each of these commentators, personified America's destructive element.

During his 1831–32 trip, in preparation for the writing of *Democracy in America*, Alexis de Tocqueville registered his doubts about the viability of democracy in the New World, particularly as it expressed itself in American cities. The French aristocrat granted that America had "no metropolis" as yet, but he looked warily at the growing size and influence of American cities, exemplified by burgeoning New York, which then contained a population of just over 200,000. Tocqueville recoiled from the "rabble" of "the lower ranks which inhabit these cities," a population that included many free blacks, who were treated as social outcasts, and immigrants from Europe, newcomers who brought Old World vices with them and were "ready to turn all the passions which agitate the community to their own advantage" by fostering urban riots. As a result, Tocqueville looked "upon the size of certain American cities, and especially on the nature of their population, as a real danger which threatens the future security of the democratic republics of the New World."[26]

As a corollary to his anxieties over majority rule in American democracy, Tocqueville saw no evidence of American literary culture. Excellence in the arts did not, he thought, mix with democratic tastes. "Americans have no poets," he affirmed, unaware that young Walt Whitman, the self-appointed poet of democracy in America, was then coming of age and preparing himself to celebrate the City and its citizens.[27]

CHARLES DICKENS VISITED THE UNITED STATES IN 1842 and described his trip in his *American Notes*, published the same year. He, like other European visitors of his day, was conditioned by suspicions about culture and democracy in the New World. America fascinated the English novelist with its splendor and its innovations, but it also shocked him with its corruptions and its deceits. Dickens was impressed by the booming commerce and the refined society of "the beautiful metropolis of America," and he was pleased by the ball given in his honor, which included some 3,000 people. Yet he was repelled by darker sides of the City: its slums at Five Points, "an ill-managed lunatic asylum, a bad jail, a dismal workhouse, and a perfectly intolerable place of police-imprisonment."[28] New York assaulted Dickens with an array of extreme images, stirred conflicting feelings, and finally pushed him to internal debate over its nature and significance.

Dickens's entry into New York, after a night-boat from New Haven, was marked by imagery of Whitmanian buoyancy: "The city's hum and buzz, the clinking of capstans, the ringing of bells, the barking of dogs, the clattering of wheels, tingled in the listening ear." Soon, however, attacks on other senses qualified his impressions of New York. The streets of the City, he discovered, were less clean and its houses were less colorfully painted than those he had admired in Boston. Although Broadway was a "great promenade," bursting with energy, the sunny, well-trod route, full of Irishmen who fueled the engines and paved the roads that ran through the Republic, held for Dickens a tinge of the satanic: "The pavement stones are polished with the tread of feet until they shine again; the red bricks of the houses might be yet in the dry, hot kilns; and the roofs of those omnibuses look as though, if water were poured on them, they would hiss and smoke, and smell like half-quenched fires."[29]

The year of Dickens's visit marked the building of the Croton Reservoir at Fifth Avenue and Forty-second Street, part of the water-supply system that became a model for large-scale systems throughout the United States and served as a lasting literary image of the City. In the next decade, behind it, was erected New York City's version of the Crystal Palace. (It was on the site of the Croton Reservoir, in 1911, that the main building of the New York Public Library would be dedicated.) New York was moving uptown and appointing itself with worthy cultural institutions. Charles Dickens saw and appreciated this side of the City, but he also noted the ominous presence of outcasts from the consensus of prosperity and progress. He was disgusted, for example, at a "Lunatic Asylum" and a nearby "Alms House" on Long Island, though he granted that such public institutions were necessary in such a large, commercial city: "New York, as a great emporium of commerce, and as a place of general resort, not only from all parts of the States, but from most parts of the world, has always a large pauper population to provide for; and labours, therefore, under peculiar difficulties in this respect."[30]

Though Dickens was celebrated on many occasions during his visit, particularly by the warring factions of the New York literati, who agreed only on Dickens's genius, he grew disillusioned, as his *American Notes* and a novel, *Martin Chuzzlewit*, later made clear. By late 1842, argues Perry Miller, "Dickens had commenced to realize that this was not the Republic of his imagination." Days after he was publicly harassed over the issue of international copyright at a dinner sponsored by the *Knickerbocker* magazine, a furious Dickens, feeling his property was being stolen by those who refused to acknowledge any point of view or interest beyond their own, wrote to a friend in England, "I believe that there is no country, on the face of the earth, where there is less freedom of opinion on any subject in reference to which there is broad difference of opinion than in this."[31] Thus Dickens's New York was at once too open in its actions, too callous in its public institutions, and too conformist in its opinions.

New York's perverse side became more evident in Dickens's night journeys through, as he saw it, its promiscuous and dangerous streets. "We have seen no beggars in the streets by night or day; but of other kinds of strollers, plenty. Poverty, wretchedness, and vice, are rife enough where we are going now." In a city where prostitutes and pigs wandered the streets, Dickens even imagined that the pigs might "wonder why their masters walk upright in lieu of going on all-fours? and why they talk instead of grunting?"[32] New York had become, in short, another version of Dickens's London; the City faded as an idealized alternative in an America no longer seen as a representation of utopia: "New York is a large town and . . . in all large towns a vast amount of good and evil is intermixed and jumbled together."[33]

Dickens's second visit, between the fall of 1867 and the spring of 1868, turned out even worse. He delivered an exhausting number of readings across America; by the time a farewell banquet was held for him at Delmonico's, in

New York City, he was visibly in pain. His success in the New World drove him to overreach himself.[34] Dickens never wholly recovered from this trip, and he died of a heart attack in 1870. For Charles Dickens New York illustrated the Republic of brutal facts, hard times, and imminent death.

BETWEEN THE TIME DICKENS FIRST VISITED THE CITY IN 1842 and the tour by another popular British novelist, Anthony Trollope, twenty years later, the population of New York, swelled by the arrival of vast numbers of poor immigrants from Europe, doubled to more than 800,000. New York had by then become a true metropolis, boasting many luxury hotels, fine restaurants (like Delmonico's), department stores (like A. T. Stewart's Marble Palace), and curiosities (like P. T. Barnum's American Museum), which could not be found elsewhere in the Republic.[35] Yet Trollope, whose account appeared in *North America* (1862), gazed in unqualified disapproval at the City, as he indicated in the opening sentence of his chapter on New York. "Speaking of New York as a traveller I have two faults to find with it. In the first place there is nothing to see; and in the second place there is no mode of getting about to see anything." Such reservations, we might reasonably conclude, should have left him little to say; however, Trollope's observations on New York were full and discriminating, though he did not comment on the phenomenon of massive immigration and he did fret fitfully about his own creature comforts. Above all, he believed that New York was quintessentially American. "That it is pre-eminently American is its glory or its disgrace, as men of different ways of thinking may decide upon."

New York was "American" for Trollope, as it had been for Dickens, in its freedom of expression, its acquisitiveness, its paucity of culture, and its lust for political power. The City lacked restraint: "Free institutions, general education, and the ascendancy of dollars are the words written on every paving-stone along Fifth Avenue, down Broadway, and up Wall Street. Every man can vote, and values the privilege. Every man can read, and uses the privilege. Every man worships the dollar, and is down before his shrine from morning to night."[36] The legend of Manhattan as a candid and mercenary place was fast taking shape.

Not that Trollope, who totted up his book royalties with the same scrupulousness that he counted his daily production of pages, scorned the pecuniary impulse. He granted that "the New Yorker has been true to his dollar, because his dollar has been true to him."[37] He admitted that with such acquisitiveness came civic obligations and wryly complimented New York for its munificence in establishing "hospitals, asylums, and institutions for the relief of all ailments to which the flesh is heir," through a system of "private liberality."[38] However, New York City for Trollope began and ended with money, not civic responsibility.

Trollope particularly disliked New York's omnibuses, on which aggressive women, trailing dirty hoop skirts, intimidated sheepish men (like him) into giving up their seats. Of course Trollope had few occasions to be so intimidated, because, as he noted, the City offered little to see. "In other large cities, cities as large in name as New York, there are works of art, fine buildings, ruins, ancient churches, picturesque costumes, and the tombs of celebrated men. But in New York there are none of these things. Art has not yet grown up there."[39] Nor did he hold out any hope that it ever would, for like Tocqueville, Trollope believed artistic excellence and democracy could not coexist: "To me it seems that such a political state [as democracy] is about the vilest to which a man can descend."[40]

Trollope did manage to travel far enough uptown to view Central Park, "the glory of New York," though he dryly observed that "its glory [is] in the mind of all New Yorkers of the present day," for the Park was "not fine, nor grand, nor beautiful." In its early stages, without fully grown trees, the Park seemed "all road"—all precarious potential, just as Stong had seen it.[41] The City, for Trollope, was better typified by its waterworks, hospitals, lunatic asylums, and schools. Anthony Trollope's New York City had neither art in its houses nor manners in its people, who revealed the dangers of unchecked liberty and undirected ambition.

DESPITE THESE GLOOMY ASSESSMENTS OF AMERICAN DEmocracy and American culture, considerable effort was invested between the Revolutionary period and the Civil War to advance both in New York City. In 1799, slavery was abolished. While De Witt Clinton was mayor (1803–15), the first black congregation was formed by members of the Methodist Episcopal Church, and all restrictions were lifted on Catholic worship in the City.[42] Above all, the open marketplace of the City provided opportunities, as Horatio Alger's parables would later demonstrate, for its citizens to pursue happiness in a wide variety of ways.

Of course, Alexis de Tocqueville was not alone in his concerns about the absence of literary culture in America. In the first issue of *Monthly Magazine* (1799), gothic novelist Charles Brockden Brown wrote an unsigned essay highly critical of his native land, "On the State of American Literature." Brown found the American character "superficial" and blamed "the love of gain" in post-

Revolutionary United States, which had become a "theater for *speculation*." America had no authors, concluded Brown, overlooking his own contributions to the profession.[43] In 1820 Sidney Smith, English clergyman and author, made his infamous attack on American culture in the *Edinburgh Review*: "In the four corners of the globe, who reads an American book? or goes to an American play? or looks at an American picture or statue?"[44] Clearly, for many observers of the American scene before and after Tocqueville, New York City had not begun to register a worthy cultural presence.

Resisting such withering dismissals, the generation of Washington Irving (1783–1859) and James Fenimore Cooper (1789–1851) did establish a lively literary presence in New York. Though both writers were ambivalent about this urban experiment in democracy, their involvement in its literary culture and their writings gave credibility to the City's nascent claims for cultural identity. Indeed, Irving was, in the memorable words of the Federal Writers' Project in 1938, "the first important American writer to deal with New York as material for literature, the first to animate it with the breath of a larger cultural world."[45]

Washington Irving, son of a Presbyterian deacon and successful merchant, was born in the spring of 1783, at the dawn of the postwar period. (He was named after the first president, who, in a chance encounter in New York, would pat young Irving on the head.)[46] Irving took a law degree, but he took more seriously his pleasures as a young man-about-town, becoming a connoisseur of the theater and the opera house. At age twenty he began to form his literary persona by contributing articles to the *Morning Chronicle*, a New York paper edited by his brother. The articles were written under the revealing name "Jonathan Old-style, Gent.," a figure of established manners and social arrangements. Along with his brother and James Kirk Paulding, another Federalist-leaning satirist, Irving began the *Salmagundi* papers, a journal of mixed commentaries and styles that was aptly named after a chopped salad. Irving, with the help of his family and friends, established the genre of "Knickerbocker Writing" in the first number of the *Salmagundi* papers in 1807. His *Salmagundi* essays, affecting the tone of knowing satire found in the *Spectator* papers, thus imposing upon humble New York the high cultural expectations of literary London, satirized the city of 60,000 in an aimless, extravagant fashion that a later generation of New Yorkers would call "camp," a style in which nothing is meant to be taken seriously. *The Whim-Whams and Opinions of Launcelot Langstaff, Esq. & Others* distanced Irving from his critical observations, allowing irony directed against the narrator to qualify the gentle satire of his observations. "Our intention is to instruct the young, reform the old, correct the town and castigate the age; this is an arduous task, and therefore we undertake it with confidence. We intend for this purpose to present a striking picture of the town; and as every body is anxious to see his own phiz on canvas, however stupid or ugly it may be, we have no doubt but that the whole town will flock to our exhibition."[47]

To gain even greater ironic distance from his native grounds, Irving included in *Salmagundi* the fictional comments of a bewildered visitor, Mustapha Rubadub Keli Khan, who, giving his impressions of Gotham, corresponded with a friend, the principal slave driver of his highness the Bashaw of Tripoli. By such a convoluted route, Irving set out to twit American politics. "Some have insisted that it savors of an *aristocracy*," writes Mustapha, while "others maintain it is a *pure* democracy; and a third set of theorists declare absolutely that it is nothing more than a *mobocracy*." Then the fabricated voice of Mustapha quickly yields to the authentic voice of Irving: "The latter, I must confess, though still wide in error, have come nearest to the truth."[48] Irving's subtle literary game was to flatter the prejudices of his aristocratic readers, in New York and London, while at the same time, by throwing his voice onto Mustapha, to protect himself from the charge of antidemocratic bias.

Though Irving's social views were indeed conservative, he gently mocked the City's Vanity Fair, of which he was a part, and he included a range of eccentric characters and stylized voices in *Salmagundi* to suggest that New York did sustain a worthy level of sophistication. Of the mass of New Yorkers, Irving knew little. In the view of Thomas Bender, "Irving barely confronted American society. In his writing style as in his residence, Irving was very little a New Yorker, even very little an American."[49] Yet Irving's works did help to demonstrate that there could be an American literature, and he did establish a New York tone of hyperbolic self-irony. It was also Irving who first named New York "Gotham," alluding to a village in Nottinghamshire and referring to the medieval tale in which the Three Wise Men of Gotham were in fact fools.[50]

Irving further developed his mode of whimsical irony and gentle satire in *A History of New York, from the Beginning of the World to the End of the Dutch Dynasty by Diedrich Knickerbocker* (1809). In the manner of Jonathan Swift's "A Modest Proposal," though with far more frivolous intent, Irving in this work perfected a literary persona whose style of narration undercuts his stated intentions. Diedrich Knickerbocker, confused and pompous, tries to make out of the history of New York an epic of national origins, an American *Aeneid*, but Irving makes it clear, through his narrator's bombast, that the history of New York has amounted only to a farce. As Peter Conrad shrewdly puts it, Irving's chronicler "gives New York a mock-epic before it has acquired an epic."[51] Irving's America had no worthy past and so, for Irving, it lacked a promising vision of the future.

Yet Irving's *History*, for all of its facetiousness, provided young New York with a sense of its rich potential, as is exemplified in Irving's playful but evocative description of the island first discovered by Dutch explorers, a passage that may have inspired F. Scott Fitzgerald's shimmering description of the New World's "fresh green breast."[52] In Irving's prose poem, Diedrich Knickerbocker describes the explorers who

> *were attracted by the transcendent charms of the vast island, which lay like a gorgeous stomacher, dividing the beauteous bosom of the bay, and to which the numerous mighty islands among which they had been wandering, seemed as so many foils and appendages. Hither they bent their course, and old Neptune, as if anxious to assist in the choice of a spot, whereon was to be founded a city that should serve as his strong hold in the western world, sent half a dozen potent billows, that rolled the canoes of our voyagers, high and dry on the very point of the island, where at present stands the delectable city of New York.*[53]

Irving, of course, was teasing in his tone, while Fitzgerald, speaking through *The Great Gatsby*'s narrator, Nick Carraway, was plaintive, but both writers envisioned the setting for the City as a woman's body, ample and inviting, and both writers imagined New York as an earthly version of the Heavenly City—an attainable aspiration. Irving, writing before modern Manhattan had evolved, saw pretension in the great expectations of New Yorkers, while Fitzgerald, writing after the disillusionments of the Great War, saw tragedy in the City's unfulfilled expectations. "MANNA-HATA," concludes the wry Knickerbocker, is "the island of Manna; or in other words—'a land flowing with milk and honey!'"[54] "For a transitory enchanted moment," wrote the rhapsodic Fitzgerald, "man must have held his breath in the presence of this continent . . . face to face for the last time in history with something commensurate to his capacity for wonder."[55] The vision of New York, then, is located in America's collective imagination, vacillating between the mock-epic description of Irving and the prose-poem threnody of Fitzgerald.

For Irving the settled island in New York Bay was nourished by far less exalted images from nature than those evoked by Fitzgerald. "No sooner was the colony once planted, than like a luxuriant vine, it took root and throve amazingly; for it would seem, that this thrice favoured island is like a munificent dung hill, where every thing finds kindly nourishment, and so shoots up and expands to greatness."[56] However, this dunghill greatness was a passing phase, for Knickerbocker ends his account with a portrait of the old and embittered Peter Stuyvesant: the man who tried to establish clear boundaries between New York and territories to the north; the man who, when war against the English colonists threatened in 1652, ordered that a fortified wall be built along the north side of town. (The path along this wall became Wall Street.) For lack of such boundaries and walls, the City lay open to the development of America; thus the Dutch colony, grown fat with its own successes, lost its integrity, suggests Knickerbocker. He could only hope that from his own remains would "spring many a sweet wild flower, to adorn my beloved island of Manna-hata!"[57] In his *History*, Washington Irving deflated New York's swollen self-image, but he also ascribed to the City theretofore unrecognized qualities of humanism and sophistication. In his deft deconstruction-reconstruction, Irving took away from the City any hint of traditional epic heroism with one hand, but he generously gave back to the City rare qualities of character and style with the other. Thus, though there is some truth in Peter Conrad's assertion that "Irving is New York's mock-epic unfounder, Whitman its belated epic founder," it must also be recognized that Irving was, however ironic, New York's true literary founder and Whitman, however celebratory, its belated denouncer.[58]

By the time Irving wrote *The Sketch Book* (1819), he had become a cosmopolitan figure. He lived for a time in England, where he was celebrated by Sir Walter Scott and was widely read. Irving's pseudonym, "Geoffrey Crayon, Gent.," revealed his reverence for the picturesque English past. However, he lacked the ironic distance from Crayon that he had previously established with Knickerbocker, so *The Sketch Book* blurs into sentimentality. It was, however, an immensely popular book on both sides of the Atlantic, establishing an attitude of Anglophilia that touched the nerve of Americans' ambivalence about their own nation and its democratic principles.

With *Bracebridge Hall* (1822), Irving had lost all critical distance on England; he wrote sentimental celebrations of English country life and Christmas rituals, fixing the image of quaint old England in the American mind. His myth of England, not New York City, was his true psychic home. Nothing that he would later write—travel books, biographies of Christopher Columbus and George Washington—qualified his alienation from the urban American experience. Irving's finest incorporations of the American scene into his fiction, "Rip Van Winkle" and "The Legend of Sleepy Hollow," tales based not upon American legends but upon German folk tales, revealed nothing about the American city he knew best. Yet Irving remained for New York an inspiring presence, a figure who showed that America could produce a writer of the first rank. Most important, Washington Irving put the "phiz" of New York City on the world's literary canvas.

WASHINGTON IRVING WAS HARDLY ALONE AMONG WRITERS who had difficulty in finding an adequate voice to describe New York City's dizzying transformations. Though Irving, it seems, was not interested in trying to compose original representations of his City and his nation, other writers were. William Cullen Bryant, who came from rural Massachusetts to spend most of his life in New York as editor of the *Evening Post*, dissolved New York into a romantic dreamscape in his "Hymn of the City" (1830), a poem deeply indebted to a sonnet by Wordsworth, "Composed upon Westminster Bridge, September 3, 1802." In "Hymn" the City was presented only to reveal surprising evidence of God's presence. "Not in solitude/ Alone may man commune with Heaven." Not only in "savage wood/ And sunny vale" is the Deity's presence felt. "Even here [in New York] do I behold/ Thy steps, Almighty!—here, amidst the crowd/ Through the great city rolled."[59] Bryant's New York, then, was redemptive in spite of its secular urbanity. But the verse that makes this claim was derived from English models, and the City still waited for an authentically native literary evocation.

James Fenimore Cooper's responses to New York were more anguished, original, and interesting. He is best known for his Leatherstocking tales, a series of novels written between 1823 and 1841, a saga of lost American primitivism and heroism, novels set in the forest primeval of upstate New York, the region around Cooperstown, the territory that enclosed the novelist's first memories. By 1822, when he was thirty-three, Cooper had established himself in New York City to enjoy the fruits of his popular success; in 1826 he left for seven years in Europe. While there he wrote *Notions of the Americans*, a book that generally praises his homeland. However, after his return in 1833, Cooper began to reexamine his commitment to democracy. *The American Democrat*, published in 1838, the same year that Tocqueville's *Democracy in America* appeared, incorporated Cooper's culture shock upon returning to an America he saw as materialistic, mediocre, and debased by democracy. "The tendency of democracies is, in all things, to mediocrity," Cooper claims in *The American Democrat*, "since the tastes, knowledge and principles of the majority form the tribunal of appeal." As a result, "we find in literature, the arts, architecture and all acquired knowledge, a tendency in America to gravitate towards the common centre in this, as in other things."[60] Americans, Cooper believed, had lost their regard for individuality and had abandoned the nation's original high purpose.

In 1838 Cooper also dramatized these attitudes in a novel, *Homeward Bound*, and its sequel, *Home as Found*. At the conclusion of *Homeward Bound* the Effingham family—composed of John and Edward, cousins, and Edward's daughter, Eve—arrive home from England and find themselves appalled at crowded, vulgar Broadway. In *Home as Found* Edward, a patriot, and John, a cynic, debate the condition of America. John's cynicism gets the stronger treatment from Cooper, who recoiled from New York's money-hunger and its needy new immigrants. After an extended and heavy-handed satire of New York society, which takes up the first seven chapters of the novel, Cooper sets the City ablaze. A fire consumes eight hundred buildings and, like a divine judgment, reveals the City's corruptions. "That Exchange, which had so lately resembled a bustling temple of Mammon, was already a dark and sheeted ruin, its marble walls being cracked, defaced, tottering, or fallen." From the pulpit a "faint voice . . . began to fancy that principles would once more assert their ascendancy, and that the community would, in a measure, be purified," but all hope for such a moral awakening in New York, Cooper's Sodom, was lost, "the infatuation [for wealth] being too wide-spread and corrupting to be stopped."[61] Cooper would not be the last writer to set an American version of the apocalypse in New York City.

AT MIDCENTURY NEW YORK WAS AMERICA'S FOREMOST city, central to the symbolic definition of the nation. Perry Miller, in his study of the New York magazine wars in this pre–Civil War era, wittily suggests that "the cause of Americanism was . . . fought as fiercely as was later fought the cause of America on Cemetery Ridge."[62] On one side magazines like the *Knickerbocker* stood for Federalist-Whig politics, European literary models, and respect for traditional class hierarchies—values encoded in a style of light irony, the better to please an audience of merchants, first families, and social climbers. On the other side the *Democratic Review* and similar publications supported Democratic politics, native American literature, and the extension of democratic opportunities—values encoded in works of strained originality, the better to please an audience of American chauvinists from many classes. Though debates raged between these two factions, with many shades of distinction in between, both sides agreed that it was only right and proper that the definition of the national character should be decided by New Yorkers. Both sides neglected to acknowledge the fact that Ralph Waldo Emerson had already declared American literary independence at Harvard in 1837, in his lecture titled "The American Scholar," insisting, "we have listened too long to the courtly muses of Europe."[63] Determinedly ignoring the established presence of the New England mind as a model, groups of New York scholars and writers set out to rescue themselves, and hence their City and their nation, from setting profit above culture. Then and later, writers who claimed New York City as the font of American culture risked the charge of provinciality.

The circle around Lewis Gaylord Clark's *Knickerbocker Magazine* was associated with Washington Irving's manners, wit, and regard for European social and literary styles. By 1840 Clark, the most stylish editor of his day, aided by his brother, Willis Gaylord Clark, had made *Knickerbocker* "the most influential literary organ in America—for years there was nothing that could compete with him."[64] Though the Clarks were committed to the goal of an independent American literature, their magazine spoke to gentlemen, thus associating money and power with culture. Washington Irving's "Geoffrey Crayon Papers" was properly published in the *Knickerbocker*.

Set against Irving and the Clarks were the Young America writers—in particular Herman Melville and Walt Whitman. Melville and Whitman, who probably never met, were born within thirty miles of each other, both on March 31, 1819. Whitman, the poet of urban perambulation, was born on Long Island, a pastoral setting resembling rural New England, while Melville, the novelist of ocean epics, was born at the clogged heart of Manhattan, on Pearl Street. Ambivalence would mark their attitudes toward the City.

Both Melville and Whitman, as Thomas Bender notes, "must forever be associated with the vision of literary democracy promoted by 'Young America' and John L. O'Sullivan's *United States Magazine and Democratic Review*" (1837–49), a Jacksonian publication allied with the reform (or Locofoco) wing of the Democratic Party.[65] O'Sullivan was a political journalist who coined the chauvinistic-imperialistic term "manifest destiny": he dedicated his journal, as he claimed in his manifesto, to "that high and holy DEMOCRATIC PRINCIPLE which was designed to be the fundamental element of the new social and political system created by the 'American experiment.'"[66] O'Sullivan published Nathaniel Hawthorne, John Greenleaf Whittier, Henry Wadsworth Longfellow, Edgar Allan Poe, and many others in his celebration of American democracy, nationalism, and literary independence.

The Young America literary group was initiated in the late 1830s by Evert A. Duyckinck, a prominent editor and book collector, and his circle in the Tetractys Club, a group devoted to literary nationalism that included William Alfred Jones and Cornelius Mathews. These three rich, young Columbia graduates, descendants of New York's first families, advanced the theory of a native American genius, though they had trouble providing an example. (Mathews and Duyckinck promoted the idea that Mathews, a novelist who saw himself as "the originator of the 'Young America' Party in the United States," might be that genius, but Duyckinck hedged his claim by calling for American critics who would discover a national bard. Notoriously, Duyckinck missed the true genius among them: Herman Melville.)[67] These Young Americans sought a forum in which they could call their forces to literary battle for the soul of America. Their journal, *Arcturus*, which ran from December 1840 to May 1842, was both New York's answer to Concord's *Dial* (1840–42), the house publication of American Transcendentalism, and Young America's response to *Knickerbocker* Whiggishness.

George Templeton Strong, a committed Whig and Knickerbocker, was disgusted with the efforts of these rash young literary democrats. "Literature pursued as an end," affirmed Strong in 1848, "for its own sake and not for the truths of which it may be made the vehicle, is a worthless affair."[68] But Duyckinck further advanced Young America when he became the editor of the *Literary World* (1847–53), where, taking exception to the pessimism of James Fenimore Cooper's *American Democrat*, he promoted his optimistic vision of the promise of democracy. He laid claim to Hawthorne, a committed Democrat, by publishing three of his tales, and Mathews insisted that American authors should deal with American subjects, thus slurring Irving and *Knickerbocker*.

Both Melville and Whitman were inspired by Young America's exhilarating spirit of literary nationalism. However, their best works, *Moby-Dick* and *Leaves of Grass*, take quite different tacks on the question of American democracy. Pessimism would increasingly mark Melville, while Whitman strained, with decreasing conviction, for a more positive vision of the country's mission. At the center of the consciousness of both writers was New York City, their daily reality and an ever-present symbol of America's future.

HERMAN MELVILLE'S NEW YORK WAS A PLACE OF DISILlusionments. Born during the 1819 postwar depression, his early years were nevertheless secure. The second son of Allan and Maria Gansevoort Melville, Herman was descended from lines of successful merchants and American patriots. When he was a boy, Herman's family moved from house to house, each time improving its social standing—from Pearl Street to Courtland, to Bleeker, to Broadway. The Melvilles employed a cook and a governess, attended the Dutch Reformed Church, and used a private carriage.[69] However, their affluent New York world fell apart in 1830 when Allan went bankrupt. The family then retreated to Albany, where the Gansevoorts gave them support. By 1832 Allan, overextended and distraught, was dead. Herman Melville would not forget that his father found ruin and death in the City.

On the opening page of *Moby-Dick*, Ishmael, the novel's narrator and Melville's reflective voice, finds himself in New York in a state of depression. With a "damp, drizzly November in [his] soul," he decides to go to sea. He walks along the City's harbor front, just as Herman as a boy had with his father. "There now is your insular city of Manhattoes, belted round by wharves as Indian isles by coral reefs—commerce surrounds it with her surf. Right and left, the streets take you waterward. Its extreme down-town is the battery, where that noble mole is washed by waves, and cooled by breezes, which a few hours previous were out of sight of land. Look at the crowds of water-gazers there." Melville's depressed, land-bound urbanites were personified in Ishmael, who yearns for the physical and contemplative release of a sea journey, for "meditation and water are wedded for ever."[70]

Melville shipped out of New York as a cabin boy aboard the *St. Lawrence*, a merchant ship, in June 1839. In England he was shocked by the poverty and sordidness of Liverpool, whose conditions he vividly described in a novel that retraces his route, *Redburn* (1849). On another voyage, in one of the best-known personal epics in American literature, Melville jumped ship in the Marquesa Islands; after living among "cannibals," he escaped, served on a whaler, then joined the crew of an American man-of-war before returning home. In all, Melville spent five years at sea, leaving New York far behind. Beginning with *Typee* (1846) and extending to *Pierre* (1852), Melville composed seven "romances" in six years; all but the last were sea centered. However, Melville would return to the City throughout his life for literary opportunities and for employment. In 1847 he settled with his family in a house on lower Fourth Avenue. In 1850 he purchased a farm, "Arrowhead," near Pittsfield, Massachusetts, but this experiment in country living ended in 1863, when, driven by the need for paying work, he traded the farm for his brother Allan's New York house, on 104 East Twenty-sixth Street.

In 1929, writing of this house, then still standing, Lewis Mumford described it as "a refuge from the city outside."[71] Melville spent the last years of his life in

New York either inside this refuge or resentfully employed as an inspector of cargoes on Hudson River docks, a forgotten man. "If I wrote the Gospels in this century I should die in the gutter," he ruefully noted.[72] Between 1866 and 1886, Melville was an inspector of customs on the Gansevoort Street pier, which must have bitterly reminded him of the decline of the Dutch in the City and of his own family, as well as his own diminished standing as an American novelist.[73] Melville's demanding and bleak works, which were criticized before the Civil War, were ignored during the Gilded Age.

When Melville was a young man, in the full flush of his powers as a writer, he was more optimistic about the possibilities of American life. He showed his Young American nativism in "Hawthorne and His Mosses," his tribute to another American romancer, an essay written while both of them resided in the Berkshires, in western Massachusetts, in 1850. Melville called attention to Hawthorne as an "American genius," noting, "it is for the nation's sake, and not for her author's sake, that I would have America be heedful of the increasing greatness among her writers."[74] So Herman Melville, anticipating the argument of Walt Whitman in *Democratic Vistas*, made the success of the democratic experiment in America dependent upon the nation's ability to acknowledge genius in its own writers. However, it is important to note that Melville wrote his tribute to Hawthorne, his praise of American writers, *not* in the persona of a New Yorker but in the guise of "a Virginian Spending July in Vermont."[75] He must have believed that he could make his argument for American genius more effective as a Virginian than as a displaced New Yorker. Virginia, after all, at least before the Civil War, evoked images of Jefferson and Monticello, while New York, for Melville, meant failure and banishment.

Melville's caustic vision of New York is best reflected in three works: a novel, a story, and a poem. In *Pierre; or, The Ambiguities* (1852), the tortured romance novel he wrote after *Moby-Dick*, Melville dramatized his reservations about New York. Pierre Glendinning, the novel's doomed hero, is a rustic innocent, a writer of love sonnets, from Saddle Meadows, a seeming Eden in upstate New York. "*It had been the choice fate of Pierre to have been born and bred in the country*," asserts Melville, with the emphasis of italics. "For the country is not only the most poetical and philosophical, but it is the most aristocratic part of this earth, for it is the most venerable, and numerous bards have ennobled it by many fine titles." The town, on the other hand, is "plebeian," characterized by its "dirty unwashed face," dressed in monotonous brick and stone; even the "town's sun is smoky paste, . . . and the town's stars are pinchbeck and not gold."[76]

Yet the beauteous country hides away its sins. Pierre, happily engaged to blond Lucy Tartan, from a prominent family, meets dark-tressed Isabel and discovers that she is his half-sister, born out of wedlock. Rather than allow his mother and his father's memory to be shamed by this revelation, Pierre, implausibly enough, pretends to marry Isabel. Along with a servant girl, Delly, later joined by Lucy, they seek a new life in New York City, where Pierre hopes to support all of them by his writing. But the young people encounter in the City an urban horror, similar to what Melville had witnessed in Liverpool: "The thieves' quarters, and all the brothels, Lock-and-Sin hospitals for incurables, and infirmaries and infernos of hell seemed to have made one combined sortie, and poured out upon earth through the vile vomitory of some unmentionable cellar."[77]

Further darkening *Pierre*, Melville included murder (when Pierre kills his threatening cousin, Lucy's brother), other deaths (of Lucy and Pierre's mother), potential incest (between Pierre and Isabel), and arrest (of Pierre). In the "low dungeon of the city prison," the Tombs, Pierre's world contracts to the size of Poe's pit: "The cumbersome stone ceiling almost rested on his brow; so that the long tiers of massive cell-galleries above seemed partly piled on him."[78] Before his sentence of death by hanging can be carried out, Pierre and Isabel, star-crossed lovers and doomed siblings, trapped in the City, commit suicide in his prison cell. In this overwrought novel, Melville codified his bleak vision of New York, mocking its false promises of success.

In "Bartleby, the Scrivener: A Story of Wall Street," a short story first published in *Putnam's* in 1853, the symbolic setting is a law firm on Wall Street. In this satire of New York commercialism, the firm's windows look out on the white wall of a skylight shaft on one side and "a lofty brick wall" on the other, making of the offices another version of the Tombs. The narrator, an elderly and smug lawyer, notes that the interval between the brick wall and his rooms "not a little resembled a huge square cistern."[79] Into this soulless setting enters Bartleby, a cryptic young man who is hired as a copyist. However, Bartleby soon repudiates his assigned work—"I would prefer not to," he says, perhaps echoing Henry David Thoreau's rejection of commerce as a means of sustaining life.[80] The narrator, while surprisingly kindhearted toward his mutinous employee, is baffled; finally, though reluctantly and guiltily, the lawyer has useless Bartleby removed from the law offices. In New York, business is business, as Melville well knew. Those who failed to do business were, like his father, removed or forced to toil in obscurity, as he himself had on the docks. Appropriating Dickens's *Bleak House*, a bitter urban satire just published in America, as one of his models, Melville dramatized the soul-smothering emptiness at the heart of the City. The case of Bartleby brings the once optimistic lawyer-narrator to a realization of life's limits: "I remembered the bright silks and sparkling faces I had seen that day, in gala trim, swan-like sailing down the Mississippi of Broadway: and I contrasted them with the pallid copyist, and thought to myself, Ah, happiness courts the light, so we deem the world is gay; but misery hides aloof, so we deem that misery there is none."[81]

Pierre and "Bartleby" can also be read as satires on the New York literary scene, which refused to recognize men of genius.[82] Melville attacked Duyckinck as a proponent of the prissy and the genteel, as one who eschewed "vulgarity and vigor," those prime Melvillian attributes; thus New York's Young America movement had subverted its own stated goals—the production of native American works of genius.

After the riots, largely by Irish immigrants, against the Draft Act in July 1863, which Melville imagined from his rooftop, he wrote the bitter poem "The House-Top," in which the City is portrayed as a landscape bereft of humanity.

> *The Town is taken by its rats—ship-rats*
> *And rats of the wharves. All civil charms*
> *And priestly spells which late held hearts in awe—*
> *Fear-bound, subjected to a better sway*
> *Than sway of the self; these like a dream dissolve,*
> *And man rebounds whole aeons back in nature.*[83]

Melville, himself a reluctant resident of the City, believed that vileness and pestilence had infested New York like swarms of diseased rodents, trapping the citizenry. While many Irish immigrants volunteered for service in the Union Army, others did not want to be drafted to fight and die for a cause they did not understand. Riots lasted for three days, causing many deaths and much destruction. Melville saw this protest as evidence of selfishness, an act of rebellion that turned New Yorkers into primitives; he was reminded of the cannibals he claims to have encountered in the Taipi Valley of Nuku Hiva. Herman Melville's New York was thus transformed, in his lifetime, from a place of civility, suitable for old, respected families, to a pit of savagery fit only for immigrants.

Walt Whitman was born in West Hills, near Huntington, in Suffolk County, Long Island, into a family of eight children, in 1819. Long Island thus became the starting point of his imagination. A poet of the shoreline, as he would be called, Whitman, from the top of Jayne's Hill, the highest point on the island, "could look over Great South Bay, Jones' Beach, and the ocean beyond—to the north he saw Long Island Sound and the Connecticut shore."[84] Whitman's poetry was characterized less by specific engagements than by the same broad perspectives he saw as a boy. In *Specimen Days* (1882), Whitman recalled his youth as a time of innocent wanderings through a pastoral Eden: "I roam'd, as a boy and man, and have lived in nearly all parts, from Brooklyn to Montauk point."[85] Forty years and more later, the sense of place of his childhood experiences was still vivid: "The soothing rustle of the waves, and the saline smell—boyhood's times, the clam-digging, barefoot, and with trowsers roll'd up—hauling down the creek—the perfume of the sedge-meadows—the hay-boat, and the chowder and fishing excursions;—or, of later years, little voyages down and out New York bay, in the pilot boats."[86]

In the spring of 1823, the Whitmans moved to Brooklyn, creating a new center for Walt, who became a stroller of streets as well as fields. In Brooklyn and later back on Long Island, he established himself as a printer's apprentice, a printer, and eventually a journalist. On the composition of *Leaves of Grass*, Whitman later urged his readers to "remember, the book arose out of my life in Brooklyn and New York . . . absorbing a million people . . . with an intimacy, an eagerness, an abandon, probably never equalled." All in all, it was, he said, "a great city," the epitome of "modern civilization."[87] In the 1850s and 1860s, he habitually crossed between Brooklyn and Manhattan on the Fulton Ferry. "What oceanic currents, eddies, underneath—the great tides of humanity also, with ever-shifting movements. Indeed, I have always had a passion for ferries; to me they afford inimitable, streaming, never-failing, living poems. The river and bay scenery, all about New York island, any time of a fine day," enthralled him.[88] In many important ways, Whitman was a crosser of borders, a man on the move who linked places and positions, unifying contraries in himself.

Whitman wrote a series of articles, titled "Brooklyniana," for the *Brooklyn Standard*, beginning June 8, 1861, pieces that showed his affection for the City. In Whitman's myth of New York, the island of Manhattan was singled out by the first settlers as a proper site for commerce, while Brooklyn was the prettier spot where these merchants preferred to live. The Dutch settlers "were ahead of all other races in their regard for moral and intellectual development." Revolution was bred in their blood. In these ways, implied Whitman, they prepared the way for bold democrats like himself.[89] Whitman argued that though New England and Virginia received primary attention in colonial accounts, New York's history holds "some points of interest transcending either of those celebrated beginnings of European colonization."[90]

Yet Whitman's Brooklyn was tinged with his nostalgia for an idyllic, pastoral past. Whitman allowed no vision of an expanded urban metropolis to enter his pages on "Brooklyniana." For example, he wrote revealingly of a painting, *Snow Scene in Brooklyn*, by Francis Guy, a Baltimore painter, a work that idealized the setting around Front and Fulton Streets, early in the nineteenth century. For Whitman, Brooklyn then resembled a New England village—"a thriving semi-country cluster of houses in the depth of winter, with driving carts, sleighs, travelers, ladies, gossips, negroes (there were slaves here in those days), cattle, dogs, wheelbarrows, poultry, etc.—altogether a picture quite curious to stand on the same spot and think of now."[91] Whitman's nervousness about the future of Greater New York was evident in this nostalgic evocation, even as the Civil War was about to change the City irrevocably.

In 1855, Ralph Waldo Emerson, the Sage of Concord, wrote to Walt Whitman, the obscure, Brooklyn journalist-poet: "I greet you at the beginning of a great career, which yet must have had a long foreground somewhere, for such a start."[92] That "long foreground" is Whitman's New York story. Among American writers, Whitman possessed a rare passion for the City.[93] If Melville's New York was a dark tomb, Whitman's was an open road. "Walt Whitman, a kosmos, of Manhattan the son," as he named himself in "Song of Myself," was a poet who presumed to speak for all of the City's citizens, indeed for all Americans.[94] In celebrating the masses, Whitman extolled their habitat, the American city, particularly New York City, where he lived and his countrymen congregated in greatest number. In *Leaves of Grass*, Whitman's much-revised spiritual autobiography, he sought his nation's soul.[95] This "Dweller in Mannahatta my city" declared in his preface to the first edition of *Leaves of Grass* "that the United States themselves are essentially the greatest poem," that New York City is essential to the establishment of both nation and poem.[96] "Whitman is New York's epic hero," writes Peter Conrad, "the individual who procreates and protects his tribe, the compound being in whose capacious 'Me myself' were housed and shielded."[97] However, Walt Whitman is also the poet of anxiety over the City's future.

Whitman's New York was far from idyllic: hogs wandered the streets, feeding from piles of garbage, and cows were herded through the muddy avenues. In the 1850s, Whitman complained of the state of the City in the *Brooklyn Evening Star*: "Our City is literally overrun with *swine*, outraging all decency, and foraging upon every species of eatables within their reach. . . . There is not a city in the United States as large as Brooklyn where the *cleanliness* and *decency* of its streets is so neglected as here." He also worried about youth gangs like the Pug Uglies and the Dead Rabbits, who wandered the streets attacking citizens. In 1856 Whitman described New York as "one of the most crime-haunted and dangerous cities in Christendom."[98]

Nevertheless, Whitman loved the City. He wandered its sidewalks, singing out its beautiful variousness, composing songs of himself for *Leaves of Grass*, even bellowing Italian arias from the tops of omnibuses while riding down Broadway. Whitman claimed that "the influence of those Broadway omnibus jaunts and drivers and declamations and escapades undoubtedly enter'd into the gestation of 'Leaves of Grass.' "[99] The City was his crowded stage, on which operatic voices blended in harmony and counterpoint. When he heard Donizetti's *La Favorita* during a summer evening at Castle Garden, for example, he sensed "a sublime orchestra of a myriad orchestras, a colossal volume of harmony" hovering over the City, a transcendent, orgiastic, mystic unity.[100]

Castle Garden reflected the promise of Whitman's vision for New York City. A former military site, it became first a public performance center (Jenny Lind, the "Swedish Nightingale," made her American debut there in 1850), and then, in 1855, it was made over to serve as the nation's chief center for processing immigrants. More than seven million immigrants passed through Castle Garden in all. After Ellis Island was opened in 1890, Castle Garden underwent another transformation, becoming the Aquarium of the City of New York, which must have pleased the sea-loving Whitman.[101]

In Whitman's day, "New York" referred only to the territory that would become the borough of Manhattan and part of the Bronx; Whitman focused on lower Manhattan, for above Forty-second Street New York was rural. Brooklyn was then an independent city.[102] Whitman, the philosophical and political advocate of union, proposed the merger of the two lesser urban centers into a Greater New York. In a memoir he suggested that "the general subjective view of New York and Brooklyn—(will not the time hasten when the two shall be municipally united in one, and named Manhattan?)—what I may call the human interior and exterior of these great seething oceanic populations, . . . is to me best of all."[103] (In 1894 Whitman's wish came true.) For Whitman, all-inclusive New York constituted a "kosmos"—"the heart, the brain, the focus, the main spring, the pinnacle, the extremity, the no more beyond."[104] He rebaptized the City, calling Long Island *Paumanok*, "the island with its breast long drawn out, and laid against the sea," and New York *Mannahatta*, "the place encircled by many swift tides and sparkling waters."[105] From "Out of the Cradle Endlessly Rocking," a poem scored to the rhythms of the ocean tides along Long Island's shoreline, his first memory; to "Crossing Brooklyn Ferry," in which his poetic persona joyously merges with the masses of Americans in motion; to "Mannahatta," a late poem in which he glosses the City's name, Whitman celebrated New York: "*A rocky founded island—shores where ever gayly dash the coming, going, hurrying sea waves.*"[106]

"Locations and times, what is it in me that meets them all, whenever and wherever, and makes me at home? Forms, colors, densities, odors," he wondered in *Leaves of Grass*, "what is it in me that corresponds with them?"[107] Whatever impelled him—personal passion, political conviction, mystical vision —Whitman exemplified what D. H. Lawrence termed the "great spirit of place" in his response to the City.[108] "Mannahatta! How fit a name for America's great democratic island city! The word itself, how beautiful! how aboriginal! how it seems to rise with tall spires, glistening in sunshine, with such New World atmosphere, vista and action!"[109] Whitman combined the contraries of New York—the aboriginal with the "tall spires," the region's Native American past and the City's ethnically diverse future.

In "Crossing Brooklyn Ferry," Whitman transcended the limits of his being, united himself with all those who "cross from shore to shore" in his own day and in the future. His mystic vision unites, indeed embraces, the City's masses—living, dead, and yet-to-be-born—into one amative whole:

> *Whatever it is, it avails not—distance avails not, and place avails*
> *   not,*
> *I too lived, Brooklyn of ample hills was mine,*
> *I too walked the streets of Manhattan island, and bathed in the waters*
> *   around it,*
> *I too felt the curious abrupt questionings stir within me . . .*[110]

"Crossing Brooklyn Ferry" extends Whitman's buoyant vision of the City into a redemptive vision of humankind.

Yet Lawrence, in *Studies in Classic American Literature*, was ambivalent about Whitman, for Lawrence doubted Whitman's full sincerity. The English novelist and poet praised the American poet and polemicist as "a great moralist," but he did not see Whitman as a true poet of the people. Rather, Lawrence saw Whitman as the poet of the "open road," ever moving on, alone, separate.[111] For all of Whitman's celebration of the urban—"Proud and passionate city—mettle-some, mad, extravagant city"—his dominant mode remained pastoral: "grass," not "streets," serves as the central image for his lifelong poetic saga.[112] For all of his rejoicing in the mass of Americans, particularly those congregated in the City—"the people, yes"—his dominant note was, as Lawrence suggests, per-sonal.[113] While it is true Whitman's poetry infused the City with pastoral pas-sion, it is also true that many of his prose responses were increasingly strained in their praise of the City.[114]

"I was never made to live inside a fence," Whitman wrote. New York City, in his eyes, provided the open vistas and democratic massings requisite to his po-etic imagination.[115] Yet he also pointed out New York's "pull-down-and-build-all-over-again spirit." This "rabid, feverish itching for change" he equated with "that father of restlessness, the Devil." At times even Whitman, for all of his commitment to optimism, despaired: "How it deadens one's sympathies, this living in a city!"[116]

Typically, Whitman aligned with *Democratic Review* writers who predicted great things for America. Like John L. O'Sullivan, Whitman assumed a "mani-fest destiny" for America. A Jacksonian Democrat, he denounced plantation and factory slavery. He became the poet of free-soil politics of the 1850s, opposing, as did the Free-Soil Party (founded in 1848), the extension of slavery into U.S. territories and the admission of slave states into the Union. Committed to the ab-olition of slavery, his attacks on the Fugitive Slave Law cost him his job as editor of the *Brooklyn Eagle*. In August 1852, Whitman wrote to Senator John Parker Hale of New Hampshire, the presidential nominee of the Free-Soil Party: "At this moment New York is the most radical city in America." However, in the fall election, Franklin Pierce, the Democratic candidate, defeated Hale and the Whig candidate, Winfield Scott.[117]

Whitman's paean to democracy, urban and pastoral, in *Leaves of Grass* was first published in counterpoint to the increasingly divisive atmosphere of the 1850s, passionate disagreements that would lead to the Civil War. His services as a "wound-dresser" during the Civil War, when he tended Union soldiers in Washington, aptly reflected his vision of the poet's role in times of crisis. His compassionate evocation of the pain and suffering of war inspired some of his best writing: the poetry of *Drum-Taps* (1865) and his prose memoir, *Specimen Days during the War* (1875).

Returning by boat to New York City from Washington after the Civil War, Whitman was struck anew by the wonder of Manhattan: "And rising out of the midst [of schooners and sloops], tall-topt, ship-hemm'd modern, American, yet strangely oriental, V-shaped Manhattan, with its compact mass, its spires, its cloud-touching edifices group'd at the centre—the green of the trees, and all the white, brown and gray of the architecture well-blended, as I have seen it, under a miracle of limpid sky, delicious light of heaven above, and June haze on the surface below."[118] Whitman sought in New York the images of unity he also hoped for in the restored nation.

Near the end of his life, in "Mannahatta," Whitman still celebrated all things associated with the City: its crowds, its tides, its ships, its "down-town streets" and businesses, its "immigrants arriving, fifteen or twenty thousand a week," its air and sun, its snows and ice, its beautiful people—"City of hurried and sparkling water! city of spires and masts!/ City nested in bays! my city!"[119] The hyperbole in Whitman's praise of the City—and by extension the democratic promise of American life—seems to override any anxieties he felt about the character and future of the city of his birth.

However, by the time Whitman published *Democratic Vistas* (1871), he had developed serious reservations about democracy in America, doubts that undermined his passion for New York City. He saw a "deep disease" infecting the land. As evidence, Whitman pointed to "the great cities," which "reek with respectable as much as non-respectable robbery and scoundrelism."[120] His reluctant task was to "look our times and lands searchingly in the face, like a physician diagnosing some deep disease." So far, he decided, democracy in America had resulted in material gain at the cost of spiritual loss. "I say that our New World democracy, however great a success in uplifting the masses out of their sloughs, in materialistic development, products, and in a certain highly-deceptive superficial popular intellectuality, is, so far, an almost complete failure in its social aspects, and in really grand religious, moral, literary, and esthetic results."[121] Whitman's pamphlet concludes in a rhetorically strained affirmation of faith in the future to redeem the Republic through the creation and appreciation of a bonding literature. In so saying, the persona of the pamphleteer, like the poet, merges into the democratic mass he began by denouncing but finally determines to affirm: "We see our land, America, her literature, esthetics, &c., as, substantially, the getting in form, or effusement and statement, of deepest basic elements and loftiest final meanings, of history and man."[122] However, Whitman's prediction of national redemption through art is qualified by the theme he sees as proper for a saga of democracy. "In the future of these States must arise poets immenser far, and make great poems of death."[123] Clearly the ravages of the Civil War, followed by the venality of the Gilded Age, particularly evident in America's "great cities," in New York City, tested even Walt Whitman's faith.

In *Democratic Vistas*, Whitman registered views about cities, democracy, and poetry in post–Civil War America that were not far from the bleak observations made by Tocqueville in Jacksonian America. Walt Whitman, the American writer who best loved New York, began and ended his days far from the City's heart. His movement from Long Island to Camden, New Jersey, was a journey of discovery—of his partially invented persona as an exuberant voice of the people, of the cities that straddle the East River, of America beyond the Hudson and Manhattan, of his mission as a redemptive national poet—and disillusionment. The Civil War, fought over the issue of union, showed him that America would not soon be united, even after victory by Union forces. New York City turned greedy and divisive, not, as he had hoped, selfless and unified. It cared more for money than poetry. "America demands a poetry that is bold, modern, and all-surrounding and kosmical, as she is herself"—a poetry, of course, like *Leaves of Grass*. "But America listens to no such poems."[124] America did not heed its self-appointed bard. Whitman had set his own standard of success when he said "the proof of a poet is that his country absorbs him as affectionately as he absorbs it."[125] He felt that his overtures of love—his poems, his myths of a unified yet various New York and America—were rebuffed by an increasingly divided populace. His last years were spent surrounded by a few disciples, but Walt Whitman died in 1892 a prophet without the honors he had hoped for in his own country, though he was not so thoroughly forgotten as was Herman Melville, who had died the previous year.

In the period that New York City was founded and developed, its character determined, the City became a symbolic center for American democracy and culture: a model through which the national experiment in governance and self-expression was examined by writers from abroad and at home. The City became the proper place for the American "new man" to compose a new self and begin a new life. As New York City went, so went the nation. New York became a city of high promise and disillusionment. New York, too, became a city that offered thematic and formal challenges for American writers—ranging from those, like Washington Irving, who looked to England and to the past for their cultural values and their literary models, to those, like Walt Whitman and Herman Melville, who looked inward, inland, and to the future for their identities and inspirations. In "Hawthorne and His Mosses," Melville insisted "that men not very much inferior to Shakespeare are this day being born on the bank of the Ohio."[126] In "City of Orgies," Whitman went further, declaring himself a literary redeemer, the nation's poet, located in the City: "I that have lived and sung in your midst," he promised New Yorkers, "will one day make you illustrious."[127] Whitman's evolving vision of the City, which moved from celebration to misgiving, embodies the arc of response followed by many other observers before and after him. At the beginning of its great career as the center of American culture, commerce, and the best example of the nation's commitment to the idea of democracy, New York City was greeted by its writers with enthusiasm, irony, doubt, and despair.

O L D   N E W
Y O R K   F A D E S

New New York

after the Civil War

WILLIAM DEAN HOWELLS, HENRY JAMES, AND EDITH
Wharton. These three novelists of manners mapped the social history of New
York City—and, by extension, American civilization—for half a century. These
stately and straight-backed artists came of age in the raucous era between the
Civil War and the Great War, when New York epitomized the brash America of
the Gilded Age—when robber barons and politicos, terms coined by Matthew
Josephson, bellied up to the Great Barbecue.[1] It was a time of extremes when
these writers sought their nation's moral center by telling tales about the life and
character of the City.

Howells, James, and Wharton were committed literary realists who nevertheless recoiled from the worst vulgarities of the new rich and granted the new
poor, mostly immigrants, their hesitant and ambivalent attentions. They
evoked a simpler, more pastoral and homogeneous City, a cohesive urban village, an idyllic old New York that never was, as the standard by which they measured the failures of new New York. They denounced the City's social pretensions and mocked the claims of economic and political opportunity in the
Manhattan of skyscrapers, ghettos, and street gangs. As New York grew into a
metropolis, these writers feared the City that was yet to be. However, at the

same time, these three American novelists saw New York as the vital center of the American dream, the place that best tested their capacities to imagine and to describe their changing homeland. They found they needed to revitalize the art of fiction to do the City justice. Each writer developed a fitting style, invented an expanded range of urban characters, and explored the forces that shaped the lives of New Yorkers.

They failed, of course, for New York City, overreaching writers' metaphors, defeats all efforts to portray its extravagance, and these three writers too often circumscribed their imaginative maps of the City to the areas, character types, and themes they knew best. New York City represented neither the urban villages they envisioned nor the cities of cultural light they encountered in Europe; indeed, New York was a city these writers could not fully comprehend. However, Howells, James, and Wharton went far in conveying a sense of New York as America's center city, the place that most openly revealed the nation's postwar soul and style, its boisterous manners and tantalizing promises. From James's *Washington Square*, set in the 1840s, through Howells's *A Hazard of New Fortunes*, set in the 1880s, to Wharton's *The Age of Innocence*, set in the 1870s but concluding in the early twentieth-century era of Teddy Roosevelt, these three novelists gave New York the respect of their considerable talents. Howells, James, and Wharton were drawn to the City as to a force field—a source of energy both for their nation and their writing.

They came from different social worlds and thus saw New York from different, if complementary, angles: Howells rose from the anonymous ranks of western pioneers and reformers; James emerged from the new middle class; Wharton freed herself from her inherited place in the City's rigid and rich upper crust. Each of them was tested to name and contain in art a city that was, in these years, expanding uptown on the peninsula of Manhattan, a city that was soon boiling over into the "outer boroughs," a city that was becoming recognized as the center of American commerce and culture. Between the Civil War and World War I, the era in which these three novelists wrote and set their best works, the "insular island of Manhattoes," as Herman Melville called it, blew open, like a volcano.[2]

William Dean Howells, Henry James, and Edith Wharton gave literary standing to the City in which they did not always feel at home. Paradoxically, the more eloquently they stated their reservations about New York, the more the City assumed symbolic standing in the American mind.

When writing about New York City, fact should precede fiction. Before examining Howells, James, and Wharton, a passing glance at the documentary record of two gentlemen of the City, Philip Hone and George Templeton Strong, whose diaries together cover half a century, carries us close to the realities of old New York's upper-class life and values, before and after the Civil War—the New York that Howells, James, and Wharton would evoke with such nostalgia.

In 1826, after his single-year term as mayor, Philip Hone began a diary that he wrote until his death, in 1854. George Templeton Strong, an important lawyer and a preservationist, began his diary in 1836 and kept it current until his death in 1875. Hone and Strong belonged to and believed in New York society. They typified the savage prejudices and the sustaining values, the vivid fears and the diminishing hopes of New York's ruling elite during the era when New York became America's Gotham. These men, the voices of the patrician class increasingly threatened by the economic and population explosions in the City, worried about a choice that had not been apparent earlier—between culture and society.[3]

On May 5, 1851, Strong noted that "half the city is being pulled down. The north corner of Wall and Broadway, an old landmark, is falling amid the execrations of pedestrians whom its ruins and rubbish drive off the sidewalk. The building on the north side of Trinity churchyard is to follow."[4] So it went: old New York, the coherent, eighteenth-century world of Washington Irving, was being razed and replaced before its residents' shocked eyes. Perhaps all diaries are momentary stays against transience, but a New Yorker's diary reflects a heightened sense of the ways all things, private and public, change utterly. What Alan Trachtenberg calls New York City's determined "destruction-construction" cycle, evident to Strong, has long been one of the ways it disorients its citizenry, making the familiar strange.[5]

Hone was a loyal Whig, well-placed in his mansion at 235 Broadway, between St. Paul's and City Hall; in this sanctuary the Hone Club held dinners for a group of gentlemen who scorned the excesses of the age of Jackson, opposed suffrage for women, and worried that the rantings of Abolitionists might lead to war. Inside their fine houses, they scorned the new immigrants, who, in their haughty eyes, littered the streets, accosted perambulating gentlemen, and vulgarized New York City.

In 1835 a major fire burned hundreds of buildings around Wall Street. U.S. Marines and militia guarded against lootings. Hone, calling this the greatest loss by fire since the burning of Moscow, somehow blamed it on Irish immigrants.

"This class of men are the most ignorant, and consequently the most obstinate white men in the world, and I have seen enough to satisfy me that, with few exceptions, ignorance and vice go together."[6] He feared that these new immigrants would bring a European level of filth, danger, and class division—fire and pestilence!—to New York. In rare moments of sympathy, Hone did imagine the disappointments of the stranger in a strange land. "Alas! how often does it prove to the deluded emigrant a land of broken promise and blasted hope!"[7] But he was certain that the newcomers threatened to ruin *his* New York. Indeed, they did help to transform the City into a place that Hone and his class could not easily recognize—a place where more than its patrician class could feel at home.

In 1857 Strong was worried about gang riots. The fight between the Dead Rabbits and the Five Pointers in July spread beyond the powers of the new metropolitan police force, so it had to be put down by the Seventh Regiment. Strong saw this street violence in ethnic and class terms in his July 5, 1857, entry: "It seems to have been a battle between Irish Blackguardism and Native Bowery Blackguardism, the belligerents afterwards making common cause against the police and uniting to resist their common enemy." He vindictively hoped, in the case of further trouble, that the police would "fire low."[8] Hone and Strong particularly hated the Irish immigrants because there were so many of them and perhaps because their Catholicism seemed to threaten old New York's Anglo-Dutch culture and values; what would become of their world when the Irish gained political power (as they soon did through Tammany Hall)? Certainly New York, as these old New Yorkers had known and loved it, would be dead and gone. Increasing democratization meant misrule by the masses to Hone and Strong. Thus majority power and patrician culture, conflicting versions of America, were juxtaposed in New York City.

Hone and Strong set themselves against change by trying to preserve emblems of the traditional urban village as sanctuaries for the future. Strong became the vice president of the New York Historical Society and he helped to foster a sense of the past in the City. However, Strong also enjoyed "Barnum's Gallery of Wonders," which represented the new side-show entertainments so pleasing to the growing masses and set the populist tone that would increasingly characterize New York. Strong also served on the Sanitary Commission, along with Frederick Law Olmsted, during the Civil War; as a result, he became a partisan of the Olmsted-Calvert Vaux plan for Central Park.

Small wonder that the Park would appeal to Strong, for Olmsted conceived it as a literal middle ground in a city divided between work and home. In "Public Parks and the Enlargement of Towns" (1870), Olmsted described the Park as an enclosed, pastoral refuge from the miseries of the City caused by commercialization. The Park should serve as an anodyne, a site of democratic encounter, and an escape valve for revolutionary impulses. "A city upon a hill within the city of destruction," Trachtenberg notes, "the park implied a scenario of recovered inner balance on one hand, and firm, elite supervision through corporate forms on the other."[9]

On June 11, 1859, Strong speculated that Central Park "will be a feature of the city within five years and a lovely place in A.D. 1900, when its trees will have acquired dignity and appreciable diameters." However, as we have seen, Strong was far from certain that the City would survive to see its trees grow, and the means by which Olmsted's dream would be realized contributed to the unpleasantness of city life: "Celts, caravans of dirt, derricks, steam engines, are the elements out of which our future Pleasuance is rapidly developing."[10]

Strong thought the street conditions of New York less severe than the sordid cities of England, but the picture he left of New York life belies the pastoral serenity found in the pages of James and Wharton. "We have our Five points, our emigrants quarters, our swarms of seamstresses to whom their utmost toil in monotonous daily drudgery gives only bare subsistence, a life barren of hope and enjoyment." Child prostitutes trooped Broadway. "And such a group I think the most revolting object that the social diseases of the great city can produce."[11] Far from callous, Strong was conscience-stricken by such sights. All that he witnessed on the streets of the City justified the documentary impulse behind his diary-keeping: "If one looks at FACTS," the realistic writer will find the composition of a diary "rather more of an achievement than the writing [of] another *Iliad.*"[12] New York, then, for Hone and even more for Strong, was a horrific place of disturbing change, yet the City presented a fascinating tableau of American energies and passions that required their testimony.

Though Walt Whitman might have passed him, unrecognized, on New York's streets, Strong searched without success for a poet who could portray the American scene. In his diary, Strong utilized the same literary devices of catalog and juxtaposition that would inform the efforts of Whitman and those of many writers after him who tried to capture the soul of the City.

> *There is poetry enough latent in the South Street merchant and the Wall Street financier; in Stewart's snobby clerk chaffering over ribbons and laces; in the omnibus driver that conveys them all from the day's work to the night's relaxation and repose; in the brutified denizens of the Points and the Hook; in the sumptuous star courtesan of*

Mercer Street thinking sadly of her village home; in the Fifth Avenue
ballroom; in the Grace Church contrast of eternal vanity and new
bonnets; in the dancers at Lewis Jones's and Mr. Schiff's and in the
future of each and all. [13]

New York required of its writers steady hands, fresh eyes, new forms, and more tolerance. For all of their disapproval, Hone and especially Strong *saw* New York, first-hand, with open-eyed wonder and shaped lasting records of their impressions.

At the end of his life, Strong placed his hopes for the future of New York in institutions designed to preserve its culture, particularly in the Metropolitan, a museum located on West Fourteenth Street: "Twenty years hence it will probably have grown into a really instructive museum." [14] Strong was right; the Metropolitan became just that in its uptown reincarnation in Central Park, by 1880 a location of majestic trees and cultivated open spaces that established patrician high culture within Olmsted's pastoral, democratic setting. Philip Hone and George Templeton Strong, despite their prejudices, despite their despair over the state of the City, not only preserved an accurate record of its past in their telling diaries, but also did much to assure New York's future.

WILLIAM DEAN HOWELLS, BORN IN OHIO IN 1837, WAS the self-educated son of a printer, a man who was devoted to free-soil politics and utopian communities. Howells was a young man from the provinces, in search of culture, self-realization, and American stories—first in Boston, then in New York.

On his first visit to the City, in 1860, Howells said he liked the impersonality of New York, but he decided that he preferred the "sense of neighborhood, . . . the secret of Boston" as he put it in a memoir. [15] He disliked the cynicism of the New York literati, the smart set who dismissed his idol, Nathaniel Hawthorne, as a shyster. Howells met Walt Whitman at Pfaff's, an uptown beer cellar, though Howells neither drank nor smoked. An illustrator for Howells's *Literary Friends and Acquaintances*, published in 1900, portrayed their brief encounter: Whitman, white-haired and bearded, looking closer to eighty than forty, wearing an open-necked shirt and a homespun suit, is leaning back in his chair and casually shaking hands with a young, slim, formally dressed Howells, who is bending slightly toward the poet, as though paying court. Howells later came to understand Whitman, the rough poet of New York's streets, in terms of his own

Boston-adopted gentility: "The apostle of the rough, the uncouth, was the gentlest person; his barbaric yawp, translated into the terms of social encounter, was an address of singular quiet, delivered in a voice of winning and endearing friendliness." Howells granted that Whitman was "a liberating force," but, looking back, he wondered just what Whitman liberated.[16] This would not be the last time Howells would seek out and then shy away from New York City's promise of release from his self-imposed moral and cultural rigidities.

The young Howells surveyed the City by riding around town on the omnibus. (By 1900, he noted, the "elevated roads" had replaced omnibuses.) Describing his early visits in his memoir, Howells waxed nostalgic for the old New York, the City as a village, which he barely knew, but intensely imagined. "Indeed, New York was really handsomer then than it is now, when it has so many more pieces of beautiful architecture, for at that day the sky-scrapers were not yet, and there was a fine regularity in the streets that these brute bulks have robbed of all shapeliness. Dirt and squalor there were aplenty, but there was infinitely more comfort."[17] When he became a New Yorker himself, Howells developed a more complex view. In *The World of Chance* (1893) he called the skyscraper "the necessity of commerce and the despair of art," recognizing the essential but problematic relationship between the two, particularly in New York City, the center of literary commerce.[18]

After such daunting first impressions, it is no surprise that Howells chose Boston over New York as the hub of his literary universe. After the Civil War he returned to New York from Venice, where he had served as consul, but he did not stay long. At the home of Bayard Taylor, in East Twelfth Street, Howells encountered Boston publisher James T. Fields, who persuaded him to come to Boston to work at the *Atlantic Monthly* as assistant editor in 1866. Though Howells began his writing career in Boston, he never forgot New York City.

Their Wedding Journey (1872), written in Boston when Howells was thirty-five, was self-consciously intended as his model of the way fiction should deal with real America. The novel's center of consciousness, Basil March, makes this clear. "Basil had said that as this was their first journey together in America, he wished to give it at the beginning as pungent a national character as possible, and that [as] he could imagine nothing more peculiarly American than a voyage to New York by a Fall River boat, they ought to take that route thither."[19] Though Basil and Isabel March, fictional surrogates for Howells and his wife, disagree over their mode of travel—finally they settle on a train journey through Worcester, Springfield, New Haven, and Stamford—it is clear that Howells wanted to show his readers that the journey to the heart of America began with the trip from Boston to New York.

When they arrive in New York in June 1870, the novel's newlyweds make an early-morning pilgrimage down Broadway. Isabel finds it "shabby" in comparison with Boston's Washington Street. But Basil is exhilarated by the panorama, witnessed from the front of Grace Church, of the "Niagara roar" and "human rapids" of crowds along Broadway. Yet his observations are ironic in tone, revealing his detachment and his (and Howells's) prejudices: "I'd have been willing to be an Irish councilman, that I might have some right to the pride I felt in the capital of the Irish Republic. What a fine thing it must be for each victim of six centuries of oppression to reflect that he owns at least a dozen Americans, and that, with his fellows, he rules a hundred helpless millionaires!"[20] Basil's sarcasm is directed at the Irishman, the Tammany Hall politician, and the editor's sympathy is saved for the millionaire—attitudes Howells would reexamine in his best New York fiction.

The Marches go to the Battery, where they see immigrants arriving. Basil wonders what it would be like to be "a friendless German boy" arriving in America: "What a smiling aspect life in the New World must wear to his young eyes, and how his heart must leap within him!" Yet the City is "too vast, too coarse, too restless" to be loved by the Marches. Though they briefly feel like Adam and Eve as they stroll along Broadway, they soon leave the City, no Eden, for Niagara Falls. Howells's complaints against urban America in *Their Wedding Journey* are mitigated by the newlyweds' buoyancy.

AT THE COMPLETION OF *THE RISE OF SILAS LAPHAM* IN 1885, William Dean Howells suffered a breakdown, perhaps in part the result of the irreconcilable conflict, portrayed in that novel of Boston, between new wealth and ambition for social status on one side and moral compromise and cultural overreaching on the other. Howells had built a grand, expensive house in Boston's Back Bay but suffered profound guilt over social injustices. After *Silas Lapham* was published, he committed himself contractually to Harper and Brothers, Publishers, and thus to New York. He also promised to write a monthly column, "The Editor's Study," for *Harper's Monthly*. New York City would provide no refuge for Howells from the conflicts he felt in Boston, but the City would inspire his best work.

In 1885 Howells traveled from Boston to New York to lunch with J. Henry

Harper, head of the publishing house, and agreed on a salary of $10,000 annually; in return he would write one short novel a year and a farce. For another $3,000, he consented to review books for the magazine. The agreement lapsed in 1891, but Howells continued to serialize works in the magazine and to publish at Harper and Brothers. He moved only gradually to New York, at first sending material from Boston to *Harper's*. Then, while residing in Manhattan during winters and in various New England sites during summers, he transformed himself—hesitantly, but definitively—into a New Yorker.

In his first "Editor's Study" column for *Harper's Monthly*, Howells imagined a comfortable, book-filled study as the proper setting for his erudite persona: "His vast windows of flawless plate look out upon the confluent waters of the Hudson and the Charles, with expanses in the middle distance of the Mississippi, the Great Lakes, and the Golden Gate, and in the background the misty line of the Thames, with reaches of the remoter Seine, and glints of the Tiber's yellow tide."[21] Settled in Manhattan, Howells, with Whitman-like expansiveness, thought of himself as living everywhere, a citizen of the world. In leaving Boston, Howells decided that he had helped to decentralize American literature and argued that America should have no literary center, that regionalism favored democratic variety and native speech. Still, he granted that "New York was the place" for the ambitious young writer from the provinces. "Once land him in New York and all would be gas and gaiters."[22]

Yet the City made him anxious. In the spring of 1888, Howells confided to a friend, "I have been trying to catch on to the bigger life of the place. It's immensely interesting, but I don't know whether I shall manage it; I'm fifty-one, you know. There are lots of interesting young painting and writing fellows, and the place is lordly free, with foreign touches of all kinds all through its abounding Americanism: Boston seems of another planet."[23]

IN EARLY 1890, HENRY JAMES WROTE TO HIS OLD FRIEND Howells to praise *A Hazard of New Fortunes*, his recently published novel of New York: "The life, the truth, the heat, the breadth and depth and thickness of the *Hazard*, are absolutely admirable." James had some reservations about some of Howells's portrayals of New York street life—"I mortally dislike the people who pass in it"—but he conceded Howells's authority over the American scene, which James thought he himself had permanently abandoned.

Sometimes James saw Howells as a provincial in his choice of America as his primary subject. In 1895 James was fascinated to hear, from Jonathan Sturgis, that Howells, while visiting Paris, had been overwhelmed by James McNeill Whistler's extravagant garden and exotic guests. During a garden party, Howells had laid his hand on the young Sturgis's shoulder and said, "Live all you can: it's a mistake not to. . . . This place makes it all come over me. . . . It's too late. It has gone past me—I've lost it. You have time. You are young. Live!"[24] Howells, overcome by Paris, seemed to suggest that neither could he "live" in New York. James was inspired to use Howells's words in *The Ambassadors* (1903) as the cry of a man who had remained too long at the American fair and, as a result, had missed the flower of life. In *The Age of Innocence* (1920), Edith Wharton, again echoing Howells, also portrayed such a New Yorker.

Just after the Civil War, when James and Howells were lean, ambitious young men, they walked the streets of Cambridge, Massachusetts, often as far as Fresh Pond, where they discussed the books they would write and speculated on prospects for their postwar nation. More than half a century after those heady literary walks, James praised Howells for his "studies of American life, so acute, so disinterested," novels that recalled "when we knew together what American life *was*—or thought we did, deluded though we may have been!"[25]

HOWELLS HAD MOVED TO NEW YORK, AND TO *HARPER'S*, IN the late 1880s, taking "the literary center of the country with him . . . from Boston to New York."[26] Boston, for Howells, was the realm of romance, an outlook derived from Hawthorne; the New England mind, reflected in fiction, was "true to an ideal of life rather than to life itself."[27] In Manhattan, the center of "life itself," Howells felt freer to advocate realism in fiction, as he made clear in "A Call for Realism" (1891): "But let fiction cease to lie about life; let it portray men and women as they are, actuated by the motives and the passions in the measure we all know." Be realistic about the ways people behave, record the ways they speak with fidelity, and all will be well, he insisted, with characteristic optimism.[28] New York, for Howells, was the landscape of the real.

To bridge the Boston–New York move, Howells began *A Hazard of New Fortunes* in 1888, for which he revived the autobiographical couple, Isabel and Basil March, from *Their Wedding Journey*. In *A Hazard of New Fortunes*, Howells sent them once again from Boston to New York. The novel has reasonably been viewed as Howells's Boston-conditioned view of "New York City and the commercial spirit that seemed to pervade the metropolis and to emanate from it, spreading over the rest of the land to the imperilment of high values." Perhaps Howells, the Ohio farm boy who transformed himself into a Bostonian, could not come to terms with the New York City of his day, but, instead, remained "the Bay State visitor, doing his best to be understanding and polite."[29] However, Howells's efforts to reflect New York's diversity, intensity, and crises in essays and fiction were inspired.

In *A Hazard of New Fortunes*, Basil March is invited by Fulkerson, a publisher, to give up the insurance business (Reciprocity Life) in Boston and to take up the editorship of a new literary journal, *Every Other Week*, in New York City. In Fulkerson's view "there's only one city that belongs to the whole country, and that's New York."[30] Howells seemed to agree. Indeed, his self-conscious reflections on New York as a proper subject for fiction are still widely praised. Kermit Vanderbilt, for example, called *A Hazard of New Fortunes* "the first extended treatment of New York art and society in the American novel."[31] Yet Howells's main characters, like himself, are reluctant and tentative New Yorkers. Isabel, a native Bostonian, thinks New York "so *big*, and *so* hideous!" that at first, despite Basil's enthusiasm, she refuses to move there.[32] Clearly the Boston–New York debate over where to live—in which city and then in which apartment in New York City—between Mrs. and Mr. March reflects Howells's own conflicting views. Boston represented traditional cultural values and restraints while New York City stood for new cultural energies and opportunities, "the poetry of the commonplace."[33]

When the Marches return to New York, fifteen years after the visit recorded in *Their Wedding Journey*, they are shocked at what the City has become. In Washington Square, the Marches see southern European immigrants as colorful newcomers, but also as outsiders, strangers to "the old-fashioned American respectability which keeps the north side of the square in vast mansions of red brick."[34] Place, even the distinctions between two sides of a public park, reveals class and character. The new El, particularly at night, seems to them an enthralling aspect of New York's vast theater. The Marches see particular drama in the glimpses of other lives in the windows they pass. They see the slums as places filled with vitality, the streets crowded with "jolly" peasants. Isabel prefers to think there is not any "*real* suffering—among those people." She does admit that the City is far filthier than it had been when they were there on their wedding journey, but the reassuring Basil says that they did not truly see it then.[35] No longer newlyweds preoccupied by their personal romance, the Marches' eyes are more open to the realities of the City.

Yet we can only wonder how much of the real New York City the Marches (or the Howellses) saw on their return visit. The City was teeming with immigrants and inequities—poor housing, political corruption, child labor—as Jacob Riis's

How the Other Half Lives, published the same year as was *A Hazard of New Fortunes*, revealed. Basil March, through whose eyes the reader views New York in the novel, seldom sees past the picturesque. Though Howells pleaded for the lives of the falsely accused Chicago anarchists of the Haymarket riot, he was curiously weak in his response to the urban poor. "Perhaps," wrote a contemporary critic of the novel, "his sympathy came from the kindness of his heart and from the conclusions of his study, rather than from close contact with the laboring classes in their everyday life. He was not a slumming novelist."[36] Still, Basil March's awareness of the City matured: "A sense of the striving and the suffering deeply possessed him; and this grew the more intense as he gained some knowledge of the forces at work—forces of pity, of destruction, of perdition, of salvation."[37] At least Howells assigned his hero and alter ego the best of intentions: to truly know the City.

Every Other Week is owned, Basil learns, by Jacob Dryfoos, a natural gas tycoon, a social climber who "came to New York . . . to spend money, and get his daughters into the old Knickerbocker society."[38] Dryfoos has hired Fulkerson to begin the journal in order to give his name respectability and provide his son, Conrad, who wants to be a minister, something practical to do. All this makes Basil feel manipulated, but he takes the job, for New York allows him to feel young again and the City releases his dormant ambitions—perhaps as it had for Howells. Howells's New York means opportunity, for good and for ill.

The journal's working staff, an odd lot, reflects Howells's determination to extend the range of his fiction with a cast representative of the social and political extremes of the City: March as editor, the dandyish and immoral Angus Beaton as art director, the Christ-like Conrad Dryfoos in charge of publishing, and Berthold Lindau, a radical German refugee who lost an arm in the Civil War, serving as translator. *Every Other Week*, from its office on Eleventh Street, places a special emphasis on life in New York. Conrad thinks "the city itself is preaching the best sermon all the time." But Basil does not fully understand.[39] Clearly New York is, for Basil, as it was for Howells, a psychodrama of conflicting perceptions and values, cautiously approached.

A strike of streetcar workers provides the climax of *A Hazard of New Fortunes*. Beaton would like to shoot some of the strikers as an example to other workers to keep their proper places in the social order. Fulkerson assigns Basil and Beaton to cover the "aesthetic aspects" of the strike. "I tell you it's imposing to have a private war, as you say, fought out in the heart of New York, and New York not minding it a bit."[40] Wall Street is indifferent to the 6,000 strikers, Dryfoos is pleased to find. When Conrad says he feels sympathy for the plight of the underpaid strikers, his father slaps him. Later Conrad watches police club strikers and assault Lindau. Pleading for peace, Conrad is killed by a bullet fired from a car and thus becomes a sacrificial victim of the forces that are pulling apart the City. Lindau's good arm has to be amputated. Thus, Howells implies, those who fight for social justice risk life and limb with no assurance of victory. Perhaps that is why Basil March, like Howells, retains his detachment, viewing the City as a performance and locating himself in the audience. In this way, although Howells's raw New York exposes all inequities and political passions, providing material for the moral realist, "*A Hazard of New Fortunes* is a novel about the scope that must be contained in the new American novel rather than the new novel itself."[41]

Though the calamitous events of the novel can hardly be said to radicalize Basil March, they do force him to contemplate the Darwinian determinism of City life: "Some one always has you by the throat, unless you have some one else in *your* grip." Is *this* what the Almighty intended? Basil objects to "the economic chance-world in which we live" but concludes that "conditions *make* character."[42] Thus the City qualifies but does not destroy his Christian idealism.

Despite its upheavals, the Marches eventually adjust to New York life; they accept, even celebrate, its dramatic extremes and condone its overt crassness: "The chief pleasure of their life in New York was from its quality of foreignness: the flavor of olives, which, once tasted, can never be forgotten."[43] In *A Hazard of New Fortunes*, Howells, the connoisseur of the commonplace, himself tasted the new, tart flavors of New York City. He extended his art into new thematic territories and he portrayed an impressive range of characters, those caught in the nets of changing social and economic "conditions." Yet Howells, like Basil March, his representative American, was finally unable to do more than glimpse scenes and problems from the passing window of an El. Howells, the committed literary realist, was still too much of a romancer to allow his alter ego to be sucked into the lower depths of the City; like Howells, March remains in New York City, making observations and drawing reassuring moral conclusions.[44]

Howells turned to utopian fiction to develop his views on New York's urban conflicts. In "Letters of an Altrurian Traveler" (1893), he describes the City through the eyes of a visitor, Aristides Homos, who writes from New York to a friend in Altruria about strikes and other conflicts, the results of mercenary competition. Homos finds New York marked by class divisions and ugliness. The Park is beautiful, but economic inequalities are evident.

In "Aspects and Impressions of a Plutocratic City," the Altrurian is horrified by the contrast between the opulence of Madison and Fifth Avenues and the squalor of the tenement districts near the Hudson. New York was a savage anarchy of unplanned buildings, vacant lots, and competing businesses. The Altrurian provided Howells with a fresh angle for his satire.

In *A Traveler from Altruria* (1894) and *Through the Eye of the Needle* (1907), Howells further dramatized his social conscience and articulated his responses both to urban strikes and to his life in New York. Altruria is an island, populated by Christians, founded by a member of the first Christian commune after Christ. In Altruria there are no labor unions and no inequities of wealth; indeed, there is no money, for each citizen works to achieve the common good. Altrurians also have eliminated cities, seeing that urban centers "were not fit dwelling places for men, either in the complicated and luxurious palaces where the rich fenced themselves from their kind, or in the vast tenements, towering height upon height, ten and twelve stories up, where the swarming poor festered in vice and sickness and famine."[45] *Through the Eye of the Needle* begins: "If I spoke with Altrurian breadth of the way New Yorkers live, I should begin by saying that the New Yorkers did not live at all."[46] Henry James would be struck by Howells's sense, in Whistler's Paris garden, of not having lived a full life in America; Howells went further, saying that no one in New York City truly lived.

Howells's best portrayal of New York is his straightforward memoir, "An East-Side Ramble," which reports his journey of the early 1890s into the most densely populated sections of the City, something of a *Pilgrim's Progress* through urban miseries, though he finds no City of Zion in the Irish and Jewish ghettos. In a crowded tenement of Irish immigrants, the fastidious Howells gazed at their unmade beds with stirrings of sexual anxiety: "They had always a horrible fascination for me. I fancied them astir with a certain life which . . . might have walked off with them."[47] Howells sought out patterns of restraint, not release. He praised the Board of Health for maintaining the principle that, "in a civilized community, the collective interest is supreme." He even envisioned the day when the board would "command the abatement of poverty when the diseases that flow from poverty cannot be otherwise abated."[48] This fine, felt statement, based on Howells's close observation of City poverty, was just the kind of sentiment he was seldom able to illustrate in his fiction.

In the "Hebrew quarter," the inquiring reporter began to adjust to the "normal" condition of poverty, even deeming most of its residents cheerful. However, he was moved anew by occasional sights of misery, like the sight of a girl scurrying like a rat out of a cellar: "I had to get away from this before I could regard them as wild beasts." But, then, "I said to myself that it was among such throngs that Christ walked, it was from such people that he chose his Disciples and his friends; but I looked in vain for him in Hester Street. Probably he was at that moment in Fifth Avenue." Howells, heavily ironic, preached no doctrine of "saving grace." Rather, he saw the journey as an occasion for realistic observations and a message of Christian socialism: "I have tried to report simply and honestly what I saw of the life of our poorest people that day. . . . Nothing but public control in some form or other can secure them a shelter fit for human beings."[49] Indeed, Howells urged a degree of public responsibility and governmental intervention in support of suffering citizens that New York would not see until the New Deal.

With the best will in the world, Howells could never wholly comprehend New York. It enticed him, intrigued him, inspired him, but he could not encompass its variety, its vulgarity, and its inequity. The City exceeded the reach of Howells's Christian socialism and the grasp of his realistic art. Yet Howells went further than any previous writer had in shaping a plausible and inclusive myth of the City; furthermore, he showed writers who followed him how to embody a parable of the American dream, its promises and its betrayals, in New York.

In 1871, Henry James, living in Cambridge, wrote about Howells in a letter to Charles Eliot Norton, who was then in Europe. James praised Howells's editing of the *Atlantic*, but he wondered about his limitations as a novelist, for he seemed, James thought, able to "write solely of what his fleshy eyes have seen," and all he chose to see was America. For James, America "will yield its secrets only to a really *grasping* imagination. This I think Howells lacks."[50] This rich and fruitful debate over the mission of the American artist would invigorate the work of both men for the rest of their lives.

Thirty-two years later, Howells, by then a longtime New York writer and the acclaimed "Dean of American Letters," received a packet of letters from Norton that included the 1871 letter from James. Perhaps Norton thought Howells needed to be reminded, by confronting James's admonition, of the strains in the nation and the failure of Howells's mission to describe convincingly the "smiling aspects" of American life. Howells responded to Norton defensively: "But I am not sorry for having wrought in common, crude material so much; that is the right American stuff. . . . I was always, as I still am, trying to fashion a piece of literature out of the life next at hand."[51] Howells's sure writing hand shaped much of the American idea, particularly its urban representation, though the "right American stuff" of New York City was, in the end, too rough and unshapely for Howells's high-minded art.

In 1920, four years after Henry James's death, Howells tried to give final shape to his impressions of their literary relationship in an "Easy Chair" piece titled "The American James." His last published words before his own death, "The American James" memorialized those days, more than half a century before, of passionate intensity when he and his friend had walked and talked their way from Cambridge to Fresh Pond. Thus William Dean Howells, that realistic chronicler of American urban life, ended his days with dreams of pastoral felicities. In fact and in imagination, both James and Howells walked away from the American city; each, sooner or later, recoiled from New York and all it meant.

DURING THE HONE ERA, IN 1842, HENRY JAMES, SR., bought a house at 21 Washington Place, just after his first son, William, was born. Ralph Waldo Emerson visited the James home to see the baby, an indication of the literary standing already established by Henry James, Sr., to be carried on in the achievements of William, Henry, and Alice James. Henry David Thoreau was also directed to the James house, "flanked on one corner by the university and on the opposite by a church," as the elder James put it. Sixteen months later, "in this home, within a stone's throw of these symbols of organized religion and systematized scholarship—from which he would always remain aloof—was born on April 15, 1843, 'another fine little boy,' as the father proudly announced to Emerson."[52] For most of his youth, New York was Henry James's principal home, as he would recall in *A Small Boy and Others*, the memoir he published in 1913, when he was seventy-one, long since "the Master" of the art of fiction, living in Rye, England. James was seized as an old man by memories of a simpler, more idyllic age, a time when New York seemed a village where boys and domestic animals safely roamed the streets and vacant lots, when New York seemed a community in which the gap between rich and poor was narrow, a time when the City had not spread uptown and into the sky with ominously tall buildings, those monuments to acquisitiveness that would appall James during his 1904 return visit to America, in preparation for *The American Scene* (1907).

In 1847 the Jameses moved to 11 Fifth Avenue; in 1848 they moved to 58 West Fourteenth Street, near Sixth Avenue. In an area bounded by Sixth and Fifth Avenues, extending from Washington Square to Union Square, young Henry explored the City, from its fenced squares to its grand City Hall. He recalled with wonder the romance he had felt while staring through iron rails at the huge house and grounds on Eighteenth Street, a place where cows, peacocks, and guinea fowl roamed. It had for him "the note of greatness—all of which shows of course what a very town-bred small person I was and was to remain."[53] More accurately, Henry James was a very small-town-bred person.

James delighted in his freedom to wander and to observe within his circumscribed world: "I see a small and compact and ingenious society screened in somehow conveniently from north and west, but open wide to the east and comparatively to the south and, though perpetually moving up Broadway, none the less constantly and delightfully walking down it. Broadway was the feature and the artery, the joy and the adventure of one's childhood, and it stretched, and prodigiously, from Union Square to Barnum's great American Museum by the City Hall."[54]

Henry's grandmother, Catharine Barber James, lived in Albany. She occupied the center of his memories of youthful visits, visits permeated by the taste and smell of her delicious peaches, a rhapsodic recollection of which opens *A Small Boy and Others*. As Henry Adams, in *The Education of Henry Adams*, would contrast Quincy (summer release) with Boston (winter duty), so too would James present Albany and New York City as symbolically alternative worlds, though James loved New York City more than Adams ever loved Boston: "The sweet taste of Albany probably lurked most in its being our admired antithesis to New York; it was holiday, whereas New York was home."[55]

At home in the City, James recalled the youthful occasion of "a dance of my elders, youthful elders, but young married people," his cousins Robert and Kitty Emmet. The sound of fiddles and the popping of corks still resounded in his memory sixty years later: "It is round that general centre that my richest memories of the 'gay' little life in general cluster—as if it had been, for the circle in which I seem justified in pretending to have 'moved,' of the finer essence of 'town'; covering as it did the stretch of Broadway down to Canal Street, with, closer at hand, the New York Hotel, . . . and rising northward to the Ultima Thule of Twenty-third Street, only second then in the supposedly ample scheme of the regular ninth 'wide' street."[56]

For James, old New York was a place of thoughtless innocence: free from aesthetic discriminations and economic pressures, open and new in its American democratic acceptance—the Jameses were, after all, nouveaux riches, newly arrived not only in the affluent class, but also in the American literary and intellectual community—a world buoyed by Emersonian optimism. Henry James's recollections from early childhood stirred in him, three years before his death, renewed vigor and amazement that "an altogether special shade and sort that the New York young naturalness of our prime was touchingly to linger with us." Amid the ghosts of people and places long gone, living far from his native grounds, James reflected on the purity of his youthful unreflectiveness in "old New York": "The special shade of its identity was thus that it was not conscious—really not conscious of anything in the world; or was conscious of so few possibilities at least, and these so immediate and so matter of course, that it came almost to the same thing."[57] For James, the New York of his childhood was another Eden, a sanctuary without any apparent source of evil.

It may well be that "James came to look with horror at New York and found in it remarkably few of the compensations that he saw in the European metropolis," as Morton and Lucia White argue.[58] This view, however, simplifies James's characteristically complex response to the City, for he loved what the City had been in his youth; he therefore wrote to remind Americans of the finer grain that had been ground down by new brutalism and to express his fears over what the City would yet become in an era of immigration and economic expansion. Still, James never knew the City as an adult as did William Dean Howells and Edith Wharton. As Wharton noted, "Wall Street, and everything connected with the big business world, remained an impenetrable mystery to [James], and knowing this he felt he could never have dealt fully in fiction with the 'American Scene,' and always frankly acknowledged it."[59]

Yet Henry James saw the City as a source of energy and inspiration, a challenge to the aspiring literary imagination. If New York was a "horror" to Henry James, it was a horror he looked upon with the curiosity of one upon whom nothing was lost. Peter Conrad argues that James recoiled from New York's openness, feeling "its abundance to be aimless and feckless. A city is by definition a place where anything can happen, a device for the multiplying of possibility. But the Jamesian novel can only exist by denying to itself this fertile freedom."[60] However, Conrad underestimates the range and play within the Jamesian novel, and he mistakenly ascribes the timorousness of James's characters, particularly in *Washington Square*, to James, forgetting that the novelist was drawn to the City in large part because it reflected infinite possibilities—dangers indeed, but also glorious opportunities for the expansion of consciousness. New York City dramatized the "complex fate" James saw as the true character of America.[61]

Washington Square (1880) shows James's fascinated ambivalence toward New York City. The novel is a true New York story of conflict over status, money, and power, though James composed it in Paris and found his inspiration for it in an anecdote he heard at a London dinner party. In his *Notebooks*, James records a story related by Fanny Kemble, the actress and writer, about her brother's engagement to a dull, rich girl. The young man had been interested in the young woman only for her money, so when her father threatened disinheritance, he refused to marry her; later, after her father died and she came into her fortune, she refused to marry her calculating suitor. James reset this tale of selfishness and "retribution in time," making it into a parable about the loss of innocence in old New York.[62] Only in Europe, then, did James gain the insight into greed and manipulativeness that allowed him to acknowledge similar vices in the City of his youth.

Washington Square is set in the 1840s, just before James's own time, in the world of assured elegance of lower Manhattan. Austin Sloper, the heroine's father, had courted Catherine Harrington, who grew up within a small world of privilege: "In 1820 she had been one of the pretty girls of the small but promising capital which clustered about the Battery and overlooked the Bay, and of which the uppermost boundary was indicated by the grassy waysides of Canal Street."[63] *Washington Square* maps the Slopers' journey, geographic and moral, uptown, from protected innocence to painful awareness of evil.

In 1835, after the deaths of his wife and son, Dr. Sloper and Catherine, his unprepossessing daughter, move to a house fronting on Washington Square, the imaginative core of old New York for Henry James. At the spot where Fifth Avenue begins, they chose "a handsome, modern, wide-fronted house, with a big balcony before the drawing-room windows, and a flight of white marble steps ascending to a portal which was also faced with white marble."[64] This far north Dr. Sloper would go, but no farther. New York would continue its inexorable development uptown, but he would resist (and teach his daughter to resist) the dangerous forces of change.

James personified the dangers of openness to the City in Morris Townsend, a mercenary suitor for Catherine's hand, but he also counted the life-denying costs, illustrated by Dr. Sloper, of closing the door against invitations to change. Lavinia Penniman, Dr. Sloper's sister, a starry-eyed romantic, encourages the Morris-Catherine courtship, while Dr. Sloper, a hard-eyed realist, a man who is always looking for the mean motive, opposes it. Dr. Sloper realizes immediately that Morris is after Catherine's promised inheritance of $80,000 a year, while Lavinia sees only true love in Morris. Realistic and romantic New York, a divided psyche, are thus at odds in *Washington Square*.

James uses the occasion of *Washington Square* to register a personal reverie of "early associations" about the area's "established repose which is not of frequent occurrence in other quarters of the long, shrill city; it has a richer, riper, more honourable look than any of the upper ramifications of the great longitudinal thoroughfare—the look of having had something of a social history."[65] However, in this setting Catherine suffers the long-term consequences of New York's cynicism and greed in ways that Henry James did not. James escaped to the heady social and literary swirl of Paris and London, where a famous actress might suggest to an aspiring young novelist the plot of his next work during a high-society dinner.

James's story of old New York is a geography of the imagination, revealing what the City was, what it would become, and what it would in time lose. His novella also contains brief excursions beyond the confines of Washington Square that hint at New York's hungry future and hard edges. Arthur Townsend, a wealthy relative of Morris's, enjoys buying a new house every three or four years, so he can move uptown with the fashionable world: "That's the way to live in New York—to move every three or four years. Then you get the last thing. It's because the city's growing so quick—you've got to keep up with it. It's going straight up town—that's where New York's going."[66]

In the end, with her father dead and with Morris, who has grown fat and bald, rejected, Catherine Sloper takes on the role of custodian of old New York ways: "Before she was forty she was regarded as an old-fashioned person, and an authority on customs that had passed away."[67] Like a princess in a perverse fairy tale, Catherine remains in her father's lower Manhattan house, in splendid isolation, while the rest of the world goes its own way. Her father's manipulativeness and her lover's cravenness might have disabused her of her innocence, but Catherine Sloper came to represent for James what was best in the old ways of New York—a sense of character, a capacity for self-denial, a belief in candor and in codes of conduct both in matters of love and money. At the same time, Catherine Sloper stands as an example of unfulfilled desire and disillusionment. She is calcified by the pressures of the City. Henry James's New York, then, was both instructive and destructive.

By THE EARLY 1880s, NEW YORK HAD BECOME "FATAL TO the imagination," as Miss Condit observes in "The Impressions of a Cousin," a lesser James tale. After years of studying painting in Europe, Miss Condit, a Catherine Sloper who escaped, has returned to live in New York, but she is appalled by all she sees, an attitude that reflects James's opinions of the period: "The city of New York is like a tall sum in addition, and the streets are like columns of figures. What a place for me to live, who hate arithmetic!" Nothing "composes" for her. "I believe I should be a good patriot if I could sketch my native town."[68] Miss Condit gives up trying to capture the City, but James did not. New York's grid plan lent itself nicely to economic expansion, less easily to artful rendering.

Sex and politics are at the heart of *The Bostonians* (1886), James's major effort to portray an American city. Though New York is not his central concern in this novel, James does give the City memorable, if passing, representation. New York, hot and flashy, stands for money and power, in counterpoint to Boston, a chill and dour city of muffled emotions and depleted idealism. The novel's male protagonist, Basil Ransom, a former Southern officer in the Civil War, comes North to make his fortune; after surveying Boston's limited offerings, he settles, of course, in New York. Ransom's ambitions, however, are thwarted by his reactionary values—he is three hundred years out of date, he is told by editors who refuse his writings—and by his desire to win the hand of Verena Tarrent, a feminist orator who has been taken up by his cousin, Olive Chancellor. The novel is a love triangle—or, more exactly, a struggle for power between Olive, the dominating Northern matron, and Basil, the acquisitive Southern gentleman, for control of Verena.

James locates Ransom, during the years when he tries to make a go of his writing and law practice, in East Twenty-fifth Street, for James knew that part of the City well. In the winter of 1875, he had lived in rooms at 111 East Twenty-fifth Street, between Lexington and Fourth Avenues. Ransom lives to the east, in a somewhat more tatty section of the City. Part of the notable "local colour" of this region centered on the El.[69] For James the El's "fantastic skeleton" suggested not romance, as it had for Howells, but a horrific vision of the City, "overhanging the transverse longitudinal street, which it darkened and smothered with the immeasurable spinal column and myriad clutching paws of an antediluvian monster."[70] When James makes clear that "a figure is nothing without a setting," it should come as little surprise for readers to discover that there is also much that is clutching and monstrous in Ransom's character. He personifies the grasping side of the City.

Yet it is in New York that Verena finds her most appreciative audience, and it is in New York that Basil draws her out; he takes Verena on the El to Central Park, where he makes his best case for her hand amid those pastoral splendors enclosed within Manhattan's urban setting: "In spite of its rockwork grottoes and tunnels, its pavilions and statues, its too numerous paths and pavements, lakes too big for the landscape and bridges too big for the lakes," Central Park "expressed all the fragrance and freshness of the most charming moment of the year," on the April afternoon of their outing.[71] The young couple visit the animals in the zoological garden, observe the swans, thread their way through the Ramble, and lose themselves in the Maze, before they sit; then Basil courts her with jokes against female emancipation. Though Verena leaves him that day, their afternoon in the Park proves to be a crucial encounter, for he will, in time, in Boston, win her away from Olive. New York City in *The Bostonians* may house the monstrous, but it is also a place where passions are released. After Ransom carries off a tearful and will-less Verena from Boston in the final pages of the novel, the prospect of a hard life in New York looms before them. Ransom, a public failure, shows every sign of becoming a private tyrant; Verena is pulled away from her public success into a life of domestic subservience to her husband.

In 1904 Henry James took the advice he had given to Edith Wharton—to choose "the *American Subject*"—when he returned to New York and opened himself to the extraordinary visions of the City that appear in *The American Scene*. During the two decades he had been away, the safe, serene village of his youth had become the nation's major urban metropolis. What was he to make of it? The self-described "restless analyst," wise in the ways of European urbanity, found himself in the paradoxical situation of the innocent who has returned from abroad to discover his home utterly changed. James was overwhelmed by the City's growth and by his conflicting impressions as he plunged into the streets and sought its true character.

James's evaluations of New York helped to shape the idea of the city in the American mind. His turn-of-the-century New York was extravagant and dangerous, an intersection of commerce and culture, an embodiment of democratic opportunities and mob tyrannies, a city strained by the pulls of the new-rich plutocrat and the impoverished immigrant, an urban memorial to a lost America, and an ominous portent of a nation eager to transform itself into something completely new. James found New York crass and vulgar; what he saw during his return to the City frightened him and made him question the survival of civilization in America. But his ambivalent experience of twenty years of change and his brave confrontation of a threatening urban future stirred his imagination into literary images and symbols commensurate with his capacity for wonder.[72]

At age sixty, Henry James found New York a polluted, but still sacred font from which he was determined to drink his fill. New York represented life for James—the place of his first consciousness, youthful innocence, and mature night-mares—and his return, for all of its shocks, meant nothing less than a renewal of life for his mind and soul.

At Hoboken, in the late summer of 1904, Henry James looked across the Hudson River, stirred by memory and desire: "One's extremest youth had been full of New York, and one was absurdly finding it again, meeting it at every turn, in sights, sounds, smells, even in the chaos of confusion and change; a process under which, verily, recognition became more difficult, like the spelling out of foreign sentences of which one knows but half the words."[73] New York was an old, beloved text, which James opened warily. Could he still "read" it, or had his native ground become obscure "foreign sentences" to him? This is the central question that preoccupies Henry James in *The American Scene.*

Compare James's encounter with Henry Adams's entry to New York Harbor, later that same year. Both men described the City in charged metaphors, but Adams's description was, like the City he imagines, hyperbolic, even hysterical.

> *The city had the air and movement of hysteria, and the citizens were crying, in every accent of anger and alarm, that the new forces must at any cost be brought under control. Prosperity never before imagined, power never yet wielded by man, speed never reached by anything but a meteor, had made the world irritable, nervous, queru-lous, unreasonable and afraid. All New York was demanding new men, and all the new forces, condensed into corporations, were demanding a new type of man—a man with ten times the endur-ance, energy, will and mind of the old type—for whom they were ready to pay millions at sight.*

Henry Adams's New York was an exploding dynamo. "The two-thousand-years failure of Christianity roared upward from Broadway, and no Constantine the Great was in sight."[74] But Henry James, despite his amazement at all that had changed, saw signs of grace in the City.

For James, "the light of the September day was lovely" in the burgeoning City. No longer the chaste village of his innocent youth, New York beckoned like the painted women of Tangier or Constantinople: "And the sun of New York rests mostly, with a laziness all its own, on that dull glaze of crimson paint, as thick as on the cheek of the cruder coquetry." Images of sexual power, absent in his youth, dominate James's renewed responses to New York. He might look warily on the City, which he personified as a painted lady, but he was also clearly seduced by her wiles and her wanton ways.[75] He met the enticing City with exquisite ambivalence, the perfect sensibility for the artist: "There was virtue evident enough in the crossing of the water, that brave sense of the big, bright, breezy bay; of light and space and multitudinous movement; of the serried, bristling city, held in the easy embrace of its great good-natured rivers very much as a battered and accommodating beauty may sometimes be 'distinguished' by a gallant less fastidious, with his open arms, than his type would seem to imply."[76] James reluctantly accepted the "easy embrace" and entered a New York he could barely recognize.

James's return stirred elusive memories and sharp tastes of his youth, the old world of Washington Square. He was overcome by his impressions of a lost past a mere three hours after his arrival. In Grammercy Park "he had felt himself a victim, up to his neck" in his "subject."[77] But he was quickly off, by steamer, to the Jersey shore, to Deal Beach, where he stayed with his publisher, Colonel George Harvey, head of Harper and Brothers. Then he left for Chocurua, the country home of his brother, William, set in the Arcadian White Mountains. So Henry James, on first returning to America, caught no more than a disconcerted glimpse of Manhattan.

In December 1904, James returned briefly to New York for a series of dinners, staying with Mrs. Cadwalader Jones, Edith Wharton's sister-in-law; he was also the guest of Wharton herself at 884 Park Avenue, where he felt himself in "elegant though very gentle bondage" to the woman who was becoming the grande dame of literary New York.[78] By then James had decided upon his dominant impression of the new New York—it was a place of "dauntless power." This power was evident in every aspect of the City, in "every floating, hurrying, panting thing." New York struck James as a "monstrous organism," growing and flinging its limbs recklessly in all directions.[79] Images of vulnerability frequently occurred to James in response to New York, as though he were seduced by its sexual enticements or physically threatened by its bullying powers. The City's streets held the dangerous allure of a painted lady and the City's skyscrapers loomed over the landscape like a rapacious monster. James was at once horrified and mesmerized.

Yet James did not cringe or flee. While he was intimidated by the new skyscrapers, he was also drawn to them as emblems of the City, as though New York were able to compose its own shape and character. The City represented an invitation to his imagination and an aesthetic challenge, a panorama of power to which James responded in Whitmanian rhapsody.

> *The aspect the power wears then is indescribable; it is the power of the most extravagant of cities, rejoicing, as with the voice of morning, in its might, its fortune, its unsurpassable conditions, and imparting to every object and element, to the motion and expression of every floating, hurrying, panting thing, to the throb of ferries, and tugs, to the plash of waves and the play of winds and the glint of lights and the shrill of whistles and the quality and authority of breeze-borne cries—all, practically, a diffused, wasted clamour of detonations.* [80]

The City, for James, was itself an artist. Its skyscrapers rose triumphant from the imprisoning gridlines of its streets, like the writer's imagination ascending from the mundane. [81]

Perhaps James, so long a displaced American, had in part assumed a European perspective on his native land. Vincent Scully, an art historian, argues that Europeans who came to America imposed their wills and their technology on the landscape. Of New York City, Scully writes, "The skyscrapers seem to rush forward to populate the tip of the island as it sails out to sea, each one clamoring to be seen from afar, as if floating on the water. Behind the skyscrapers the man-made grid stretches the length of the island, dramatizing its length as the great avenues rush uninterrupted to the north." [82] Henry James was similarly struck by the City's magnitude and force.

James found traces of old New York, but they were overpowered by the presences of the new "tall buildings." Trinity Church's spire was "so cruelly overtopped and so barely distinguishable" that traditional religion seemed forced into silence and submission by the castles of Mammon. However, James's mind reeled to stupefaction when he discovered that the skyscraper that loomed over Trinity to the north—"a south face as high and wide as the mountain-wall that drops the Alpine avalanche, from time to time, upon the village, and the village spire at its foot"—had been sanctioned by Trinity's trustees. [83] God and Mammon were, then, a consenting couple in new New York, located far east of Eden, near Sodom. (In 1908 Trinity's role as a Lower West Side slumlord was exposed, so the church tore down tenements and built office buildings and warehouses in their places.) [84]

James granted New York its greatness after viewing it from the perspective of a ferry-boat ride around the island. When he returned to New York from Washington, on his way to Boston, in the spring of 1905, his Pullman was carried by barge around the tip of Manhattan; from this angle he saw "the most extravagant of cities, rejoicing, as with the voice of mourning, in its might, its fortune, its unsurpassable conditions."[85] James's extraordinary meditation suggests his intense realization of the City's destructive powers, but it also demonstrates his abilities to rise to the occasion in imaginative response. "The universal *applied* passion struck me as shining unprecedentedly out of the composition; the bigness and bravery and insolence, especially, of everything that rushed and shrieked; in the air as of a great intricate frenzied dance, half merry, half desperate, or at least half defiant, performed on the huge watery floor."[86] No longer a beloved old book, New York became James's *tabula rasa*, "the vast white page that awaits beyond any other perhaps the black overscoring of science," a page James was determined to mark with his own impressions.[87]

The towers of Wall Street drew James's particular wrath and inspired him to overreaching tropes, though he was far less apocalyptic than Adams had been. For James, "the multitudinous" skyline "looked like extravagant pins in a cushion already overplanted, and stuck in as in the dark, anywhere and anyhow," though the huge buildings "have at least the felicity of carrying out the fairness of tone, of taking the sun and the shade in the manner of marble."[88] More felicitously, he also compared these new buildings with long-stemmed American Beauty roses, poised for pruning. Close-up, James could see that they were neither marble- nor roselike. (He did not comment on the more obvious metaphorical implications of the Fuller Building, erected in 1903, a triangular-shaped tower on East Twenty-third Street that was compared by others to a bow of a ship or a locomotive; it finally became known as the Flatiron.)[89] James hated not only the bulk and scale of such buildings, but also their glassy impenetrability, by-products of the new technique of steel-frame construction. He condemned, as well, elevators, the other crucial new technology that made such building heights possible. He disliked the confinement of elevators, their speed, and the sense of powerlessness he felt inside them.[90] "The thousand glassy eyes of these giants of the mere market" were, for James, "the most piercing notes in that concert of the explosively provisional into which your supreme sense of New York resolves itself."[91]

James's visit to Ellis Island, his confrontation with the "alien" newcomers who entered America through New York, was further evidence that New York's citizens lived in a time and place after the Fall. The naive visitor to Ellis Island, he says, returns transformed, knowing: "He has eaten of the tree of knowledge, and the taste will be forever in his mouth."[92] James's visit to Ellis Island altered his sense of what it meant to be an American. He was concerned by the implications of so many immigrants for American culture as he knew it. The immigrants were displaced citizens, men and women without countries; their presence made, in a sense, all New Yorkers aliens and redrew the implicit social contract by which urban peoples lived: "We must go, in other words, *more* than half-way to meet them; which is all the difference, for us, between possession and dispossession."[93] The sights and sounds of the diverse voices he encountered at Ellis Island haunted Henry James and made him feel the City had been taken from him when he returned to Manhattan and walked its suddenly unfamiliar streets.

James's metaphors encompass his search for a sense of unity in the City. The City was filled with different notes, but it was also "a keyboard as continuous, and as free from hard transitions, as if swept by the fingers of a master-pianist." Or the City was a banquet in which the memory of each dish recalled the entire meal: "The whole feast affects one as eaten—that is the point—with the general queer sauce of New York."[94] Yet, James wondered, how could the "aliens"—if aliens these newcomers could be called in a nation of immigrants—be incorporated into his perception of unity? Everyone riding the new "electric cars" appeared separate to James, but all of them were home, James granted, in New York.

In assuming a new, "American" identity, many of the immigrants, Italians in particular, seemed to James to have sacrificed the charm and color that they possessed in their own country. James had little to say about the Irish, even less about New York's unassimilated blacks, but he found much to report about immigrant Jews, whom he met in a visit to the Lower East Side. There Jewish children filled the streets, and residents appeared caged in tenements that were enclosed by metal fire escapes. In the Cafe Royal, a coffeehouse where the air was filled with Yiddish and broken English, James was struck with worry over the future of the English language and literature as he knew it in America: "The accent of the very ultimate future, in the States, may be destined to become the most beautiful on the globe and the very music of humanity (here the 'ethnic' synthesis shrouds itself thicker than ever); but whatever we shall know it for, certainly, we shall not know it for English—in any sense for which there is an existing literary measure."[95] Later James attended a Yiddish theatrical performance, with Jacob Gordin, a Yiddish dramatist, as his guide, but perhaps disturbed because he was unable to follow the play, he walked out. In the final passages on New York in *The American Scene*, James portrayed himself walking alone, not quite sure where he was, amid the Jewish crowds of the Lower East

Side. He savored the sense of indefiniteness and uncertainty he felt, for, he realized, *that* was New York to the core: "It breathed its simple 'New York! New York!' at every impulse of inquiry; so that I can only echo contentedly, with analysis for once quite agreeably baffled, 'Remarkable, unspeakable New York!' "[96]

Had James remained in New York for a few years, he would have been interested in Israel Zangwill's popular play, *The Melting-Pot* (1908), which dramatized the acculturation of David Quixano, a Russian Jewish immigrant to New York who wants to write a symphony expressing the union of American "races" and to marry a young Christian woman, Vera. In the play's climactic scene, David rhapsodizes before the bedazzled Vera as they survey the City from the roof garden of a settlement house: "There she lies, the great Melting-Pot—listen! Can't you hear the roaring and the bubbling? Ah, what a stirring and a seething! Celt and Latin, Slav and Teuton, Greek and Syrian,—black and yellow." Behind them shines the torch of the Statue of Liberty. The strains of "My Country, 'tis of Thee" rise as the curtain falls. Henry James's cauldron, New York City, was indeed shaping an "American" character.[97]

However, James fled New York's noisy present and ominous future, seeking safe haven in emblems of the past. "The precious stretch of space between Washington Square and Fourteenth Street had a value" for James; it "had even a charm, for the revisiting spirit," which served as an anodyne to crass, new New York.[98] Amazed that that humble world, characterized by its "lamentable little Arch of Triumph," would turn out to be the preserve of New York's "tone," James saw Washington Square as "the old ivory of an overscored tablet."[99] James sought in his old Washington Square world the symbols by which he would redesign his sense of the City.

He was pleased to discover that the school he had attended as a boy, where he had been taught by an Irish woman, still stood, but he was appalled to find that the house in which he was born had been "ruthlessly suppressed," or razed, a stark fact that called up images of emasculation: "The effect for me, in Washington Place, was of having been amputated of half my history."[100] He had imagined that a tablet, commemorating his birth, might someday be placed on the wall of that house, but he found the wall "smashed" and so he concluded that such memorials in New York are "unthinkable." (Such a plaque has since been placed on the New York University building erected on the site of James's birthplace.) The grand uptown homes that had risen along upper Fifth Avenue since James's youth also stood as poignant reminders of the transient ways of all things lovely in New York: "I found myself recognizing in the New York predicament a particular character and a particular pathos. The whole costly up-town demonstration was a record, in the last analysis, of individual loneliness; whence came, precisely, its insistent testimony to waste—waste of the still wider sort than the mere game of rebuilding."[101] The rich houses of New York's upstart aristocracy struck James as "pompous" and "flagrantly tentative." While New York obliterated the symbols of his childhood, the City was itself a greedy child, "living but in the sense of its hour and in the immediacy of its want," lawless, boundless, irresponsible.[102]

Even when the City was at its best, offering places of recreation or education to its citizens, in Central Park and in the new Metropolitan Museum—"a palace of art, truly, that sits there on the edge of the Park"—the new New York daunted James.[103] The Park, he thought, strained too much to please, like an actress in a company without other actresses; as a result, "she assumes on successive nights the most dissimilar parts and ranges in the course of a week from the tragedy queen to the singing chambermaid."[104] For James the Park's efforts to blend the pastoral and the urban were ultimately a failure.[105] Yet he was touched by the Park's democratic openness—to immigrants in their colorful garb who seemed at ease with more staid City residents—and by its efforts at "ingratiation." Despite his description of it as a "palace of art," he found little to admire in the new Metropolitan, which seemed a vast expense, perhaps of spirit as well as money, a futile effort to educate, another vulgar, New York "demonstration." Of course, James confessed, the new Metropolitan failed in part because it brought to mind the old Metropolitan, on Fourteenth Street, of his childhood. Like his parents' home, it too had been razed—it had "vanished as utterly as the Assyrian Empire"—in that characteristic New York manner that constantly reminds the observer that this too shall pass.[106] James took greater pleasure in an evening of repose at an old German beerhouse on the Upper East Side—perhaps like the one in which Howells met Whitman—a near-European haven of quiet and slow time that stood in counterpoint to frenzied, modern Manhattan.

The beleaguered James also found brief refuge in the Church of the Ascension, where he took pleasure in viewing a mural, depicting the Ascension, by his old friend, John La Farge. Though James had no religious convictions, he found the occasion "wonderful" because the church's cool and artful recesses removed him from the heat, noise, commerce, and other destructive elements of the streets of Manhattan, the glaring City outside. While he studied La Farge's art, an allegorical struggle for the City's soul began to shape itself in James's imagination: Art vs. Commerce: "Here was the loveliest cluster of images, begotten on the spot, that the preoccupied city had even taken thought to offer itself; and here, to match them, like some black shadow they had been condemned to cast, was this particular prepared honour of 'removal' that appeared to hover about them."[107] Everywhere James looked, emblems of the artful were surrounded and subverted by fresh examples of the vulgar.

The Waldorf-Astoria Hotel, a central symbol of Manhattan's overreaching commercial impulses, came under James's ironic scrutiny. His attention there was properly fixed, for the location of this vast hotel, at Fifth and Thirty-fourth, held the history of much of New York's evolving sense of itself. It had been the site of Mrs. William Astor's home, built in the 1850s, where she gave balls for New York's "four hundred," its social elite. The mansion had been torn down in 1897 and replaced by the Waldorf-Astoria, which would in turn be torn down in 1929 and replaced by the Empire State Building.[108]

James's arrival at the Waldorf-Astoria, out of the sleet and slush of January 1905 was to him a "revelation": "New York told me more of her story at once, then and there, than she was again and elsewhere to tell."[109] He saw that the hotel is the true expression of the American character. There American gregariousness, commerce, and transience met. James, unnerved as he had been by skyscrapers, millionaires, and immigrants, beheld with wry amusement the Vanity Fair of democracy on parade in the lobby of the Waldorf-Astoria: "It sat there, it walked and talked, and ate and drank, and listened and danced to music, and otherwise rebelled and roamed, and bought and sold, and came and went there, all on its own splendid terms and with an encompassing material splendour, a wealth and variety of constituted picture and background, that might well feed it with the finest illusions about itself."[110] In this "gorgeous golden blur," this "paradise peopled with unmistakable American shapes," James felt he had come to the heart of what matters to New York—showy, self-centered, opulent, pretentious, and presumptuous.[111] Having found what he sought, an epiphany of the new America, Henry James vowed never to return.

JAMES WROTE *THE AMERICAN SCENE* IN ENGLAND, WHERE he spent most of his remaining years and where he died, having become an English citizen in the midst of the Great War, in 1916. However, New York was never far from his mind during his final decade. For more than four years he worked on a collected edition of his works—twenty-three volumes, for which he did considerable revising and composed eighteen extended prefaces, essays that stand as his artistic autobiography and credo—which he called his "New York Edition." In a way, this was an odd designation, for James dropped many of his

American tales from the collection, including *Washington Square* and *The Bostonians*, though he did include his late, definitive stories of New York. The "New York Edition" emphasized James's international fiction—he was described as "the representative cosmopolitan novelist" in the publisher's prospectus—and it was designed to remind readers of Balzac's twenty-three volume *Comédie humaine*.[112] James wanted his collected works to stand as a tribute to his first home, as he made clear in a 1905 memo to his New York publisher, Scribner's: "I should particularly like to call it the New York Edition if that may pass for a general title of sufficient dignity and distinctness. My feeling about the matter is that it refers the whole enterprise explicitly to my native city—to which I have had no great opportunity of rendering that sort of homage."[113] James's designation of his collection suggests that one of the major concerns of his last years was to reaffirm his identity as an American—in particular, as a New Yorker. He also seized the opportunity to render homage to the City in three late tales: "The Jolly Corner" (1908), "Crapy Cornelia" (1909), and "A Round of Visits" (1910), works in which he returns to the fictional territory he had surveyed nearly thirty years before.

In "The Jolly Corner" James returns again to the relations between love, money, and character in New York, themes he had first treated in *Washington Square*. In this mature tale, James recombines the elements of his early novella—making the New York woman into a matron of modest means who is eager to marry and the reluctant suitor a well-off dilettante who has spent most of his life in Europe—and reenforces the image of New York as a place where money and power destroy innocence.

James wrote "The Jolly Corner" in 1906 after a visit to his Rye home by Hamlin Garland, a westerner and a disciple of William Dean Howells. "The mixture of Europe and America which you see in me has proved disastrous," James told this "son of the middle border," whose nativism stirred James's nostalgia for America. "If I were to live my life again I would be American—steep myself in it—know no other."[114] James's reflection on his life-not-lived inspired him to compose, months later, an eerie tale about a fifty-six-year-old American, Spencer Brydon, who has lived more than three decades in Europe. Brydon, a Jamesian alter ego, comes home again to New York to confront the man he might have been had he not decided to leave New York at age twenty-three. Young Brydon had left behind Alice Staverton, who remained in Irving Place, scraping by on little money, but maintaining her social station and her fidelity to her reluctant, long-absent suitor; Alice, then, is a variation on Catherine Sloper, just as Brydon is a recasting of Morris Townsend. Alice and Brydon renew their acquaintance on his return, but more comes of it than came of the renewed suit by Morris for Catherine's hand.

Brydon has ostensibly returned to oversee his properties in lower Manhattan, that idyllic territory of James's first memories around Washington Square. Brydon owns two houses: one on the "jolly corner" where he had been reared, another "two bristling blocks westward" of "the comparatively conservative [Fifth] Avenue."[115] Rents from these houses had been subsidizing his long stay in Europe. Though he had long before chosen a life of culture over business, Brydon finds he enjoys overseeing the conversion of the lesser of his houses into an apartment building. The ironic Alice thinks that if Brydon had remained at home he might have been one of those "new men" who razed and rebuilt the City. He would have had power and money, those new New York traits, in exchange for his European manners and culture, a polish that has been gained, Alice points out, because he was too selfish to share his life with anyone. In this tale, James wonders not only what might have been the personal cost of a truly American success but also what an American might have sacrificed for a life committed to European culture.

Alice has seen what Brydon might have been in a dream; in a late-night hunt through his "jolly corner" house, Brydon pursues this ghost of himself, an apparition whose hands cover his face; two fingers on one hand are "reduced to stumps, as if accidentally shot away."[116] Perhaps, James hints, money and power would have been purchased at the price of disabling the shaping, artistic hand.

When Brydon confronts his other self, he faints. Soon, however, he is awakened by the attentive Alice. "Alice Staverton had made her lap an ample and perfect cushion to him," and she brought him back to consciousness, to "life," he grants. *She* could accept the "black stranger," the American Brydon might have become, as she could welcome the expatriate he had in fact become. Indeed, Spencer Brydon seems a tense composite of his divided selves, for he was now both a New York builder, "living in luxury on *those* ill-gotten gains," as Alice wryly reminds him, *and* an aesthete.[117] Perhaps as her lover (of sorts), Spencer Brydon will learn to share his life, an ambiguous fate for James.

To Garland, James said that he had become "a man who is neither American nor European. I have lost touch with my own people and I live here alone."[118] "The Jolly Corner" suggests that "Europe" meant a life of manners, culture, genteel poverty, selfishness, and celibate loneliness—particularly for one, like Brydon, who had no hand for art—and "New York" meant money, power, maiming, vulgarity, and heterosexual union. Perhaps, after all, James's story implies, his choice for what James Joyce called a life of "silence, exile and cunning," emigration for the sake of art, was the wiser course.

In "Crapy Cornelia," Henry James uses the devise of the reluctant suitor to satirize new New York. At age forty-eight White-Mason sits in Central Park, amid colorfully dressed immigrants, "the daughters of the strange native—that is the overwhelmingly alien—populace."[119] He decides to propose marriage to the wealthy Mrs. Worthingham, thus turning from the company of the "alien" newcomers to the alienating new rich, the two groups that have transformed Manhattan. Indeed, "the gloss of new money" is more intriguing to White-Mason than the faces of immigrants.[120] However, when he visits Mrs. Worthingham, he recoils from her ostentatious display and her eagerness for a New York in which the wealthy will further remove themselves from the rest of the population. From the large window of her East Side house, a perfect and possessive view of the City is framed; by her side he could be secure, within a sanctuary of affluence, but he realizes that the price will be too high. Mrs. Worthingham understands neither him nor his world—the fading realm of old New York, which existed before the newcomers, rich and poor, took over the City. Searching for echoes of that world, White-Mason visits an old friend, Cornelia, a woman of modest means who recalls, as Mrs. Worthingham does not, "the New York of 'his time,'" that is, the New York of James's youth.[121] White-Mason decides to spend his final years at the side of Cornelia—not married to her, but as a frequent visitor to her humble home—indulging in remembrances of things past, and not as Mrs. Worthingham's husband, a pet bird in the gilded cage of new New York.

Finally, in "A Round of Visits," James portrays a world of grotesque display and personal corruption—a city of swindlers in which a young man, compromised by greed, commits suicide. Mark Monteith, recently disembarked from a long stay in Europe, is the instrument of James's renewed observations of horrific Manhattan. Monteith is plunged into a disorienting snowstorm that at once masks and symbolizes the City's frozen soul: "a blinding New York blizzard" gives him "a deep sore inward ache."[122] Perhaps James drew this story from one of the anecdotes in his notebooks about the City's vulgar hotels so that he could, one last time, portray all that he hated about the new New York. "The great gaudy hotel"—the Pocahontas—in which Monteith seeks refuge, is "carried out on 'Du Barry' lines—made all about him, in blocks and tiers and superpositions, a sufficient defensive hugeness; so that, between the massive labyrinth and the New York weather, life in a lighthouse during a gale would scarce have kept him more apart."[123]

Having established the New York hotel as something of a floating iceberg, James switches to tropical imagery to suggest the extravagance of its effects. The lobby of the Pocahontas, where the ridiculous newly rich parade, gives the impression of "a tropical forest, where vociferous, bright-eyed, and feathered creatures, of every variety of size and hue, [are] half smothered between undergrowths of velvet and tapestry and ramifications of marble and bronze."[124] James wrote "A Round of Visits" from the safety of his small house in Rye, far from New York and its hotels. But he had been, during his own return visit, attentive to the threatening City—like a lighthouse keeper in a gale, or a game hunter in the jungle.

If Lambert Strether, hero of *The Ambassadors*, returned from Paris to Wollett, Massachusetts, with nothing more than his "wonderful impressions," then Henry James returned from New York to Rye with similar baggage—a renewed and renewing vision of place.[125] New York was at once wondrous and horrific, a dreamscape of the past and a nightmare vision of the future. Above all, it was America. New York City—though rich, spicy, nearly indigestible—was a moveable feast for Henry James, the ambivalent expatriate.

A GENERATION AFTER THE BIRTHS OF HOWELLS AND JAMES, Edith Wharton was born in 1862, into a New York family of long-standing social prominence. The City offered her a youthful idyll, similar to James's urban village, though one more socially exacting and stultifying as she came of age and married. She defined her adult literary career by turning on the New York that had misshaped her; then, after the horrors of the Great War, she qualified her charges, finding good in New York's old ways. "When I was young," Wharton wrote in her memoirs, "it used to seem to me that the group in which I grew up was like an empty vessel into which no new wine would ever again be poured. Now I see that one of its uses lay in preserving a few drops of an old vintage too rare to be savoured by a youthful palate."[126]

Edith Wharton's first memory, as she recalls in *A Backward Glance*, her post–World War I memoir, is of walking up Fifth Avenue with her beloved father: "the old Fifth Avenue with its double line of low brown-stone houses, of a desperate uniformity of style, broken only—and surprisingly—by two equally unexpected features: the fenced-in plot of ground where the old Miss Kennedys' cows were pastured, and the truncated Egyptian pyramid [between Fortieth and Forty-second streets] which so strangely served as a reservoir for New York's water supply." When they encountered relatives, her cousin Daniel lifted

Edith's veil and kissed her on the cheek. She was, she says, "wakened to conscious life by two tremendous forces of love and vanity."[127] New York City would remain for Wharton throughout her life a balanced antithesis, an ambivalence, a net of contraries. She looked fondly on old New York as a girl, waking to first consciousness, and then again as an old woman, remembering worthy things past, but in midlife, at the peak of her literary powers, New York was her Vanity Fair, an overreaching city that deserved her scornful cautionary tales.

Edith Newbold Jones was born into a distinctly unmodern world, before so many inventions in communication and transportation changed the ways people lived. The Rhinelander and Stevens families supplied her with a fixed, privileged Dutch-English heritage. She was reared in a world still shaped by "an old tradition of European culture," which by the time her memoir was published in 1934 "the country [had] totally rejected." For her, Massachusetts, where her Stevens forebears first settled, represented religious fanaticism, while New York was more "easy-going"—"New York, where people seem from the outset to have been more interested in making money and acquiring property than in Predestination and witch-hunting." Edith Jones's New York was Episcopalian, which gave her an appreciation of "the noble cadences" of *The Book of Common Prayer* and "reverence for an ordered ritual in which the officiant's personality is strictly subordinated to the rite he performs." Her old New York stood as well for education, good manners, and "scrupulous probity in business and private affairs." Wharton's psychic map framed an enclosed world—from Twenty-first Street to the Park, along Fifth Avenue—with vague hints of the wondrous doings beyond its boundaries that stirred her cloistered imagination.[128]

She recalled New York after the Civil War as ugly, "its untended streets and the narrow houses so lacking in external dignity, so crammed with smug and suffocating upholstery," but her New York years of lead became, in retrospect, her era of gold. The certainty that it represented, however smothering, had been replaced by dangerous unpredictability.

> *What I could not guess was that this little low-studded rectangular New York, cursed with its universal chocolate-coloured coating of the most hideous stone ever quarried, this cramped horizontal gridiron of a town without towers, porticoes, fountains or perspectives, hidebound in its deadly uniformity of mean ugliness, would fifty years later be as much a vanished city as Atlantis or the lowest layer of Schliemann's Troy, or that the social organization which that prosaic*

setting has slowly secreted would have been swept away to oblivion with the rest. Nothing but the Atlantis-fate of old New York, the New York which had slowly but continuously developed from the early seventeenth century to my own childhood, makes that childhood worth recalling now.[129]

Edith Jones's New York was an overly fine and excessively private place, an overstuffed living-room world. She was born into a social system where women, whatever their intelligence, were allowed no public presence beyond social decoration and ceremony. Women could not vote and were legally barred from holding property in most states; women of society were trained only for marriage and were expected to be subservient to their husbands. Certainly they were not encouraged to do anything of lasting public value, or to say anything memorable. In this world, particularly in New York society, "women did not *create* beauty," notes Cynthia Griffin Wolff. "Women *were* beautiful."[130]

The social minuet was the only dance in town. Lucretia and Frederick Jones, Edith's parents, sent her older brothers to ivy league schools, but their daughter was educated by tutors in modern languages (correct usage) and proper manners. The Joneses discouraged her desire to write as unseemly; indeed, they removed writing materials from her presence and restricted her access to contemporary novels. Though Edith Jones "came out" at one of Mrs. Morton's balls, at her home on Fifth Avenue she still felt bottled-up.

Edith married Edward Wharton in April 1885, at Trinity Chapel, New York City. "Teddy" was a handsome, popular, purposeless young man of sufficient social standing for the Joneses. The newlyweds moved first into Pencraig Cottage, located on Edith's mother's Newport estate, then into a small house on Madison Avenue in the City. Seldom free from her mother's supervision, Edith Wharton's world was fixed in New York's social season, bounded by summers in Newport, and punctuated by regular visits to Europe. As a young wife, she gave every appearance that she willingly conformed to the designated script for a woman of her station. However, tensions exacted by a life devoted to fulfilling the expectations of her class led to a breakdown in 1892.

Tentatively, Edith began writing; a few poems and eventually some stories were accepted by *Scribner's* and other magazines. When she and Teddy bought Land's End, their own Newport estate, in 1893, she worked with Ogden Codman on the decoration of its interior. In time this resulted in *The Decoration of Houses* (1897), a study of the interior arrangements of upper-class city homes.

Certainly Codman's professional expertise was invaluable to the completion of the book, but its theme and its style were driven by Wharton's passion to reimagine her life.

The Decoration of Houses was shaped around an aesthetic of organicism. Wharton believed that "the interior of a house is as much a part of its organic structure as the outside, and that its treatment ought, in the same measure, to be based on right proportion, balance of door and window spacing, and simple unconfused lines."[131] Yet this bland and high-minded statement of the book's theme, as described in Wharton's *A Backward Glance*, omits the hard intent that lurks between the lines of *The Decoration of Houses*. For Edith Wharton was, at age thirty-three, indirectly attacking old, aristocratic New York on its own grounds by finding the interior arrangements of its houses, like the one in which she was reared on West Twenty-third Street, wanting—dark, cold, formal homes of "exquisite discomfort."[132] *The Decoration of Houses*, then, came close to Edith Wharton's declaration of independence, for, it implies, if a higher vision of taste can so alter traditional arrangements in small ways, so too can a person of independent vision and will change her life in large ways. Taste, here, became Wharton's political weapon and an artistic credo. When she said she found New York "ugly," she was saying no small thing. In the arrangement of her houses and in her life, Edith Wharton rejected Victorian stuffiness and clutter. Rather, she sought space, balance, and light.

With the purchase of a 113-acre property in Lenox, Massachusetts, in 1901 and the construction of a house modeled on Christopher Wren's Belton House in Lincolnshire, Edith Wharton broke out of her bell jar: "At last I escaped from watering-place trivialities to the real country."[133] She would have lived there year-round, but Teddy disliked the cold winters of western Massachusetts and he wanted to keep up his New York City social life, which was centered at 884 Park Avenue. Edith Wharton's geographical removal was followed by her psychic distancing from New York society in her writing, in which she revealed the awkward and repressive social arrangements within her City.

In the summer of 1902 Edith Wharton, a beginning novelist at age forty, sent Henry James, an accomplished novelist at age fifty-nine, a copy of *The Valley of Decision*, her recently published novel about the Italian aristocracy in the eighteenth century. James replied with faint appreciation, but he encouraged her to profit from his own example and not make his mistake of straying too long from home. He urged her to choose "the *American Subject*," to "take hold of it and keep hold, and let it pull you where it will." Above all, she should write from experience—"*Do New York!* The first-hand account is precious."[134] New York, for James, was the American subject writ large, as he implied to Howells and to Wharton. Though in her career she wrote in and on many different places, it can be said that Edith Wharton took James's advice with a passion and *did* New York in a series of striking works, particularly in *The House of Mirth* (1905), *The Custom of the Country* (1913), *The Age of Innocence* (1920), and finally in her artful recasting of her past, *A Backward Glance* (1934).

Furthermore, though James may not have realized it when he wrote to her, Edith Wharton had already done New York in her first novel, *The Touchstone* (1900). It is the novel that marked her turn from the myth of innocence, from her youthful vision of old New York society, to the portrayal of intrinsic evil lurking beneath its display of manners. Manipulation, deceit, and cupidity characterize Wharton's revised version of New York in *The Touchstone*, just as it did for James in *Washington Square*.

The Touchstone centers on Glennard, a lawyer, a man with more culture than money. Glennard is a cold conformist who recoils from passion and disapproves of intelligence in women—a woman like the late Margaret Aubyn, whom he had known before she became a famous novelist. Glennard wants to marry Miss Alexa Trent, but he lacks the money to do so until he sells for publication the passionate letters Margaret had sent to him. With the money he receives for the letters, Glennard marries Alexa and buys a small house in the country. However, guilt over what he has done eats at Glennard, though not enough to make him confess his shameful deeds to his wife, for he has no idea how she will receive the revelation that he has betrayed the trust of another woman. *Margaret Aubyn's Letters* is published and causes much conversation, even in Glennard's social circles, where books are not often read. Clearly Wharton is saying that "frivolity," the excessive regard for money, goes far in destroying this conventional man. However, in the end his suffering makes him a better man, for Alexa learns the truth and forgives him.

Wharton's New York in *The Touchstone* is characterized by a weak, scheming man who uses women to get what he can from them to better his condition. He plays one off against the other; he betrays the trust of one and he refuses to trust the other. It is a silly, social world that overvalues appearance and turns from commitment. In the end, however, it is the woman of passion (Margaret) who provides the test of character and the occasion of self-recognition for Glennard and the woman of spirit (Alexa) who correctly interprets the lesson.

"Fate had planted me in New York," Wharton wrote in *A Backward Glance*, "and my instincts as a story-teller counselled me to use the material nearest at hand, and most familiarly my own." Her artistic challenge was to make something worthy of the trivial lives of New York's social elite. She decided that "a frivolous society can acquire dramatic significance only through what its frivolity destroys. Its tragic implication lies in its power of debasing people and ideals."[135]

T_{HE} *House of Mirth* WAS EDITH WHARTON'S BREAK-through novel. With it she both defined herself as a professional writer—meeting the demands of serialization in *Scribner's* in 1905 and achieving a vast success, with sales of more than 100,000 copies—and distanced herself from the hothouse world of New York society. After she wrote this novel, she also escaped the New York-Newport circle; she lived longer periods at the Mount, where Henry James visited, and the rest of the year abroad, within the social and literary orbits of London and Paris.

The House of Mirth traces the precipitous decline and fall of a young woman of fashion—Lily Bart, age twenty-nine, who has great beauty and social connections but little money—over a seventeen-month period, from her great expectations of a brilliant marriage to her death from an overdose of chloral. Edith Jones had been nicknamed "Lily" in her Newport days, before her own socially successful marriage, but unlike the wealthy and industrious author, the heroine of the novel is a lily of the field who neither toils nor spins; Lily Bart hopes that her beauty, her glory arrayed, will be sufficient to bring her marital and social success.

Wharton considered calling her novel *A Moment's Ornament*, a title that would have stressed Lily's role as an object of art, or *The Year of the Rose*, a title that would have emphasized her transient beauty.[136] The title Wharton finally chose derives from Ecclesiastes 7:4: "The heart of the wise is in the house of mourning, but the heart of fools is in the house of mirth." That is, *The House of Mirth* is a cautionary tale, illustrating the foolishness of overreliance on feminine charms for salvation, even for survival, in the wicked City. Cynthia Griffin Wolff is right in saying that Wharton chose to kill off Lily Bart: "That choice implies a judgment upon the elements of femininity that Lily embodies: they are not viable, not worth preserving."[137]

However, when *Scribner's* included the passage from Ecclesiastes on the title page, Wharton asked that it be removed because it too openly insisted on the book's moral. When William Roscoe Thayer, a Boston writer, suggested she had "stripped" New York society, Wharton replied in ambiguous defense of her native grounds: "New York Society is still amply clad, & the little corner of its garment that I lifted was meant to show only that little atrophied organ—the group of idle & dull people—that exist in any big & wealthy social body." However she did admit to Thayer that in New York "the social organization" was "more harmful in its influence" than elsewhere, "because fewer responsibilities attach to money with us than in other societies."[138] Clearly, *The House of Mirth* stands as Edith Wharton's satirical separate peace with New York society, her complaint against the glossing of its avarice for money and status with a veneer of manners and morals. Lily Bart thus became New York society's sacrificial victim and Edith Wharton's representative woman in the City.

Lily Bart, as Louis Auchincloss points out, was a woman between worlds, with links to the upright, hypocritical society of old New York and ties to the avaricious, amoral social climbers of new New York. "Mrs. Wharton saw clearly enough that the invaders and defenders were bound ultimately to bury their hatchet in a noisy, stamping dance, but she saw also the rich possibilities for satire in the contrasts afforded by the battle line in its last stages and the pathos of the individuals who were fated to be trampled under the feet of those boisterous truce makers."[139] Lily Bart gets caught in the crossfire between two armed camps that will soon declare a truce and form a bond—a bond that affirms the alliance between social standing and money that still defines the character of modern New York City.

The reader first encounters Lily Bart as she is caught in the rush of Grand Central Station; we see her through the admiring eyes of Lawrence Selden, a diffident bachelor. She is on her way to visit the Trenors at Bellomont, in Rhinehart, a country house where she is desperate to land a rich husband, though she also wants more from a man than money. We meet Lily, fittingly enough, between trains, with time on her hands, torn between what she should do for her own best advantage and what she wishes she could do; that is, Wharton locates her heroine between calculating designs of the head and self-destructive impulses of the heart.

Lily seems to stand apart, as though she is waiting for someone. She "roused speculation" in Selden, but little passion.[140] Selden will not heroically take Lily up in her times of need. Indeed, that special someone, the rescuing hero for whom she waits, will never appear—probably does not exist, Wharton implies—and Lily will fall farther away from the fashionable crowd. Still, as they stroll up Madison Avenue, Selden is struck by Lily's *value*, in a particularly New York sense of the term: "He had a confused sense that she must have cost a great deal to make, that a great many dull and ugly people must, in some mysterious way, have been sacrificed to produce her." Perhaps not surprisingly for someone so valued, Lily recoils from the City, declaring, "what a hideous place New York is!"[141]

Then Lily does something stupid. Unchaperoned, she accompanies Selden to his rooms in the Benedick for tea. She is drawn to Selden, for he seems to retain "a happy air of viewing the show objectively, of having points of contact outside the great gilt cage in which they were all huddled for the mob to gape at."[142] With him she sees the triviality of her set. However, she knows that she must marry a man with far more money than Selden possesses, for she is addicted to luxury—"It was the only climate she could breathe in."[143] Yet Lily Bart's one false move, entering Selden's rooms, takes her over the precipice of New York society's moral code. At this and other crucial moments in her life, Lily Bart follows the whims of her heart. She stoops to folly and becomes a social outcast in a society that rewards calculation and hypocrisy, calling them manners. Like many other failures before her and after her in works about the City, she comes to see suicide as her only way out.

John Updike has observed that Edith Wharton denied her characters the liberation she found for herself.[144] Perhaps Wharton wished to underline the murderous powers beneath the velvet gloves of old New York. The stories of Edith Wharton and Lily Bart, told in counterpoint, are true New York tales of success and failure, illustrating one woman's artistic pluck and another woman's social bad luck.

Yet on another fictional occasion, Wharton extended sympathetic understanding to the City's true have-nots. First written in 1892, but not published until it was revised in 1916, "Bunner Sisters," a short story, recounts the sad lives of Ann Eliza and Evelina Bunner, proprietors of "a very small shop, in a shabby basement, in a side-street already doomed to decline," near Stuyvesant Square.[145] Their precarious lives, confined to the shop and a room in the back where they live, begin to fall apart when Ann Eliza steps beyond the boundaries of the familiar and ventures forth into the City to buy a present, an expensive clock, which they cannot afford, for Evelina's birthday: "The mere act of going out from the monastic quiet of the shop into the tumult of the streets filled her with a subdued excitement which grew too intense for pleasure as she was swallowed by the engulfing roar of Broadway and Third Avenue, and began to do timid battle with their incessant cross-currents of humanity."[146] Ann Eliza meets an immigrant German shopkeeper, Herman Ramy, who brings ruin to their lives when he marries Evelina and carries her off into a life of hellish misery. At the end of the story, Evelina is dead, the shop is lost, and Ann Eliza is left to an uncertain fate in the City. R. W. B. Lewis imagines that Mrs. Edward Wharton of Madison Avenue, like the aristocratic lady with puffed sleeves who appears in the story, patronized just such shops, where she acquired material for this story.[147] Written by an author who had been smothered with privileges, "Bunner Sisters" is a tale that, like *The House of Mirth*, illustrates the City's harsh treatment of penniless women.

Edith Wharton's *THE CUSTOM OF THE COUNTRY*, published by Scribner's in 1913, echoed Howells's satire of the social-climbing new rich who defied custom and fought their way into the "country" of old New York. As in James's *The American Scene*, Wharton's ironies cut in several directions—against the new-rich "invaders" and across her own caste. In her New York, just before the shocks of the Great War modified her views, all was vanity. However, *The Custom of the Country* is not a rewriting of *The House of Mirth*. In her earlier satire of New York society, Wharton had made the ambivalent Lily Bart into something of a tragic heroine. In *The Custom of the Country*, Wharton makes the rapacious Undine Spragg into a grotesque success. As a result, the stuffy and self-important society diminishes in importance and increases in sympathy, pointing a new thematic direction for Wharton's late works.

Ralph Marvell, a dabbling Manhattan lawyer and occasional poet, represents old New York at its mannerly best in the novel, though there is less to him than meets the eye. What matters most to Marvell is that he be thought a "gentleman." Ralph lives in Washington Square, which he calls the "Reservation for his world," the world of "aboriginal New York," populated by a soon-to-be-extinct species. When, after a night at the opera, Ralph contemplates his "Dutch interior," he thinks that New York society is much like the houses in which they dwell: "a muddle of misapplied ornament over a thin steel shell of utility."[148]

Since he has no other meaningful occupation, Ralph is intrigued by those social-climbing newcomers who have muscled their way into the City, "the Invaders," particularly by the Spraggs, a family from Apex City, where Mr. Spragg has made his fortune in pure water. The beautiful Undine Spragg, staying in Hotel Stentorian with her compliant mother and her coarse father, is conducting her siege of New York society, plotting her move from the West Side, across the Park: "Fifth Avenue was where she wanted to be!" Undine is Wharton's version of a literary archetype, the new American girl—beautiful, vain, common, brave, materialistic, pampered, a bundle of contradictions. "Undine was fiercely independent and yet passionately imitative."[149]

Ralph sets out to save her presumed innocence from corruptions by the vulgar and shallow rich, but in the end, he and his world are undone by the ambitious Undine. In this New York, the best, like Ralph, lack the courage of their convictions, and the worst, like Undine and her showy circle, are full of passionate intensity, grasping for the gaudy and the meretricious. Undine marries Ralph, neglecting to tell him about Elmer Moffett, her first husband, a blackmailer. Quickly impatient with Ralph's high standards of personal conduct, Undine leaves him for flashier company. After a divorce she marries the marquis Raymond de Chelles, who also cramps her style. Thus Undine seizes and quickly disposes of both an American and a French aristocrat in her search for social success.

Ralph finally realizes that he and his kind have been defeated by the Invaders: "He stood at the corner of Wall Street, looking up and down its hot summer perspective. He notices the swirls of dust in the cracks of the pavement, the rubbish in the gutters, the ceaseless stream of perspiring faces that poured by under tilted hats."[150] He then goes home and shoots himself, adding to the list of literary suicides in Manhattan fiction. But Undine's hunger for success is insatiable. She again marries Elmer Moffett, now a billionaire, and she carries on, with only a glimmer of self-realization. As Undine receives people in their Paris home, she realizes that "even now, however, she was not always happy. She had everything she wanted, but she still felt, at times, that there were other things she might want if she knew about them."[151]

If Henry James created Spencer Brydon as an alter ego and an antitype in "The Jolly Corner," so too did Wharton create Undine Spragg as a similar counterself in *The Custom of the Country*. Undine Spragg is Edith Wharton without the redeeming qualities of morality, culture, and talent.[152] Undine is a young woman from Middle America (Apex City, Kansas), desperate for self-transformation. She falls in love with an image of New York, and she sets out on a quest to dominate the world of her dreams: "Even in Apex, Undine's tender imagination had been nurtured on the feats and gestures of Fifth Avenue. She knew all of New York's golden aristocracy by name, and the lineaments of its most distinguished scions had been made familiar by passionate poring over the daily press."[153] Culture and talent gave Edith Wharton, who transcended the limits of New York, old and new, the detachment to delineate the ascent of a young woman from the provinces who comes to a city that offers her every opportunity to develop her most destructive values. In *The Custom of the Country*, Wharton views Undine Spragg and the old New York that she seizes with a combination of irony and pity.

After the Great War, all was changed for Edith Wharton: "Before the war you could write fiction without indicating the period, the present being assumed. The war has put an end to that for a long time, and everything will soon have to be timed with reference to it. In other words, the historical novel, with all its vices, will be the only possible form of fiction."[154] Edith Wharton had spent much of the Great War in Paris, working to rescue children, orphans of war. After World War I, when she wrote again of the world of her childhood, Wharton saw that old New York—the society that had stifled her when she came of age, the overstuffed and rigidly patterned world whose furniture she had tried to rearrange, the tyrannical realm of status distinctions she had bitterly satirized—had been blown asunder. Once the pressures of its presence had lifted, Wharton was free to come to terms in a new way with old New York through the genre of historical fiction.

If irony, as Paul Fussell argues, is the dominant literary attitude that emerges from the Great War, nostalgia for a lost world of coherence cannot be far behind.[155] In the words of R. W. B. Lewis, "Edith Wharton went in search, imaginatively, of the America that was gone" and she "located the lost America in the New York of her girlhood," in the 1870s.[156] The working title for her reassessment of things past was, fittingly, *Old New York*, but she changed that geographic and temporal designation to one that made a moral point: *The Age of Innocence*, a novel that became one of the touchstone works in the definition of the idea of the City. *The Age of Innocence* begins in irony, but it ends in reconciliation. "After all, there was good in the old way," concludes the novel's hero, clearly speaking for Wharton, as he looks back more than thirty years, from 1907, upon old New York.[157]

In the novel's opening pages, set in early 1871, members of old New York's "four hundred" gather at the Academy of Music on East Fourteenth Street and settle into its "shabby red and gold boxes" as though their world could never change.[158] The Academy would be driven out of business by the opening of the Metropolitan Opera House at Broadway and Thirty-ninth Street in 1883, so Wharton has deliberately placed her characters in a museumlike setting. These cautious, rule-bound people have come to hear Gounod's *Faust*, though most of them would sell their souls to keep from knowing the truth: "In reality they all lived in a kind of hieroglyphic world, where the real thing was never said or done or even thought, but only represented by a set of arbitrary signs." In *The Age of Innocence*, Edith Wharton, as though she were Margaret Mead in Samoa, sets out to expose "this elaborate system of mystification," but aware of the horrors of war and the social disruptions to come, she also finds redeeming virtues in New York's old ways.[159]

Wharton's representative figure in this world is Newland Archer, a polished product of the New York "system," as is his fiancée, May Welland, a "creation of factitious purity, so cunningly manufactured by a conspiracy of mothers and aunts and grandmothers and long-dead ancestresses."[160] Newland is, like so many of the New York society men in Wharton's novels, a tepid prig, a type against whom she lets loose her irony: "Few things seemed to Newland Archer more awful than an offense against 'Taste,' that far-off divinity of whom 'Form' was the mere visible representative and viceregent."[161] Yet Newland possesses a tentative intellectual adventurousness, which leads him to read books that give him some critical distance on the world he inhabits.

Into this stylized and pretentious world enters Ellen Olenska, a figure of light and grace. Descendant of a New York first family, the Mingotts, Ellen, after her parents died, was reared in Europe by an eccentric aunt; she has since married a Polish nobleman, Count Olenski, who has been unfaithful and cruel to her. She too is at the Academy to hear *Faust*. Having left her unworthy husband, Ellen has returned to a place she presumes to be secure and supportive, as it had been when she was a young Mingott. "I'm sure I'm dead and buried, and this dear old place is heaven," Ellen says to Newland at the opera.[162] Ellen will learn that New York society is a nest of vipers who are ready to turn on her for flaunting their values: to maintain marriages at whatever cost and, above all, to remain financially solvent. In turn, Ellen will teach Newland to see some of his world with fresh eyes. At first, when he observes New York from her point of view, "as through the wrong end of a telescope, it [looks] disconcertingly small and distant."[163] In this novel, Newland makes a journey across his social world that brings him from smug celebration to renunciation and, finally, to reconciliation.

The Age of Innocence is something of a morality play in which Newland is torn between two women who represent conflicting values. Newland gives his hand to May, for he is truly wed to the circumscribed world of old New York she represents, but he gives his love to Ellen, for he sincerely yearns for escape to her world of knowledge and experience. At one point, in the midst of a carriage ride through a winter storm, Newland begs Ellen to run off with him to some other country, where they can be free to love each other "and nothing else on earth will matter." But Ellen asks, "Oh, my dear—where is that country?"[164] Her European experience educates his American innocence. She cannot build her happiness on the betrayal of another. Paradoxically, the only way they can retain their love is to renounce it. Finally Newland *sees*; he stops their cab and he steps out into the winter winds of Manhattan, where his tears freeze to his face—an apt symbol of frozen passions in Wharton's New York.

Ellen leaves New York, eventually settling in Paris, and Newland recommits himself to May. Their marriage proves sound, though it is not based upon shared intimacies, and their children, Dallas, Mary, and Bill, incorporate the best of their parents' values while leading "a larger life and [holding] more tolerant views." Thinking of how they have turned out, Newland concludes, "there was good in the new order too."[165]

Newland remains "a good citizen," but he never becomes an active participant in the world, as does a younger member of his class, Teddy Roosevelt, who encourages Archer in his brief foray into politics. As Newland, musing in the library of his house at East Thirty-ninth Street, recalls his cautious past, he realizes that he has missed "the flower of life."[166] In assigning Newland these carefully chosen words, Wharton evokes the grieving William Dean Howells in Whistler's Paris garden and the despairing Lambert Strether of James's *The Ambassadors*—other provincial Americans struck by the emptiness of their world and by visions of richer, European life.

When Newland and Dallas visit Paris, where Ellen lives, the elder Archer refuses the invitation to see her, though nothing stands in the way of their reunion; perhaps he hangs back because he is fearful either that the vision he holds of his lost love might be compromised by seeing her or, alternatively, that renewing his love for Ellen might make a mockery of the life he has led with May. For Cynthia Griffin Wolff, Newland Archer has gained more than he lost; he has arrived at maturity through his late realizations: "Newland had escaped the narrow limitations of old New York in the only way that was ever *really* available to him, by achieving an inner peace that transcends time and place altogether."[167] However, that peace has been purchased at the price of a lifelong misunderstanding. Long after May's death, Newland learns from Dallas that she had always known about his love for Ellen, but May also told her son, on her deathbed, that Newland would, in the best way of old New York, honor all his vows. But she and Newland had never discussed any of this. So when Newland says he missed the flower of life, referring to his unrequited love for Ellen, he still does not realize that his wife had been that flower, within his reach in New York while he yearned for romance in foreign climes. Like Howells and Strether, Archer felt "life" resided in Europe, more exactly, in his mental image of a liberating and romantic European culture. But *The Age of Innocence* makes it clear that Wharton believed that life was there for the plucking if one only *saw* it—rich, various, and honorable—in old New York. In *The Age of Innocence*, Wharton treated her once-scorned home both with vengeance and forgiveness.

OCCASIONALLY, EDITH WHARTON'S PASSIONS TO DO—IN effect, to do in—New York led her to exaggeration and simplification. So determined was she to convey her sense of the destructive City that she created cartoon characterizations and plotlines that reduced her stories to stark parables with pat ironies and inescapable morals. This occurs in *Old New York* (1924), a gathering of four novellas composed in the early 1920s.

The first of these, "False Dawn," set in the 1840s, tells the story of Lewis Raycie, heir of the "monumental" Halston Raycie, lord of High Point, an estate overlooking Long Island Sound. Lewis is sent on his Grand Tour of Europe so that he might see, as his father puts it, "those older civilizations whose yoke it has been our glory to cast off."[168] A man who controls his wife's money and his children's every move, the elder Raycie personifies the patriarchal tyranny of old New York. He hopes to shape his son—a young man who is in love with a plain cousin and likes to hear Edgar Allan Poe read his poetry—into old New York's version of the "cultivated gentleman."[169] To this end, Halston Raycie, a man of invincible ignorance and uninformed tastes, charges Lewis with the responsibility of buying old masters in Europe. Lewis is to collect the core of the planned Raycie Gallery, which is intended to bring esteem to the family. Old New York money will then be ennobled through its translation into classic paintings by Correggio, perhaps even by Raphael.

Predictably, Lewis, who has all of Wharton's sympathetic identification, ignores his father's instructions and goes his own way. Under the sway of a "blue-eyed gentleman" he meets in Switzerland, who turns out to be John Ruskin, Lewis, while examining frescoes in a Venetian church, is overcome by a beautiful rendering of Saint Ursula. When Lewis returns to New York with a collection of works by little-known artists, works that portray saints and madonnas, his father is appalled. He disinherits Lewis, leaving him only the paintings and a small allowance. Lewis marries his beloved cousin, who faithfully supports his efforts to make the collection known by opening a "Gallery of Christian Art" in a huge, rotting house on the corner of Third Avenue and Tenth Street. Its failure further alienates Lewis from the rest of the Raycie family.

It takes half a century for Lewis's aesthetic vision to be justified. By then all traces of the once-proud Raycies have disappeared: "These old New Yorkers, who lived so well and spent their money so liberally, vanished like a pinch of dust when they disappeared from their pews and their dinner-tables."[170] A distant relative of Lewis Raycie, by then deceased, discovers the paintings in an attic, sells them, and, with the profits, buys a new house on Fifth Avenue. Wharton's case is completed in this heavily ironic touch: old New York was oppressive, ignorant, and pretentious, a society that thwarted its most sensitive children, failed in its artistic judgments, and traded its true treasures for status possessions. "False Dawn," then, is Wharton's "Ozymandias of Egypt"; in her story, as in Shelley's poem, the mighty inevitably fall, but art endures to mock their presumptions.

WILLIAM DEAN HOWELLS, HENRY JAMES, AND EDITH Wharton—three American novelists of manners who created compelling myths of New York in their works of fiction. These novelists emphasized the City's social discriminations, and invidious distinctions of money and manners composed the essential drama of their work. While Walt Whitman's poetic persona sings out acceptance amid the crowd as he strolls Broadway, these novelists' characters usually stay behind heavy doors, withdraw from the raucous City, or make only tentative forays into the life of its streets. The New York of Howells, James, and Wharton is a threatening presence.

Despite the varied perspectives of these authors, something of a monomyth of the City emerges from their fiction. Once upon a time New York had been a simple place, for James and Wharton in particular, a place of innocence, free from awareness of economic exploitation, class or ethnic differentiation, and sexual knowledge. For all three writers, the post–Civil War City was a circus of conspicuous consumption and display. Their urban village had become an engine of capitalistic expansion, defined by its vulgar hotels and cathedrals of commerce, its pretentious mansions and pathetic tenements. The City was, moreover, an arena of dangerous social conflicts populated by avaricious social climbers and desperate immigrants. Thus for each novelist, especially Howells,

New York tested the limits of the American dream of democratic polity. Yet the City stood as well for the possibilities of American life—the opportunity for transformation, self-realization, and even, for Wharton after the Great War, the preservation of redemptive values. For each of these writers, New York City also represented the supreme test to the artistic powers of imagination.

FIN DE SIÈCLE
NEW YORK CITY

New York's "New People"

and New Era

Wᴜ̆ᴜ̆ᴜ̆ᴜ̆ᴀᴍ Dᴇᴀɴ Hᴏᴡᴇʟʟs, Hᴇɴʀʏ Jᴀᴍᴇs, ᴀɴᴅ Eᴅɪᴛʜ Wharton portrayed old New York as a city under assault from the "new people"—invaders, rich and poor, from the heartland or from Europe. The reserved, old New York rich moved uptown, where their hastily erected gates were crashed by the ambitious, new-moneyed class. The simultaneous arrival of poor immigrants in vast numbers made Manhattan an island of cruel contrasts: uptown and inland opulence vs. downtown and coastal poverty.

The arrival of new New Yorkers changed the story of the City between the Civil War and World War I. Americans from the provinces—Horatio Alger, O. Henry, Stephen Crane—reinvented the City in different ways. Alger and O. Henry were two marginal men who, having committed crimes and indiscretions in the heartland, sought the haven of anonymity in the City. They wrote tales of sadness, sentiment, and success set in the hard heart of New York, while Crane, an ambitious and adventurous young man, came with more purposeful intent—to tell the story of the City's have-nots with the eyes of a literary realist and the light, ironic touch of a poet. Jacob Riis's photographic record and his reports on the dispossessed shocked the nation into a belated realization of urban inequities. Jewish authors, particularly Abraham Cahan and Anzia Yezierska, confirmed the truth of Riis's gritty pictures in their fiction, but they also provided a map of assimilation and achievement: from Ellis Island, through the Lower East Side to a new vision of America. The Irish-American voice, telling the tale of a similar journey, was registered by George M. Cohan, Finley Peter Dunne, James W. Sullivan, William L. Riordon, M. A. Sadlier, and others, further amplifying the City's tone and style. The increasing presence of African-Americans in Harlem was celebrated by one of its best writers, James Weldon Johnson, who foreshadowed and then chronicled the Harlem Renaissance. Theodore Dreiser's myths of the City evoked New York as a place of awesome power that seized the imaginations and shaped the fates, for better or worse, of those who were drawn to it, as though by a strong magnet. Before and after the turn of the century, young writers of promise sought their own success and self-transformation in New York by inventing parables about those who attempted and often failed to fulfill the promise of American life on its gridlike streets. As New York realized its potential, its writers chronicled, more accurately and vividly than ever before, its powers to create and destroy.

By 1900 NEARLY THREE AND A HALF MILLION PEOPLE, MORE than a third of them foreign-born, lived in Greater New York, a rich and mighty city, newly lighted by electricity, its sections linked by new bridges and rail lines. South of Central Park, open spaces were filled in with grand houses and tall buildings—"hideous, top-heavy nightmares" to George Templeton Strong, but "cloud touching edifices" to Walt Whitman.[1] New York had become a city of dramatically contrasting images and attitudes. Paralleling the "Millionaires' Row" of Fifth Avenue, for example, was the presence of nickel-and-dime businesses along Sixth Avenue.[2]

Such territorial and class distinctions increasingly divided New Yorkers after the Civil War. No road easily linked these two worlds. Broadway bisects lower Manhattan, from the Battery to Tenth Street, but then bends up the West Side, along the old Bloomingdale Road, eventually reaching into Yonkers. Many of New York's new immigrants and other urban poor clung to the Bowery, an avenue that provided an actual but symbolically difficult route uptown. "The dichotomy between Broadway and the Bowery began early," writes Luc Sante, "as their respective theatrical districts came to epitomize respectability in the case of the former and cheap flash in the latter, and as the years went on, these qualities expanded in the popular mind, so that the two avenues came, however inaccurately, to stand for moral poles."[3]

Society abandoned its old center, the Gay White Way of homes and clubs along lower Broadway. Fashionable New York went its own way uptown, isolating itself from the increasingly distasteful Bowery and ignoring Broadway's westward turn. In 1850, Bishop Hughes decided to build St. Patrick's Cathedral at Fifth Avenue and Fiftieth Street; when completed in 1879, it stood at the center of New York's society, culture, and commerce. Henry Vanderbilt, son of Cornelius, built a mansion at Fifth Avenue and Fifty-first Street, starting the uptown movement of wealth and fashion. It was a time when, as Oliver Allen notes, "aristocracy—such as it was—had yielded to plutocracy."[4]

With the completion of Central Park in the 1870s, Fifth Avenue, above Fifty-ninth Street, became style's new center. Easter parades, ostentatious displays of conspicuous consumption, were held along upper Fifth Avenue. The new Metropolitan was set at Seventy-ninth Street in 1880. The new plutocrats built the Metropolitan Opera House at Broadway and Thirty-ninth Street in 1883, driving the old Academy, on East Fourteenth Street, an aristocratic institution memorialized in *The Age of Innocence*, out of business within two years. "Conservatives cherished the [Academy of Music] for being small and inconvenient, and thus keeping out the 'new people' whom New York was beginning to dread and yet be drawn to," wryly noted Wharton.[5] When the Academy became a vaudeville theater, the downtown cultural decline was confirmed. Uptown, Carnegie Hall opened its doors to new and old money in 1891. The Waldorf-Astoria Hotel was built in 1897. The Plaza Hotel, at Fifth and Fifty-ninth Street, was completed in 1907, joining the Netherlands and the Savoy at the Park's entrance. Delmonico's relocated its opulent restaurant in 1897 to Fifth Avenue and Forty-fourth Street. By the turn of the century, skyscrapers dominated the skyline of Manhattan: notably the Tower Building on Broadway (1889) and the Park Row Business Building (1898), which reached 392 feet.

New York was quickly being opened to influences that would change its socially restrictive character. The Roeblings' Brooklyn Bridge was completed in 1883. The elevated railway opened northern Manhattan to easy access. Grand Central Terminal was built by Cornelius Vanderbilt in 1871. More important, the proportion of foreign-born New Yorkers rose rapidly from 11 percent in 1825 to more than 50 percent in 1855; more than half of these immigrants were Irish. Between 1880 and 1919 more than twenty-three million Europeans came to America; some seventeen million landed in New York City. Many long-standing New Yorkers felt their world crumbling under the weight and needs of these newcomers.[6] New New Yorkers were making the City their own.

In 1892 Ellis Island opened to accommodate the increased traffic, replacing

Castle Clinton as a clearinghouse for immigrants. The Irish arrived in staggering numbers, settling in the Lower East Side, Hell's Kitchen, and dispersing to many parts of the City. Italians moved into the area around Canal Street, which became known as "Little Italy." Jews, who soon composed a quarter of the City's population, settled around Hester Street, on the Lower East Side. By World War I, emigrating African-Americans from all parts of the nation had altered the face of Harlem. In 1894 five counties united: New York (Manhattan), Brooklyn, Queens, the Bronx, and Staten Island. On January 1, 1898, the City of Greater New York came into being—an urban metropolis spread over 320 square miles. By the early years of the twentieth century, New York City had shaped its modern character.

However, the more inclusive and imperial New York became, the more the "Greater City" revealed unresolved opposites.[7] "New people," foreign and domestic, rich and poor, strained its polity. This becomes clear when we examine the dominant myths of New York as codified by the writers—in addition to Howells, James, and Wharton—who responded to the idea of the City from the end of the Civil War to just after the turn of the century. These writers contrived original images to represent New York, a city transforming itself before their eyes. They developed new plots, new voices, and new artistic designs to represent the City's increasingly fragmentary, melodramatic, and stark contrasts. For some writers New York was a place of random and disconnected circumstances, but for others New York was a closed system of intersection and moral consequence. A new generation of writers strained to depict a city that defied credible description. Hyperbole came to define New York literary style. For all of these writers New York was a city divided, a city whose citizens affirmed their identities through individual and group struggles for survival.

This period saw the emergence of writers who spoke for new New Yorkers, for those who neither derived from nor deferred to the City's traditional culture. The Gilded Age saw a radical democratization of American letters, led by New York voices. Voices from the street were heard: in particular, Horatio Alger and O. Henry composed modern myths of New York, a city that held its terrors, guaranteed melodrama, but sanctioned access to, even on occasion fulfilled its promise of, success and happiness. Both men wrote about New York's previously ignored "little" people, in Upton Sinclair's words, "the obscure and exploited masses of New York, the waitresses and hat-pressers, soda-jerkers and bums, the taxi drivers and policemen, O. Henry's 'Four Million.' "[8] Popular fiction thus extended the democratic covenant to include most New Yorkers.

These and other writers gave the New York story new range, texture, and complexity. Their New York, a place insistently economic in its measurement of its citizens, was, as well, an Oz of romance and adventure.

IN MORE THAN ONE HUNDRED NOVELS PUBLISHED BETWEEN 1867 and 1899, Horatio Alger portrayed the romance of urban life, the exhilaration of Manhattan, for a rural and provincial America that was making the difficult transition to the urban and urbane. In a typical Alger plot line, a young man, innocent and full of virtue, winningly naive, comes from his village to the City to seek his fortune; there he suffers tests of character and trials of fate. However, in the end, through rectitude and good fortune, he succeeds in his endeavors. Or, alternatively, Alger portrays an urban street urchin whose worthiness is, after various tests of will and value, acknowledged and rewarded. Pluck and luck prevail in Alger's City—a place that, though full of evil, yields to the power of a pure heart. The Alger hero saw his opportunities in New York and he took them, but unlike the Tammany lords of his day, he did not need to resort to "graft." In Alger's myth, the City, in the long run, is benign, even beneficent. The Alger heroes are baptized into the secular religion of ethical capitalism, reeducated into the manners of the bourgeoisie, and either restored to their rightful inheritance or granted the opportunity for success. Indeed, Alger's novels were success manuals for young men from America's provinces; they were didactic tracts illustrating the worthiness of the Protestant ethic, the providence of American life in the City, which paradoxically served as both a haven for Alger's heroes and a vast stage on which they acted out their dramatic lives.

Horatio Alger's own route to success in New York City was even more circuitous than the melodramatic courses of his heroes. He was born in Revere, Massachusetts, on January 13, 1832. His father was a Unitarian minister who urged his reluctant son to follow in his profession. After schooling in Marlborough, Massachusetts, Alger attended Harvard, where he graduated in the class of 1852. He dropped out of Harvard Divinity School in 1853, but eventually returned to complete his degree in 1860. He took a trip to Europe, financed through an inheritance from a former landlord, a solicitous substitute father—establishing the pattern of paternalistic rescue in Alger's imagination. On his return, he accepted a pastorate at the Unitarian church in Brewster, on Cape Cod, where he continued his writing.[9] During the Civil War he published *Frank's Campaign* (1864), a novel about a young man who takes care of the family farm so that his father can fight for the Union. However, Horatio Alger would not remain a stay-at-home in pastoral America.

Alger's lifelong interest in young men led to his removal from the pulpit. Accused of homosexual encounters with boys, he was dismissed from his ministry at Brewster. Critic Carl Bode argues that Alger spent the rest of his life doing penance by taking up the cause of needy young men of the City and telling their tales.[10] Certainly Alger focused his personal and literary energies on the street boys of New York, where he arrived in 1866, a month after his dismissal.[11] Through Charles L. Brace, a philanthropist who was concerned with the welfare of homeless boys, Alger discovered the Newsboy's Lodging House, where he stayed and gathered material for his books; there he found his models for Ragged Dick, Tattered Tom, and other appealing urban waifs. In 1867 William T. Adams, editor of *Student and Schoolmate*, accepted a story, the basis for *Ragged Dick*, and Alger's extraordinary literary career was under way.

Alger's tales demystified the awesome City; they assured American youth and their parents that dangers could be averted and success achieved without the loss of moral character, which was the price of success in Howells's more realistic urban novels. For Alan Trachtenberg, the Alger hero progresses by "converting Bunyan's linear allegory through a symbolic landscape into a vertical rise within the city." *Ragged Dick; or, Street Life in New York* (1867) teaches a valuable lesson. "Not to be abandoned to the cheats of Vanity Fair and thugs, . . . the city must be recovered, recaptured as the city upon a hill."[12] Alger, a product of Harvard and the "New England mind," echoed John Winthrop's quest for a heavenly city. Yet, like essayist and editor Norman Podhoretz after him, Alger was also concerned with "making it" in this world, in worldly Manhattan. Alger's heroes, too, would have it both ways—by achieving their success through manners and morality, by acquiring money and attaining grace. Americans, Podhoretz notes, are contradictorily encouraged to strive for wealth and made to feel guilty for pursuing "the bitch-goddess SUCCESS," as William James called "our national disease."[13] The solution to this dilemma for Alger was to contrive a hero who preserved his sense of decency and character at the same time that he pursued the dream of success. Alger adapted to his own purposes Ben Franklin's myth of the impoverished, idealistic young American who enters a strange city and, through hard work, an exemplary character, shrewdness, and good fortune, eventually triumphs.

Johnny Nolan, an Irish bootblack whom Alger met in Manhattan, served as the model for Ragged Dick, though Alger made over the shiftless Nolan into a meritorious model, thus imposing his own ennobling myth upon the compromising facts of a New York life. Though Alger may have been banished from his pulpit, his didactic, urban adventure stories provided another way for him to preach to the youth of America.

In *Ragged Dick*, Alger's touchstone book, his hero is a fourteen-year-old, orphaned, shoeshine boy who works in the Bowery. Though a "real boy" who swears, smokes, gambles, and enjoys Barnum's, Dick will not steal: "His nature was a noble one, and had saved him from all mean faults."[14] All he needs is a rescuer. Fortuitously, Dick is taken up by a Mr. Whitney, whose nephew, Frank, wants to see the City and requires a guide. When Mr. Whitney has Dick wash and don one of Frank's suits so he will be presentable, his transformation into a gentleman commences.

Dick has as much to teach the Whitneys about survival in the City as he has to learn from them about gentlemanly ways. Even crossing Broadway against the traffic is an adventure, an illustration of Dick's (and Alger's) awareness of New York. Dick, the street urchin, is also surprisingly knowledgeable about the composition and costs of elite dwellings: "As the boys pursued their way up Broadway, Dick pointed out the prominent hotels and places of amusement. Frank was particularly struck with the imposing fronts of the St. Nicholas and Metropolitan Hotels, the former of white marble, the latter of a subdued brown hue, but not less elegant in its internal appointments. He was not surprised to be informed that each of these splendid structures cost with the furnishings not far from a million dollars."[15] Despite such touches of realism in *Ragged Dick*—Alger's footnotes point out the precise locations of landmarks or note the exact distance between City Hall and Central Park—the novel is a Christian-capitalist parable in which a worthy young man rises from rags to riches.

Alger puts opportunity in his hero's path. In a classic Alger scene, Dick, ever in the right place at the right time, rescues a boy, Little Johnny, after he falls from a ferry boat. Little Johnny's father, Mr. Rockwell, tells Dick to come to his counting room on Pearl Street, where he is offered employment as a clerk, at a salary of ten dollars a week. Ragged Dick is thus transformed into Richard Hunter, "a young gentleman on the way to fame and fortune," notes another street urchin.[16]

The City rechristened Alger's representative young men, providing them with new names and identities. In one of his last works, *Adrift in New York* (1902), Alger once again showed how a young man, removed from his rightful station in life, is restored to his inheritance. *Adrift in New York* opens on John Linden, still disconsolate over the loss of his son, Harvey, who had been kidnapped at the age of four some fourteen years before. John's untrustworthy nephew, Curtis War-ing, age thirty-five, argues that even if Harvey is alive "he is a rough street-boy, perchance serving his time at Blackwell's Island, a hardened young ruffian, whom it would be bitter mortification to recognize as your son."[17] John's young niece, Florence, an orphan, is optimistic about the lost boy's fate and character—thus she assumes the role of heroine. This, then, is the essential theme of the novel: whether inherited family values of probity and decency can survive the corrupting effects of the City. Through a convoluted and characteristically melodramatic plot, the answer is never really in doubt.

John Linden has made two wills. One divides his property between Florence and Curtis. The other leaves all to Harvey. (In Alger's vision, a test of character is also a test of fortune.) John, a petty Lear, misjudges the characters of these young people; he misses Curtis's manipulatory evil and ignores Florence's uncompromising goodness. (The City, in Alger, educates the young, who, in turn, reeducate the old.) John encourages Florence to marry Curtis; when she refuses, he banishes her from his house. Before Florence leaves, Tom Dodger, a reluctant thief, enters, but he accidentally (providentially) encounters Florence. She can tell, somehow, that Dodger could become a good man. After she informs him of her plight, the young thief invites her to come home with him. Inspired by her kindness and goodness, he promises never again to steal. John discovers them and accuses Dodger of thievery. Alger here plots heavy structural irony, for "Tom," of course, is the long lost Harvey, who had been kidnapped by the evil Curtis and sent off to Australia; now known as Dodger—no doubt after Dickens's artful thief—Harvey is back in New York, employed by a saloon keeper. Thus Alger sets his hero on a quest to regain his identity and to restore his true name.

The reader is offered glimpses of what it is like to be young, lonely, and aimless in New York, though Alger can never approach the psychic terror of Melville's characters, similarly adrift, in *Pierre*. Florence goes to the City with Dodger and gets a job as a governess. Then the already murky plot thickens into a soupy fog when Dodger is tricked by Curtis onto a ship bound for San Francisco. However, one thing remains clear: Alger's world is a closed system of internal references and fortuitous accidents. Everything that arises must converge in revelation and moral righteousness. Thus Dodger returns to New York to right all wrongs.

Finally, John Linden realizes that Curtis is the cause of all his family's bad fortune. John is reunited with his son. "Florence and Dodger (now known as Harvey Linden) live with him," though "in the midst of their prosperity Florence and Dodger will never forget the time they were adrift in New York."[18] A possible marriage is hinted, and the novel ends with a restored family unit, with

Harvey and Florence (more brother and sister than lovers) assuming the roles of children to the paternalistic John Linden. New York has served as a necessary backdrop to the testing of a worthy young man; the City also has been a quickening agent for the resolution of conflicts and the revelation of characters.

For Alger a man's character, not his environment, no matter how compromising, is his fate. This must have been a difficult credo to hold onto when Alger saw around him the actual plight of the boys who were adrift in the real New York, often living in hovels, constantly victimized by street predators, and frequently dying young. Speaking of the actual homeless and wayward youth of Alger's day, Luc Sante writes:

> *If it seems that these children must have very early used up the entire stock of adult pleasures—sex, drink, gambling, extortion, racketeering, fraud, intimidation, unfair competition, price-fixing, terrorism—it should be remembered that the life expectancy for kids growing up under those conditions could not have been very high. The whole adult order of high and low sensations had to be experienced in fifteen or twenty years at best before they succumbed to disease, malnutrition, exposure, stab wounds, or gunfire.*[19]

Alger's novels, then, are triumphs of hope (or wishful thinking) over experience; their vast popularity tells us much about what Americans wanted to believe about themselves and about the America they saw in New York City.

THE TYPICAL O. HENRY TALE, LIKE THE STANDARD ALGER success story, is inextricably bound in the popular imagination with New York City. Both men wrote about what has come to be known as the underclass—not the elite "four hundred," but the vast and often nameless "four million" who comprised the true "voice of the city," in phrases used as titles for two collections of O. Henry's stories.[20] In "The Pride of the Cities," O. Henry treated with heavy irony the attitude of entitlement that kept privileged New Yorkers from acknowledging their less fortunate fellow residents: "New York was empty. Two hundred thousand of its people were away for the summer. Three million eight hundred thousand remained as caretakers and to pay the bills of the absentees. But the 200,000 are an expensive lot."[21] In his preface to *The Four Million*, O. Henry justified the expanded scope of his fictional concerns: "A wiser man has arisen—the census taker—and his larger estimate of human interest has been preferred in making out the field of these little stories of the 'Four Million.' "[22]

Like Horatio Alger, O. Henry came to the City from the far reaches of the Republic. William Sidney (later Sydney) Porter was born in 1862, in Greensboro, N. C.. His father, Dr. Algernon Sidney Porter, was a beloved and prominent physician. His mother was the daughter of a newspaper editor; she had graduated from Greensboro Female College. His parents provided a background of solid, middle-class success, a standard to which their son could never measure up, just as Alger could not emulate his father's values. Both writers were dropouts from middle-class proprieties and the Protestant ethic.

Porter's schooling ended in his teens, when he went to work for his uncle, W. C. Porter, in a drugstore, where he was employed for three years. He then spent years in Texas, where he was married in 1887, and worked as a draftsman. In 1894 young Porter began a journal, the *Rolling Stone*, while working as a teller in the First National Bank of Austin. However, the financial strain of leading a life both as a publisher and a bank employee led him to the crime of embezzlement. Under suspicion, Porter fled to New Orleans, then to Honduras, but he eventually returned to Austin in 1897, the year his wife died. There he published his first stories. In 1898 Porter was arrested, tried, found guilty of embezzlement, and sentenced to a five-year imprisonment at a federal penitentiary in Ohio, though he was released in 1901. Porter's self-protective "O. Henry" persona was developed while in prison, where he wrote fourteen stories.

After a stay in Pittsburgh, where he wrote more stories, Porter came to New York in 1902, invited by Gilman Hall, editor of *Ainslee's*. He would live in New York for eight years, a period during which he wrote more than 125 stories about the City. In the impersonal metropolis, Porter hoped to hide his criminal past. "If ever in American literature the place and the man met, they met when O. Henry strolled for the first time along the streets of New York," wrote an early biographer.[23] Yet Porter, despite his increasing success, remained elusive and secretive; he lived in obscure hotels, where even his publishers could not find him. He prowled the streets for material, drank two bottles of liquor a day, and produced reams of stories. In 1903 he signed a contract with the *Sunday World* to supply a story each week for the fee of $100. He moved to 55 Irving Place, where he felt the ambience of Washington Irving, like him a stroller and literary sketcher of Manhattan.

From his window on the City, Porter watched the passing parade, imagining what New Yorkers' lives might be like, preparing his tales.[24] But his dwelling was also conveniently located near bawdy houses, saloons, and Tony Pastor's vaudeville theater, for O. Henry was drawn to low-life haunts and characters. He was a divided man, pulled between raffishness and respectability. He was most comfortable playing the role of the big spender with other socially marginal New Yorkers who sought to allay their insecurities in public displays. Driven by ambition and by economic desperation, he wrote for the *World* 113 stories in two years, a form that was an appropriate reflection of urban dwellers' fragmented lives. As Peter Conrad notes, "the story's shortness institutionalizes the city's ruthless concision—its editing of existence."[25]

Despite the brevity of his tales, O. Henry's New York is a place of extravagant metaphors and dramatic struggles, in his words, "a combination of Delilah, green Chartreuse, Beethoven, chloral and John L. in his best days." His Manhattan holds an elusive beauty, "like a great river fed by a hundred alien streams. Each influx brings strange seeds on its flood, strange silt and weeds, and now and then a flower of rare promise. To construe this river requires a man who can build dykes against the overflow, who is a naturalist, a geologist, a humanitarian, a diver, and a strong swimmer."[26] In an arrestingly mixed trope, he evokes the spirit of the City as a living being, hunted and consumed by its inhabitants: "Silent, grim, colossal, the big city has ever stood against its revilers. They call it hard as iron; they say no pulse of pity beats in its bosom; they compare its streets with lonely forests and deserts of lava. But beneath the hard crust of the lobster is found a delectable and luscious food."[27] O. Henry's New York is, then, a kind of wilderness, in which seekers struggle for survival and seek their prey—prey that in turn seeks them. "Robert Walmsey's descent upon the city resulted in a Kilkenny struggle," he writes in "The Defeat of the City." "He came out of the fight victor by a fortune and a reputation. On the other hand, he was swallowed up by the city."[28] O. Henry, for his part, ingested New York.

O. Henry wrote stories about Jews, Germans, and Irish immigrants; he also wrote about victimized shop girls and good-hearted prostitutes. All were material for his urban operettas: "In the big city the twin spirits Romance and Adventure are always aboard seeking worthy wooers. As we roam the streets they slyly peep at us and challenge us in twenty different guises."[29]

Of course O. Henry's New York was not all glitter and sentiment. In "The City of Dreadful Night," he portrays Irish immigrants who, on a boiling summer night, are evacuated from their slum residence, Beersheba Flats, and ordered to sleep in Central Park. But the "dreadful" aspect turns out, after all, to be a matter of low comedy, featuring restless sleepers, rolling over each other in the grass, and thin irony: the owner of Beersheba Flats raises the rents of the poor by

15 percent because they have been provided "the grass and trees that give extra benefits to a man's tenements."[30]

O. Henry's most telling parable of Manhattan occurs in "The Duel," a story from an aptly titled 1910 collection, *Strictly Business*. O. Henry sets out to show that "New York stands unique among the cities of the worlds." Though New York's millions have arrived in various ways, they all have to battle the City— "and, oh, the city is a general in the ring." Either the citizen becomes a New Yorker or "the rankest outlander and Philistine." So it is with William and Jack, friends from the West who seek their fortunes in New York: "William was for business; Jack was for Art." This story gives O. Henry the opportunity to point out, as powerfully as Crane or Dreiser, the power of the City to draw in and alter the outsider, unfitting him for his original home: "Not only by blows does it seek to subdue you. It woos you to its heart with the subtlety of a siren." For O. Henry, however, the City's attractions were largely beneficent.

Four years after they arrive, William and Jack meet over lunch to compare their conditions. Jack decides that William has been gobbled up by the City. New York, for Jack, is "a leech. It drains the blood of the country." Or, in an even more elaborate metaphor, "it is a juggernaut, a moloch, a monster to which the innocence, the genius, and the beauty of the land must pay tribute." Jack despises "its very vastness and power" and wishes to return to the clean air of the West. However, later, when he receives a telegram from his beloved Dolly, who begs him to return home, he finds he cannot leave the City.

The strategy of sudden reversal, crucial to the structure of so many O. Henry stories, is here utilized to lend a sense of romance to the City, which persuades Jack, the suspicious outsider, to stay. Sitting at his window at midnight, Jack finally realizes New York's magic. "Far below and around lay the city like a ragged purple dream." The caverns and brightly lit gulches of the urban landscape are too wondrous for him to abandon: "There below him lay all things, good and bad, that can be brought from the four corners of the earth to instruct, please, thrill, enrich, despoil, elevate, cast down, nurture or kill. Thus the flavor of it came up to him and went into his blood."[31] Though O. Henry glazed his vision of New York with sentiment and contrived situations of cloying melodrama, his City, in its vast powers to shape the wills and color the minds of its residents, anticipated Dreiser's hallucinatory vision of New York.

IN 1896, TWO BRIEF NOVELS WERE PUBLISHED THAT EXtended the resources of that genre beyond those advocated by William Dean

Howells with their realistic portrayals of what Jacob Riis called "how the other half lived." Abraham Cahan's story of a young Jewish immigrant's ambition to become an American, *Yekl: A Tale of New York*, and Stephen Crane's *George's Mother*, which chronicles a poor young man's decline into alcoholism, experiment with narrative point of view and the vernacular to achieve a more authentic New York voice. These works, which expanded the form of the urban novel, were what Melville called "inside narratives," locating readers not as observers, as in Howells's fiction, but inside the minds of those caught in constricting worlds. The influence of this urban realism can also be seen in the dramatic accounts of hard times in the City underpinning the fiction and autobiography of Anzia Yezierska.

Abraham Cahan, born in a Lithuanian village in 1860, arrived in the United States in 1862 and was quickly appointed as editor of the *Jewish Daily Forward*, a newspaper published in Yiddish for the Jewish community, a position he held from 1897 until his death in 1951. Cahan became an accomplished writer of journalism and fiction, and an ardent socialist. He also developed a reverence for American writers—for Hawthorne, James, and in particular, Howells, whose works he translated for his *Forward* readers. In 1892 Howells, seeking information about union organizers for *A Traveler from Altruria*, sought out Cahan. Howells, who had been a young man from the provinces seeking "gas and gaiters" in New York, recognized Cahan as a fellow literary seeker, despite their different backgrounds. New York was America's literary marketplace, our crass Paris, where writers from elsewhere came, exchanged their works, and joined the discordant chorus.

In 1880 some eighty thousand Jews, most from Germany, lived in New York, making up 4 percent of the city's population. Following a large influx from eastern Europe, that fraction grew to 25 percent by 1910. By the time immigration quotas were set in 1924, some two million Jews dwelled in New York City.[32] With such a presence, a Jewish-American literature quickly developed. Yiddish poets, called the "sweatshop school," told of the miseries of manufacturing. Just after the turn of the century, a group of immigrants who called themselves "Di Yunge" (Young Ones) and then, in the 1920s, another group, "In Zich" (Introspectives), brought a new level of artistic consciousness to the immigrant's story, inspiring works by Sholem Asch and I. J. Singer, Sholom Aleichem, Isaac Bashevis Singer, and many more.[33] Yiddish theater and journals thrived in the City, a story eloquently told in Irving Howe's *World of Our Fathers*. Above all others, Abraham Cahan was crucial to the legitimizing of Jewish-American writing in Manhattan and in the American mind.

In 1895, having read a Cahan story, "A Providential Match," Howells invited Cahan to his home overlooking Central Park and encouraged him to write a novel about the ghetto. The result was *Yankele the Yankee*, which Howells deftly retitled *Yekl: A Tale of New York*, thus localizing the story's focus.[34] Howells himself had included glimpses of immigrant life in *A Hazard of New Fortunes* and in "East-Side Ramble," but his stance showed the compassionate detachment of a high-minded, Christian reformer. *Yekl*, on the other hand, a work written from inside the ghetto, was more an evocation and analysis than an exposé and moral allegory. *Yekl* is the first novel, notes Jules Chametzky in his study of Cahan, "*by an immigrant wholly about the immigrant experience.*"[35] Cahan was far closer to the experience, of course, than Howells could possibly have been, but Cahan's is no mere cautionary tale designed to elicit sympathy for the dwellers of Hester Street and its environs. Instead, it is a complex work that suggests Cahan's divided view of the experience of acculturation he describes.

In *Yekl* we follow the transformation of the eponymous hero, an immigrant garment worker on the Lower East Side, into "Jake," an American who has put aside old-country ways. "One must not be a *greenhorn*," Yekl tells his fellow garment workers.[36] Cahan was able to reflect Yekl's bicultural world by italicizing English words into "the Yiddish of the characters of this novel," as he explains in a footnote.[37] "*F caush* you don't, *becaush* you are a bedraggled *greenhorn*, afraid to budge out of Heshter Shtreet," says Yekl to his timorous peers.[38] The linguistic system Cahan devised for his characters' dialogue constituted his brave effort to place the English readers inside the verbal world of immigrant Jews. That is, Cahan, from inside the Jewish community, confronted the same problem—translating immigrant experience into American literature—that James and Howells as outside observers had addressed.

Indeed *Yekl* is told in two voices: in both immigrant vernacular and in formal diction, from inside and outside points of view, an uneasy blending. The novel's omniscient narrator, whose "purity" of English diction Howells admired, establishes an ironic distance from the halting and contorted speech of Yekl and the other ghetto residents. This narrative voice—indistinguishable from Howells's own studied diction, which echoed literary Boston and repudiated his own Ohio upbringing—served Cahan best to guide the reader smoothly into a survey of New York ghetto life:

> *Suffolk Street is in the very thick of the battle for breath. For it lies in*
> *the heart of that part of the East Side which has within the last two or*
> *three decades become the Ghetto of the American metropolis, and,*

indeed, the metropolis of the Ghettos of the world. It is one of the most densely populated spots on the face of the earth—a seething human sea fed by streams, streamlets, and rills of immigration flowing from all the Yiddish-speaking centers of Europe.[39]

This poised, omniscient narrative voice, lifted far above the yearnings of Suffolk Street, betrays no mark of ethnic origins. Indeed, the assured voice of the narrator is just what Yekl aspires to possess—an "American" voice unmarked by regional or ethnic traits. (Unlike Yekl, Cahan achieved fluency and acceptance in two languages.) Thus did Cahan's new man strive for full cultural acceptance in the "Promised Land of today."[40]

However, *Yekl* is not *The Melting-Pot*. Unlike Israel Zangwill, whose hero celebrated America as God's crucible, Cahan expressed an exquisite ambivalence about the cultural heritage Yekl was losing through his craving to transform himself into Jake. As Irving Howe says, "It seemed at times as if having been granted a dour vision of the final outcome of the whole Yiddish enterprise, Cahan took it as his special burden to carry through that vision to the end."[41]

Cahan portrays a representative immigrant pulled between two worlds of conflicting values, worlds symbolized by two women—Gitl, the wife he has left behind, and Mamie, the Americanized Polish girl he desires. When Gitl arrives in New York, Yekl's crisis intensifies. He feels responsibility for Gitl, but "at the same time his heart was thirsting for Mamie, and he felt himself a wretched outcast, the target of ridicule—a martyr paying the penalty of sins, which he failed to recognize as sins, or of which, at any rate, he could not hold himself culpable."[42] Cahan's genius resided in his ability to evoke, with a balance of sympathy and irony, both the sincere sentiments and the self-serving justifications of the greenhorn. "No Yiddish writer," notes Howe, "was as acute as he in grasping the desires of the Jews for spiritual gratification, material easement, and a way of life that might yoke the two."[43] At the end of his story, Yekl divorces Gitl and, having become the Jake of his heart's desire, sets out to marry Mamie. But he carries a heavy heart into his new life, for he has begun to realize that in order to become a "new man" he has sacrificed his former self, everything that "Yekl" stood for, and the coherent, Yiddish world that defined him.[44]

The Rise of David Levinsky (1917), Cahan's masterpiece, strikes the same note of ambivalence about the transformation of a poor Jewish immigrant into a successful American. "Sometimes, when I think of my past in a superficial, casual way, the metamorphosis I have gone through strikes me as nothing short of a miracle," writes Levinsky, in the first words of what appears to be the boastful, nostalgic, self-justifying memoir of a man who has risen from poverty to a position of money and power in New York, around the turn of the century.[45] However, this long novel proves to be the testimony (perhaps the cathartic confession) of a man who is trying to come to terms with his life, for Levinsky is forced to confront his own darker self, another beast in the jungle of the City.

Cahan, a committed socialist, had published in 1913, in New York's leading muckraking journal, *McClure's Magazine*, a series called "The Autobiography of an American Jew," pieces that served as the basis for *David Levinsky*.[46] Clearly Cahan took Howells's *The Rise of Silas Lapham* as his model, but he went beyond Howells by having his representative businessman serve as his own story's narrator, a strategy that dramatizes the contradictions beneath the surface of Levinsky's self-satisfaction. The divided voices of *Yekl*, comprising both the participant who employs the vernacular and the observer who uses formal diction, merge in the ambivalent character of David Levinsky.

In 1913, the fifty-two-year-old Levinsky looks back at his childhood *shtetl* life in Russia, his immigration, and his "rise" to affluence and influence in New York. Cahan must have had in mind, as well, Andrew Carnegie, whose credo, *The Gospel of Wealth*, was published in 1900.[47] As did Carnegie, Levinsky exults in his wealth and power: "I was born and reared in the lower depths of poverty and I arrived in America—in 1885—with four cents in my pocket. I am now worth more than two million dollars and recognized as one of the two or three leading men in the cloak-and-suit trade in the United States." David Levinsky illustrates the American dream of success; yet, unlike Carnegie (but like Yekl), he is unfulfilled: "My present station, power, the amount of worldly happiness at my command, and the rest of it, seem to be devoid of significance."[48] The narrative, ostensibly a parable of success, is in fact a meditation upon the loss of cultural identity and spiritual certainty.

Cahan depicts Levinsky's early life in Russia in great detail, showing the powerful pull of the past upon the narrator. Levinsky came from a harsh but loving and coherent world of family and village; he thus left an important part of himself behind when he emigrated. As Chametzky puts it, "Despite everything, one kind of Paradise was lost. The rite of passage from one state to another was so much more than symbolic: the ocean crossing, the cutting off from one culture and the emergence in a new one, was absolute, complete, traumatic—a second birth."[49] Levinsky became the "new man," born anew in America, but who is this man without a past? Henry James worried about the ways the immigrants would change America; Abraham Cahan examined the ways America transformed the immigrant.

Levinsky recalls his first vision of America, seen from the boat off Sandy Hook, in terms of a spiritual rebirth. On a June morning, looking out on Staten Island, America "unfolded itself like a divine revelation." Levinsky insists upon the supernatural sense of the experience: "When I say that my first view of New York Bay struck me as something not of this earth it is not a mere figure of speech."[50] When such expectations are aroused, disillusionment is inevitable—neither America nor he can measure up to the promise of his first vision of the New World.

With the help of Gitelson, a fellow immigrant who lends him ten dollars, Levinsky moves from peddler to apprentice sewing-machine operator. He also picks up practical information about the devious ways of American politics from a prostitute. He does what he has to do to get ahead. He seduces a friend's wife, sets himself up in business, where he exploits Orthodox Jews who work for less than union wages, and, like Carnegie, becomes something of a social Darwinist, seeing himself as one of the fittest, a man who is worthy of survival.

Twenty-five years after his arrival at Hoboken, Levinsky invites Gitelson to a celebratory dinner at the Waldorf-Astoria, but the occasion turns out badly. Levinsky, full of sentiment for "Landing Day," the day the two greenhorns passed through Castle Island immigration, insists upon repaying the ten-dollar loan. However, Gitelson, who has not been a success in New York, demands that Levinsky pay considerable interest on the loan. Furiously, Levinsky writes out a check for five hundred dollars. He then returns to his work, disappointed: "In the evening I went home, to the loneliness of my beautiful hotel lodgings. My heart was still heavy with distaste and sadness."[51] There is nothing to celebrate. Money is the only measure of worth, the currency of affection, in New York. Levinsky, a success, has accepted New York's inequities, while Gitelson, a failure, naturally enough seeks recompense. But money cannot buy happiness, Levinsky realizes. He sees he may have taken the wrong course in not attending, as he had wished, City College, in not having "a life of intellectual interest." He feels the yearnings of an unfulfilled artist: "I cannot escape from my old self. My past and my present do not comport well. David, the poor lad swinging over a Talmud volume at the Preacher's Synagogue, seems to have more in common with my inner identity than David Levinsky, the well-known cloak-manufacturer."[52] New York City, America, has transformed the idealistic innocent into a hard-nosed realist. Levinsky has sold his soul, betrayed his "inner identity," for a mess of pottage. If his autobiography is an illustrative tale of the successful immigrant businessman who wants to have it both ways—for Levinsky retains his affluence and power while he insists upon his sense of loss—it serves even more as an effective way for Cahan, a socialist and a satirist, to portray the cultural and moral costs of success in America. New York City, with its extremes of wealth and poverty, its embodiment of the American dream of success and its reminders of the personal and cultural sacrifices necessary for that success, provides the fit setting for this literary realist. The wandering Jewish man encounters soul-destroying temptations in the relatively tolerant atmosphere of New York, which entices him to repudiate his identity and his past.

THE WANDERING JEWISH WOMAN FACED HER OWN SET OF problems, problems well articulated by Anzia Yezierska in a number of memorable books, particularly *Bread Givers* (1925), an autobiographical novel, and *Red Ribbon on a White Horse* (1950), a memoir. She arrived at Ellis Island from the Russian part of Poland when she was sixteen years old, in 1901, and found work first as a servant, then in a sweatshop and a factory, while living in a tenement with her family in the Lower East Side. Leaving home at age seventeen, she was determined to learn English at night school and make something of herself: "I burned to do something, be something."[53] When she took classes at Columbia, she impressed John Dewey when she declared, with characteristic emphasis, "I want to make from myself a person!"[54]

Yezierska's novels and stories—*Hungry Hearts* (1920), *Salome of the Tenements* (1922), *Children of Loneliness* (1923), *Arrogant Beggar* (1927), and others—were cries from the heart by an intense woman thwarted by circumstances, even in the brave new world of New York City. Following her own example, Yezierska's heroines rebel against their pious, oppressive fathers, their passive mothers, and their Jewish ghetto. Like Edith Wharton at the other end of town and the economic scale, Yezierska escaped through her writings. However, her two marriages failed, her success in Hollywood quickly passed, and she was poor and obscure at the time of her death in 1970.

Bread Givers and *Red Ribbon on a White Horse* both begin on Hester Street, legendary center of Jewish consciousness, culture, and commerce in America. In both works, an immigrant heroine moves through Hester Street in search of her "America." Sara Smolinsky, Yezierska's alter ego in *Bread Givers*, is disappointed to discover that the nation in which she has arrived is not, as she had dreamed, a land of plenty; rather, she finds herself dwelling in a dark, crowded room, under the Old World thumb of her righteous father, a poor rabbi. Yet when Sara becomes a fish peddler, she develops a sense of her own powers. A twenty-five cent profit from the sale of herring makes her feel like Rockefeller:

"It began singing in my heart, the music of the whole Hester Street. The push-cart peddlers yelling their goods, the noisy playing of the children in the gutter, the women pushing and shoving each other with their market baskets—all that was only hollering noise before melted over me like a new beautiful song."[55] However, Sara finds she must search well beyond Hester Street to find herself and to discover America.

In the story "How I Found America," Yezierska's heroine is inspired by a passage from Waldo Frank: "We go forth all to seek America. And in the seeking we create her. In the quality of our search shall be the nature of the America that we create."[56] The America that Anzia Yezierska created as she evolved from a Hester Street worker to novelist, to Hollywood screenwriter, to WPA guidebook writer was recounted in *Red Ribbon on a White Horse*, a dramatic memoir that was critically well received but went largely unread when it was published in 1950. In this account, she leaves Hester Street, leaves New York City, and encounters an America far more ample and various than what she had known, an American landscape where she can transcend the oppression, economic and emotional, of her ghetto background. Her memoir concludes in a pastoral retreat, Fair Oaks, New Hampshire, with words that might have been written by Henry David Thoreau: "The power that makes grass grow, fruit ripen, and guides the bird in its flight is in us all." At least rhetorically, Anzia Yezierska believed she had risen "above the accidents of fortune" that ruled her "outer life" as an immigrant to New York City.[57]

In *HOW THE OTHER HALF LIVES* (1890) AND *THE CHILDREN of the Poor* (1892), Jacob Riis, an immigrant from Denmark who became a police reporter for the *New York Tribune*, stunned American readers with accounts of the conditions affecting urban outcasts, particularly the miserable state of the tenement children of the Lower East Side, in the Mulberry Street area. (Some one million Irish, German, and Jewish immigrants, it is estimated, were living in approximately 37,000 tenements in 1880.)[58] Riis's noble battle against crowded tenements, child labor, prostitution, and other plights of the poor enlisted the support of Theodore Roosevelt—who advanced from head of the City's police board, to governor, to president—and prepared the nation for legislation to alleviate such conditions.[59]

Riis's still-striking account also traced the decline of the City. The first tenements, he noted, were sectioned out of some of old New York's finest homes: "Nothing would probably have shocked their original owners more than the idea of their harboring a promiscuous crowd; for they were the decorous homes of the old Knickerbockers, the proud aristocracy of Manhattan in the early days."[60] The bucolic wholesomeness of old New York had been violated, suggested Riis. An ancient cow-path became the Mulberry Street "Bend," the "foul core of New York's slums," for example. "Echoes of tinkling bells linger there still, but they do not call up memories of green meadows and summer fields; they proclaim the home-coming of the rag-picker's cart. In the memory of man the old cow-path has never been other than a vast human pig-sty."[61]

Though he indulged in demeaning ethnic stereotypes, Riis balanced moving portraits of misery with sharp complaints against those who benefited from inequity. His photographs, anticipating those of Lewis Hine, framed the poor, the children of the slums, with dignity. In a chapter called "The Reign of Rum," he wrote, "the rumshop turns the political crank in New York. The natural yield is rum politics."[62] In such conditions, the City was turning its young men into toughs and its young women into exploited workers and prostitutes—the very models Stephen Crane would soon employ in *Maggie: Girl of the Streets* (1893). Furthermore, Riis helped to popularize the Darwinian notion of environmental conditioning, thus removing blame from the City's victims. America's slums, he pointed out, were little better than those in Europe, from which immigrants in New York had fled. Yet Jacob Riis believed that America held a promise of social redemption that was unavailable in Europe.[63]

THE ROLE OF THE WRITER, STEPHEN CRANE MUST HAVE concluded from reading Riis, was to expose the hard truth of the urban condition to readers, who were themselves conditioned by comforting tales designed to distract them from urban miseries, and to awaken the conscience of the nation. Crane, like Riis, became a literary explorer of the City's darker streets, but Crane was more artful, less given to ethnic stereotypes, and less moralistic.

In *Maggie: A Girl of the Streets*, Crane portrayed the life of New York's Lower East Side firsthand, though his background would not seem to have prepared him for such a mission. Crane was the fourteenth son of a Methodist minister and a mother who wrote tracts against the evils of alcohol. In *George's Mother*, his second novel of City slum life, Crane obliquely told the story of his strained relationship with her. In the novel, George Kelcey becomes a drunkard to escape his demanding mother. Crane was a rowdy drinker at Syracuse University, which he chose to leave (or was told to leave) in order to immerse himself in the life of the Bowery. Manuscript evidence from *Maggie* suggests that New York City stood as a vivid image of depravity for Crane even before he saw it. He began writing about the City while he was still living in Syracuse, where he practiced being down-and-out and where he watched suspects being booked at the courthouse.

In "An Experiment in Misery" (1894), a sketch of urban life, Crane described a nation whose callous indifference toward the displaced was symbolized by New York's arrogant buildings. They were "emblematic of a nation forcing its regal head into the clouds, throwing no downward glances; in the sublimity of its aspirations ignoring the wretches who may flounder at its feet." Crane's prose registered the shock of an outsider, in a language of select, symbolic details. "The roar of the city to him was the confusion of strange tongues, babbling heedlessly; it was the clink of coin, the voice of the city's hopes were to him no hopes," but he strained to identify with the "other half." Crane's persona, wearing tattered garb, conducts "an experiment in misery" by living among the lowly. Perhaps Crane's experiment had as much to do with literary realism (an experiment in depiction) and the extension of authorial consciousness as it did with the eliciting of public sympathies or the rectification of social injustices.[64] At the end of his report, he tells a friend that he may not have discovered the poor man's point of view, "but at any rate I think mine own has undergone a considerable alteration."[65] New York, city of oppression and opportunity, transformed Stephen Crane's view of the world, just as he knew it would.

In "The Men in the Storm" (1894), Crane registered more awe than moral outrage at the sight of long-suffering men who stood in line waiting for a "charitable house" to open its doors. Their individualities were muffled by miseries and their identities were lost in the moving mass of the crowd. As Peter Conrad suggests, convincing tales of urban life were difficult to relate, from Dickens to O. Henry: "There are a million or—in O. Henry's calculation—four million stories in New York, but you're prevented from telling them because you can't extricate from the crowd the people to whom they're happening." Whitman's celebratory merging of the individual with the crowd was, by the 1890s, a thing of the past.[66] Again, in "Men in the Storm," the young reporter crosses from the known world and enters a surreal section of the City, where middle-class standards of conduct are missing: "In a certain part of a dark West-side street, there was a collection of men to whom these things were as if they were not."[67] His reconstruction of the lives of the New York poor—like his imaginary participation in the Civil War, *The Red Badge of Courage* (1894), or his fictional account of hours spent adrift at sea, "The Open Boat" (1897)—provided Crane with further opportunities to transcend his middle-class consciousness and to enter a wonderland of lost souls.

After the *Red Badge* became a success, Crane's New York novellas were revised and published in 1896. Crane was publicly grateful to Howells for showing him the way. However, in many ways, Crane outdid Howells; his fiction portrayed New York "low life" much more vividly, from the inside, and he explained the determining environmental forces, as Howells noted, without resort to moral judgment. While praising *Maggie*, Howells admitted that he had no taste for the "inarticulate and blasphemous life" Crane depicted. Yet Howells saw in Crane a successor, one who could tell the truth without the social and literary "trammels" that Howells knew held him back.[68]

In *Maggie*, Crane evoked a world in which characters were driven and broken by forces beyond their comprehension and control. Maggie Johnson, a beautiful but passive product of "Rum Alley," an invented slum region of lower Manhattan, never has a chance. Her violent father, her alcoholic mother, and her tough young brother provide a tense family nexus from which she flees into the arms of a bartender; he first seduces her and then abandons her to prostitution and, finally, suicide. Death for Crane was the only exit for the "children of the poor."

"A very little boy stood upon a heap of gravel for the honor of Rum Alley." In this sentence, which opens *Maggie*, Crane establishes the narrow boundaries of his characters' world. Here Jimmie Johnson, Maggie's brother, battles Irish lads for territorial supremacy: "He was throwing stones at howling urchins from Devil's Row who were circling madly about the heap and pelting at him."[69] "Rum Alley" is located at the center of Crane's imaginative map of the City.

Hamlin Garland, in his 1893 review of *Maggie*, praised Crane as "the voice of the slums," but he was more.[70] Crane's observations of slum life confirmed his bleak vision of the world and inspired him to create images to match that vision. His slums serve as sparsely lit backdrops for the pathetic life of his doomed heroine. New York is represented in lurid flashes of the beer gardens and saloons in which Maggie loses her way. Familiar urban sites are adapted to reinforce Crane's thematic concerns. Thus, at the Central Park Menagerie and Museum of Arts (the zoo) Pete, Maggie's seducer, identifies with a combative monkey who, after his tail is pulled, threatens to thrash the other monkeys. Clearly, Crane's New Yorkers are little better than battling animals, and culture is merely a lie that glosses that hard truth. At the theater, the sentimental Maggie "rejoiced at the way in which the poor and virtuous eventually surmounted the wealthy and wicked." The zoo, then, enables Crane to depict the Darwinian struggle for existence in the City and the theater provides occasion for heavy irony at the expense of Maggie: "The theater made her think. She wondered if the culture and refinement she had seen imitated, perhaps grotesquely, by a stage heroine, could be acquired by a girl who lived in a tenement house and worked in a shirt factory."[71] In Crane's realistic allegory, the answer is obvious. The lives of the New York poor were nasty, mean, brutish, and short. It was Crane's ambitious determination, through the artful use of fiction, that their desperate lives should be known.

William Dean Howells, who found a commercial publisher for *Maggie*, admitted that he had learned much from Stephen Crane, the young man who had experimented with his life and art by living among the miserable. As Howells wrote in a moving letter to Cora Crane after her husband's death in 1900, "He never came without leaving behind him some light on the poor, sad life he knew so well in New York, so that I saw it more truly than ever before."[72]

W HEN JIMMIE JOHNSON BATTLED IRISH LADS TO DETERmine who would rule a "heap of gravel" in Rum Alley, he was participating in a struggle for ethnic hegemony. Crane could see that New York was becoming, as Daniel Patrick Moynihan later described it, "an Irish city." The spirit of Irish-Americans' patriotism was enshrined in the American mind in the Broadway plays and music, particularly in "You're a Grand Old Flag," of George M. Cohan, whose statue stands in Times Square. The image of Irish-American truculence and charm was projected by another New Yorker, James Cagney, in his many memorable films, beginning with *Public Enemy* (1930), where he played a combative, doomed gangster. In *The Fighting 69th* (1940) Cagney paid tribute to New York's Irish soldiers of the Great War, where the image of Irish aggressiveness was converted to ardent patriotism. When Cagney acted the part of the winning Cohan in the 1942 film *Yankee Doodle Dandy*, the New York Irish-American archetype became a national figure.[73] When Cohan saw the film he said, "That Cagney. What an act to have to follow!" Within a year of the film's screening, Cohan was dead; after his solemn requiem Mass, the organist of Saint Patrick's cathedral played "Over There," Cohan's World War I anthem.[74] Cohan had helped to establish the Irish presence over here, in New York and in the nation. Cagney justly called him "the real leader of our clan."[75]

An Irish-American style—mixing charm, combativeness, wit, and occasional sentimentality—became part of New York's way. The New York Irish also influenced the City's diction. A. J. Liebling—a writer whose own voice was shaped by New York and who, in turn, helped to shape the literary voice of the *New Yorker*—even suggests that "basically, New Yorkese is the common speech of nineteenth-century Cork, transplanted during the mass immigration of the

South Irish."[76] Cohan, it might be said, incorporated that street voice into popular, patriotic songs. Cohan had first titled his most famous patriotic song "You're a Grand Old Rag," but he decided that wording was too shockingly colloquial. As Cagney imitated East Side corner-boys' gestures, he used in his films street phrases he had heard as a boy, like "Whattya hear, whattya say?" Cagney recalls, "There was a gal in the neighborhood, I think she was a hooker—I never found out, really—and she came out with that one day. One of her boyfriends used to say it, so I dropped it in."[77] By such circuitous routes a native American diction of the City developed.

As Finley Peter Dunne, the most famous Irish-American writer of the turn of the century, has Mr. Dooley say, "When we Americans are through with the English language, it will look as if it had been run over by a musical comedy."[78] If Henry James, after spending time in a Jewish coffeehouse on the Lower East Side, worried about the future of the English language in the new America of immigrants, one notable immigrant had as much trouble with James's many-layered syntax. Edith Wharton gleefully recorded that Dunne was "floundering helplessly in the heavy seas of James's parentheses" when he heard James converse. Dunne spoke of his delight at meeting James but "mournfully" added, "What a pity it takes him so long to say anything! Everything he said was so splendid—but I felt like telling him all the time: 'Just 'pit it right up into Popper's hand!' "[79] America, like England, was becoming a nation divided by a common language. Old manners and locutions were rapidly fragmenting in New York City.

The saga of the Irish in New York has been recorded in widely various works, from nineteenth-century tales written to please the new immigrants to Eugene O'Neill's plays, which challenged his community to confront its darker sides. Unlike their Jewish counterparts, the Irish in New York showed little literary sophistication in the New World. Their early writings were tribal self-justifications, acts of literary propaganda lacking the ethnic self-criticism found in Cahan, Yezierska, and others.

Mary Anne Sadlier, the voice of the post-Famine generation of Irish immigrants in America, wrote eighteen didactic novels on Irish history and immigration between 1850 and 1870. Her husband, James, was cofounder and manager of the D. & J. Sadlier Company, the largest Catholic publishing house in America. They also owned the *New York Tablet*, a newspaper that printed her fiction before it appeared in book form. The Sadlier homes on East Broadway and at Far Rockaway became gathering sites for Catholic intellectuals of the day. Sadlier, then, represented the values of bourgeois Irish-America.

Sadlier also helped to establish the Irish immigrants' presence in the American mind. Her works lack self-irony and complexity of characterization, for she wrote mainly to flatter and to justify her kind. For example, *Willy Burke; or, The Irish Orphan in America* (1850), as Sadlier states, was "written for the express purpose of being useful to the young sons of my native land, in their arduous struggle with the tempter, whose nefarious design of bearing them from the faith of their fathers, is so artfully concealed under every possible disguise." The American way to wealth, asserted the wealthy Sadlier, drew the immigrant from his true mission: "that of spreading the true faith."[80] In *Willy Burke*, one immigrant son, Peter, renounces his faith and breaks his mother's heart, but another son, loyal Willy, retains his Catholicism and is rewarded by a legacy of $5,000, money inherited from his employer, a German Protestant who converts to Catholicism.

In *The Blakes and Flanagans* (1855), Sadlier contrasts two families: the Flanagans, who are "good, old-fashioned Catholics," and the Blakes, who value ambition over religion. Young Harry Blake goes to public school, where he loses his faith; after attending Columbia College, he becomes a "Broadway swell." Then Harry completes his slide to perdition by becoming a lawyer, a Freemason, and the husband of an anti-Catholic Protestant. He inevitably finds his true home in Tammany politics. The Flanagans, in contrast, attend parochial school, remain loyal to their family values, and sustain their Irish Catholicism. With such contrived melodramas, Sadlier manipulated experience to emphasize her narrow vision. (Alger's stories, while equally manipulative, presented the City as a far more open and various place.) Nevertheless, as Charles Fanning points out in *The Irish Voice in America*, "The Sadlier American-set novels are the most graphic fictional examples available of the jarring collision in the 1850s and 1860s of the profoundly dissimilar Irish Catholic and American Protestant cultures."[81] In particular, they showed New York as a city of increasingly sharp ethnic, cultural, and class divisions.

The darker side of the Irish story in New York was told in *Tenement Tales of New York* (1895), by James W. Sullivan, a journalist and novelist who tried, as Cahan did in *Yekl*, to portray the process of assimilation both with sympathy and with an understanding of the price it exacted from the immigrants. In "Slob Murphy," Sullivan describes the brief life of a street urchin who dies in an accident at age eight. The story is narrated by "Steamboat," a lodger in the tenement in which young Pat Murphy lives with his neglectful family. Sullivan establishes a point of view that is close enough for sympathy, but detached enough for understanding. Pat steals a dollar from Steamboat, who is not surprised at "the unpleasant traits in little Pat's character," for the boy is a product of the harsh influences that have shaped Steamboat himself. Pat's mother is dead, his father a drunkard, and his world is defined by New York's mean streets. However, the boy never has a chance to develop his potential for evil, for he is run over by a horse car. His dying prayer, composed in "his down-town New York Celt dialect," is a model of purple pathos: "T'y will be done on eart' as it is in heaven—on eart' wi me fader, so he won't git drunk. Give us dis day our daily bread—dat's fur do oders; I don't need none no more. An' furgive us our trespasses—dem's sins—as we furgive dose who trespasses 'ginst us. And lead us not into temptation—dat's fur me fader, too." Steamboat underscores Sullivan's point in more formal diction: "Dirty, ragged, bad Slob had had goodness in him which ought to have had a chance."[82]

From Sadlier's conscience-torn, middle-class immigrants to Sullivan's victimized tenement dwellers, Irish writers portrayed their countrymen as victims of New York City: either they were ignored, left to suffer and to die in miserable and murderous tenements, or, with a few noble exceptions, they were corrupted (measured by the loss of their Catholic values) by the City's temptations to success. To get beyond ethnic pieties and sentimentality to the street level where canniness and wit defined the Irish in New York, the reader has to turn to politics, the most assured means of ascent available to Irish-Americans in the City.

The Tammany political machine and the Democratic Party—which, along with the Catholic Church, became the defining institutions for Irish immigrants and their descendants in the last quarter of the nineteenth century—controlled New York.[83] Through an intricate system of a shadow-governmental hierarchy, from district to assembly to county committees, Tammany maintained its power. For the Irish, who came from villages, all politics was local and personal, a system of loyalties rather than legalities. The political boss, like the parish priest, served as his clan's leader.[84] From William R. Grace, the City's first Irish Catholic mayor, whose election in 1880 demonstrated the power of the Tammany organization, to the era of Al Smith, 1928 presidential candidate, and Mayor Jimmy Walker, first elected in 1925, who, it was said, "wore New York in his buttonhole," the City was governed by Irish Catholic Democrats.[85]

Tammany's leaders were Irish-American tribal chieftains, noted for their arrogance. "Well, what are you going to do about it?" became the credo of William W. "Boss" Tweed, the third largest holder of real estate in Manhattan in the 1860s, behind John Jacob Astor and A. T. Stewart.[86] "Honest" John Kelly's domination of Tammany so appalled Herbert Spencer, visiting in 1882, that he said New York resembled the Italian republics of the Middle Ages, where freedom existed only in form.[87] Kelly's successor, Richard Crocker, known as the "Master of Manhattan," enriched himself at the public's expense by, among other things, selling City jobs. Under pressure from investigating commissions in the early 1890s, Crocker "retired" to his English estate, where he oversaw his thoroughbreds.[88] After Al Smith, a product of Tammany politics, lost his bid for the presidency and after Jimmy Walker resigned his office in disgrace over charges of corruption in 1932, the Irish lost their grip on the City.

The Irish political machine, despite its corruptions, provided services (jobs, emergency funds, etc.) to the immigrant poor, including all groups who voted, which the long-established (Dutch-English Protestant) government had refused to supply. Richard Crocker claimed—self-servingly, but not incorrectly—that Tammany was responsive to an otherwise ignored constituency: "Think what New York is and what the people of New York are. One half, more than one half, are of foreign birth. . . . They do not speak our language, they do not know our laws, they are the raw material with which we have to build up the state." Tammany "looks after them for the sake of their vote, grafts them onto the Republic, makes citizens of them."[89] Certainly Tammany grafted the American Irish to the power elite of New York City.[90]

The best book about Irish-American politics in New York, indeed, one of the best books about the American political system of the turn of the century, was written by William L. Riordon, a reporter for the *New York Evening Post*. Riordon was fascinated by "the mental operations of perhaps the most thoroughly practical politician of the day—George Washington Plunkitt," Richard Crocker's most trusted lieutenant.[91] While clearly selecting, editing, and shaping Plunkitt's discourse, Riordon seems merely to provide the vehicle for Plunkitt's soliloquies on politics—an Irish-American version of Machiavelli's *Prince* or, as Riordon would have it, Rousseau's *Confessions*. Of course, Riordon was to Plunkitt what Dunne was to Dooley—an artful mediator between the street-Irish vernacular voice and the presumably genteel reader.

Plunkitt's extemporaneous insights into the savage yet comic art of politics in a new land were delivered from his "rostrum"—the New York County Court House Bootblack Stand, a mock-heroic throne for this representative leader of the new clan that ruled New York politics. Plunkitt's observations confirmed the charges of those who accused Tammany leaders of narrow self-aggrandizement at the same time that his aphorisms disarmed his critics: "I seen my opportunities and I took 'em," Plunkitt said. There was no need to commit crimes, he reasoned, for New York was full of opportunities for "honest graft."[92] For example,

Plunkitt bought up land he knew the City would need, then resold it to the City for a profit and, in the process, was viewed as a "statesman," not a crook. Politics, he explained, should be accepted as a business based upon trust and reciprocity, that is, patronage in exchange for votes.

Therefore, civil service reform, in Plunkitt's eyes, was a "curse," the enemy of political organizations and a barrier to opportunities for advancement of immigrant youth. "Hayseed" legislators from Albany (or Brooklyn) also interfered with the perfect running of the Tammany machine, so Plunkitt predicted that New York City would break away from New York State to become an autonomous state. If Walt Whitman's vision of the City was adhesive, drawing adjacent territories and various peoples into its ever-expanding being, George Washington Plunkitt's vision of New York was exclusive. His ideal New York City would be a version of "Sinn Fein" (Ourselves Alone). Outsiders, he held, had to adapt to the City's ways to become "a real New Yorker. . . . Even a Jap or a Chinaman can become a New Yorker, but a Brooklynite never can."[93] Though Plunkitt had no use for the poverty he associated with the practice of poetry, and little sense of poetry (or any other kind of literature) as a means of cultural transformation, he confessed that the shimmering vision of statehood for New York City, with Tammany in control, "takes me sometimes to yell poetry of the red-hot-hail-glorious-land kind."[94] Political power was the prime passion, for better or worse, and the prevailing poetic mode of the Irish-American in New York City. At the same time, as Irish-American writers suggest, the range and rhythms of their talk, the style of their walk, and the lift of their songs altered the culture and character of their City.

FOLLOWING THE GREAT IMMIGRATION OF IMPOVERISHED Europeans to New York was the "Great Northern Migration" of yet another group of newcomers who were seen as "rabble" by established New Yorkers: African-Americans. The City's black population doubled, reaching some three hundred thousand by the 1920s.[95] Segregation fostered cultural differentiation. Harlem became "Black Manhattan"—in the words of poet, novelist, and composer James Weldon Johnson—the nation's "Negro capital, . . . a black city, located in the heart of white Manhattan, and containing more Negroes to the square mile than any other spot on earth. It strikes the uninformed observer as a phenomenon, a miracle out of the skies."[96]

Johnson sustained the vision of Manhattan as a "miracle," though he was well aware of the City's pattern of discrimination. In his sonnet "My City," Johnson weighs what he will miss most when he dies.

> *But, ah! Manhattan's sights and sounds, her smells,*
> *Her crowds, her throbbing force, the thrill that comes*
> *From being of her a part, her subtle spells.*
> *Her shining towers, her avenues, her slums—*
> *O God! the stark, unutterable pity,*
> *To be dead, and never again behold my city!*[97]

Johnson notes in his autobiography, *Along the Way* (1933), "One of my prime purposes in writing" *Black Manhattan* (1930), a history of African-American life in New York City, "was to set down a continuous record of the Negro's progress on the New York theatrical stage."[98]

James Weldon Johnson was born into relatively privileged circumstances in Jacksonville, Florida, in 1871, to parents who nurtured his artistic gifts for music and literature. He attended Atlanta University and he taught in Georgia and Florida schools. Johnson became a lawyer, an editor, and a composer, famous for writing "Lift Every Voice and Sing," a song so stirring it became known as the Negro national anthem. In 1901 Johnson went to New York, where he joined his brother, J. Rosamond, and a musical comedy performer, Bob Cole. They were known as "Cole and the Johnson Brothers" where they played, at Jimmie Marshall's Hotel, located near the Fifty-third Street Theater district, and on Tin Pan Alley.[99]

Cole and the Johnson Brothers wrote "Under the Bamboo Tree," "Congo Love Song," and other hits, giving the genre of "coon songs" a fresh cleverness and gentility. Johnson set out to "clean up the caricature," using "mild dialect" for his love songs that would meet the "genteel demands of middle-class America."[100] But Johnson's songs also anticipated a New York style of jazz. He even set the spiritual "Nobody Knows the Trouble I've Seen" to ragtime, syncopating its rhythm and "ragging" on its lyrics.

While composing in New York, Johnson studied literature at Columbia University, where he began his novelized autobiography. During his years in the diplomatic service—he was a U.S. consul in Venezuela and Nicaragua—he continued to write poetry and he completed *The Autobiography of an Ex-Colored Man* in 1912. When the book was published, anonymously, by a small Boston firm, it caused little stir. However, it is an important novel, written by a man who was most conscious of the development of a special relationship between African-Americans and New York City.

The narrator's entry into New York, by boat, through New York Harbor, recalls the wary fascination of Henry James's reentry into the City. Johnson's unnamed speaker sees the towers of Manhattan shining "in a reflected light which gave the city an air of enchantment; and, truly, it is an enchanted spot. New York City is the most fatally fascinating thing in America." Seen closer, New York becomes for Johnson, as it had for James, a temptress, a "great witch at the gate of the country, showing her alluring white face and hiding her crooked hands and feet under the folds of her wide garments—constantly enticing thousands from far within, and tempting those who come from across the seas to go no farther. And all these become the victims of her caprice." The City is irresistible, as Johnson's hero realizes while walking its crowded streets. [101]

New York meant opportunity for the migrant in Johnson's eyes, not inevitable defeat, as it had for Crane. On arrival, Johnson's narrator quickly wins two hundred dollars in a poker game. In the "Club," the hero discovers the "center of colored Bohemians and sports." [102] He finds work rolling cigars, but his real passion is for gambling. At the Club he plays ragtime, which earns him money and respect, particularly when he rags Mendelssohn's "Wedding March" for the cakewalking patrons. After a scene of jealous violence, he has to flee New York and the country with a rich, white patron, for whom he plays the piano. In Europe's white society, this "ex-colored man" becomes a success.

Near the end of his autobiography, Johnson's narrator returns to New York and becomes a real estate entrepreneur, making money and mixing with a crowd of wealthy New Yorkers who have no idea he is not white. "The most serious question of [his] life" arises when he falls in love with a blonde, blue-eyed woman, "as white as a lily." [103] When he finally tells her he is black, she cringes from him: "This was the only time in my life that I ever felt absolute regret at being colored, that I cursed the drops of African blood in my veins and wished that I were really white." [104] However, in time love conquers racial barriers and they are married. They have two children, but he never ceases to worry that she might find some flaw in him that she could attribute to his race. After she dies, he weighs his life and finds it wanting. "I have sold my birthright for a mess of pottage," concludes Johnson's narrator.

In *Harlem Renaissance*, Nat Huggins explores the implications of Johnson's theme: "The tragedy, as he saw it, was not merely the protagonist's abdication of his art (and his essential self) but, more, that the society had lost the cultural synthesis that might have been possible through the genius of this marginal man."[105] The ex-colored man's spiritual loss, despite his financial gain, is also, then, New York's loss, for his life illustrates that a black man cannot be accepted in the City's restrictive world of business and society. Johnson's narrator will remain "white" for the sake of his children, but what will they, young men without an authentic heritage, be like? More important, *who* will they be?

Like Cahan's David Levinsky, Johnson's ex-colored man employs the format of the autobiography to confess his ambivalence about a life he has no intention of resolving. That is, both men, business successes in Manhattan, are determined to retain their wealth, but both also feel the need to express public regret for their losses of cultural (ethnic or racial) heritage. Through the guarded confessions of these representative immigrants to New York, Cahan and Johnson reminded their readers of the need to retain the vital cultural heritages that they brought to the City. However, there was no chance, in either case, that these men could either return to old-country ways or be fully integrated into mainstream American life. Perhaps, then, these fictionalized autobiographies are the only places in which the disparate elements of New Yorkers' lives can be drawn into a cultural synthesis.

Johnson's *Black Manhattan* capped his extensive labors, as a writer and an editor, to create a positive sense of racial identity and a vital black community in Harlem, to develop an "Afro-centric tradition," in the 1920s. A leader in the NAACP, Johnson also wrote poetry, *Fifty Years and Other Poems* (1917); in addition, he and his brother edited two volumes of Negro spirituals. Most important, Johnson edited *The Book of American Negro Poetry* (1922), "the book that really kicked off the New Negro Movement known as the Harlem Renaissance."[106] In his introduction to this volume, Johnson equated artistic expression with cultural achievement, just as Whitman had in *Democratic Vistas*: "The final measure of the greatness of all people is the amount and standard of the literature and art they have produced." As a result, "what the colored poet in the United States needs to do is something like what Synge did for the Irish; he needs to find a form that will express the racial spirit by symbols from within rather than by symbols from without."[107] What John Millington Synge was to the Irish Renaissance, Johnson was to the Harlem Renaissance—both writers created a new literary language derived from folk tradition and both inspired successors to surpass their work.

Black Manhattan traces the development of African-Americans in New York

City from the Dutch settlers to the Harlem Renaissance. Only New York, Johnson suggests, would welcome Claude McKay, who arrived from Jamaica in 1911, and celebrate his cruel but beautiful poem, "America":

> *Although she feeds me bread of bitterness,*
> *And sinks into my throat her tiger's tooth,*
> *Stealing my breath of life, I will confess*
> *I love this cultured hell that tests my youth!*[108]

In *Black Manhattan*, Johnson also calls attention to Countee Cullen, who was born in New York, and Langston Hughes, who came to New York from Joplin, Missouri. Though both poets rebelled against the "propaganda" poetry of racial consciousness, in Johnson's eyes both writers' works were inspired by the "idea of race."[109] This combination of racial pride and artistic achievement became the driving force of the Harlem Renaissance. For Johnson, New York proved that "two hundred thousand Negroes have made themselves an integral part of New York citizenry." His New York exemplified the triumph over slavery and bigotry. Johnson saw blacks' cultural achievements as proof of their cultural value.

> *The Negro in New York still has far, very far yet, to go and many,*
> *very many, things yet to gain. He still meets with discriminations and*
> *disadvantages. But New York guarantees her Negro citizens the funda-*
> *mental rights of citizenship and protects them in the exercise of those*
> *rights. Possessing the basic rights, the Negro in New York ought to be*
> *able to work through the discriminations and disadvantages. His rec-*
> *ord beginning with the eleven [slaves among the first settlers] three*
> *hundred years ago proves that he can; and he will.*[110]

Despite Johnson's optimism, *Black Manhattan* appeared at a time when the Renaissance he was celebrating was, in fact, fading, and the Great Depression was converting Harlem into a ghetto.[111] A new generation of informed observers saw Harlem fall far from the miraculous. However, Johnson's novel and his study of black Manhattan established the importance of the African-American experience to any understanding of New York City.

IN THE SPRING OF 1896, THEODORE DREISER, THEN AGE twenty-four, another awkward but ambitious newcomer, wrote an impressionistic tribute to the City during a temperate May, that brief respite between winter cold and summer heat. The intensity of Dreiser's prose, despite its clumsiness, confusion of tenses, and repetition, captures the transient beauty of the City he had inhabited for the past two years: "The myriad shop lights, the patter of pedestrians upon the pavements below, the lolling creatures, talking from out the windows, the thin smoke curling from distant chimneys, the stars—these, blended, blurred, merged until none are distinct and all are softened, makes for them the city, such as it is, vast, sad, romantic, the city as it is, in May."[112] Writing under the name "the Prophet," Dreiser was determined to represent all sides of the City for *Ev'ry Month*, a monthly magazine featuring sheet music, which he began editing in 1895. The City "such as it is," New York "as it is," was Dreiser's concern.

To this end, Dreiser read Balzac and listened to Howells. In the spring of 1900, Dreiser, like other disciples before him, met with Howells in his apartment overlooking Central Park. Howells was depressed over the state of the City. "The great city surprises me. It seems so much a to-do over so little—millions crowding into it to obtain subsistence in a region where subsistence is least. . . . This little island is cold and bleak a great many months of the year. Nothing is grown here." Dreiser must have been pleased to learn that Howells's vision had come to encompass more than the "smiling aspect" of urban life.[113]

New York for Dreiser was typically a place of extremes, lurid and romantic, steaming or freezing; above all the City was a site of initiation, knowledge of the best and worst that life could offer. For Dreiser, born in Terre Haute, Indiana, New York was a book of revelations that he was determined to recompose in his stories for the uninitiated, for other young men and women from the heartland. It was a city of dynamic change and dramatic contrast—just the place for a young man with a melodramatic turn of mind. As he would note in *The Color of the City* (1923), "The thing that interested me . . . about New York . . . was the sharp, and at the same time immense, contrast it showed between the dull and the shrewd, the strong and the weak, the rich and the poor, the wise and the ignorant."[114] Yet Dreiser recoiled from an "immense, congested, smoky" City "smeared by millions of insignificant people," diminished by "too many unidealistic Jews." He was nostalgic for turn-of-the-century New York, "more varied and arresting and, after its fashion, poetic and even idealistic than it is now."[115] New York City never satisfied Dreiser, but it also never ceased to fascinate him. From first to last, Dreiser saw New York as an energizing city of conflict; he saw no need for resolution in his stories of the City.

When Dreiser first arrived in New York in the summer of 1894, his brother,

Paul Dresser, a savvy New York songwriter, showed "Thee" the City, as they walked uptown from the ferry stop at Cortlandt Street in lower Manhattan. At first Theodore was put off by the dirty, crowded streets, but debonair Paul fed his brother's imagination: "Wait'll you see Broadway and Fifth Avenue."[116] They visited their sister, Emma, who lived with L. A. Hopkins, a fugitive from Chicago. Hopkins had stolen $3,500 from the tavern where he had worked as a cashier and, leaving his job and wife, fled with Emma, first to Montreal and then to New York. He returned most of the money but he also turned out to be unfaithful to Emma. Though Dreiser hated Hopkins, the novelist adapted their story in his most fully realized work of fiction, *Sister Carrie* (1900). Thus the first fable Dreiser chose for the City involved the betrayal of an innocent young woman by a corrupt urbanite. While Paul, a city slicker, drew his brother to the uptown world of glamor and success, "Thee," a rube, was preoccupied by a downtown tale of failure.

On that first visit, Paul and Theodore strolled up Broadway, seeing the "parade" of wealth, passing through Tin Pan Alley, crossing the vice-ridden Tenderloin, gazing at the upscale department stores, finally arriving at the Hotel Metropole on Forty-second Street, where Paul greeted cronies. Later in the week, Paul took his brother to a "French" brothel, where Theodore indulged, but felt guilty afterward. During a Sunday stroll on Manhattan Beach, the novelist had an epiphany of New York's wonder, spread out around him—a city lit by fireworks. He would long remember Paul's advice: "Sometimes you ought to write about these things, Thee. . . . The people out West don't know yet what is going on, but the rich are getting control. They'll own the country pretty soon. A writer like you could make 'em see that."[117] As the City brought Theodore Dreiser to a higher consciousness, so too would he, in his writings, bring the nation to awareness of "what was going on" in New York.

Dreiser created a mythic encounter with New York in *The "Genius"* (1915), a novel in which his young hero, Eugene Witla, a dreamy painter from Illinois, comes to do battle with the City. His confrontation with this dragon he sets out to slay is an initiation into new worlds of sexuality, money, and artistic challenge. He emerges from the conflict wiser but sadder. Eugene's moment of self-realization occurs in the Museum of Natural History, where he contemplates the skeletons of long-extinct animals: creatures who once thrived, but who then were cast aside by an indifferent Nature.[118] Eugene is a success both as an artist and a businessman but a failure in his private relations. Failure is built into the natural order and so is inevitable in Dreiser's vision of the tempting but finally indifferent City.[119]

Yet for the young provincial who was determined to become an important and successful American writer, there was nowhere else to go: "If you have it in you to be great you must come to New York," he wrote.[120] After Dreiser was rebuffed in his efforts to get a reporter's job at the *World*, he sat beside other destitutes in City Hall Park. There "the idea of *Hurstwood* was born," Dreiser's first vision of the tragic presence in *Sister Carrie*—a sympathetic treatment of Hopkins. Dreiser was struck, not by the idea of Carrie, who personified success, but by the idea of Hurstwood, who embodied failure, a figure who exemplified an American tragedy. Though Dreiser was hired at the *World*, he was always conscious in Manhattan of the prospect of failure.[121]

Indeed, after he left the *World*, Dreiser lived, down and out, in the Bowery, sleeping in flophouses, like those spectral figures described by Riis and Crane. "I sank to the bottom of human misery," he wrote.[122] However, with Paul's help, Dreiser became editor of *Ev'ry Month* and the voice of "the Prophet." Paul Dresser's career peaked when he composed the plaintive song, "On the Banks of the Wabash," to which his brother contributed.[123] Despite their success, in his "Reflections" for *Ev'ry Month*, Dreiser was haunted by those who were driven to suicide by their disappointments in the City: "Between the time when the voices of abundant hopes call a young man to the city, and his later desponding self-sought death, God only knows what may intervene." Then "suicide looms large."[124]

During a strike of sweatshop workers in 1896, Dreiser recorded his views on the City's allure. For Dreiser, as it had been for James and Johnson, New York was a tempting woman of the night: "Like a sinful Magdalen the city decks herself gaily, fascinating all by her garments of scarlet and silk, awing by her jewels and perfumes, when in truth there lies hid beneath these a torn and miserable heart, and a soiled and unhappy conscience that will not be still but is forever moaning and crying 'for shame.'" But, even though city workers were starving, Dreiser thought there was nothing that could or should be done to alter their fate.[125]

For Dreiser, nature's face could best be revealed not in Darwin's outbacks but in the City. Throughout his *Ev'ry Month* columns, Dreiser praised Herbert Spencer's adaptation of Darwin's survival-of-the-fittest theory to social success and failure. "It is only the unfit who fail—who suffer and die," wrote "the Prophet" in 1897.[126] In "Curious Shifts of the Poor" (1899), an urban sketch, Dreiser calls attention to the destitutes who stand in abject contrast to the flashy rich along Broadway. He traces a representative man of underground New York, "the Captain," en route to a flophouse, somewhere below Tenth Street. (Dreiser adapted this and other reports he wrote on the City into *Sister Carrie*, giving that novel its documentary underpinnings.) Describing the homeless who were lined up outside a mission on Fifteenth Street during a cold January day—a sketch that owes much to Crane's "The Men in the Storm"—Dreiser goes out of his way to mute his readers' sympathies: "Their parade before us should not appeal to our pity, but should awaken us to what we are—for society is no better than its poorest type. . . . Wealth may create an illusion, or modify a ghastly appearance or ignorance and error, but it cannot change the effect. The result is as real in the mansions of Fifth Avenue as in the midnight throng outside a baker's door."[127]

In his journalistic excursions of the late 1890s, which took him into New York's darkest corners, Dreiser prepared himself to write his finest novel, *Sister Carrie*. This novel offers no temperate zone of moderation, only triumph or destruction. As he would later write in *The Color of a Great City* (1923), a memoir, New York becomes dull when its extremes are muted: "The glory of the city is its variety. The drama of it lies in its extremes."[128]

Retelling his sister's story in *Sister Carrie*, Dreiser has Hurstwood and Carrie, the guilty lovers in flight, take a flat on West Seventy-eighth Street. After returning $1,300 of the stolen money, Hurstwood buys half interest in a saloon on Warren Street, but he is eaten up by nostalgia and guilt. While living in the City, he discovers there stands within it an inaccessible, walled sanctum of ease and privilege: "He began to see it as one sees a city with a wall about it. Men were posted at the gates. You could not get in. Those inside did not care to come out to see who you were. They were so merry inside that all those outside were forgotten, and he was on the outside. Each day he could read in the evening papers of the doings in this walled city."[129] After *Sister Carrie* was written, Dreiser, close to Hurstwood's voice, bemoaned "the utter isolation and loneliness of heart forced upon the average individual" in the City.[130] Indeed, after *Sister Carrie* was reluctantly published by Scribner's, Dreiser had his worst period of poverty and despair, during which he contemplated suicide and again had to be rescued by his brother.[131]

In *Sister Carrie* Dreiser portrays a man who never truly believes in the possibility of success. Hurstwood recoils from the City. Meanwhile, Carrie is introduced to the City's wonders by her neighbor, Mrs. Vance, "the typical New Yorker in many things, some of which were dressiness, jollity, love of metropolitan life, crowds, theaters and gentlemen companions."[132] The magic of the theater, a fancy restaurant, and rich crowds along Broadway stir Carrie's ambitions.

At the same time, Hurstwood begins to fade in her imagination, just as her Chicago lover had previously faded in the presence of Hurstwood. Apparently, those who are successful in the City, as in nature, possess adaptable identities and bear few attachments.

After Hurstwood loses his money in the saloon investment, he cannot find work. He and Carrie have to move downtown, to Thirteenth Street, near Sixth Avenue. Out of work, he sits in the lobby of the Broadway Central, watching the more fortunate parade past. However, Carrie finds a place in a chorus line of comic opera. The lines of their lives, which intersected in Chicago, now clearly have crossed and are headed in opposite directions, Carrie moving up and Hurstwood slipping down.

Overwhelmed by the magnitude of New York City, Hurstwood loses what is left of his vitality. He briefly becomes a scab motorman during a strike in Brooklyn. After he is beaten by a striker, he quits. Meanwhile, Carrie becomes a huge success on the stage. With her $150-a-week salary, she moves to a new apartment and abandons Hurstwood, as he had abandoned his Chicago family for her. Carrie is now safely inside the walled city of privilege. Her adapted name (made up by her first lover) shines in lights along Broadway and her image presides: "At Broadway and 39th Street was blazing, in incandescent fire, Carrie's name. 'Carrie Madenda,' it read, 'and the Casino Company.' All the wet, snowy sidewalk was bright with this radiated fire. It was so bright that it attracted Hurstwood's gaze. He looked up, and then at a large gilt-framed poster-board on which was a fine lithograph of Carrie, life-size."[133]

Hurstwood's decline and fall is Dreiser's best articulation of the lethal powers of the City and illustration of the brutal Darwinian laws of life. When Hurstwood and Carrie first enter New York, Dreiser lectures the reader on the fixity of "the social atmosphere of the city." He adds, "Whatever a man like Hurstwood could be in Chicago, it is very evident that he would be but an inconspicuous drop in an ocean like New York." Dreiser then plots a cautionary tale that confirms his thesis. Chicago is a small pond compared with New York—an oceanic city in which weak men drown: There "the sea was already full of whales. A common fish must needs disappear wholly from view, remain unseen. In other words, Hurstwood was nothing."[134] Finally, Hurstwood gasses himself inside a Bowery flophouse. "What's the use," he says, giving up the ghost of his life.[135]

As Dreiser was writing *Sister Carrie*, it is reported, he would rock and sing "Wabash." His brother's lyrics evoke an idealized, lost past:

Oh, the moonlight's fair tonight along the Wabash,
From the fields there comes a breath of new mown hay.
Thro' the sycamores the candle lights are gleaming,
On the banks of the Wabash far away.[136]

Thus, while Dreiser was filling out the details in his parable of success and failure in the City, he was sustained by a sentimental lyric idealizing his boyhood days, a song that also struck chords of nostalgia, perhaps in compensation for disappointments, in the hearts of so many adopted New Yorkers—émigrés from the American heartland who, like the Dreiser brothers and sister, had been eager to trade the confines of pastoral America for the possibilities of urban life. Far enough removed from the realities of life along the banks of the Wabash and surrounded by the imperatives of living in the City, they could well imagine a lost Eden.

Dreiser, an "ambivalent urbanite" like Howells, never resolved his attitude toward New York City.[137] While he experienced some of the success Carrie felt, Hurstwood held his full sympathies. For Dreiser, whether you were a success or failure, New York seized control of you, obliterated your former self. It either buoyed you or broke you. As another of New York's adopted sons would say, once you come to the big City, you can't go home again.

Horatio Alger and O. Henry offered redemptive myths of the City in hundreds of tales for Americans who were eager to know about New York in the Gilded Age. Irish-American writers offered reassuring or illustratively moving urban stories and songs to the newcomers. But other writers between the Civil War and World War I—Abraham Cahan, Anzia Yezierska, Jacob Riis, Stephen Crane, James Weldon Johnson, and Theodore Dreiser among them—described a darker, more destructive New York City.

FLAPPERS AND

PHILOSOPHERS

New York

in the Twenties

After the great war, New York City became, more distinctly than ever, another country, an island unto itself, separated by its opulence, extravagance, and power from the heartland—particularly from middle-class, Middle West, nineteenth-century America. Yet New York City, the center of the nation's publishing businesses and the engine of its culture, also served as a model for those who sought to understand or to explain America during its transit from the postwar exhilaration after 1919, through the Crash of 1929, and into the Great Depression. After the Great War, the City was increasingly linked to, yet symbolically separated from, the mainland by bridges, ferries, and trains—those emblems of beauty, vehicles of realization and transformation, as the City's memorialists in story and song so often and so eloquently noted. In *The Great Gatsby* (1925), F. Scott Fitzgerald's narrator, riding into the City from Long Island with Gatsby driving "his gorgeous car," is enthralled: "The city seen from the Queensboro Bridge is always the city seen for the first time, in its first wild promise of all the mystery and the beauty in the world."[1] Coming and going, the City was a place of drama and freedom, particularly for its writers. Manhattan, ever a site and an occasion for hyperbole, became the place to be for the literary modernist and the political radical.

Paul Rosenfeld's *Port of New York* (1924) spoke to the new cultural energies in the City and the nation: "We are content to remain in New York. In the very middle of the city, we can feel the fluid of life to be present. . . . The circle of the globe commences here, too."[2] Rosenfeld's grandiose claim must have seemed reasonable even to the most dispassionate observer of New York City in the 1920s. Then New York was on a boom and bust cycle, a place full of charm, corruption, and idealism. The City was also a place of paradox: one long, alcoholic, acquisitive party, paced to the rhythms of jazz, during the era of Prohibition, a place of plenty that ignored its outcasts. For Fitzgerald especially, but also for other writers born around the turn of the century, the City staged American dramas that paralleled their own coming of age and disillusionment. From the heady days of celebration and promise after the Great War, to the Crash and Depression, the City's story was an informing parable of the nation's rise and fall.

A NUMBER OF FACTORS COMBINED TO GIVE A NEW CHARacter to the City after the Great War. The Emergency Quota Act of 1921 limited immigration from each nation to the 1910 quotas; then the Johnson-Reed Immigration Act of 1924 scaled the quotas back to the 1890 limit, thus lowering the numbers of people entering the country and maintaining the preponderance of northern European immigrants. In the words of Oliver E. Allen, "For New Yorkers it was an odd, unexpectedly quiet interim. The calm came to an end only in the mid-1930s when the city began welcoming Jewish refugees from Hitlerite Germany and the partial reopening of the Golden Door brought back some of the old sense of energy."[3]

However, in this "interim" new urban energy was evident in class mobility. During this postwar period, the City's middle class grew rapidly, expanding into the boroughs of Queens and the Bronx. They were primarily commuters to the City's center, which was increasingly dedicated to financial and commercial concerns. Having risen out of the working class, these New Yorkers sought better homes and greater opportunities. As Robert A. Gates suggests, "Movement was considered the sign of success, for no one upwardly mobile was expected to stay in any one place for too long. The City became restless and experimental, even daring, in its approach to life."[4]

Money, more than ever, served as the measure of value in New York, and Wall Street became the center of the nation's postwar financial boom. New buildings, taller than ever, symbolized the City's new assurance. At the same time, New York became more and more impersonal. Even H. G. Wells was shocked by what the City, a "steel-souled machine room," portended for the future; for him New York was a place where "individuals count for nothing . . . the distinctive effect is the mass . . . the unprecedented multitudinousness of the thing."[5]

Lands beyond Manhattan were made more accessible during this period. By 1925 the Bronx River Parkway—which would be followed by the Henry Hudson Parkway and other highway projects, tied the City's boroughs to Manhattan. In 1927 the Holland Tunnel opened, linking Jersey City with Manhattan. In 1931 the George Washington Bridge, then the longest suspension bridge in the world, opened, spanning the Hudson and joining New York with New Jersey.

Prohibition added to the City's sense of danger and adventure, for speakeasies flourished. Cafe society was sustained by corruption, as police were bribed to keep drinking establishments open, and organized crime, supplying liquor and protection, reigned. Dutch Schultz, a bootlegger, and Frank Costello, who went from bootlegging to gambling, controlled Tammany Hall judges and therefore ran much of the City's nightlife.[6]

Popular culture took over Times Square; high culture moved uptown, near Central Park, centered at Carnegie Hall, on West Fifty-seventh Street. The Yankees, the "Bronx Bombers," dominated the American League in Yankee Stadium on 161st Street. In Harlem, writers and jazz musicians flourished, giving rise to the Harlem Renaissance. The *New Yorker* was founded in 1925; the magazine, at once whimsical and sophisticated, was "not edited for the old lady in Dubuque" by editor Harold Ross. *Time* began its publication in 1923, under the visionary and dictatorial direction of Henry Luce. *Vanity Fair*, established in 1913, under the editorship of Frank Crowninshield, appealed to the high style and expensive tastes of New Yorkers and would-be New Yorkers in the 1920s; however, by 1936, in the trough of the Great Depression, it would cease publication.

The City's artists congregated at the Algonquin Hotel, at one end of the aesthetic and political spectrum, and in Greenwich Village at the other. After a while, as Malcolm Cowley says in *Exile's Return*, aspects of the Greenwich Village "idea"—its veneration of youth and self-expression, its iconoclasm and hedonism, its advocacy of women's rights, and its idealization of Europe (far from the American Midwest)—would become accepted attitudes throughout the nation, but not without a struggle against those mainstream, mid-American values so relentlessly dissected in Sinclair Lewis's *Main Street* (1920).[7] Edna St. Vincent Millay, Eugene O'Neill, and others became legends of the Village, which, as it had before and during World War I, represented one side of the City's sensibility—radical in life and art, both creative and self-destructive. The Algonquin Round Table, which included Robert Benchley, Alexander Woollcott, and Dorothy Parker, represented another side—brilliant in wit and enterprise, but also self-indulgent and self-destructive. In the 1920s, New York was both heaven and hell for American writers who were drawn to its heat and its lights.

F. SCOTT FITZGERALD CAME TO THE CITY FROM THE heart of the heart of the country; for this ambitious and imaginative young man, New York, above all, meant personal and professional drama. As he put it in his notebooks, he responded to "the city's quick metropolitan rhythm of love and birth and death that supplied dreams to the unimaginative, pageantry and drama to the drab."[8] The City was the site of his most extravagant gestures; it inspired his best fiction and it symbolized his greatest losses.

Fitzgerald's story began in St. Paul, Minnesota, where he was born in 1896, and ended in Hollywood, where he died in 1940, but New York City was at the center of his life's purpose and meaning. By way of a New Jersey prep school, Princeton, and wartime service in the South, he prepared himself for the City, a fitting stage for a life centered on love, luxury, and literature. While stationed in Montgomery, Fitzgerald met Zelda Sayre, "the most beautiful girl in Alabama *and* Georgia," thought the smitten second lieutenant.[9] After his military service, served stateside, Fitzgerald laid siege to New York City, determined to make a success for himself as a writer and win Zelda's hand in marriage.

Fitzgerald came to New York in 1920, a heady period during which he projected his own élan and determination onto the City. "New York had all the iridescence of the beginning of the world," he said.[10] When *The Romantic Egotist*, a novel, was rejected by Scribner's, Fitzgerald was afraid he might have lost the ambitious Zelda. At the time Fitzgerald lived in the Bronx, where he rewrote this novel in a room on Claremont Avenue, "one room in a high, horrible apartment-house in the middle of nowhere"; he worked for the Barron Collier agency, writing advertising jingles.[11] He was a young man suspended between a dreary present and an uncertain future:

> *In a haze of anxiety and unhappiness I passed the four most impressionable months of my life. . . . As I hovered ghost-like in the Plaza Red Room of a Saturday afternoon, or went to lush and liquid garden parties in the East Sixties or tippled with Princetonians in the Biltmore Bar I was haunted always by my other life—my drab room in*

the Bronx, my square foot of the subway, my fixation upon the day's letter from [Zelda, in] Alabama—would it come and what would I say?—my shabby suits, my poverty, and love. . . . I was a failure—mediocre at advertising and unable to get started as a writer.[12]

When Scribner's finally accepted his revised and retitled novel, *This Side of Paradise*, Fitzgerald crossed the line from failure to success, moving from that small room in the Bronx to a suite at the Plaza in Manhattan.[13] Success meant magical transformation. Suddenly, wrote the amazed Fitzgerald, "I was adopted, not as a Middle Westerner, not even as a detached observer, but as the arch type of what New York wanted."[14]

In March 1920 *This Side of Paradise* was published; in April Scott and Zelda were married in the rectory of St. Patrick's Cathedral. However, Fitzgerald always retained a sense of guilt about one of the costs of success: the loss of his Catholic faith. Charles Fanning describes Amory Blaine, the central character of Fitzgerald's first novel, as "the first Irish Catholic protagonist in a novel by an Irish Catholic American whose *bildungsroman* ends in the rejection of his faith."[15] Edmund Wilson, Fitzgerald's Princeton classmate, recalls that as early as 1916 Fitzgerald saw himself in a morally divided world, a testing ground in which New York stood for temptation and destruction. "Why can't I go up to New York [from Princeton] on a terrible party and then come back and go into the church and *pray*—and mean every word of it, too!" he wondered. When he lost his Catholicism, speculates Wilson, Fitzgerald was left "with nothing at all to sustain his moral standards or to steady him in self-discipline."[16] In his own terms, Fitzgerald went "to New York on a terrible party," and in a sense he never returned. He swung between hedonism and moralism, with no middle ground on which to stand.

In *This Side of Paradise*, a semiautobiographical novel, the City is portrayed as a garden of earthly and heavenly delights, where innocents confront temptations. The novel's epigraph—"The victor belongs to the spoils"—reveals Fitzgerald's obsession with the destructive element of New York success.[17] In his first novel, Fitzgerald imagines a dashing, young alter ego, Amory Blaine, who is overwhelmed by his first vision of the City. Amory comes from a family of rich midwesterners who are accustomed to foreign travel, people who are "attached to no city."[18] Amory, like Fitzgerald, passes two years at a nearby prep school. While at St. Regis, on the Hudson, Amory encounters New York City and discovers himself, all in one memorable night of intoxication and revelation: "New York burst upon [Amory] on Washington's Birthday with the brilliance of a long-anticipated event. His glimpse of it as a vivid whiteness against a deep-blue sky had left a picture of splendor that rivaled the dream cities in the Arabian Nights; but this time he saw it by electric light, and romance gleamed from the chariot-race sign on Broadway and from the women's eyes at the Astor, where he and young Paskert from St. Regis' had dinner."[19]

After dinner the two novices-about-town go to the theater, where "everything enchanted": "The play was 'The Little Millionaire,' with George M. Cohan, and there was one young brunette who made him sit with brimming eyes in the ecstasy of watching her dance." After the play, as they emerge onto Broadway, Amory is struck by a clarifying vision of his future: "He was going to live in New York, and be known at every restaurant and cafe, wearing a dress-suit from early evening to early morning, sleeping away the dull hours of the forenoon." Of the actress in the play who has so enchanted him, Amory decides, "Yes, sir, I'd marry that girl tonight!"[20] New York, for Amory, no doubt as it had been for young Fitzgerald, is a city of romantic possibilities, best seen by the new electric lights, which artfully reorder reality by masking and highlighting; a city best discovered in the theater, viewing a play about a "little millionaire."

Amory's play embodies Fitzgerald's three passions: art, romance, and finance; it also stars that most prominent Irish-American New Yorker, George M. Cohan. Success in the City is symbolized by an unattainable, beautiful young woman, who is playing the role of the temptress. All is art and artifice in Fitzgerald's primal meditation upon Manhattan. No mention is made of the kind of *work* that might be necessary to sustain such a sybaritic life. Thus the elegantly lounging and longing Amory Blaine personifies Fitzgerald's personal, romantic enthusiasm for New York and foreshadows that self-destructive, overreaching idealist, Jay Gatsby—though Fitzgerald had to learn the hard work of the writer's trade to bring this figure to life.

Amory Blaine is a character who is seen often in New York stories—stylish and self-indulgent, "spoiled," in the trope of his day; a young man who falls in love with love, a dreamer who is half in love with easeful death; a shallow, self-indulgent, sophisticated, charming, and doomed lad. Amory attends Princeton, then he serves in France as a lieutenant. He returns to learn that his former beloved has chosen wealth (a rich husband) over love (Amory). Amory even has to work—in advertising. All of this postwar disillusionment permits him to drown his sorrows in bouts of drink and to indulge in a brief fling with a similarly egocentric young woman. At age twenty-four, the self-pitying Amory is left with nothing but a sense of emptiness. In "May Day," a story set in and probably written during 1919, another of Fitzgerald's sad young men, also bereft over his losses of love and money, shoots himself "in a bedroom of a small hotel just off Sixth Avenue."[21] Fitzgerald built his literary career upon such New York cautionary tales.

In his first flush of success, Fitzgerald realized that he "knew less of New York than any reporter of six months standing and less of its society than any hallroom boy in a Ritz stag line," but there he was, magically transformed, living in the Plaza or other posh palaces: a celebrated author, with the former Zelda Sayres of Montgomery beside him; they became, of course, *the* couple of the Jazz Age.[22] Those were the days of the legendary Scott and Zelda pranks—riding down Fifth Avenue atop taxis, diving into the fountain at Union Square, or most notoriously, plunging into the Pulitzer fountain in front of the Plaza. They were young, talented, and famous, but frequently drunk. But like most earthly heavens, New York City in the early twenties turned out to be a transitory pleasure for the Fitzgeralds, a prelude to their fall from grace.[23]

At first, the less Fitzgerald actually understood of the workings of the City, the more easily he was able to appropriate it to the requirements of his imagination. In this way, his ignorance was his bliss; in another sense, though, his lack of specific knowledge allowed him to reach beyond the quotidian and grasp at the larger meaning of the City. Looking back from 1931, in "Echoes of the Jazz Age," Fitzgerald said, "It all seems rosy and romantic to us who were young then, because we will never feel quite so intensely about our surroundings any more."[24]

Fitzgerald conveyed a more vivid sense of the City's betrayal of youthful promises in his second novel, *The Beautiful and Damned* (1922). He intended the novel as social satire, according to the dust-jacket description (which he probably wrote): "It reveals with devastating satire a section of American society which has been recognized as an entity—that wealthy, floating population which throngs the restaurants, cabarets and hotels of our great city."[25] In his second novel, the Scott-and-Zelda fictional projections, Gloria and Anthony Patch, go rapidly from self-indulgent success to self-destructive degradation. Anthony naively imagines that he can get by in New York without effort by separating himself from the money that sustains him. He only visits Wall Street once a week, to check on his investments, but he lives uptown, in a posh apartment house on West Fifty-second Street. Sudden ascent and descent—uptown/downtown, climbing/falling—were the routes to revelation in Fitzgerald's vision.[26] Indeed, Anthony Patch learns that what goes up must come down.

Anthony's slide into infidelity and alcoholism, portrayed in the most vivid part of the novel—he makes a drunken journey through the City, trying to borrow money, and he ends up in a fistfight—recalls the slow decline and fall of Hurstwood in Dreiser's *Sister Carrie*. During their social and moral deterioration, Anthony and Gloria move to Claremont Avenue, near the Hudson. Though the City by then is losing its shine for the Patches, Anthony still seeks signs of romance in its vistas: "Across the water were the Palisades, crowned by the ugly framework of the amusement park—yet soon it would be dusk and those same iron cobwebs would be a glory against the heavens, an enchanted palace set over the smooth radiance of a tropical canal."[27] New York, once an amusement park for the Patches, as it had been for the Fitzgeralds, would soon close, but it would not entirely lose its twilight glow.

In the fall of 1922, Scott and Zelda, still buoyed by New York's wonders, moved to Great Neck Estates, Long Island, less than forty-five minutes from Broadway on the Long Island Express. Celebrities lived there—Lillian Russell, George M. Cohan, Ring Lardner, and others. Many lavish parties marked their stay. But their drinking soon grew destructive, as Scott and Zelda egged each other on, beyond old-fashioned limits. "They complemented each other like gin and vermouth in a martini, each making the other more powerful in their war with dullness and convention," notes Andrew Turnbull.[28] Yet out of this period of wretched excess Fitzgerald drew the material for his finest fiction, *The Great Gatsby*.

That novel opens in the spring of 1922, when Nick Carraway—narrator, center of consciousness, ambivalent participant in the postwar boom—moves to West Egg, into a small house beside Gatsby's mansion, which looks across the Sound to glittering East Egg. The portrayal of Carraway allowed Fitzgerald to recount and revise his own past. Fitzgerald, after returning from the Great War, had not been able to remain in the suddenly confining Middle West—or the "West," as he often put it, thus extending the gap between Minnesota and Manhattan—where families expected you to "settle down." Fitzgerald, who sought his release from his Irish-American background in St. Paul, has Nick realize that "instead of being the warm center of the world, the Middle West now seemed like the ragged edge of the universe." Fitzgerald came East to learn the fiction business; Nick decides "to go East and learn the bond business."[29] "East," of course, means New York.

Carraway arrives in New York better connected than Fitzgerald had been. Daisy Buchanan, Nick's wealthy, distant cousin, lives on Long Island, "on that slender riotous island which extends itself due east of New York," in East Egg, just across the bay from his humble home.[30] However, Nick's enchantment with Daisy is brief, for he senses her power to destroy as well as seduce. Nick shifts his fascination to Gatsby after he sees his mysterious neighbor standing at the end of his long lawn, stretching out his arms—personifying all of the inchoate aspirations Nick is afraid to seek with abandon. Gatsby appears to be a man who yearns for far more than Nick can imagine. Later Nick learns that Gatsby was gazing only at the green light that marks the end of her dock, beyond which lives his lost love, Daisy Buchanan.

Between West Egg and New York, trains pass through the "valley of ashes," a landscape presided over by an advertising sign displaying "the eyes of Doctor T. J. Eckleburg," eyes that, though "dimmed a little by many paintless days under sun and rain, brood on over the solemn dumping ground." Thus the symbolism of T. S. Eliot's *The Waste Land* (1922) provides the conceptual and symbolic background for this novel. In *The Great Gatsby*, Fitzgerald portrays a passage of enlightenment from the place of glittering mansions to the hot City: through the burnt-out country, where George B. Wilson (agent of Gatsby's doom) and Myrtle Wilson (victim of the Buchanans' destructiveness) live above Wilson's garage. Nick makes his passage into the City first with Tom, Daisy's husband, by train; they are joined on their way by Tom's mistress, Myrtle.[31] There are then, Nick learns, two ways into Manhattan—the high road of bright prospects over the Queensboro Bridge, or the low road of sexual and economic power through the valley of ashes. Nick has to go both ways before he can learn the full meaning of his quest.

On that trip into New York with Tom and Myrtle, Nick is quickly drawn into the City's destructive element. While Tom and Myrtle squabble in a cramped apartment, Nick gets drunk and yearns for escape: "I wanted to get out and walk eastward toward the park through the soft twilight, but each time I tried to go I became entangled in some wild, strident argument which pulled me back, as if with ropes, into my chair." The sordid situation in which he finds himself in the City gives Nick the ambivalence necessary to his role as observer-interpreter: "I was within and without, simultaneously enchanted and repelled by the inexhaustible variety of life." This scene of petty revels climaxes in Tom's breaking Myrtle's nose.[32]

Divided between the allure of Gatsby's lavish parties at West Egg, held to entice Daisy, and his job at the Probity Trust in lower Manhattan, Nick becomes a lonely romantic, wandering the streets of the City. "At the enchanted metropolitan twilight [he] felt a haunting loneliness sometimes," thinking he might be "wasting the most poignant moments of night and life."[33] In the tea garden of the Plaza Hotel, Jordan Baker, Daisy's friend, tells Nick about the romance that developed in Louisville, where Gatsby, then a young officer, met Daisy.

This story in turn inspires Nick's attraction to Jordan. Walking through Central Park, they kiss.[34]

Nick sees a side of the City where the worst extremes of human nature are displayed after his trip over the Queensboro Bridge with Gatsby. In a Forty-second Street cellar, they meet with Meyer Wolfsheim, a notorious criminal, who shows Nick his cuff links made of human molars. Gatsby shocks Nick with the information that Wolfsheim fixed the 1919 World Series. The City is full of revelations, romantic and horrific.

An eventful journey, something of a motorcade, into and out from the City, climaxes *The Great Gatsby*. During a summer heat wave even East Egg is sweltering, and Daisy is petulant:

> *"What'll we do with ourselves this afternoon?" cried Daisy,*
> *"and the day after that, and the next thirty years?"*
> *"Don't be morbid," Jordan said. "Life starts all over again when it gets crisp in the fall."*
> *"But it's so hot," insisted Daisy, on the verge of tears, "and everything's so confused. Let's all go to town!"*[35]

Daisy implies that a trip into the City will clarify their life's journeys, as indeed it does, though in the most disastrous manner. Tom, Gatsby, Jordan, and Nick agree to meet at a suite in the Plaza, where they quickly get drunk. There Gatsby and Tom argue bitterly over Daisy's love. Daisy cannot convincingly say, as Gatsby urges her to, that she *never* loved Tom. As they all start back for Long Island—Daisy drives Gatsby's car, with Gatsby as passenger—Nick, traveling in another car, realizes he has turned thirty, but he takes some comfort in the presence of Jordan: "As we passed over the dark bridge her warm face lazily against my coat's shoulder and the formidable stroke of thirty died away with the reassuring pressure of her hand. So we drove on toward death through the cooling twilight."[36] Journeys to and from the City are confrontations with mortality.

The accident—Daisy runs down Myrtle in Gatsby's car—was waiting to happen, an inevitable result of the combustible mixture of "Westerners" gathered in New York and a dramatic embodiment of Fitzgerald's moral judgment on the City. New York, then, stands as both the geographic and symbolic center of this novel. These Westerners, dislodged by the Great War, come East in search of meaning (love and money). They gather on separate sides of Long Island, at the edge of the continent, where America began. They periodically journey into Manhattan, where they find clarification in confrontations. Nick alone comes to understand the meaning of their quests and the extent of their losses. After Gatsby's death at the hands of the confused George B. Wilson, who thinks that Gatsby was Myrtle's lover and murderer, Nick knows he can no longer stay in New York. As he walks the shore, in front of Gatsby's mansion, on his last night in the East, the full realization of the significance of Gatsby's journey—to recapture lost innocence—comes home to him:

> *I became aware of the old island here that flowered once for Dutch sailors' eyes—a fresh, green breast of the new world. Its vanished trees, the trees that had made way for Gatsby's house, had once pandered to the last and greatest of all human dreams; for a transitory enchanted moment man must have held his breath in the presence of this continent, compelled into an aesthetic contemplation he neither understood nor desired, face to face for the last time in history with something commensurate to his capacity for wonder.*

Greater New York, as it would become, was the site observed in that dream of transcendence for the Dutch sailors, but Nick makes it clear that this has been a false dream for his band of expatriates from the West. Nick realizes "that this has been a story of the West, after all—Tom and Gatsby, Daisy and Jordan and I, were all Westerners, and perhaps we possessed some deficiency in common which made us subtly unadaptable to Eastern life."[37]

Gatsby pursued his dream, made a symbol out of the green light at the end of the Buchanan dock, and a graven image of a woman. "He did not know that [his dream] was behind him, somewhere back in that vast obscurity beyond the city, where the dark fields of the republic rolled on under the night." The American dream was not to be discovered in the tantalizing promises of American life associated with New York City.[38]

When Scott and Zelda returned from a stay in Europe in 1926, Fitzgerald caught the City's grandeur, its sweep, in baroque language: "As the ship glided up the river, the City burst thunderously upon us in the early dusk—the white glacier of lower New York swooping down like a strand of a bridge to rise into uptown New York, a miracle of foamy light suspended by the stars. A band started to play on deck, but the majesty of the city made the march trivial aad tinkling. From that moment I knew that New York, however I might leave it, was home."[39] From St. Paul, the city he wanted to forget, Fitzgerald found a problematic, transient, symbolic "home" in New York, the only city adequate to the requirements of his ambition, his stylistic hyperbole, and his penchant for moral judgment.

By the time he wrote "My Lost City" in 1932, Fitzgerald was ready to reconsider the romantic symbolism of his youthful discovery of New York, so lusciously evoked in *This Side of Paradise*. What had been lyric was reinterpreted as a lament for lost felicities. Nostalgia and regret for some unnamed, lost thing had replaced his great expectations.

> *There was first the ferry boat moving softly from the Jersey shore at dawn—the moment crystallized into my first symbol of New York. Five years later when I was fifteen I went into the city from school to see Ina Claire in* The Quaker Girl *and Gertrude Bryan in* Little Boy Blue. *Confused by my hopeless and melancholy love for them both, I was unable to choose between them—so they blurred into one lovely entity, the girl. She was my second symbol of New York. The ferry boat stood for triumph, the girl for romance. In time I was to achieve some of both, but there was a third symbol that I have lost somewhere, and lost forever.*[40]

Fitzgerald saw himself as a representative man of his era, identifying his own heady rise and fall during the 1920s with the state and styles of the nation. "My wife and I were married in New York in the spring of 1920," he wrote in "How to Live on $36,000 a Year" (1934), "when prices were higher than they had been within the memory of man. In the light of after events it seems fitting that our career should have started at that precise point in time."[41] Thus New York was the heart of his own and his land's revealing drama: "The ten-year period that, as if reluctant to die outmoded in its bed, leaped to a spectacular death in October, 1929, began about the time of the May Day riots in 1919." Then "the police rode down the demobilized country boys gasping at the orators in Madison Square." Such events made the young men of his generation cynical and narcissistic. Sexual and other traditional behavioral standards fell ("petting" and smoking increased; cocktail parties commenced), and the Jazz Age began its two-step toward the Crash of 1929—in Fitzgerald's eyes, proper punishment for an age of moral corruption. With the passing of the era of "flappers and philosophers," as Fitzgerald named it in a 1920 collection, a sense of youthful romantic optimism also passed from the land.[42]

Fitzgerald composed no "account of the city's changes but of the changes in this writer's feeling for the city." Indeed, in his alcoholic swirl, he and Zelda "felt one with New York, pulling it after us through every portal."[43] Fitzgerald's tendency to self-dramatization and self-pity was encouraged by the City's dramatic contrasts. He recalled once even bawling in a Manhattan taxicab because "I had everything I wanted and knew I would never be so happy again." Pleasure resided in the realization of irretrievable losses for Fitzgerald: "For us the city was inevitably linked up with Bacchic diversions, mild or fantastic."[44]

In the 1930s, Fitzgerald's sense of New York became frantic and greedy. Only momentarily could he hold onto his original vision of the City. He recalls "riding south through Central Park at dark toward where the facade of Fifty-ninth Street thrusts its lights through the trees. There again was my lost city, wrapped cool in its mystery and promise. But that detachment never lasted long—as the toiler must live in the city's belly, so was I compelled to live in its disordered mind." In his mind's eye, Fitzgerald came to see a city "bloated, glutted, stupid with cake and circuses," a city marked by a new vulgarity and aggressiveness, a combative style embedded in the phrase "Oh, yeah?" Fitzgerald revised his vision of New York's morality play: "I once thought that there were no second acts in American lives, but there was certainly to be a second act to New York's boom days."[45]

By 1931, after again returning from Europe—this time as part of the generational migration portrayed in Malcolm Cowley's *Exile's Return*—Fitzgerald saw a sobered-up New York, a city hungover and depressed. Before he left for Europe he had bid the City farewell from the Plaza roof; on his return he greeted the City from the newly opened Empire State Building, "the last and most magnificent of towers." There, high above Manhattan, Fitzgerald suddenly understood that New York "*had limits*—from the tallest structure he saw for the first time that it faded out of sight and mind into the country on all sides, into an expanse of green and blue that alone was limitless. And with the awful realization that New York was a city after all and not a universe, the whole shining edifice that he had reared in his imagination came crashing to the ground." Fitzgerald could not go "home" again to New York.[46]

"New York was a dreamland to Fitzgerald," says Alfred Kazin. "No writer born to New York's constant pressure can ever associate so much beauty with it—can ever think of New York as the Plaza Hotel."[47] Kazin, author of many works on the City, speaks with the savvy voice of a born New Yorker. However, Kazin's approach does not preclude Fitzgerald's vision of the City as a dreamscape in which a diamond can seem as big as the Ritz. "The dreamer within the city is its character," notes Philip Fisher, "as the shepherd is *the* character of the pastoral world."[48] At one extraordinary moment in *The Great Gatsby*, Fitzgerald shows how his romantic imagination could transform the mere facts of New York: "We drove over the Fifth Avenue, so warm and soft, almost pastoral, on the Summer Sunday afternoon that I wouldn't have been surprised to see a great flock of white sheep turn the corner."[49] No one "born to New York's constant pressure," like Kazin, could ever think of New York's streets as a field of sheep or imagine himself as a dreamy shepherd. Fitzgerald, the outsider, could appreciate the mere glaze of man-made appurtenances imposed upon the island's grounds.

Yet Fitzgerald's City was no pastoral retreat; for it too often took the shape of a nightmarish hallucination. In "The Lost Decade," a 1939 story, Orrison Brown, the minor editor of a Manhattan newsweekly, is asked to take the writer Louis Trimble, another alter ego for Fitzgerald, to lunch. Trimble has been away from New York City for ten years, since 1928, when the Empire State Building was going up. They walk up Fifth Avenue, and they stop to lunch at a restaurant where the waiter does not recall Trimble. Everything is unfamiliar, and Trimble is neither interested in the new buildings nor in the luncheon. He is interested, however, in the people and the rhythms of New York. He recalls that Cole Porter came back to New York in 1928 to catch the new music of the City. (By 1938 Cole Porter had been immobilized by an accident that would haunt him for the rest of his life.) After they shake hands and part, Brown realizes that Trimble has been drunk for a decade, but the long party is finally over.

When Fitzgerald sobered up, he too realized that New York had limits. Porter could write "I Happen to Like New York"—Porter said he liked not only the sight and the sound, but also the *stink* of it—but not Fitzgerald: "Sometimes I wish I had gone along with (Cole Porter and Rogers and Hart and that gang), but I guess I am too much a moralist at heart and really want to preach at people in some acceptable form, rather than to entertain."[50] New York City finally became F. Scott Fitzgerald's heart of darkness and the occasion for a series of sermons on lost virtues and graces.

I F F. SCOTT FITZGERALD SAW NEW YORK THROUGH THE teary eyes of a moralist, his friend and fellow novelist, John Dos Passos, saw the City through the cold eyes of an aesthete turned political satirist. As Dos Passos recalled more than four decades later in *The Best Times*, one day in October 1922 their differences became clear: He had been invited to lunch with Scott and Zelda at the Plaza. In Manhattan "everything [had] the million dollar look" in the eyes of Dos Passos, who had just returned from war-scarred Europe. On this "crisp autumn day," the sky was blue, the clouds were white, the girls were pretty in their autumn dresses, and the windows of tall buildings sparkled with reflected sunlight. At the Plaza "the elevator man's buttons flashed like gold sovereigns."

In the Fitzgeralds' suite, Dos Passos met another author he admired, Sherwood Anderson. There they dined on lobster croquettes and talked about writing; they drank Bronx cocktails and champagne, for "Scott had good bootleggers." After lunch Anderson left, and the rest of the party were chauffeured out to Long Island in the Fitzgeralds' red touring car to find a house for Scott and Zelda to rent. After they finished touring "gentlemen's estates," they called on Ring Lardner in his mansion, but he was too drunk to talk. On their way back to Manhattan, the party stopped at a carnival, where Scott stayed in the car, drinking whiskey, while Dos Passos and Zelda rode on the Ferris wheel. After repeated turns, Zelda refused to get off and, when Dos Passos insisted that they leave, she sulked all the way back to Manhattan, where they parted "under the gilt Sherman in front of the Plaza."

The Fitzgeralds and Dos Passos went their separate ways. "For the Fitzgeralds that was the beginning of their Great Neck period, which Scott made *aere perennius* in *The Great Gatsby*. For me it was the beginning of something quite different."[51] Dos Passos turned away from Scott and Zelda's conspicuous consumption and riotous emotional excursions. Dos Passos's New York, where little guys were shoved around by brutal forces, had small room for "gentlemen's estates" and endless rides on a Ferris wheel.

Dos Passos named New York "the City of Destruction," an allegorical site of personal and national testing, and he seized every opportunity to leave it. However, like so many other American writers, he could neither stay away nor cease imagining New York.[52] Ambivalence was in his nature and background. The protagonist of Dos Passos's novel, *Chosen Country*, is "a double foreigner . . . A Man Without a Country."[53] John Dos Passos, born John R. Madison, thought of himself the same way. He was born in a Chicago hotel, out of wedlock, to John Randolph Dos Passos and Lucy Addison Sprigg Madison in 1896. Because of his anomalous family situation and the demands of his father's business interests, young John had a "horrible childhood," spent traveling from city to city, in America and abroad.[54] His father was a successful lawyer who had also written a book, *The Anglo-Saxon Century and the Unification of the English-Speaking People* (1903), that affirmed the Anglo-Saxon basis of American values. Late in his life, when Dos Passos himself had become so determined a defender of traditional American values that he could legitimately be called his father's son, he recovered his father's property in Westmoreland, Virginia, just the kind of "gentleman's estate" he had scorned decades before.

Dos Passos had been reared to be a gentleman, but he rebelled. After John attended Choate, his father insisted that he go to Harvard, though he wanted to go to sea. At Harvard, along with other young men of his generation (class of 1916), he discovered the aestheticism of Walter Pater, an influence reflected in his undergraduate writings and early fiction, *One Man's Initiation* (1920) and *Streets of Night* (1923). But he also read Thorstein Veblen's expositions on the injustices of capitalism.

While he was a Harvard undergraduate, Dos Passos railed against "the cossack tactics of the New York police force" during a riot; rejecting his father's legacy, he was drawn to "foreigners," particularly to the Jews of the Lower East Side.[55] There he talked about the Russian Revolution with Yiddish journalists and poets, or he went to Minsky's, the famous burlesque house on Second Avenue. Dos Passos found his voice in the pages of the *Masses*, which began publication in 1912, with Max Eastman as editor—a journal that described itself as "A Revolutionary and not a Reform Magazine, a Magazine with a Sense of Humor and no Respect for the Respectable; Frank; Arrogant; Impertinent; Searching for the True Causes . . . A Free Magazine."[56] The magazine's anger spoke to Dos Passos, who grew quickly cynical about the war to end all wars, thinking it meant an end to civilization. In November 1917, Eastman, John Reed, managing editor Floyd Dell, and others were charged with subverting the nation's war efforts, so the *Masses* ceased publication in 1918, but within three months it was reborn as the *Liberator*, becoming formally affiliated with the Communist Party in 1922. Dos Passos made a similar transit from random rebelliousness to focused political radicalism.

After Harvard, Dos Passos went to Spain to study architecture, but in 1917, after his father died and war broke out, he joined the Norton-Harjes ambulance unit, serving first in France, then in Italy with the Red Cross ambulance service and the U.S. Army Medical Corps. In Paris his job required him to carry buckets of amputated limbs from an operating room. These shocking experiences were exploited in *Three Soldiers* (1921), and his rage at war's waste can be seen in the social and political themes of his novels.

After the disillusionments of the Great War, New York held considerable wonder for Dos Passos. On his return in 1920, after a three-year absence, he was overwhelmed by the City, finding it a kind of "Babylon gone mad." Like Fitzgerald and so many others, Dos Passos felt called upon to compose a response of sufficient scope and imagination, to develop a prose capable of meeting the grandeur and the terror of the City. "New York—after all—is magnificent," he wrote. It seemed "a city of cavedwellers, with a frightful, brutal ugliness about it, full of thunderous voices of metal grinding on metal and of an eternal sound of wheels which turn, turn on heavy stones. People swarm meekly like ants along designated routes, crushed by the disdainful and pitiless things around them." Dos Passos forced the denunciatory zeal of Isaiah into the lyricism of Rodgers and Hart: the City reminded him of "Nineveh and Babylon, of Ur of the Chaldees, of the immense cities which loom like basilisks behind the horizon in ancient Jewish tales, where the temples rose as high as mountains and people ran trembling through dirty little alleys to the constant noise of whips with hilts of gold." He assumed the role of the prophet: "O for the sound of a brazen trumpet which, like the voice of the Baptist in the desert, will sing again about the immensity of man in this nothingness of iron, steel, marble, and rock." But Dos Passos's imagination also danced on the ceilings of the City's towers: "Night time especially is both marvelous and appalling, seen from the height of a Roof Garden, where women with raucous voices dance in the amber light, the blue-grey bulk of the city cut up by the enormous arabesques of electric billboards, when the streets where automobiles scurry about like cockroaches are lost [in] a golden dust, and when a pathetic little moon, pale and dazzled, looks at you across a leaden sky."[57]

At other times, Dos Passos reached for more comic analogies. "New York is rather funny," he wrote to John Howard Lawson in September 1920, "like a badly drawn cartoon—everybody looks and dresses like the Arrow-collarman."[58] The next month, he wrote to Robert Hillyer: "New York is silly and rather stupendous, rather like a badly drawn cartoon in the self-style funny section of a Sunday paper."[59] However, Dos Passos's images became more threatening; by 1925 he was writing to Hillyer, from shipboard, on his way back to France, that a week in New York "was like being rolled naked in metal filings."[60]

Dos Passos always saw himself as "the visitor, the tourist on his way to the railroad station."[61] He was like the symbolic figure who opens his epic trilogy, U.S.A. (1936): "The young man walks by himself searching through the crowd with greedy eyes, greedy ears taut to hear, by himself, alone."[62] This peripatetic persona resembles both Walt Whitman's buoyant democrat celebrating New York's citizenry and those morose urban wanderers, Melville's Bartleby and Poe's man of the crowd. In *The Big Money*, the final volume of *U.S.A.*, Dos Passos made his debt explicit by declaring, "I too am Walt Whitman," but as his biographer points out, it was the Whitman of *Democratic Vistas*, not "Song of Myself," that Dos Passos invoked as a model. He identified with the Whitman he described in *Century's Ebb*, who feared that the "fervid and tremendous *Idea*" of American democracy was stuck in "solid things" during years of "unprecedented material advancement."[63]

In the early 1920s, Dos Passos felt more at home in New York, his "chosen country."[64] He enjoyed sitting at the Brevoort, a cafe at the corner of Fifth Avenue and Eighth Street, where Emma Goldman, Isadora Duncan, Theodore Dreiser, Eugene O'Neill, Edna St. Vincent Millay, John Reed, and Max Eastman could often be found. Dos Passos's political views became increasingly "red"; he meditated upon the destruction of Harvard and all it stood for.[65] In 1922 he settled into Greenwich Village and "La Vie Litteraire," as he titled his chapter on this period in *The Best Times*.

In the 1920s, while he alternated living in New York and Europe, Dos Passos often visited E. E. Cummings and Esther Andrews in the Village. At Andrews's house on Commerce Street, Dos Passos joined something of a salon, where he met Dawn Powell, Whittaker Chambers, and others who prided themselves on their failures to fulfill themselves as artists. "Esther Andrews' New York was a sort of mirror image of the Fitzgeralds' city of glitter and success. Everything was the other way around. Anybody who wasn't a celebrity was welcome to Melancholia Villa."[66] Though intrigued by these new artistic currents, Dos Passos disliked the sense of superiority he saw in many Village bohemians of the time.

Dos Passos saw himself as a socialist and an artist, so he supported the *New Masses*, a journal begun in 1926 that combined the commitment to artistic experimentation of the old *Masses* with the political radicalism of the *Liberator*. Editor Mike Gold, writing as though he had Dos Passos in mind, declared he wanted "to conduct a cultural defense of the revolution" and to create a journal for artists and intellectuals "wanting to do and say something to solve the bloody mess we are all in."[67]

In the late 1920s, Dos Passos combined his artistic and political radicalism by directing plays for three years at the New Playwrights' Theater, which John Howard Lawson and Michael Gold had founded in imitation of the Russian revolutionary theater. Through the *New Masses* crowd he also became involved in the Sacco-Vanzetti case, joining Lillian Hellman, Dorothy Parker, Edna St. Vincent Millay, and others to protest the Sacco-Vanzetti death sentences in Boston. After their executions in 1927, Dos Passos declared he had "privately seceded" from the nation. Soon, however, he also became alienated from his associates in New York who prided themselves on their own alienation from America, feeling cramped by the rigid Marxist ideology of groups like the New Playwrights. In the theater and in politics, Dos Passos came to see himself as a writer who had been used by the Communist Party, so he left New York in 1929.

In *Most Likely to Succeed* (1954), a late novel, Dos Passos looked back on his New York days with satirical bitterness. Jed Morris, an ambitious young playwright, goes from bright promise to disaster in New York in a few years. When he returns from Morocco in the mid 1920s, all things seem possible for Jed, who is young, talented, and a Communist:

> *Jed's entrance into New York was magnificent. He came swooping down out of the noisy sunlight. His ears were full of the hoot of tugs and the crying of gulls. His eyes were dazzled with the tall buildings that rose, sparkling with windows like mica, to meet him as the liner nosed into the harbor. Walking down the first class gangplank, briefcase under his arm, he squinted through the glare to try to make out the faces scattered like spilled peas in the shadow of the pier below him.*[68]

Images of descent and darkness foreshadow Jed's involvement with a radical theater company. He acquiesces to the Communist Party's demands on his play. His director, Kenneth, is so distressed by Party pressures that he commits suicide, leaving Jed to carry on in his career of artistic compromise in Hollywood. As this recasting of his autobiography makes clear, by the mid 1950s, when Dos Passos had become politically conservative, he had turned savagely against the art and politics that had so absorbed him in New York in the twenties.

Dos Passos's New York, like Fitzgerald's, was contained in that period between the Armistice and the Crash. By the mid 1930s, as he was completing *U.S.A.*, he had "rejoined the United States."[69] However, before he enlarged the scope of his concerns, John Dos Passos wrote one of the great books about New York, *Manhattan Transfer* (1925).

In the spring of 1923, Dos Passos had promised a friend, "I shall start knocking together a long dull and arduous novel about New York and go-getters and God knows what besides." Then he went again to Europe. When he returned, he moved to Far Rockaway to finish "a novel," as he told another friend, "that I hope will be utterly fantastic and New Yorkish." After another trip, he again returned to the City, moving into an apartment building at 106–110 Columbia Heights, in Brooklyn, where Hart Crane also lived. The building faced the East River and the Brooklyn Bridge, giving both writers a broad perspective of Manhattan. *Manhattan Transfer*, a "collective novel," features the City as its central character, in all of its awesome power to shape and to break the lives of its citizens.[70]

The second chapter of *Manhattan Transfer*, titled "Metropolis," begins with a meditation upon skyscrapers: "Crammed on the narrow island the millionwindowed buildings will jut glittering, pyramid on pyramid like the white cloudhead above the thunderstorm."[71] Beneath these looming towers walk diminished and pathetic searchers. Bud Korpenning, for example, arrives in New York from "upstate," having trudged fifteen miles that morning to get away to the City. (Bud has murdered his father, so he is a perverse version of the Alger hero, who typically sought refuge in the City.) "How do I get to Broadway?" Bud asks. "I want to get to the center of things." He is told by a cook in a lunchwagon that "it's looks that count in this city." New York is a place of style, not substance; manner, not matter; edge, not center.[72]

Bud travels down Broadway from the point where it is a walkway of weeds to the region where planks are laid, and he slogs on until he finds himself treading on sidewalks. He asks for work at a construction site, but he is told that he cannot get a job without a union card: "He shuffled his feet uneasily and walked on. If I could get more into the center of things." Bud stops at a traffic incident, "one o them automobile riots," says a butcher's boy. The boy tells Bud, in that wise-guy way New Yorkers speak to obvious hicks, to continue down Broadway to City Hall, to "the center of things," and ask the mayor for a seat as an alderman.[73]

Bud continues his trek and becomes Dos Passos's man of the City—lost and doomed. "He walked down Broadway, past Lincoln Square, across Columbus Circle, further downtown towards the center of things where it'd be more crowded."[74] Between the East River and Fifty-third Street, Bud encounters a gray-haired woman at a pile of coal. He tells her he is from Cooperstown. "And what did you want to come to this horrible city for?" she asks. "Couldn't stay on the farm no more," Bud answers. The gray-haired woman at the coal pile underlines Dos Passos's theme of a lost pastoral: "It's terrible what's going to become of this country if all the fine strong young men leave the farms and come into the cities."[75] Cooperstown suggests James Fenimore Cooper, who came to recognize the threats New York City held. *Manhattan Transfer*, then, derives in part from the doubts over civic polity previously expressed in Cooper's *The American Democrat*.

Bud gives up his search in his final moments of life, which find him atop the Brooklyn Bridge. "The sun has risen behind Brooklyn. The windows of Manhattan have caught fire. He jerks himself forward, slips, dangles by a hand with the sun in his eyes. The yell strangles in his throat as he drops." Dos Passos's New York has no coherent center. It is a force of dispersal—like Henry Adams's Dynamo.[76] The Bridge, which Hart Crane strained to make into an emblem of redemption, is Dos Passos's center of destruction. In their most important works on the City, both Dos Passos and Crane placed American youth atop the Brooklyn Bridge, poised to jump.

Bud Korpenning occupies only one of the several intersecting storylines in *Manhattan Transfer*. Emile, an émigré, believes in opportunity: "That's why I came to New York." Marco, an anarchist, argues that the City will betray them. Dos Passos makes it clear that both young men are caught in a net of circumstances: "At a corner they looked up Broadway that was narrow and scorched as if a fire had gutted it."[77] Indeed, fire is a principal trope for the City and its yearning citizenry. Stanwood Emery, who had wanted to be an architect, literally ignites himself. A burning desire for transformation characterizes this group of have-nots in prosperous New York. However, even those who are transformed, those who do become successful, find themselves against a wall, confronting their own emptiness. "The terrible thing about having New York go stale on you," says George Baldwin, a successful lawyer and politico, "is that there's nowhere else. It's the top of the world. All we can do is go round and round in a squirrel cage."[78] Although Dos Passos would eventually leave New York, his characters are stuck there.

In counterpoint to Bud Korpenning stands Jimmy Herf, Dos Passos's alter ego. Jimmy is first seen as a boy, arriving in New York by boat from Europe, on July Fourth, 1904. Through Jimmy's awed eyes, we move past the Statue of Liberty and Governors Island, with local landmarks prominent: the Brooklyn Bridge, the Battery, the spire of Trinity Church, the Pulitzer Building—standards of the bright promise of American life. When he is sixteen, Jimmy's mother dies and leaves him $5,500. His Uncle Jeff then tells Jimmy to work hard, for "if a man's a success in New York, he's a success!" However, Jimmy does not want success on New York's terms. Outside the Customhouse, he "stares long up the deep gash of Broadway, facing the wind squarely. Uncle Jeff and his office could go plumb to hell."[79]

Near the end of the novel, Jimmy, who has been a reporter, a chronicler of the City's corruptions, is out of work and his marriage has gone bust. His former wife, Ellen Thatcher, who came to Manhattan to become an actress, has lost all of her idealism, so she marries an aging politician for security. "Life in New York had seemed full of possibilities, but because of her inner emptiness they come to nothing."[80] Jimmy becomes a cynic, like his author. "Pursuit of happiness, unalienable pursuit . . . right to life liberty and. . . . A black moonless night; Jimmy Herf is walking alone up South Street" and he is "stumped." He can only see two choices: to "go away in a dirty soft shirt or stay in a clean Arrow collar. But what's the use of spending your whole life fleeing the City of Destruction?"[81] Yet, on the novel's final page, Jimmy does finally flee New York. At a lunchwagon on the edge of town, he asks a truck driver for a ride. "How fur ye goin?" asks the driver. "I dunnoo. . . . Pretty far," says Jimmy Herf, concluding *Manhattan Transfer*.[82] In Dos Passos's stark vision, Manhattan lures America's young men, native and immigrant, to urban death or failure. Dos Passos does not make it clear what young men like Bud and Jimmy should do, since lives in Cooperstown or in Europe are not presented as viable alternatives. "What is certain," as Robert A. Gates notes of this novel, "is that within the confines of New York, life is too fast to be understood clearly, too hectic to be truly appreciated, and too selfish to be kind."[83]

Manhattan Transfer is a striking combination of modernist vigor and political pessimism. From Joyce's *Ulysses* and Eliot's *The Waste Land*, Dos Passos drew the license to experiment boldly and to portray the City as an alien environment.[84] This jazzy, multifocused novel was the result of Dos Passos's conscious efforts to capture the rhythms, the sharply contrasting sights and sounds, of the City. It reflected the techniques of French modernists, particularly its painters, and incorporated the jumpy, documentary style of New York's young filmmakers. "The artist must record the fleeting world the way the motion picture film recorded it," declared Dos Passos. "By contrast, juxtaposition he could build reality into his own vision: montage. New York was the first thing that hit me when I got back home [in the early 1920s]. I started rapportage on New York. . . . The narrative must stand up off the page. Fragmentation. Contrast. Montage. The result was Manhattan Transfer."[85] Each of Dos Passos's characters live in incoherent, uncentered fragments of experience. New York, as Peter Conrad notes, "ascends beyond the reach or comprehension of Dos Passos's trudging pedestrians, who traipse through the city or disconsolately sit in it but are disjointed from it."[86]

Manhattan Transfer constituted something radically new—a combination of technique and vision that reconceived the City. So argued Sinclair Lewis in an essay in the *Saturday Review*, an essay that was quickly printed as a brief book. Lewis even wondered if Dos Passos's novel might "be the first book to catch Manhattan." He rejected previous portrayals of the City by Whitman as provincial; by Howells, Wharton, and James as both provincial and mannered; and by the "reporters of the Jazz Age" as "but foam on the beer!"[87] Though he went too far in denigrating others in order to praise Dos Passos's originality, Lewis did capture the excitement stirred by *Manhattan Transfer* in the mid 1920s.

In the *New Masses*, Mike Gold called the novel "a barbaric poem of New York" that reflected Dos Passos's "bewilderment." Gold may have been right when he suggested that "Dos Passos suffers with nostalgia for a clean, fair, joyous and socialized America" of a hundred years ago.[88] After reading *Manhattan Transfer*, Edmund Wilson wondered whether Dos Passos's hatred of capitalist America was not becoming a "distaste for all the beings who compose it."[89]

In fact, *Manhattan Transfer* was planned as a tragedy, so Dos Passos's characters had little latitude. They were doomed by the formal requirements of the tragic mode and by the determining vision of their author. "Jimmy Herf goes away" is how Dos Passos closed his early set of notes for the novel: "Manhattan Manhattan Manhattan The flight of [Jimmy] and the deaths of old m[an and] child."[90] As the City circumscribed their choices, so too did this modernist novelist.

In "Newsreel L" of *The Big Money*, Dos Passos picked up a jaunty refrain of the day: "And if you should be dining with a little stranger/ Red light seem to warn you of a danger/ Don't blame it all on Broadway."[91] But Dos Passos *did* blame much of the crisis in America on Wall Street and on plutocrats like his father who sold out the promise of American life: "Listen businessmen collegepresidents judges America will not forget her betrayers," he wrote in *U.S.A.*[92] Above all other American places, New York was Dos Passos's city of betrayers, America's city of destruction.

John Dos Passos appears as Hugh Bammon, a character in Edmund Wilson's novel *I Thought of Daisy* (1929), a satire of Greenwich Village types. Wilson gently mocks Dos Passos by portraying Bammon as a failed bohemian uncomfortable with the new manners and morals of the Village, its drinking and its bold "new women."[93] In Wilson's novel Bammon, who is "really on close terms with no one," is a man in rebellion against the "single culture" of his father, a "clever lawyer."[94] Dos Passos and Wilson had to come to terms with the America of their fathers—both of whom were Progressives and American chauvinists during the Gilded Age—in an era of political disillusionment and international literary modernism. Neither writer ever felt fully at ease in the American Zion of capitalism, but at the beginning of their careers, Wilson defined his commitment to the idea of "America" by faulting Dos Passos for willfully alienating himself from his chosen country.

Though he, too, grew disillusioned, Edmund Wilson, as a young man, embraced the City and enthusiastically took up Village ways. In 1919 Wilson got a job at *Vanity Fair*—he became managing editor in 1921—working with John Peale Bishop. There they both fell in love with Edna St. Vincent Millay, the legendary young woman of their generation—beautiful, outspoken, sexy, and poetic.

THE VILLAGE EPITOMIZED THE CITY'S ARTISTIC FREEDOM and political radicalism both before and after World War I. For women in particular, as Liz Heron points out, urban culture (which Village life in many ways defined) offered opportunities of self-expression, experimentation, and independence: "Fictions [and poems] of the city suggest that, whatever the social restrictions imposed on women's mobility, the city itself offers initiation enough to women to ignore these and to follow their inclinations. The very danger that conformity warns against may thereby be a lure."[95] In a satiric sketch of Village life, written in 1916, Djuna Barnes, who lived there, noted the Village's spiritual isolation: "The greater part of New York is as soulless as a department store; but Greenwich Village has recollections like ears filled with muted music and hopes like sightless eyes straining to catch a glimpse of the beatific vision."[96]

Seekers and satirists flocked to lower Manhattan. Along with novelist John Dos Passos and critic Edmund Wilson, poet E. E. Cummings, political radical Mike Gold, playwright Eugene O'Neill, and many more personified the rebellious élan of the Village in those years. "When I think of Greenwich Village, it is almost with tears," noted Wilson in 1922. "For there this battered battalion dress their guns against the whole nation. Where the traffic, gnashing iron teeth, no longer oppresses the pavement, where the toned red bricks of low houses still front an open square . . . from the darkest corners of the country they have fled for comfort and asylum."[97] Edna St. Vincent Millay, portrayed as the arty and promiscuous poet Rita Cavanagh in Wilson's *I Thought of Daisy*, both embodied and articulated this Village state of mind.

Millay was born in 1892, in Rockland, Maine, a far country from Greenwich Village. After her undergraduate years at Barnard and Vassar (where she received her degree in 1917), years filled with poetry and challenges to college proprieties, she moved to the Village, to the heart of the new bohemia. Though she was only there for a few years—she married and moved to the Berkshires in 1923—Millay left her mark on all who knew her with her unforgettable presence and her haunting lyrics, some of which served as a credo for postwar freedom. Famously, in "First Fig," she declared, "My candle burns at both ends;/ It will not last the night;/ But ah, my foes, and oh, my friends—/ It gives a lovely light!"[98] Millay cast her own light as an actress and director at the Provincetown Playhouse. She and her sister Norma lived in an unheated room with a fireplace on Waverly Place, then in a house on Charlton Street. "She lived in that gay poverty," wrote Floyd Dell, "which is traditional of the village, and one may find reminiscences of that life in her poetry."[99]

As Millay enchanted the young men who were drawn to her brief flame, so her romantic vision of Manhattan enticed young men and women away from dull provinces all across America. "We were very tired, we were very merry—/ We had gone back and forth all night on the ferry," she sang in "Recuerdo."[100] The world she conjured is long gone, but the beauty of her brief presence in the Village, the assurance of her oddly archaic verse, and the poignance of her message linger still.

UNDER MILLAY'S GUIDANCE, EDMUND WILSON ENTERED the world of 1920s bohemia, in Greenwich Village—"the speakeasies, the parties, the passionate and sometimes tortured sex," in Leon Edel's words.[101] Millay, whom Wilson was never able to forget, taught him some of her bittersweet tones of love and loss. He recalled, in his tribute after her death in 1950, a time when they rode along Fifth Avenue in a bus while she recited a sonnet about a failed love affair with another man: "Here is a wound that will never heal, I know." Wilson felt only "chagrin" that he was not that man, sensing that she would be his wound that would never heal. Yet he concluded his tribute with an image of Millay at her most winning, just after she had come from Vassar to New York: he sees her running around a corner at Macdougal Street, in Greenwich Village, laughing "like a nymph." For him, she *was* New York in the 1920s, vibrant and beautiful.[102]

Born in New Jersey in 1895, Wilson came to the center of this cultural circle from Princeton in 1916 to work as a reporter on the *Evening Sun*, at fifteen dollars a week. He lived on West Eighth Street, in rooms with other young men. In his spare time Wilson composed his impressions of the City in symbolist journal entries. In his fervid eye, "the old iron fence on the north side of Washington Square flowers into flat iron chrysanthemums."[103] New York provided him with new inspiration for his cerebrations, evocations, and denunciations.

At the *Liberator*, the *Dial*, and the *New Republic*, where he began as an associate editor in 1926, Wilson, in essays of rare understanding, introduced modern European literature, particularly the works of Joyce and Eliot, to American readers. He also reported on New York's low life, with a sympathetic eye for those who sought their epiphanies in back alleys and burlesque houses. He attended burlesque shows at the National Winter Garden on Second Avenue and Houston Street, and he sought out "burlesque in its more primitive form" at the Olympic on Fourteenth Street, where the dancers left the audience mute at a "vision of erotic ecstasy."[104]

Critic Sherman Paul imagines a map of Wilson's world that stretches from New Jersey towns (Red Bank, Lakewood, Princeton) to Wellfleet, on Cape Cod, to Cambridge, Massachusetts, to Talcotville, in upstate New York: "Toward the center are New York City and Stamford, Connecticut," which Wilson named "Hecate County" in his fiction.[105] Like the characters in *Manhattan Transfer*, Wilson was long searching for "the center of things." This bright, ambitious young man from Red Bank looked first in Manhattan.

Like his more impressionable Princeton classmate, Scott Fitzgerald, Edmund Wilson seemed most sensitive to impressions of Manhattan upon moments of entry and departure. "*The skyscrapers in November.* From the Jersey City ferry, on a gray morning of November, the skyscrapers stood out distinctly in a hard light and seemed no more dignified, but only larger, than the hideous utilitarian buildings of the small towns—like them, of the drabbest and most grimy colors and of a square machine-made architecture which excluded imagination."[106] Wilson also showed himself to be more detached, accepting, and cynical about skyscrapers than Henry James had been. Anticipating Fitzgerald's set piece in *The Great Gatsby*, Wilson tried out a meditation upon entering the City from another angle: "As we went over the Queensboro Bridge, the factories and main streets and gas tanks looked strange in the obscure dawn and the blue of the water struck a curiously clear note. We looked back and saw that all the sky was suddenly suffused with lucid yellow.—And before we were over the bridge, we had met the sour smells of the city."[107] Wilson clearly was less enchanted by Manhattan than was Fitzgerald, who saw Wilson as the consummate urbanite. Like Fitzgerald and Dos Passos, Wilson used the Plaza to represent the City, though he viewed the hotel neither with Fitzgerald's awe nor with Dos Passos's political jaundice: "*Cold June.* The Plaza rose from Fifth Avenue like some high white sea cliff, and the whole scene, in a pale setting sun, had a certain bleakness of marine skies—the statue of Sherman, at the entrance to the park, showed a spiny and black silhouette."[108]

Wilson, who served as Fitzgerald's conscience and literary advisor, understood the limitations of his gifted classmate from St. Paul. Both were men of the 1920s, as Wilson thought of it, but Fitzgerald was different, more naive and romantic than most. Fitzgerald brought the values of "the more prosperous strata" of Middle West cities to New York, wrote Wilson in 1922. "In *The Beautiful and Damned*, for example, we feel that he is moving in a vacuum; the characters have no real connection with the background to which they have been assigned; they are not part of the organism of New York."[109] Both Fitzgerald and Wilson were newcomers to New York, but the more cultivated and prosperous society of nearby Red Bank provided Wilson with a sense of access to the City that Fitzgerald, who traveled East on those long train rides through the heartland, lacked.

Wilson was determined to know New York, not be swept off his feet by it. Above all, New York gave Wilson a new level of self-awareness, evident in a journal entry in which he imagines himself as a character: "He comes to New York, reads the papers, sees the theater advertisements and begins calling up friends,—Even before calling up the friends, he says to himself, 'I love this!' "[110] Indeed, Wilson became one of the great chroniclers of New York in the 1920s, describing its "drinks, animated conversation, gaiety, brilliant writing, uninhibited exchange of ideas." He wrote about all of it, from Stravinsky to the Moscow Art Theater, from Georgia O'Keeffe to Houdini.[111] Yet, though he loved New York for all that it offered a young writer, Wilson was often appalled by what it said about the American experience.

Wilson was not seeking asylum in the City, but, rather, freedom of expression—in art, sex, and politics. An essay self-consciously titled "Greenwich Village in the Early Twenties," published in April 1925, reveals Wilson's attitudes at the time. It is the story of a woman from the American interior who marries young, bounces around, and ends up in the Village. "I tell you," Wilson has her say, "the West is alright, but it's a great relief to get some place where you can feel a little bit free."[112] If provincial America was bondage, then the Village was freedom. Yet Wilson's Arcadia had its dark and empty places. He came to see, as Daniel Aaron points out, pretension and shallowness at Village parties—"the pit of ashes at the bottom of the gin mill."[113]

Wilson's New York meant speed: "fast taxi ride through New York streets when you are drunk: impression that you are plunging through all obstacles at exhilarating giddy speed; nothing can interfere with your progress." His City mixed elegance and nausea: coming home along Broadway one night, he was vomited upon by a drunk, who was leaning out from a second-story window. The City was also Wilson's sexual marketplace: "*Marie*. I picked her up somewhere in the Forties or Fifties coming out of a hotel." While his marriage to actress Mary Blair deteriorated in the late 1920s, Wilson took up with Anna Pennington, a dancehall girl and waitress; he kept a careful record of their erotic life in his journals and incorporated her into "The Princess with the Golden Hair," in *Memoirs of Hecate County* (1946). Indeed, New York offered a range of erotic and romantic possibilities. Wilson imagined "a thousand girls resurrecting themselves in the afternoon from dark and messy rooms," dressing "and emerging, like butterflies from cocoons, enchanting and romantic creatures to exert their magic in the streets, to wander and draw men's glances."[114]

Even before the Crash of 1929, Wilson saw the City as a modern wasteland, an arid place lacking in soul and spirit. Wilson began *The American Earthquake* in 1925 with images of displacement—St. John's Chapel in Varick Street, already squeezed between the Sixth Avenue El and the freightyards of the Central Railroad, was threatened by construction of a new subway: "The old spire itself, with its multiple tiers, was beginning to lurch a little, like the mast of a sinking ship. And now, indeed, the office buildings, the freightyards and the factories have closed over it and swallowed it up, imposing a monotony as blank as the sea." In the East Forties, looking down from a high window, Wilson contemplated "the monstrous carcass of Grand Central Station and Palace, with its myriad skylights and its zinc-livid roofs, stretched out like a segmented seaworm that is almost unrecognizable as a form of life." The City presented Wilson with strange sounds, lurid images, and odd sensations that suggested an earthquake: "the drilling of granite teeth, the cackling of mechanical birds, the thudding of Cyclopean iron doors; accelerating avalanches of brick, the collapse of deserted warehouses; explosives that cause no excitement, pistol shots that are quite without consequence. Nor does one care to find out what these noises are. One goes on with whatever one is doing, incurious and wholly indifferent."[115] Detached and speculative, Wilson here epitomizes the high modernist artist viewing the City.

However, at times he sounded less like James Joyce and more like Henry James, for Wilson, too, was horrified at what had happened to Washington Square and all that it stood for. He noted, for example, in 1927, how "the big red houses of the north and west sides had already been gutted of their grandeurs and crammed with economized cells, the cubbyholes of modern apartments, and the sooty peeling fronts of the south side, with their air of romance and mystery, had already been replaced by fresh arty grays and pinks." Monstrous apartment buildings came to dominate Wilson's Village: "these huge coarse and swollen mounds—blunt, clumsy, bleaching the sunlight with their dismal pale yellow sides and stamping down both the old formal square and the newer Bohemian refuge."[116] Looking back on these years in 1957, reflecting on the work of photographer Alfred Stieglitz, "something of a mesmerist," Wilson developed his image of the City. Stieglitz, he decided, had long been working for modern art, "trying to make beauty of—in Paul Rosenfeld's words—the 'strange brazen human emptiness' of the City in which I then lived and of which, as will be plain from these pages, I was irked by the recent overbuilding and increasing ugliness. I could remember when New York was as bracing, as electric and full of light, as San Francisco had been; when the Flat Iron Building was a wonder, the tallest thing on the skyline."[117]

Wilson's finest impressionistic sketch of New York, however, remains his description of the newly completed Empire State Building, which opened on May 1, 1931. Wilson was not impressed by the dedication ceremonies, which featured laudatory remarks by Al Smith (president of the owning company that constructed the building), President Herbert Hoover, Governor Franklin Roosevelt, and Mayor Jimmy Walker. His own picture was far darker:

> *Here the light of the setting sun strikes that scrambled mass of upright rectangles and broken-off graceless towers, bringing out in raw stone and drab brick their yellows without delicacy or brightness, their browns without depth or warmth. Brooklyn, Long Island City, Bronx, Englewood, Hoboken, Jersey City: rigid streets, square walls, crowded bulks, rows of rectangular windows—more than ten million people have been sucked into the vast ever-expanding barracks, which has scarcely a garden, scarcely a park, scarcely an open square and whose distances in all directions are blotted out in pale slate-gray. And here is the latest pile of stone, brick, nickel and steel, the latest shell of shafts and compartments, that outstacks and outmultiplies them all—that, most purposeless and superfluous of all, is advertised now as a triumph in the hour when the planless competitive society, the dehumanized urban community, of which it makes the culmination, is bankrupt.*[118]

The device of juxtaposition here provided Wilson with the opportunity to condemn the values of the Republic, exemplified in the hubristic Empire State Building.

In his late years, Wilson spent little time in the City. He divided his days between Wellfleet and Talcotville. The center of his world was still New York, but Wilson lived more on the edge of America, alienated from the mainstream of its culture, as he pointed out in "The Author at Sixty": "I live mainly in two old-fashioned country towns: Wellfleet, Massachusetts, and Talcotville, New York, with visits of days, weeks or months to New York City and Boston, where I see my old friends and transact my business."[119] Wilson's real business carried him far from New York and far from contemporary America. He spent months in the Mideast, studying for his book on the Dead Sea Scrolls. However, even abroad, New York and all that it represented stayed on his mind: "In Europe, I think of New York with nostalgia I shouldn't have expected. . . . We all had it in common that we were struggling with New York, stimulated by New York. More interesting, and perhaps more profitable—after all—than Europe. This is where the new culture, the new civilization, has really been being produced; the new American internationalism."[120]

In two works of fiction, *I Thought of Daisy* and "The Princess with the Golden Hair," a novella from *Memoirs of Hecate County*, Edmund Wilson revealed his deepest ambivalences about the City of New York, its immediate surroundings, and the Republic it represented. In each work Wilson personified the urban culture's values in a woman. In each work the narrator, clearly a stand-in for Wilson, vacillates between women who embody different sides of his own mind and represent conflicting aspects of the world around him: from aristocratic to common, from high poetry to low passions. In *I Thought of Daisy*, as Diana Trilling has suggested, the protagonist moves from the heady but stultifying realm of aesthetics, represented by a young poet, to the world of another, more common, woman—a journey symbolized in a trip to Coney Island. In "The Princess with the Golden Hair," a work of fiction informed by Wilson's experiences in the Great Depression and his study of Communism for *To the Finland Station* (1940), the intellectual hovers indecisively between his fascination for a rich but neurotic princess and a sexually engaging working-class woman.[121] Taken together, these women represent for Wilson, not only the body and soul of the City, but the character of America itself.

After the Great War, the narrator of *I Thought of Daisy* could not "go back . . . to living indifferently or trivially."[122] Drawn by his friend and foil, the nihilistic Hugo Bammon, the narrator does go to a Village party, after which he spends the night talking with Rita Cavanagh, a woman more passionate about poetry than sex, in his Bank Street flat. "Now the Village was at last revealed to me; it had that day come alive about me, and I felt myself part of its life. I, like them, had turned my back on all that word [world?] of mediocre aims and prosaic compromises; and at that price—what brave spirit would not pay it?—I had been set free to follow poetry!"[123] But the narrator also meets and is drawn to the more commonplace Daisy Coleman, who is the symbolic opposite of Fitzgerald's exotic, destructive Daisy Buchanan. The commitment by Wilson's narrator to transcen-

dence through art is balanced by his desire to root himself in her, the embodiment of the culture. Daisy and Rita stand for perhaps irreconcilable aspects of
America. The narrator senses this when he returns from his Coney Island outing
with Daisy. He sees a New York filled with bright shops and

> *girls in their summer dresses, hatless, with bobbed heads and pink or*
> *tan stockings, strolling out, alone or in couples. . . . That was the*
> *America to which I had returned when, coming back after the War*
> *from France, I had been greeted by that other suburban street-lamp*
> *on the Staten Island shore! That was the America to which tonight I*
> *felt myself returning again—those neat and new little shops, those*
> *girls wandering out in the evening between the drug-store and the*
> *building-lots—hardly knowing what they expected but half hoping for*
> *some new turn in their lives! Had not Daisy been once such a girl,*
> *walking out in the streets of Pittsburgh—had not Rita, in her up-state*
> *town?*[124]

Only the narrator—that is, the sensibility of Edmund Wilson—can join these opposites into a coherent whole. Thus only in art can the opposite forces of American life become unified. Rita and Daisy serve their purposes in providing a balanced education for the young artist who is determined to know this City and
this nation. He decides Daisy is a simple American girl, not just the product of
Broadway and the Village. They make love in his rooms. Wilson's stand-in per-
ceives Daisy as his last chance to connect with American reality.

Wilson's quest to understand New York and the nation through sexual and
cultural contact is extended in "The Princess with the Golden Hair," which is
set in New York after the Crash, Depression, and World War II. Again a man of
letters crosses the cultural and territorial lines of New York. He takes an apartment on East Twelfth Street, between Fifth and Sixth Avenues, and he walks
the streets of the Village, looking to pick up working girls. There, he meets
Anna, a dancehall girl and a waitress who lives in Brooklyn. She tells him lurid
stories about her many mistreatments and exploitations; as a result, the narrator
decides that Marx was correct about capitalism. Their romance is brief, but intense and instructive for both. Anna has a hysterectomy, and the narrator soon
finds Communism a simplistic solution. However, he is grateful to Anna for in-
troducing him to the realities of City life.

Imogen Loomis, ethereal, detached, married to an advertising man, is the
fairy-tale character of the title. The narrator tries to make himself worthy of her

by getting a job at the Metropolitan Museum and by moving to an expensive apartment. He has trouble getting her into bed, and when he finally does, he finds it disappointing, for she wears a brace, the result of spinal disease. When the narrator decides her disease is caused by her neurosis, he feels free from his obsession. In the end, the narrator rejects Imogen as unreal, and has a new appreciation of Anna: "It was Anna who had made it possible for *me* to recreate the actuality; who had given me that life of the people which had before been but prices and wages, legislation and technical progress, that new Europe of the East Side and Brooklyn for which there was no provided guidebook."[125]

In an essay on *Memoirs of Hecate County*, John Updike isolates Wilson's tortured attitudes toward America: "America seemed incorrigibly alien to Wilson, though fascinating, and intrinsic to his destiny. Like Dante, he is a tourist *engagé*."[126] In his journalism, his memoirs, and his fiction, Edmund Wilson most eloquently demonstrated that rich ambivalence in his writings on New York—a city of romance and degradation but, more important for Edmund Wilson, a city of education into new realities of life and art. New York City allowed Edmund Wilson to make his own spiritual journey through the Inferno.

HART CRANE, BY ALL ACCOUNTS, WAS A BRIGHT, HANDsome, engaging young man who reveled intemperately in art and life. As the Fitzgeralds drank to excess and plunged into the pool outside the Plaza, Crane drank to excess and reeled to the hypnotic, overinsistent rhythms of Ravel's *Bolero*. Crane's dance macabre, personal and poetic, was elegant, but frantic and brief. Like the dancers in "The Masque of the Red Death," by Edgar Allan Poe, a writer invoked by Crane as a model, Crane's "revel went whirlingly on, until at length there commenced the sounding of midnight on the clock."[127] The frenzied dance was halted in mid-stride by Crane's suicide, only months before his thirty-third birthday, in 1932.

"He was an American Mid-westerner, a homosexual, and an alcoholic," notes William Pritchard, but above all, Crane was a poet.[128] This combination of location, inclination, addiction, and dedication made New York City his inevitable, self-elected "home." He had left his grandmother's house in Cleveland in the spring of 1923, his twenty-third year, to live in New York, where previously he had only visited. He then felt, as he confided to a friend, "directly connected with Whitman . . . in currents that are positively awesome in their extent and possibilities." The yea-saying Walt Whitman of "Crossing Brooklyn Ferry" inspired Crane at the same time that the nay-saying Poe of "A Man in the Crowd" embodied his fears of personal isolation and national pessimism.[129]

For all of his articulated confidence, a streak of anxiety accompanied Crane's quest for love and poetry through the streets of the modern metropolis, as was clear in his response to his early days in the City: "The N.Y. life is too taxing. New York takes such a lot from you that you have to save all you can of yourself or you simply give out."[130] Crane never saved anything of himself, and within a decade, he simply gave out. By 1930 he had come to detest New York. The City "became for him a symbol of his weakness—both symbol and temptation—and he tried very hard to locate places in which he would be able to sober up," writes John Unterecker in *Voyager: A Life of Hart Crane*.[131] What remained of Crane's voyage carried him over the edge, to a place of deeper immersion.

Yet Crane fulfilled his promise in *The Bridge* (1930), an epic, semicoherent poem that describes his leap of faith, his poetic transcendence in the soaring curves of the Brooklyn Bridge. The Bridge became his symbol for the poetic impulse—this dreamlike structure of steel and cables that rose out of the mechanized life of the City. However, by the spring of 1932 Crane had reached and passed over the apogee of his arc, in life and art. Returning by boat from Mexico, where he had been involved in a risky love affair, Crane leaped overboard and was, as his tombstone inscription fittingly says, "lost at sea."[132] The most determined celebrator of modern New York, at the end of his days, could not face a return to the City.

Crane had grown up in Garretsville, Ohio, the son of a bourgeois father, a candy manufacturer, and a possessive, religious mother; he was the product of a troubled marriage. He sought escape from this fractious family situation and from middle-class, midwestern values by making the traditional American pilgrimage east, to New York, the city of freedom. There he could, without restraint, practice his homosexuality, consume alcohol freely, and most important, commit himself to poetry.

Crane met Malcolm Cowley in 1923, when Cowley was working as a copywriter for Sweet's Catalogue Service. They were brought together by poet Alan Tate at a Greenwich Village party. Crane himself was then a copywriter for the J. Walter Thompson Agency. Each of these bright young literary pilgrims to Gotham (Cowley was from Pittsburgh) had contributed to "little magazines" that celebrated modern poetry, *Broom* and *Secession*. Later Crane joined Cowley to work at Sweet's. Thus were the antitheses of American culture—poetry and advertising—briefly bridged.

Cowley recalls a visit with Tate to Crane's apartment in Brooklyn Heights in the spring of 1924. Crane had disparaged Poe, but he reconsidered when Cowley read aloud Poe's "The City in the Sea." After a while the young men left the room, wandered through the streets of Brooklyn, and found themselves at the base of the Bridge, looking toward the "proud towers," as Poe had put it, of Manhattan: "Suddenly we felt . . . that we were secretly comrades in the same endeavor: to present this new scene in poems that would reveal not only its astonishing face but the lasting realities behind it."[133] Yet Poe's poem, read with the knowledge of Crane's fate, holds an eerie air of doom: "Lo! Death has reared himself a throne/ In a strange city lying alone . . . / Resignedly beneath the sky/ The melancholy waters lie./ So blend the turrets and shadows there/ That all seem pendulous in air,/ While from a proud tower in the town/ Death looks gigantically down."[134] The City, with its looming towers and its soaring bridges, thus provided a symbol of indifference and an appropriate setting for the plunge into the abyss.

Hart Crane strained to find symbols of life in the "proud towers" and other emblems of the modern, urban age. In "Modern Poetry" (1929), an essay, Crane weighed "the function of poetry in a Machine Age." The "firm entrenchment" of machinery in the modern world, he believed, "has already produced a series of challenging new responsibilities for the poet. For unless poetry can absorb the machine, i.e., *acclimatize* it as naturally and casually as trees, cattle, galleons, castles and all other human associations of the past, then poetry has failed of its full contemporary function." Success for Crane "demands, however, along with the traditional qualifications of the poet, an extraordinary capacity for surrender, at least temporarily, to the sensations of urban life. This presupposes, of course, that the poet possesses sufficient spontaneity and gusto to convert this experience into positive terms." Paradoxically, in surrender Crane sought renewal; his artful leap into the abyss was meant to be a Joycean flight past the nets. For Crane, Whitman, "better than any other, was able to coordinate those forces in America which seem most intractable, fusing them into a universal vision which takes on additional significance as time goes on." However, leaving room for himself and his epic poem, Crane added, Whitman's "bequest is still to be realized in all its implications."[135] In *The Bridge*, a single poem in fifteen sections, Crane at once celebrated and surrendered himself to a central symbol of the machine age.

Crane began the poem that would become *The Bridge* in 1923, while still living in Cleveland. It would be an epic, a "mystical synthesis of America," as he anticipated it. Out of his spiritual affinity with Whitman, Crane set out to repudiate Eliot's *Waste Land*. In Crane's personifying myth, he decided, before he even came to New York to live, that Eliot would serve him "as a point of departure toward an almost complete reverse of direction." Where Eliot had been pessimistic about modern, urban life, Crane would be "ecstatic."[136] That is, Hart Crane (much like Stephen Crane) tried to impose his ideological will upon the City, even before he had seen it.

From 1923 to 1932, while composing his mystic epic, Crane lived mostly in Brooklyn Heights—in a room with a view of the Bridge. In 1924 he lived, as he more ominously put it, "in the shadow of the bridge," at 110 Columbia Heights, in the same house in which John Augustus Roebling and his son, Washington, who built the Brooklyn Bridge, had once lived.[137] Indeed, it has been said, Crane converted the massive Bridge into pure idea. "Hart Crane saw the structure as an idea; to the Roeblings the idea was only in the structure," suggests Alfred Kazin.[138]

Crane's views of his project, which occupied him for seven years, swung from depression to optimism. In 1926 he wrote, "The form of my poem rises out of a past that so overwhelms the present with its worth and vision that I'm at a loss to explain my delusion that there exists any real links between that past and a future destiny worthy of it. . . . The bridge as a symbol today has no significance beyond an economical approach to shorter hours, quicker lunches, behaviorism and toothpicks." However, less than two months later, his enthusiasm had revived. In May 1930, Crane said the poem was "an affirmation of experience," that it should be seen as " 'positive' rather than 'negative' in the sense that *The Waste Land* is negative."[139] The poem was first and last a deeply personal encounter with the central symbol of New York and the modern age: "I have attempted to induce the same feelings of elation, etc.—like being carried forward and upward simultaneously—both in imagery, rhythm and repetition, that one experiences in walking across my beloved Brooklyn Bridge."[140] The poem, combining awe, promise, and fear, preserves the wonder of Crane's first vision of the City.

Despite its rhetorical and structural confusions, the plotline of *The Bridge* is straightforward. For twenty-four hours, beginning at dawn, the reader witnesses a day in the life of a young poet, alone in the City. It can be seen as a modern *Divine Comedy*, in which a poet is adrift in the urban jungle. Crane has no single guide (no Virgil), no rescuing woman (no Beatrice), and no sustaining faith in a redeeming God, though the Bridge does serve as his graven image. All he has to bolster him is his innate sense of virtue and his poetic mind, teeming with associations.

Those associations include Whitman's "Crossing Brooklyn Ferry," a poem in which Whitman seeks mystical union with those who "cross from shore to shore" in his own day and in the future. Crane also draws from a modern prose epic, Joyce's *Ulysses*, which portrays another young writer's wanderings in another alienating city. Crane further invokes legends from American history, from Columbus to Rip Van Winkle, and he combines them with images from the urban present to form a nervous synthesis.[141] Further, he moves through time and space, seeking more disparate emblems to fit into his collage. "In a sense, the entire day is a dream; the poet journeys through his own consciousness toward an awakening," suggests Alan Trachtenberg. The reality of New York City dissolves into visionary Cathay, the land Columbus sought. "He seeks to learn the meaning of American history which, in so far as that history is inseparable from his own memories, is the meaning of himself: Cathay, which designates the end of the journey, or the discovery of the new world, Crane wrote, is 'an attitude of spirit,' a self-discovery."[142] The City and the world, then, are metaphors serving Crane's true passion: "self-discovery."

Or self-destruction, as is made clear in the poem's first section, "Proem: To Brooklyn Bridge." There the Bridge stands in all of its mystery, embodying an idea of freedom. The Bridge looms in God-like detachment, while the poet contemplates: "Under thy shadow by the piers I waited;/ Only in darkness is thy shadow clear." The Bridge promises transcendence: "O Sleepless as the river under thee,/ Vaulting the sea, the prairies' dreaming sod,/ Unto us lowliest sometimes sweep, descend/ And of the curveship lend a myth to God."[143] However, this freedom attracts "a bedlamite" who climbs atop the Bridge and threatens to leap to his death, while a voice from the crowd jests, urging the jumper on. We never learn whether the bedlamite jumps or is rescued—an ominous opening. The curve of the Bridge promises to lead to a revelation of God, the God Columbus sought, but His presence is uncertain.

"The Harbor Dawn," the next section of the poem, is set in New York in the 1920s. It invokes images of the "Cyclopean towers across Manhattan," which glitter in the sun.[144] "Van Winkle" shows Irving's hero down and out in contemporary Manhattan; he is sweeping a tenement on Avenue A. "The River" carries the reader from the East back to the heartland, then from the present to the sixteenth century of DeSoto. In "Cape Hatteras" recollections of the Wright brothers show that modern dynamos have taken over. The Wright brothers have wrought a revolution in mechanized motion. They soon merge into the picture of Whitman celebrating America. The poet asks Whitman "if infinity/ Be still the same as when you walked the beach/ Near Paumanok—your lone patrol—and heard the wraith/ Thorough surf, its bird not there a long time falling . . ." Could it be the same for Crane as it was "for you, the panoramas and this breed of towers,/ Of you—the theme that's statured in the cliff"?[145] For Trachtenberg " 'Cape Hatteras' poses the key questions of the poem: 'What are the grounds for hope that modern history will not destroy itself?' 'Where lies redemption?' 'Is there an alternative to the chaos of the City?' "[146] The answer is found in the person of Walt Whitman, who guides Crane through the destructive "Tunnel" to the Bridge.

In "The Tunnel" Crane's poet rides the subways. "And so/ of cities you bespeak/ subways, rivered under streets/ and rivers . . ." Poe is discovered as a mere subway straphanger, a mechanized, modern man of the crowd. Finally, the poet arrives at East River, returning to the Bridge. "And this thy harbor, O my City, I have driven under,/ Tossed from the coil of ticking towers. . . ."[147] In "Atlantis" the Bridge seems to affirm God's promise. Here Crane transforms the Bridge into musical and mystical imagery. The cable strands become "the flight of strings" and the Bridge's granite and steel become "transparent meshes" where "sibylline voices flicker, . . . as though a god were issue of the strings."

The Bridge suffers from the excesses of its author's intentions, from the overextension of his language, and the incoherence of his vision. For William Pritchard, the poem is damaged by Crane's ambitions to match the forms of classic epic (the *Aeneid*) and structure (the Sistine Chapel): "In a very real sense he had nothing to say, beyond reiterated appeals for moving onward and upward toward 'New thresholds, new anatomies' or, as in the final supplication from 'To Brooklyn Bridge'—'Unto us lowliest sometimes sweep, descend/ And of the curveship lend a myth to God.' " Thus the poem is less about the greatness of America, as Alan Tate deemed it, and more a verbal exercise, an incantation of sometimes unfocused "self-discovery."[148]

The deeper failure of *The Bridge* may, however, derive from Crane's lapse of faith in his own vision of a redemptive symbol rising out of the modern City. Perhaps the poem's blur and excess indicate his determination to override, through rhetorical intensification, his own anxieties. Atlantis, after all, was a submerged city.[149] If New York is Atlantis, it is a drowned city, no matter how high the Bridge (connecting what with what?) soars in Crane's incantations. At best the Bridge becomes, for Crane, a modern deity, mysterious and mechanical, but worthy of worship: "Migrations that must needs void memory,/ Inventions that cobblestone the heart,—/ Unspeakable Thou Bridge to Thee, O Love."[150] However, this "Love" passes clear understanding, for the deity demands the loss of memory and creates a hardness of the heart—"unspeakable" conditions for its worshipers.

Despite his reach for exotic imagery, Hart Crane may have succeeded best as a regional poet, for he reinvented the image of the City by reprocessing Walt Whitman's nineteenth-century Brooklyn Ferry into a new image of the twentieth-century colossus that America had become. At least that is how *The Bridge* has struck critics and poets who weigh Crane's achievement. Alan Williamson, for example, says, "The America one remembers from Crane's poetry is New York, even more than it is the Midwest: the 'Crap-shooting gangs in Bleecker'; the 'penguin flexions' of people entering the subway; the new Art Deco towers whose 'ribs palisade/ Wrenched gold of Ninevah'; 'The Harbor Dawn' where 'steam/ Spills into steam, and wanders, washed away/ —Flurried by keen fifings.'"[151] And Robert Lowell, who wrote "Words for Hart Crane" in *Life Studies*, said in 1961 that Crane "somehow got New York City; he was at the center of things in the way that no other poet was."[152] It might be said that New York, fact and symbol, city of shimmering possibilities and hard limitations, soaring heights and watery depths, in turn got Hart Crane.

HAROLD ROSS FOUNDED THE *NEW YORKER* IN 1925— the year, James Thurber reminds us, of *The Great Gatsby*, *Arrowsmith*, and *An American Tragedy*, the year Rodgers and Hart wrote their hit song "Manhattan," for *Garrick Gaieties*.[153] Ross's humor magazine was characterized, like Rodgers and Hart's songs, by ebullience and wit. Its survival into today's *fin de siècle* New York is an impressive achievement, though the magazine has altered its style considerably.

The *New Yorker* ideal was best articulated by William Shawn, the magazine's most esteemed editor, in a tribute to the magazine's founder. Harold Ross resolved "never to publish anything, never to have something written, for a hidden reason: to promote somebody or something, to pander to somebody, to build somebody up or tear somebody down, to indulge a personal friendship or animosity, or to propagandize. Everything published in *The New Yorker* was precisely what it purported to be, was published for its own sake."[154] Brendan Gill, in his memoir *Here at the New Yorker*, paid tribute to Harold Ross as "a secret idealist," a man with a high vision of what the *New Yorker* should be.[155]

The years with Ross were defined by the brittle wit of the Algonquin Round Table set. Harold Ross had worked with Alexander Woollcott and with Franklin P. Adams, columnist for the *New York World*, and Ross adopted the Algonquin style. He sold the idea of the magazine to Raoul Fleischmann of Fleischmann's Yeast, who became cofounder and financial backer of the humor magazine.

When Ross added E. B. White (1926) and James Thurber (1927) to his staff, the voice of the magazine—elegant, ironic detachment—was established. "*The New Yorker* was not really angry," wrote Thurber. "It just didn't give a good goddamn."[156]

The Algonquin Round Table was founded at a luncheon, in 1919, in honor of Woollcott, who was the influential drama critic for the *Times* and, later, for the *Herald* and the *World*. "The Ten Year Lunch," as it has been called by Aviva Slesin—by 1929 most of the luncheon set had gone to Hollywood—drew from Manhattan's literary elite of journalists, essayists, and dramatists a group that included Robert Sherwood, a film critic; James Thurber and Robert Benchley, humorists; Dorothy Parker, a short story writer and an acid wit; Donald Ogden Stewart, an essayist and screenwriter; Marc Connelly and George S. Kaufman, who collaborated with each other and with others on a number of Broadway dramatic hits. This group met for lunch or drinks—along with Edna Ferber, playwright and novelist, and Ben Hecht and his partner Charles MacArthur, playwrights—to amuse each other and to promote each other's careers.

The temper of the Algonquin Table can best be appreciated by recounting one of Dorothy Parker's famous cracks. When challenged to use the word "horticulture" in a sentence, Parker replied, "You can lead a whore to culture but you can't make her think." Their humor was designed more to amuse than enlighten, to characterize the speaker as sophisticated, and to flatter listeners into believing they were in on the joke. *The Man Who Came to Dinner* (1939), by Kaufman and Moss Hart, a play based upon Woollcott, starred Monty Wooley as lecturer Sheridan Whiteside, a curmudgeon with a broken hip who is forced to live with his pretentious *nouveau riche* hosts. The play is, as Caryn James notes, one of many Kaufman "social satires that cozy up to the rich, only to discover that they are as wonderfully foolish as poor folk. (That, basically, is what the Algonquinites did in life, too.)"[157] Even Dorothy Parker came to complain that "people romanticize" the Round Table group, which did not include the "real giants" of the literary world of the day. Instead, "the Round Table was just a lot of people telling jokes and telling each other how good they were."[158]

The City "got" Dorothy Parker, as it had Hart Crane, though later than she might have expected it would when she was the boast of the town in the twenties. She died at age seventy-three in 1967, alone but for a dog, in a Manhattan hotel room where she had been living on alcohol. A pale imitator of Edna Millay, Parker too gave off a brief, though a less lovely, light. Instead, we are left with the sharp crack of her worldly-wise, world-weary New York voice, which was too sophisticated to live and too jaded to die. "Razors pain you," she noted, beginning a catalog of discomforts induced by suicide and concluding, "You might as well live."[159] Not for Parker the romantic commitment to self-destruction of Hart Crane. Her razors were directed against others, particularly in her *New Yorker* reviews.

Parker's repartee sparkled on West Forty-fourth Street, at the Algonquin Round Table, amid the company of those who valued wit above all other accomplishments. Seen from a distance, Parker's poems, stories, and reviews seem, like so much of the Algonquin circle's work, mannered and blasé. As Brendan Gill has noted, Parker lacked Millay's poetic ambition and assurance. The first poem in Parker's first book was called "Threnody," a piece that resembles one of Cole Porter's bitter lyrics about love: "Lips that taste of tears, they say,/ Are the best for kissing."[160]

Born Dorothy Rothschild, in 1893, in West End, New Jersey; married to and divorced from two husbands; contributor to *Vogue*, *Vanity Fair*, the *New Yorker*, *Esquire*, and the central art journals of literary New York; Hollywood screenwriter—Parker lived a long and generally unhappy life. Her life, like the lives of so many writers of her generation who came to New York in search of recognition, is a story of progressive disillusionment. Behind her cynicism stands a deep pessimism that has long found its place at the center of the City. There is nothing good in life, she said and believed, that will not be taken away from you. At its best this voice expressed sympathy for those whose lights had been extinguished. It is said that after Scott Fitzgerald died in Los Angeles in 1940, Parker contemplated his corpse and repeated the words of "Owl-eyes" at Gatsby's funeral: "The poor son of a bitch."[161] The phrase might also be a fitting epitaph for Dos Passos, Wilson, Millay, Crane, and the men and women of their stories and poems: characters who came to New York with great expectations, but who eventually left the City with bitter tastes in their mouths—or who died there, alone.

POET AND CRITIC MARIANNE MOORE'S NEW YORK EXperience was far more sustaining than Dorothy Parker's quick rise and long fall. Perhaps Moore was better prepared for its challenges. Born in a suburb of St. Louis in 1887—ten months before T. S. Eliot, who would come to inspire her poetic vocation, was born in the same city—Moore attended the Metzger Institute and Bryn Mawr College (a biology major), taught in the U.S. Indian School in Carlisle, Pennsylvania, and lived in a parsonage in Chatham, New Jersey, with her mother and brother, John, a Presbyterian minister. Though she published a few poems in prestigious journals, the *Egoist* and *Poetry*, Moore turned thirty-one before she, along with her mother, came to live in Greenwich Village in 1918, a month after the Armistice. Though she had to work as a private tutor, a secretary, and later as assistant at the Hudson Park Branch of the New York Public Library, for the first time in her life she was, she felt, where she belonged, at the heart of the American modernist movement. In the eyes of Helen Vendler, "for the first thirty years of her life, Marianne Moore had no literary society to speak of; after 1918, when she and her mother moved to New York, she lost her isolation and, with it (though this can only be conjectured), some measure of her gift for despair, dismissiveness, and denunciation."[162] If New York City strained Crane's optimism, it also qualified Moore's pessimism. Her first volume of verse, *Observations*, appeared in an American edition in 1924.

From her apartment in St. Luke's Place, Moore could see ships in New York Harbor. In "Dock Rats," she sees the City's intimidations from the point of view of a wharf rat, but she also echoes Walt Whitman in her rhapsodic celebration of the sights, sounds, and odors of harbor ships. When two of her poems were accepted by the *Dial* in 1920, Moore felt she had found her true home in the City. The journal took its name from Ralph Waldo Emerson's 1840 journal. It appeared in Chicago from 1880 to 1917; then it was moved to New York. In 1920, under new ownership, editors set out to present in the *Dial* models of literary modernism from its offices on West Thirteenth Street: "the best of European and American art, experimental and controversial." (In the *Dial* T. S. Eliot first published *The Waste Land*.) Marianne Moore served as editor of the *Dial* from 1925 until it ceased publication in 1929.[163]

Moore, like Hart Crane, lived in Brooklyn, moving there in 1929. For her, Brooklyn provided a villagelike contrast to booming Manhattan. The rhythms of the City inspired Moore, as they had Crane. She found, for example, material for poetry when, in 1931, construction of the new IND Eighth Avenue subway line, which would connect Manhattan with Brooklyn, undermined the foundation of the Lafayette Avenue Presbyterian Church and a steeplejack was hired to remove the steeple. Like Crane's *The Bridge*, Moore's "The Steeple-Jack" opens in a broad perspective of the City, then focuses on specifics. But Moore's poem—which begins in Brooklyn, but subsumes all other American towns—is far more reassuring, for in it she finds an emblem of hope in the star that is placed on the restored steeple.[164]

Moore loved the many sides of the City, from the Bronx Zoo to the Brooklyn Dodgers, writing with equal admiration about a leopard who insults a crocodile by batting him on the nose and Don Zimmer's losing his hat in his dash for a backhand catch at Ebbett's Field.[165] At the same time, Moore was not uncritical of New York. Like so many writers before and after her, she mocked its soul-searing dedication to commerce. In "New York," a poem of the early 1920s, she envisioned "the savage's romance" giving way to "space for commerce," for, Moore pointed out in a note, "New York succeeded St. Louis as the center of the wholesale fur trade." But her poetic mission in New York surpassed mockery, and her vision of New York transcended commerce. The poem's final lines remind us of the City's true mission by adapting a phrase taken from Henry James: "It is not the plunder,/ but 'accessibility to experience'" that most matters in New York.[166]

B EFORE AND AFTER THE GREAT WAR AND INTO THE GREAT Depression, New York solidified its hold on the American imagination through the mighty and varied voices that wrote of the City's powers. For its writers, New York City held both the dream of success and the nightmare of failure; in concentrated, dramatic ways, the City told the essential American tale. New York City liberated talented young men and women from the main traveled roads of the American provinces, inspired them to acts of self-expression, placed them amid likeminded, adventurous souls, tested their powers of endurance, and brought them to new pitches of passion and levels of awareness. Simultaneously, paradoxically, wondrously, New York was a city of destruction and the nation's creative center.

B L A C K
M E T R O P O L I S

Harlem from the Renaissance

to the 1990s

 H ARLEM TALKS AMERICAN, READS AMERICAN, THINKS American."[1] Despite James Weldon Johnson's bold and characteristically optimistic words, African-Americans live, it might be said, in another country, even when they dwell in the same city as white Americans. Certainly the vision of America contained in black literature of twentieth-century Harlem is unique; it is, by and large, far more intense, dramatic, violent, and alienated than the image of New York life reflected in works by white writers. Black writing consistently reveals ambivalent relations between races in the nation's cities—and, by extension, divisions in the national consciousness and inequities in American society. The literature that portrays black life in New York City, particularly from the end of World War I to the present, illustrates the wisdom in Henry James's observation that it is a complex fate to be an American.

 A FRICAN-AMERICANS BEGAN TO EMIGRATE TO NEW YORK in large numbers around the turn of the twentieth century. When Malcolm Little, who later became known as Malcolm X, first arrived in New York at the beginning of World War II, he was amazed by the presence and authority of blacks in Harlem and wondered how such a city-within-the-City came to be. Harlem had been home to a succession of ethnic groups—Germans, Dutch, Irish, Italians, Jews—while "Negroes had been in New York since 1683, before any of [these ethnic groups] came, and had been ghettoed all over the city." Black communities had moved from the Wall Street area to Greenwich Village, then to the present Pennsylvania Station region. "And then, the last stop before Harlem, the black ghetto was concentrated around 52nd Street, which is how 52nd Street got the Swing Street name and reputation that lasted long after the Negroes were gone."[2] But it was, above all, in Harlem that blacks made their most memorable mark in New York City.

Harlem achieved political presence for African-Americans before and after the Great War. In those years, voices demanding justice and fair treatment for American blacks rose up most resonantly from Harlem. "Negroes throughout the country were looking to New York City and to Harlem for the most advanced thought and opinion," notes Nathan Huggins.[3] But these voices and their suggested solutions to America's "Negro problem," as it was then known, differed sharply. W. E. B. Du Bois articulated the reformist-integrationist approach in his journal, the *Crisis*, and in his many influential writings. So, too, did the National Urban League and their journal, *Opportunity*. Marcus Garvey spoke for the radical separatist view in his Universal Negro Improvement Association and in his newspaper, *Negro World*, which conveyed his popular back-to-Africa vision. Garvey was Harlem's most charismatic leader until he was imprisoned for mail fraud in 1924. The "New Negro" movement, which became known as the Harlem Renaissance, contained elements of Garveyite Africanism, but it generally reflected the values—integration, patriotism, social acceptance through cultural achievement—of the NAACP and the Urban League.

Following the lead of Du Bois, most of the Harlem Renaissance figures believed that art and culture could bring the divided races together; however, their sense of culture was "high" and therefore restrictive, often cutting them off from the vital street culture of Harlem. Except for Langston Hughes and Claude McKay, Harlem's cultural leaders ignored jazz, perhaps the greatest African-American cultural creation, and other popular cultural expressions, which they saw as vulgar.[4] Bessie Smith, "King" Oliver, Eubie Blake, "Fats" Waller, and others captured the imagination of Harlemites, but they did not win the approval of most of those who shaped the Harlem Renaissance, who gave lip service to folk culture only after Zora Neale Hurston's prodding. Yet what these writers of the Harlem Renaissance accomplished was amazing; they created a body of literature that emphasizes the richness, the complexity, and the centrality of black experience in New York City. Despite all of its problems, they believed in

Harlem, as a place and a vision, and they sustained their community's faith in the importance of their work. "An arts-and-letters legacy" was established in Harlem, suggests David Levering Lewis, "of which a beleaguered and belittled Afro-American could be proud, and by which it could be sustained. If more by osmosis than conscious attention, Mainstream America was also richer for the color, emotion, humanity, and cautionary vision produced by Harlem during its Golden Age."[5]

The Harlem Renaissance of the 1920s was a flowering of the arts from the theater to poetry, a culmination, in the words of William L. Andrews, of "creative expression that had long been bottled up within black America by the constraints of segregation."[6] Its intellectual underpinnings were established primarily by W. E. B. Du Bois, James Weldon Johnson, Charles S. Johnson, and Alain Locke; its poetic voice was shaped by Claude McKay, Countee Cullen, Langston Hughes, and many more; its fictional accounts were written by Hughes, McKay, Nella Larsen, Wallace Thurman, and others. Its influence has reached well past its brief duration—notably in the works of Ann Petry, Ralph Ellison, James Baldwin, and Toni Morrison, who have used Harlem as a setting for some of their most important works. Harlem, then, has been a defining territory and a compelling state of mind for the best African-American writers. The literature of Harlem is indispensable to an understanding of New York City.

The Harlem Renaissance was the product of various forces: the establishment of Harlem, after the turn of the century, as the cultural center of black America (though Harlem remained a mixed community and its property was still largely white-owned throughout this period); the influx of new residents from the South and the return of the black veterans of World War I, who cherished the hope that, during the postwar years of economic boom, America would keep its promise of justice and opportunity. In the 1912 election, Du Bois supported Woodrow Wilson's candidacy; Du Bois believed that a hundred thousand northern blacks, voting for Wilson, contributed to his election. Despite the segregation of black troops, Du Bois urged black Americans to support Wilson's war efforts. Self-determination of ethnic groups was one of the Allied war aims. As Wilson promised freedom for Europe's small nations, many African-Americans believed he would grant justice and economic freedom to them as well.[7] However, that promise was not kept. In the first year after the war that, as Woodrow Wilson put it, would make the world safe for democracy, more than seventy African-Americans were lynched in the nation—ten of them black soldiers in uniform. In the last six months of 1919, some twenty-five race riots occurred in the nation. James Weldon Johnson called this bloody time the "Red Summer."[8]

Thereafter, a conscious effort was made by a group of Harlem intellectuals and political leaders to establish identity and acceptance for blacks through the arts. For most Harlem intellectuals, the acceptable arts excluded popular musicals like *Shuffle Along* (1921), a peppy Broadway production written (by Aubry Lyles and Flournoy Miller), performed, and directed by blacks. But for Langston Hughes, *Shuffle Along* was the most important black theater of the 1920s, defining the age: "Certainly it was the musical review, *Shuffle Along*, that gave a scintillating send-off to that Negro vogue in Manhattan, which reached its peak just before the crash of 1929, the crash that sent Negroes, white folks and all rolling down the hill toward the Works Progress Administration."[9]

Whites, too, were caught up in the "Negro vogue" of the period, as illustrated by the popularity of Dubose Heyward's play, *Porgy* (1925), and Carl Van Vechten's portrayal of exotic Harlem in a novel, *Nigger Heaven* (1926). Van Vechten's portrait of Harlem—in a book detested by many black Harlemites—appealed to white Americans who were pleased to see Harlem as a wondrous nighttime alternative to the daytime America of the Protestant ethic. Black jazz—symbolized by the spirited genius of Louis Armstrong's "Hot Five," or the elegant rhythms and arresting harmonies of Duke Ellington's orchestra—meant that Prohibition America retained a rich, semisecret, inner life, centered in Harlem. At the segregated Cotton Club, white New Yorkers and tourists could thrill to Ellington's "jungle music." Thus the "New Negro" was circumscribed and qualified by the contradictory expectations of both blacks and whites. White influence was strongest in the first phase of the Harlem Renaissance, notes David Levering Lewis, in the early 1920s. The New Negro establishment dominated in the mid 1920s; from the late 1920s to the Harlem riot of 1935, artists and writers increasingly shaped the movement.[10]

Blacks, too, saw Harlem as the center of American vitality. In *Black Manhattan*, James Weldon Johnson praised Harlem for being known worldwide as "exotic, colorful, and sensuous; a place of laughing, singing, and dancing; a place where life wakes up at night." A stroll through Harlem, he added, "is not simply going out for a walk; it is more like going out for adventure."[11] Harlem, then, in its mythic configurations bore the burden of expectations—nothing less than America's compensatory dreamscape—which it could not long deliver. For Harlem eventually failed white Americans who sought brief release from bourgeois America, just as it failed to grant black Americans the transformation of status and culture they sought. Harlem would neither truly become another country, sufficient unto itself, nor would it wholly blend in as part of mainstream America, though no physical barriers separated Harlem, located just to the north of Central Park, from the rest of Manhattan. "When Harlem was in Vogue," as Langston Hughes put it, black Harlem was located between 130th Street and 145th Street, a territory that later became known as Central Harlem.[12]

Yet, despite their disillusionments during the 1920s, black Americans were still inspired to travel to New York. Langston Hughes came from the West and Zora Neale Hurston came from the South to discover their artistic missions in Harlem. "Harlem was like a great magnet for the Negro intellectual, pulling him from everywhere," recalled Hughes. "Or perhaps the magnet was New York— but once in New York, he had to live in Harlem" to afford rooms and to try to escape prejudice.[13] Harlem would be a new home for black Americans, serving both as a sanctuary from white prejudice and as a way station to success in America. Looking back on the "Negro Renaissance" thirty years after his journal, *Opportunity*, sponsored a series of gatherings where awards were distributed to black writers, Charles S. Johnson recalled "a period, not only of the quivering search for freedom, but of a cultural, if not a social and racial emancipation. It was unabashedly self-conscious and race-conscious. But it was race-consciousness with an extraordinary facet in that it had virtues that could be incorporated into the cultural bloodstream of the nation."[14]

Just as James Weldon Johnson wrote of an "ex-colored man" who traded his racial identity and his soul for success in the City, so did other African-American writers set out to create myths by which New York City in general and Harlem in particular could be better known and understood. In the black literary experience the City figured as an alternative to racist, repressive America far more dramatic than that imagined by white writers in opposition to Winesburg, Spoon River, Gopher Prairie, or to any other smothering American village. In African-Americans' eyes, New York City held out a bright future, but inevitably, as in white myths of the City, it chastened, disappointed, and often destroyed those who sought new lives there. As ever in American history, blacks suffered more than whites in the City. From Paul Laurence Dunbar, who wrote just after the turn of the century, to Toni Morrison, who writes just before the turn into the next century, Harlem has been the central symbolic site, the defining territory of fact and imagination, for black American writers.

PAUL LAURENCE DUNBAR'S BEST NOVEL, *THE SPORT OF the Gods* (1902), was the first extended literary treatment of Harlem. Published at the turn of the century, when Harlem was taking on the identity of a black community, it is a cautionary tale of the City's destructive powers over black innocents abroad in its dangerous streets. Born in Dayton, Ohio, in 1872, to parents who had been Kentucky plantation slaves, Dunbar was long concerned with the problems of a race in transition, of the "Folks from Dixie," as he titled a collection of stories. Booker T. Washington dubbed the precocious Dunbar the "Poet Laureate of the Negro Race" for good reason. His poetry—*Oak and Ivy* (1893), *Majors and Minors* (1896), and *Lyrics of Lowly Life* (1897)—paid tribute to worthies like Harriet Beecher Stowe ("At one stroke she gave/ A race to freedom and herself to fame"). He celebrated and idealized black life in his poems, as in "The Poet": "He sang of life, serenely sweet,/ With, now and then, a deeper note."[15] But the deepest note Dunbar struck during his brief life—he died in his thirty-fourth year, in 1906—was *The Sport of the Gods*, a novel that questioned whether African-Americans could find happiness in northern cities.

In Dunbar's view, the South, with all of its obvious injustices, was a far better place in which to live than New York, with all of its promises, could ever be. In Dunbar's eyes, racism in the South was more overt and intelligible, less insidious than it was in the City. Though Dunbar understood the attractions of New York, he portrayed them as addictive enticements that seduced and betrayed its naive victims.

In the novel, Berry Hamilton, a faithful servant of a southern white family, is arrested and convicted for a theft he did not commit. Forced to leave the South, his family seeks refuge in Harlem. Their arrival allows Dunbar to reflect upon the mystery of the City, particularly for the black internal émigré: "To the provincial coming to New York for the first time, ignorant and unknown, the city presents a notable mingling of the qualities of cheeriness and gloom." However, after the newcomer adjusts to this strange, new world, the magnetic attractions of the City pull him in:

> The real fever of love for the place will begin to take hold upon him. The subtle, insidious wine of New York will begin to intoxicate him. Then, if he be wise, he will go away, any place,—yes, he will even go over to Jersey. But if he be a fool, he will stay and stay on until the town becomes all in all to him; until the very streets are his chums and certain buildings and corners his best friends. Then he is hopeless, and to live elsewhere would be death. The Bowery will be his romance, Broadway his lyric, and the Park his pastoral, the river and the glory of it all his epic, and he will look down pityingly on all the rest of humanity.[16]

After five years, Berry is released from prison, comes North, and finds his family destroyed: his son is in jail; his daughter has become a selfish and soulless actress; his wife has married another man. As Robert A. Bone puts it, *The Sport of the Gods* "reiterates the plantation-school thesis that the rural Negro becomes demoralized in the urban North."[17]

Dunbar stressed the literary naturalists' vision of the City as a maelstrom that sucks its victims, particularly its black victims, down to the lower depths of depravity and destruction. His account concludes with the nearly destroyed Hamiltons returning to the South: "They knew they were powerless against some Will infinitely stronger than their own."[18] Dunbar's Hamiltons thus fare little better than Crane's Maggie, girl of the streets, who was seduced to her death, or Dreiser's Hurstwood, who was driven to suicide by the heartless City. For Dunbar even urban success destroys. Kitty Hamilton, following the path of Dreiser's Carrie, becomes a success on the New York stage, but she pulls away from her family in the process; when her brother Joe is arrested, she does nothing about it, leaving New York on a theatrical tour instead.

"Whom the Gods wish to destroy they first make mad," said Dunbar, paraphrasing Euripides. But who are these gods? Rather than isolate racism or economic discrimination as the forces oppressing African-Americans, Dunbar blamed "New York"; he portrays the City as a malign, overpowering presence that offers provincials many opportunities to destroy themselves. New York rots their characters by making them feel superior to the traditional (religious and familial) ways of black folks, as lived in the South, where they were indeed persecuted but also where their characters were protected by humility: "The first sign of the demoralization of the provincial who comes to New York is his pride at his insensibility to certain impressions which used to influence him at home." Harlem, then, could never be home for Dunbar. In the City the rural black "grows callous. After that he goes to the devil very cheerfully."[19] For Dunbar "the South had its faults . . . and its disadvantages, but . . . even what they suffered from these was better than what awaited them in the great alleys of New York." In the South black bodies would be chastened, but in Harlem "the soul would fester."[20]

On February 17, 1919, the Fifteenth Infantry Regiment of New York's National Guard (attached to the French Army as the United States 369th Infantry Regiment)—a black unit that had served heroically in France—marched up Fifth Avenue, striding to the music of Big Jim Europe's band, with Bill "Bojangles" Robinson leading them as the regimental drum major.[21] The parade passed a reviewing stand at 130th Street, then it broke up in celebration, but the memory of that march still reverberates three quarters of a century later as a defining moment in black American history, a point of high hopes that blacks, too, might be able to reap the rewards of American life. "Make way for Democracy!" wrote Du Bois in "Returning Soldiers." "We saved it in France, and by the Great Jehovah, we will save it in the United States of America, or know the reason why."[22] There, it might be said, began the Harlem Renaissance.

Nathan Huggins properly sets Harlem within the urban myth of great expectations. "Harlem for blacks, like New York for whites, was synonymous with opportunity, the release of the individual spirit. . . . For all—black and white—New York was the occasion for breaking away from small town life, the restrictions of family control, and for growing up."[23] Like Greenwich Village at the other end of New York City, Harlem promised personal freedom.

Jazz, a novel published in 1992 by Nobel Prize winner Toni Morrison, reviews and dramatizes this process of transition, transformation, expectation, disillusionment, and adjustment for the generation of African-Americans whose lives the writers of the Harlem Renaissance described. As Henry Louis Gates Jr. points out, the story on which Morrison based *Jazz* was taken from Camille Billops's *The Harlem Book of the Dead*, which contains Van Der Zee's photographs of Harlem lives and deaths from the 1920s. One of these photographs is of a young woman who has bled to death, refusing to reveal the man who cut her, just as does a young woman in *Jazz*.[24] Clearly, Toni Morrison set out in writing *Jazz* to examine the heritage of pain and purpose handed down from the era of the Harlem Renaissance.

Morrison's *Jazz* opens on Lenox Avenue in early January 1926—seven years after the Armistice and that memorable parade up Fifth Avenue. The novel deals with the disillusioning aftermath to this moment when everything seemed possible. Her plot centers upon an incident that reveals the continuing warfare within black lives, lives circumscribed by a racist society. Joe Trace, husband and salesman of Cleopatra beauty products, shoots and kills Dorcas, his eighteen-year-old lover. Violet, Joe's wife, then attacks Dorcas's corpse with a knife at the young woman's funeral. Thus the promises resounding in the parade of returning soldiers for peacetime prosperity for black Americans has quickly devolved into a series of self-inflicted wounds. Morrison's characters seem to have no part of a Harlem rebirth of spirit. The City serves as a paradigm of possibilities qualified by dark undercurrents that test their faith in the future: "Word was that underneath the good times and the easy money something evil ran the streets and nothing was safe—not even the dead."[25]

"I'm crazy about this City," reflects the narrator of *Jazz*. "Daylight slants like a razor cutting the building in half. . . . A city like this one makes me dream tall and feel in on things. Hep." The narrator thinks that in 1926 Harlem residents are happy, that the "sad stuff" is behind them, that "at last, everything's ahead."[26] "Nobody says it's pretty here; nobody says it's easy either. What it is is decisive, and if you pay attention to the street plans, all laid out, the City can't hurt you."[27] As it turns out, she is quite wrong; the twists and turns of the City embedded in its serpentine jazz tones and syncopated rhythms belie the regularity and the reassurances of its street design. Morrison's novel serves, then, as something of a deconstruction of myths about Harlem and the City, showing the deviousness and anguish that lie beneath its ordered surfaces, the depths of pain reflected in the blues that the narrator abhors, and the violent, passionate acts of its citizens.

Violet and Joe first meet in Vesper County, Virginia, in 1906. They arrive in New York, dancing on the train, seeking a return of the love they already feel for the City: "Like a million more they could hardly wait to get there and love it back." For them, as for Dunbar's Hamiltons, the City holds the hope of escape from the racism, violence, and injustice they have left behind in the South. The City promises freedom from the past: "When they fall in love with a city, it is forever, and it is like forever. As though there never was a time when they didn't love it."[28]

This wave of "country people," called the Great Migration, arrived in enormous numbers, and most of them, too, quickly fell in love with New York, for "there, in a city, they [were] not so much new as themselves: their stronger, riskier selves." [29] However, twenty years after their arrival, Violet and Joe's marriage goes numb, and Joe begins his doomed affair with young Dorcas. The City transforms them all. Alice, Dorcas's aunt—who detests that "lowdown music," jazz—"had worked hard to privatize her niece, but she was no match for a city seeping music that begged and challenged each and every day. 'Come,' it said. 'Come and do wrong.' "[30] As in Dunbar's work, the City seduces black pilgrims and undermines their rural morals.

Yet the City, for Morrison, is a force and a mystery beyond her narrator's understanding. In the end, the unidentified narrator of *Jazz* admits all that she does *not* know of the City: "It was loving the City that distracted me and gave me ideas. Made me think I could speak its loud voice and make that sound human.

I missed the people altogether." (The narrator is sure that one of the three re-maining characters will kill another, but this does not happen. Joe goes unpun-ished; he and Violet even renew their marriage.)[31] "So I missed it altogether," concludes the puzzled narrator.[32] Morrison's novel may be a parable of the writer's difficulty in truly portraying Harlem, a place of contradictions, where narrative lines are unpredictable, where conventional expectations and moral glosses seem not to apply. Or Morrison may be drawing upon the many con-tending sounds of Harlem for her narrator's choral voice. As Gates suggests, "Morrison's . . . novel serves to redefine the very possibilities of a narrative point of view. Like Duke Ellington, Morrison has found a way, paradoxically, to create an ensemble of *improvised* sound out of a *composed* music."[33] Morrison's improvisatory narrator is able to suggest the mystery and possible redemption at the heart of Harlem. *Jazz* redefines the ways we think about New York in the 1920s, the "Jazz Age," revealing black experience at the City's core, and the novel reminds us of the symbolic importance of Harlem in the American mind.

On March 21, 1924, Charles S. Johnson, editor of *Opportunity* and author of *The Negro in Chicago: A Study of Race Relations and a Race Riot*, planned a dinner at the Civic Club (Twelfth Street, near Fifth Avenue) to honor "Negro" literature. The guest of honor was Jessie Fauset, whose first novel, *There Is Confusion*, had just been published. Fauset was a fitting figure for celebration by those who sought racial-cultural revival and reconciliation in Harlem.

One of Harlem's most prominent women writers, Jessie Fauset was born in 1882 to a Philadelphia family of wealth and status. She earned a Phi Beta Kappa key after studying classical and modern languages at Cornell University, class of 1905. In 1919 she earned an M.A. in French at the University of Pennsylvania. Reflecting her own experience, the moral of her fiction, as stated in her foreword to her novel *The Chinaberry Tree*, is that the genteel black American "is not so vastly different from any other American, just distinctive."[34] Fauset thus ex-pressed the high-minded, integrationist goals of the conservatives within the Harlem Renaissance.

However, Fauset's fiction has a satirical edge and a formal inventiveness that most critics of her day missed. As Deborah E. McDowell points out, Fauset's *Plum Bun* (1928), her best novel, is only superficially a novel of "passing." The work is also a manipulation of popular conventions found in the fairy tale and the woman's romance. "It comments specifically on the Harlem Renaissance and the literary straightjacketing that pervaded the movement, violating many writers' artistic integrity and autonomy."[35] *Plum Bun* also conveys a vivid sense of urban place, particularly in its contrast between white downtown and black uptown. The novel's heroine, Angela Murray, comes from Philadelphia to New York, where she passes as white while she is the mistress of a wealthy white man. When she first arrives, Angela lives on Fourteenth Street. On an "exquisite afternoon" she explores Harlem: "She was amazed and impressed at this bustling, frolicking, busy, laughing great city within a greater one. She had never seen coloured life so thick, so varied, so complete." Yet black Harlem makes this woman uncomfortable. As she departs Harlem on the lurching El train, she is glad she has "cast in her lot with the dwellers outside its dark and serried tents."[36] Though Angela eventually reconsiders her choice, finding betrayal in the white downtown world and discovering a cultural heritage in the black uptown world, Jessie Fauset makes it clear that there is no true home in the City for her black alter ego. *Plum Bun* closes in Paris, where Angela still searches for a husband and a home.

Perhaps Fauset's most important contribution to the movement came through her role as literary editor, under W. E. B. Du Bois, of the *Crisis*. There she solicited work from a wide range of writers, many with views of art and politics more radical than her own. Among others, she published Claude McKay, Jean Toomer, Anne Spencer, and Langston Hughes. Fauset had an eye for talent, as she illustrated in a letter to Hughes: "You assuredly have the true poetic touch, the divine afflatus, which will someday carry you far."[37]

At the Civic Club dinner honoring Fauset, James Weldon Johnson spoke, representing the first generation of black literary culture in the City. Johnson had articulated his cultural goals in *The Book of American Negro Poetry* (1922), where he wrote, "Nothing will do more to change the mental attitude and raise his status than a demonstration of intellectual parity by the Negro through his production of literature and art."[38] Carl Van Doren, white editor of *Century* magazine, also spoke at the dinner of the younger generation of Negro writers. "What American literature decidedly needs at this moment is color, music, gusto, the free expression of gay or desperate moods. If the Negroes are not in a position to contribute these items, I do not know what Americans are."[39] Many black writers and intellectuals in attendance that evening were ready to take up the challenge. The Civic Club dinner led, for example, to a special issue of *Survey Graphic* (March 1925) devoted to Harlem culture, "Harlem: Mecca of the New Negro," edited by Alain Locke.

The principal task of defining and representing the Harlem Renaissance fell to Alain Locke, master of ceremonies at the dinner. Locke, a forty-year-old assistant professor of philosophy at Howard University in Washington, edited *The New Negro* (1925), an amplification of his *Survey Graphics* issue. *The New Negro* was at once an anthology and a manifesto, perhaps the most important book of the movement. Locke, who came to be known as "the Proust of Lenox Avenue," was, like Fauset, the product of a wealthy Philadelphia family. Educated at Harvard, the first African-American Rhodes scholar at Oxford, the debonair and well-traveled Locke became, as Charles Johnson called him, a natural "press agent" for the Harlem Renaissance.[40]

The New Negro has been called the Bible of the Harlem Renaissance because it both defined the boundaries of the literary movement and articulated its worth.[41] In *The New Negro*, Locke stressed the transformative powers of urban life for its black Americans. In Locke's ideal vision of the City, the Negro would be more complex and sophisticated, more open to culture, and as a result, more valued by white New Yorkers. Paradoxically, racial consciousness would result in integration. For Locke, Harlem was not only the largest concentration of blacks worldwide, it was a place that brought together a wide variety of backgrounds and experiences: "In Harlem Negro life is seizing upon its first chances for group expression and self-determination. It is—or promises at least to be—a race capital."[42] On the other hand, as Huggins points out, the Harlem Renaissance also sought to celebrate pre-Harlem roots in the South and in Africa, thus subverting its own assertion of Harlem as a black Mecca. Furthermore, Harlem in the 1920s was entwined with white culture. Indeed, the Harlem Renaissance, depending as it did upon white patrons, promoters, and publishers to produce its works, was, in part, a *product* of white America, at least in its early years.

In his foreword to *The New Negro*, Locke declared that "this volume aims to document the New Negro culturally and socially—to register the transformations of the inner and outer life of the Negro in America that have so significantly taken place in the last few years." His volume offered "the first fruits of the Negro Renaissance."[43] In his manifesto essay, "The New Negro," Locke celebrated the potential of Harlem to improve black life: Migration leads to transformation, "in the Negro's case a deliberate flight not only from the countryside to the city, but from medieval America to modern. Take Harlem as an instance of this. Here in Manhattan is not merely the largest Negro community in the world, but the first concentration in history of so many diverse elements of Negro life." Locke associated the Harlem Renaissance with other recent literary and cultural manifestations by subjugated peoples: "Without pretense to their political significance, Harlem has the same role to play for the New Negro as Dublin had for the New Ireland or Prague for the New Czechoslovakia. Harlem, I grant you, isn't typical—but it is significant, it is prophetic."[44]

Selections in *The New Negro* describe conditions both in and beyond Harlem of the 1920s. In Rudolph Fisher's story, "The City of Refuge," King Solomon Gillis escapes from racist North Carolina, where he shot a man. Gillis comes to New York City, where he assumes that a black man can find freedom. In Harlem, Gillis sees "Negroes at every turn; up and down Lenox Avenue, up and down One Hundred and Thirty-fifth Street; big, lanky Negroes, short, squat Negroes; black ones, brown ones, yellow ones. . . . This was Negro Harlem." For him it is "the city of refuge." He decides that he has "done died an' woke up in Heaven" when he sees that Harlem even has "cullud policemans."[45] However, Gillis, duped by a black con artist, is eventually arrested for dope-peddling. Fisher's bitter story ends with Gillis waiting to confront another "cullud policeman."

The value of jazz, the folk music of Harlem, was also debated in *The New Negro*. J. A. Rogers, in "Jazz at Home," acknowledged jazz's energies, but he also said "it vulgarizes" and should be lifted "into nobler channels."[46] In contrast, Langston Hughes's poem "Jazzonia" celebrated "a whirling cabaret," where "six long-headed jazzers play."[47]

The writers included in *The New Negro* were fully aware that they were creating a myth of place and identity, a black version of Emerson's "American Scholar." Charles S. Johnson, for example, in "The New Frontage on American Life," distinguished between "New York City with its polite personal service and its Harlem—the Mecca of the Negroes the country over. Delightful Harlem of the effete East!" There "a new type of Negro is evolving—a city Negro. . . . In ten years, Negroes have been actually transplanted from one culture to another."[48] Johnson's essay illustrated the community's hopes for Harlem's future.

Despite the honors conferred upon Jessie Fauset, the Harlem Renaissance, like most reform and utopian movements, consigned women to a second level of importance. Segregation and feminism remained secondary concerns for most of the male leaders of the Harlem Renaissance.[49] But a few women's voices were heard. In *The New Negro*, for example, Elise Johnson McDougald, in "The Task of the Negro Womanhood," argues that the health of a culture is measured by the prosperity of its women: In Harlem, "modern city in the world's metropolis, . . . the Negro woman is free from the cruder handicaps of primitive household hardships and the grosser forms of sex and race subjugation."[50] Zora Neale Hurston was also represented in the anthology by "Spunk," a story about black folk customs in Florida, her native grounds. Hurston went on to write *Their Eyes Were*

Watching God (1937), becoming a major figure of the Harlem Renaissance without writing much about Harlem. (She discussed the Harlem Renaissance for only two paragraphs in her autobiography, *Dust Tracks on a Road*.)

Yet Hurston's influence on the movement was enormous. Born in an exclusively African-American town, Eatonville, Florida, in 1901, she studied at Howard University under Alain Locke and arrived in Harlem in 1925. A woman of great vitality, wit, and magnetism—Hughes found her the most amusing member of the Harlem literati—Hurston quickly found herself at the center of the arts movement.[51] "I love it," she wrote to a friend about her new life in New York. "I am just running wild in every direction, trying to see everything at once."[52] Soon her life found a direction. She became the live-in secretary to Fanny Hurst, a popular white novelist who promoted black artists. Hurston also resumed her studies at Barnard. She took up the cause of the "New Negro," aligning herself with the integrationist position of Du Bois and Locke and mocking the separatist stance of Garvey. Though Hurston was included in Locke's anthology, she established her own ideological ground by advancing the value of black folk art.[53] She joined other young black writers, including Hughes and Thurman, in publishing the journal *Fire!!*, which survived only one issue.[54] In her writings, Hurston expanded the reach and reference of the Harlem Renaissance. In the words of Robert E. Hemenway, Hurston's biographer, "she tried to reconcile high and low culture by becoming Eatonville's esthetic representative to the Harlem Renaissance, and when she discovered that this was an unsatisfactory role, she turned to the professional study of folklore as an alternative," studying at Barnard under Franz Boas.[55]

For all of Locke's efforts to be inclusive, *The New Negro* did not represent every important writer of the period. The absence of writings by Jean Toomer and Nella Larsen was particularly unfortunate. William Stanley Braithwaite, in "The Negro in American Literature," celebrates Jean Toomer's novel *Cane* (1923) as the supreme achievement of black literature. This label is ironic, for Toomer himself hoped to transcend the limitations of racial designations; like Whitman, he yearned to be "the first American" of a newly fused race.[56] Born in 1894 into the black bourgeoisie of Washington, D.C., Toomer in time would become a mystic, a disciple of Georges I. Gurjieff, leaving Harlem and racial issues far behind.

Nevertheless, with *Cane*, his tales of the South, the enigmatic Toomer helped to launch the Harlem Renaissance. The book appeared just as Louis Armstrong was making himself known in New York with "King" Oliver's band. Black musicals had made only brief appearances on Broadway. Only one major

Renaissance text had then been published—*Harlem Shadows* (1922), by Claude McKay.[57] Yet *Cane* struck not only an artful but also a bleak, premonitory note for Harlem Renaissance literature: In the final story of *Cane*, Toomer portrayed a northern black artist-intellectual who travels to the South, but there he finds that he has no place to go in America, so he indulges in self-destructive sex and drink; finally, he figuratively goes underground. In a sense, Toomer's *Cane* anticipated, but in reverse pattern, Ralph Ellison's *Invisible Man*, a novel in which a southern black intellectual-artist travels to Harlem, where he literally becomes an underground man.

Nella Larsen was another somewhat mysterious but centrally important writer in the Harlem Renaissance. Racial identity, the state of black women, and the search for home were the primary themes of her fiction—themes that grew out of her own experiences. She claimed to have been born in Chicago in 1891 but may in fact have been born that year in New York; her father was African-American and her mother was Danish. Nella Larsen spent time in Denmark and studied at Fisk University for a year, before graduating as a nurse from the Lincoln Hospital Training Program in New York City. She also worked as a children's librarian at the Harlem (135th Street) branch of the New York Public Library from 1922 to 1929. She married a Fisk professor, but the marriage ended in a bitter divorce. After her brief writing career, Larsen returned to nursing at Gouveneur Hospital in New York City.[58]

In *Quicksand* (1928), her first novel, heroine Helga Crane discovers Harlem: "Her existence was bounded by Central Park, Fifth Avenue, St. Nicholas Park, and One Hundred and Forty-fifth Street." Within these confines, Helga finds the entire range of the human condition: "Everything was there, vice and goodness, sadness and gaiety, ignorance and wisdom, ugliness and beauty, poverty and richness. And it seemed to her that somehow of goodness, gaiety, wisdom, and beauty always there was a little more of vice, sadness, ignorance, and ugliness. It was only riches that did not quite transcend poverty."[59] But Helga, highstrung and ambivalent, also of mixed racial background, does not long feel at home in Harlem; she decides it is provincial in its blackness. As in Dunbar's *The Sport of the Gods*, the heroine marries and retreats to the South, for a life of drudgery.[60] In Larsen's *Passing* (1929), two light-skinned black women choose different paths. Clare tries to "pass" in the white world, while Irene stays in Harlem.[61] After Clare marries a white bigot, she returns to Harlem for a party, where she falls in love with Irene's black husband, who hates whites. Clare's suspicious husband traces her to another Harlem gathering, where, during their confrontation, Clare falls to her death from a window. Once again the paradoxical condition of American blacks, damned no matter which way they turn, leads to tragedy. In a reading of her fiction, Bernard W. Bell suggests that Nella Larsen, like Jessie Fauset, rejected "the romantic extremes of nationalism and assimilation in favor of cultural dualism."[62] However, neither woman saw the likelihood of developing such cultural dualism, in or out of Harlem. "The very structure of things," argues Michael G. Cooke, speaking of Larsen, "in Harlem or out, seems to suggest that no vision of life is tenable."[63]

James Weldon Johnson, founding father and chronicler of black Manhattan, offered a far more celebratory vision of Harlem in *The New Negro*. In his essay, "Harlem: The Cultural Capital," Johnson argues that "Harlem is not merely a Negro colony or community, it is a city within a city, the greatest Negro city in the world. It is not a slum or fringe, it is located in the heart of Manhattan and occupies one of the most beautiful and healthful sections of the city." For Johnson, Harlem was a transforming vision: "To my mind, Harlem is more than a Negro community; it is a large scale laboratory experiment in the race problem." Johnson was insistently optimistic about the positive possibilities of black life and culture in Harlem: "I believe that the Negro's advantages and opportunities are greater in Harlem than in any other place in the country, and that Harlem will become the intellectual, the cultural and the financial center for Negroes of the United States, and will exert a vital influence upon all Negro peoples."[64] Thus commenced the Harlem Renaissance—in a celebratory dinner for one of its own and in the publication of an anthology that put the best face on Harlem—though many of its best writers were already expressing reservations about life in Harlem, in New York City, in America.

B EFORE THE HARLEM RENAISSANCE WAS ESTABLISHED, Claude McKay was creating a black consciousness in New York. Born in Jamaica in 1889, McKay studied at Tuskegee Institute and Kansas State College before he arrived in Harlem in 1921. First publishing his poetry in *Seven Arts*, McKay helped to edit, along with Michael Gold, the *Liberator*, under the direction of Max and Crystal Eastman. At the *Liberator*, McKay developed his aesthetics and his politics. In a review, for example, he celebrated the street energies of the Broadway musical *Shuffle Along*, seeing in it a repudiation of a demand for respectability that had stifled black artists: "In Harlem, along Fifth and Lenox avenues, in Marcus Garvey's Hall with its extravagant paraphernalia, in his churches and cabarets, [the black man] expresses himself with a zeal that is yet to be depicted by a true artist."[65] That depiction became McKay's goal. Yet his attitude toward Harlem remained ambivalent, as his alter ego in the novel *Home to Harlem* (1928) expresses: "Harlem! How terribly Ray could hate it sometimes. Its brutality, gang rowdyism, promiscuous thickness. Its hot desires. But, oh, the rich blood-red color of it! The warm accent of its composite voice, the fruitiness of its laughter, the trailing rhythm of its 'blues' and the improvised surprises of its jazz."[66]

McKay became known to many of his contemporaries as "the *enfant terrible* of the Harlem Renaissance" when he wrote his manifesto poem, "If We Must Die," in 1919 after a series of race riots. McKay urged African-Americans to fight "like men" to the death rather than submit to slaughter "like hogs."[67] He was still concerned with violence in Harlem when he reported on the riot of 1935 in "Harlem Runs Wild" for the *Nation*: "One Hundred and Twenty-fifth Street is Harlem's main street and the theatrical and shopping center of the colored thousands. Anything that starts there will flash through Harlem as quick as lightning. The alleged beating of a kid caught stealing a trifle in one of the stores merely served to explode the smoldering discontent of the colored people against the Harlem merchants."[68]

McKay's pessimism was articulated in a variety of powerful metaphors. In "The Tropics in New York," a poem included in *The New Negro*, McKay juxtaposes the lushness of the tropics against the sterility of the City and weeps. *Harlem Shadows* (1922), a collection of sonnets, helped to define that city-within-the-City. In "The Desolate City," McKay writes after the fashion of Eliot, "My spirit is a pestilential city,/ With misery triumphant everywhere." In "Harlem Shadows," he expresses similar disenchantment: "Ah, heart of me, the weary, weary feet/ In Harlem wandering from street to street."[69] McKay's Harlem wanderer was, as McKay would become, a man without a country.

In his autobiography, *A Long Way from Home* (1937), McKay described his distance from "the Negro elite," characterizing them as figures perpetually attired in dress suits, with some élan: "I have never had the slightest desire to insult Harlem society or Negro society anywhere, because I happen not to be of it."[70] Though *Harlem Shadows* made him into the most prominent and influential black poet of his day, in 1922 McKay, seeking an alternative world, went to the Soviet Union. He fled Harlem, notes David Levering Lewis, to "escape from the pity of sex and poverty, from domestic death, from the *cul-de-sac* of self-pity, from the hot syncopated fascination of Harlem, from the suffocating ghetto of color consciousness."[71] Yet, in time, the Soviet Union also failed the ideologically restless McKay. In 1923 he moved to Berlin, where he remained for eleven years.

McKay's best novel, *Home to Harlem*, surpassed Van Vechten's *Nigger Heaven* in its celebration of Harlem low life—the "debauched tenth," as Du Bois called them. McKay's *Home to Harlem* portrays two representative black men: Jake, an army deserter who returns to the City and becomes consumed by his search for a woman, and Ray, a Jamaican writer who goes beyond Jake's simple, sensual response to Harlem. McKay's novel is clearly hostile to the black bourgeoisie; he took such pride in his racial heritage that the novel is even anti-mulatto. Inspired by D. H. Lawrence, McKay's novel sought to present a black Harlem of passion and blood knowledge rather than a sanctuary of culture and cerebration.

In *Home to Harlem*, Harlem is discovered, celebrated, and then lost. When Jake arrives in Harlem, he goes out for a promenade down Seventh Avenue: "He thrilled to Harlem. His blood was hot. His eyes were alert as he sniffed the street like a hound. Seventh Avenue was nice, a little too nice that night." So Jake turns off onto Lenox Avenue, in search of women, reveling in Harlem's blackness: "Harlem! Harlem! Little thicker, little darker and noisier and smellier, but Harlem just the same. The niggers done plowed through Hundred and Thirtieth Street. Heading straight for One Hundred and Twenty-fifth. Spades beyond Eighth Avenue. Going, going, going Harlem! Going up! . . . Oh Lawdy! Harlem bigger, Harlem better . . . and sweeter."[72] Through Jake's eloquent street talk, McKay presents Harlem from an insider's perspective. The wonder of local place persists throughout the novel. In the end Jake finds his woman, aptly named Felice, but restless Ray ships out for Europe, seeking a better world. Between the two characters, one at home in Harlem and the other an alienated wanderer, "stands Claude McKay reflecting on his own unfulfilled search for an intellectual and spiritual home."[73]

McKay followed *Home to Harlem* with *Banjo* (1929), a novel in which Ray and Jake arrive in Marseilles, where they meet another bardic spirit, Banjo. Leaving the reluctant Jake behind, Ray and Banjo respond to modern alienation, compounded by the color of their skin, by wandering aimlessly around Europe. McKay, too, left Harlem behind in his later works of fiction, which are centered on Jamaican experiences: *Gingertown* (1932), a collection of stories, and *Banana Bottom* (1933), a novel. He returned to New York in 1934, however, to work as a journalist and as a member of the New York Federal Writers' project during the 1930s. Both his autobiography and his sociological study of working-class life, *Harlem: Negro Metropolis* (1940), show that he could never truly leave Harlem.[74]

McKay's poem "The White City" summarizes his vision of Harlem as simultaneously seductive and destructive. Within the self-imposed confinements of the Shakespearean sonnet form, McKay expressed his lifelong hatred, qualified by his consuming love, for the City. Indeed, his "dark passion" for the City was his sustaining life force. He saw "the mighty city through a mist" of towering spires, passing trains and ships, leading him to the poignant final couplet: "The tides, the wharves, the dens I contemplate,/ Are sweet like wanton loves because I hate."[75]

Unlike Claude McKay, Countee Cullen was a child of Harlem, though he may not actually have been born there, in 1903, as he claimed. His values were shaped by his foster father, Frederick A. Cullen, a Methodist minister who introduced him to European culture on summer trips abroad. After De Witt Clinton High, Countee Cullen won awards at NYU for his poetry, which celebrates black life and letters. Graduating Phi Beta Kappa from NYU, Cullen went on to Harvard and earned an M.A. in 1926. He returned to Harlem to write a column, "The Dark Tower," for *Opportunity*, the journal of the Urban League. As a young man, Cullen defined a personal aesthetic designed both to celebrate his race and to transcend parochial propaganda: "If I am going to be a poet at all, I am going to be POET and not NEGRO POET."[76] For Cullen, poetry was a means by which blacks could be accepted as Americans.[77] Cullen derived from and spoke for the genteel tradition of African-American expression, the so-called talented tenth of black elite.

In 1928 Cullen was briefly married to W. E. B. Du Bois's daughter, Yolande, a marriage that confirmed his spiritual lineage; however, it was a marriage more fitting as idea than as experience and they soon separated. At the beginning of the Harlem Renaissance, in 1925, after the publication of his first collection of poems, *Color*, Cullen, then age twenty-two, replacing Claude McKay, was deemed, inside and outside Harlem, the most celebrated black writer in New York, perhaps in America.[78] Yet Cullen's "race" poetry emphasized his alienation from American culture, black and white.[79]

"Heritage," his best-known poem—memorized for decades by black school children—reveals both his interest in and his artful detachment from the claims of color. "What is Africa to me?" he asks. The black continent is a book he thumbs through listlessly, not a tie that binds; he is a Christian, so Africa's "heathen gods" mean little to him.[80] Indeed, for Cullen, as it had for Phillis Wheatley in Revolutionary-era Boston, Christianity became the means of affirming and transcending blackness and other earthly considerations. "The Litany of the Dark People," as Cullen put it in a poem from *Copper Sun*, promises that Bethlehem and Calvary will merge in Paradise.[81]

Cullen's only novel, *One Way to Heaven* (1932), shows his divided attitudes, for passages satirical of Harlem Renaissance figures do not fit into the main plot of the novel, which concerns the adventures of a one-armed black con man. Arriving in New York from the South, "Sam Lucas, striding through the raw, mordant December night felt that he had chosen an ill moment in which to come to Harlem. New York was bright and gay, and these colored people looked happy, as he had been told he would find them; but they also seemed too intent upon their own affairs to promise much attention to an ill-starred stranger."[82] Harlem is a challenge for Cullen's fictional hero, one that he only seems to overcome, for in the end, a churchgoing young woman, Mattie Johnson, brings out the best in this small-time hustler.

Lucas enters Mount Hebron African Methodist Episcopal Church, where he works his con game. He moves to the mourners' bench, tosses a deck of cards and a razor on the floor as evidence of his conversion, then collects donations from pitying churchgoers. Yet his false conversion results in the true conversion of Mattie. They marry, but Sam leaves Mattie for another woman. When he is dying from pneumonia, he returns; he tries to fake a deathbed conversion, but it turns sincere—thus proving Cullen's thesis that there is more than one way to heaven. Though the novel takes place in Harlem, it is a morality tale that could have been set anywhere.

Scattered throughout this narrative uneasily is Cullen's thin satire of Harlem Renaissance figures. Mattie works for Constance Brandon, a Harlem hostess who holds parties in her fourteen-room house on Striver's Row, on Sugar Hill, for white and black literary and cultural figures. "The novel respected what it mocked," notes David Levering Lewis, "so lacked the proletarian grit of *Home to Harlem* and the bitterness of [Wallace Thurman's] *The Blacker the Berry*."[83] Furthermore, Cullen makes no thematic link between the two parts of his novel. His attitude toward black Harlem is reflected in the structural uncertainty of *One Way to Heaven* and in the divided view of black identity that is reflected in many of his writings. Countee Cullen found it difficult both to transcend Harlem and to engage it in his art.

In *INFANTS OF THE SPRING*, WALLACE THURMAN WROTE a far better satirical novel of the Harlem Renaissance. Indeed, some critics accuse him of presiding over the movement's demise. Nathan Huggins, for example, calls Thurman's *roman à clef* "an obituary of the Harlem Renaissance."[84] Robert A. Bone, too, identifies Thurman as its "undertaker," a writer filled with self-hatred and self-destructiveness.[85] Certainly Thurman did think that Harlem writers, including himself, failed to fulfill their artistic potential. Langston Hughes's portrayal of Thurman in *The Big Sea* catches his ambivalence of character (an ambivalence reflected in his fiction): "a strange kind of fellow who liked to drink gin, but *didn't* like to drink gin; who liked being a Negro, but felt it a great handicap; who adored bohemianism, but thought it wrong to be bohemian."[86] These internal tensions and artistic frustrations were never resolved, for Thurman died in Bellevue Hospital from tuberculosis at age thirty-two in 1934, at the depths of the Great Depression. His personal Harlem renaissance quickly turned into a requiem.

Indeed, Thurman's busy and brief life paralleled the rise and fall of the New Negro era. He was born in Salt Lake City, Utah, in 1902. He came to Harlem in 1925, straight out of the University of Southern California, and was hired as editor of the *Messenger*, a radical monthly, in 1926. He helped to publish two black journals, *Fire!!* and *Harlem*, and coauthored, with William Jourdan Rapp, a play called *Harlem* (1929), which was successfully presented at the Apollo Theater on Broadway. "*Harlem*: A Forum of Negro Life," editorials printed in two issues of *Harlem*, was Thurman's manifesto for young black writers; his magazine, he promised, would "give them a medium of expression and intelligent criticism."[87]

In two novels, *The Blacker the Berry* (1929) and *Infants of the Spring* (1932), Wallace Thurman expressed disillusionment over the betrayed promises made to postwar blacks in Harlem. In *The Blacker the Berry*, Thurman attacks those, black and white, who show prejudices against black skin. His heroine, Emma Lou Brown, experiences such discrimination growing up in Boise, Idaho: "Not that she minded being black, being a Negro necessitated having a colored skin, but she did mind being too black."[88] Emma has been trained to think this way by her grandmother, who hates blackness and who presides over an elite mulatto society in Boise. After three years of college in Los Angeles, Emma comes to Harlem, where she finds she is not hired as a secretary because she is too black. She then becomes a maid for a black actress. The novel tracks Emma through Harlem, on the job and on the town—rent parties, dances, theaters—and traces her relations with many men. Throughout, the burden of her blackness weighs on her mind. Emma even tries to bleach her skin.

She gets a job as maid for one Clere Stone, a former actress who has retired and married a famous writer, Campbell Kitchen. Kitchen, like Carl Van Vechten, upon whom the character was modeled, "had become interested in Harlem. The Negro and all things negroid had become a fad, and Harlem had become a shrine to which feverish pilgrimages were in order."[89] Kitchen, too, has written a book about Harlem, a work that sensationalizes the community, in the manner of *Nigger Heaven*.

Emma eventually becomes a teacher in Harlem. She makes herself up heavily and gets involved with two black men, who still deem her too black. Walking along Seventh Avenue, "the gorge into which Harlem cliff dwellers crowded to promenade," she does not know where to go.[90] Where, if not in Harlem, can a black woman go? Thurman set out to show the wisdom in the black folk saying "The blacker the berry, the sweeter the juice"; however, his Harlem is bitter fruit for a black woman.

In *Infants of the Spring*, the brightest figures of the New Negro movement suffer "contagious blastments," just as Laertes warns Ophelia that she may if she unmasks "her beauty to the moon," in a passage from *Hamlet* that serves as the novel's epigraph. Black bohemianism is the canker in the rose of the Harlem Renaissance for Thurman. Paul, a dissipated writer, and Raymond, another failed writer, stand as representative figures of Harlem's "infants of spring." They live in Niggeratti Manor, where they spend most of their time talking, rather than painting or writing. (The term "niggeratti," or "niggerati," was coined by Wallace Thurman and Zora Neale Hurston, a combination of "nigger" and "literati.")[91] The novel's set piece is centered on a party hosted by Dr. Parkes (Locke) and attended by Sweetie May Carr (Hurston), who cleverly plays the roles expected of her by white patrons; also attending are Tony Crews (Hughes); and De Witt Clinton (Johnson), "the Negro poet laureate," who claims to have been equally inspired by Keats and the Bible. Parkes, "a mother hen clucking at her chicks," urges them to use artistic beauty as a weapon that "will cause the American white man to re-estimate the Negro's value to his civilization." Paul and Ray, speaking for Thurman, see the affirmation of African ancestry, indeed, any strict ideology, as destructive. The party, held to celebrate black art, declines into bickering and feuds.[92] At the end of the novel, Paul, in despair, commits suicide; in the process, he destroys his manuscript, leaving only the title page, which pictures Niggeratti Manor caught in beams of white light. The last words of the novel constitute Thurman's epitaph for the Harlem Renaissance: "The foundation of this building was composed of crumbling stone. At first glance it could be ascertained that the sky-scraper would soon crumple and fall, leaving the dominating white lights in full possession of the sky."[93] In Wallace Thurman's apocalyptic vision of Harlem, white obliterates black.

In Langston Hughes's vision of Harlem, on the other hand, black is beautiful. Hughes seldom suffered the personal and racial anxieties experienced by Cullen and Thurman. Hughes came from a comfortable and well-educated background in the black aristocracy of Missouri, Kansas, and Illinois. After completing Central High School in Cleveland, Hughes persuaded his father to send him to Columbia University to study engineering, though his real purpose was to get to Harlem: "More than Paris, or the Shakespeare country, or Berlin, or the Alps, I wanted to see Harlem, the greatest Negro city in the world."[94] In Harlem he quickly found a new identity, a new profession, and a new father in W. E. B. Du Bois. In 1921, the poem that revealed his distinctive voice, "The Negro Speaks of Rivers," inspired by his first crossing of the Mississippi, was accepted for publication by Jessie Fauset in the *Crisis*. Alain Locke sought him out, enlisting him in the Harlem Renaissance, though Hughes went well beyond the high-minded Locke in finding inspiration in the street vernacular and jazz rhythms of Harlem.

In 1922 and 1923, Hughes served as a messboy on a boat that traveled up and down the west coast of Africa; though he spent little time ashore, the sight of the continent expanded his vision and the scope of his poetry. A Whitmanian note was struck in several of his poems included in Locke's *The New Negro*; Hughes, the "darker brother," sang America, for, he said, "I, too, am American."[95] If Brooklyn was America's imaginative source for Walt Whitman, then Harlem was America's vital root for Langston Hughes:

> *Harlem was like a great magnet for the Negro intellectual, pulling him from everywhere. Or perhaps the magnet was New York—but once in New York, he had to live in Harlem, for rooms were hardly to be found elsewhere unless one could pass for white or Mexican or Eurasian and perhaps live in the Village—which always seemed to me a very arty locale, in spite of the many real artists and writers who lived there. Only a few of the New Negroes lived in the Village, Harlem being their real stamping ground.*[96]

His first book, *The Weary Blues* (1926), features a black musician who plays the blues on Lenox Avenue—Hughes's ideal bard. In his autobiography, Hughes says he tried to write "poems like the songs they sang on Seventh Street—gay songs, because you had to be gay or die; sad songs, because you couldn't help being sad sometimes. But gay or sad, you kept on living and you kept on going."[97]

As Hughes makes clear in his seminal essay "The Negro Artist and the Racial Mountain," jazz rhythms and blues tones give blacks a separate identity and supply "the tom-tom of revolt against the weariness in a white world. . . . We younger Negro artists who create now intend to express our individual dark-skinned selves without fear or shame."[98] The essay served at once as a personal credo and a call to artistic arms for black Harlemites.

At the same time, Hughes, like Hurston, utilized opportunities offered by downtown whites who were enamored with black Harlem. Van Vechten helped to place Hughes's *Weary Blues* at Knopf, for example; Hughes and other black writers appeared in *Vanity Fair*, aided by Van Vechten, who served as a go-between, linking Harlem's black writers with the white world of publication, parties, and patronage. Hurston and Hughes were supported at various times by a Park Avenue matron whom Hurston called "Godmother." Hughes finally broke away from her patronizing beneficence, but he sometimes mourned the loss of her support.[99]

In "Slaves on the Block," from *The Ways of White Folks* (1934), a story collection, Hughes offered a parable in which a young black man is taken up by Michael and Anne Carraway, a wealthy and artistic white couple who "went in for Negroes." They bring Luther into their house to have him pose for Anne's painting. By a process of natural attraction, Luther and the black maid, Mattie, get together: "They didn't understand the vagaries of white folks, neither Luther nor Mattie, and they didn't want to be bothered trying." When Michael's snobbish mother criticizes Luther for being overly familiar in his speech, he denounces her and, with Mattie, leaves. Hughes's black characters regain their dignity by denouncing patronizing whites, renouncing dependence, and going off on their own.[100]

Langston Hughes's poems were loosely formed, reading like spontaneous combustions, his stories both simple and rhetorical, and they caught Harlem life, its joys and its angers, better than the works of any other Renaissance writer. Hughes's Harlem embodies the dream deferred for black Americans, but at least it *is* a version of the American dream, one not easily denied, as he makes clear in his complex, touching poem "Passing," which celebrates those who live in hope in "Harlem of the bitter dream."[101]

In Harlem, just after the Great War, for a few years "everything was pollinated by the spirit of self-determination which pervaded the world at that time," writes Nathan Huggins. So there is "little wonder Harlemites anticipated the flowering of Negro culture into a racial renaissance." There is little wonder, as well, that American cultural racism and economic discrimination soon wilted the hopes of Harlem's citizens.[102] Langston Hughes gave voice both to Harlem's vigor and its despair.

T HERE WAS A COLD NOVEMBER WIND BLOWING THROUGH 116th Street." Ann Petry's *The Street* (1946) opens with a bleak image that sums up her vision of post-Renaissance life in Harlem. Cold wind cuts through her Harlem, just as fog shrouds Dickens's London. In Petry's novel, the wind "did everything it could to discourage the people walking along the street" and "lifted Lutie Johnson's hair away from the back of her neck so that she felt suddenly naked and bald."[103] Petry's beautiful heroine and her eight-year-old son, Bub, are looking for a place to live. They are fleeing her abusive husband. Though she locates a small, airless apartment, out of the wind, in the long run Lutie finds that there is no true place for them in Harlem, where her son's life is destroyed.

Petry's *The Street*, appearing long after the collapse of the Harlem Renaissance, is as defeatist and as deterministic about life in Harlem as Dunbar's *The Sport of the Gods*, written long before Harlem's heyday. More exactly, *The Street* echoes Richard Wright's *Native Son* (1940), a novel set in Chicago, for in each work the central character is driven to murder by the conditions of American racism. But, as Mary Helen Washington points out, Petry's novel has far different concerns: "to put a black woman in a central position and talk about both the sexism and racism affecting that woman's life. [Petry] also deals with a single mother trying to bring up a child."[104]

Ann Petry's experience in Harlem was far more satisfying and successful than her fictional heroine's. Petry and her husband first arrived in the City from Old Saybrook, Connecticut, in 1938, when she was thirty. In Harlem she sold advertising for the *Amsterdam News*, acted in American Negro Theater productions, and became a reporter for the *People's Voice*. While doing volunteer work for a school, Petry was shocked at the condition of abandoned children in Harlem, where, she said, "the street reached out and sucked them up."[105] This concern for its victims is the foundation for her literary vision of Harlem.

After taking a writing course at Columbia in 1942, Petry embarked on a successful career as a fiction writer. Her first story, a characteristic parable of disillusionment, appeared in the *Crisis*. In "On Saturday, the Siren Sounds at Noon," a man returns home from the Great War, only to discover his wife in bed with another man. Petry then wrote her first and most popular novel, *The Street*. The novel was celebrated both in *Ebony* and in New York's white literary community; this success allowed Petry and her husband to leave Harlem and buy a house in Old Saybrook, where she has remained.

In *The Street*, Petry sought "to show how simply and easily the environment can change the course of a person's life."[106] Filth, depravity, and violence circumscribe the lives of Lutie and her son. "No one could live on a street like this and stay decent," Lutie decides. The street attacks its victims, like a vampire: "It would get them sooner or later, for it sucked the humanity out of people—slowly, surely, inevitably."[107] By the end of the novel, the grown-up Bub has been arrested for a crime he was forced to commit by the building superintendent who also assaulted his mother. When Lutie tries to borrow money to release her son, she is nearly raped by the musician she appeals to for help—the man she then kills. As Lutie escapes and her train leaves New York City behind, she blames Harlem for what has happened to them. The wind of the novel's opening paragraph is transformed into the snow of the final page. "All she could think was, It was that street. It was that god-damned street."[108]

Petry's novel struck a nerve in the black community when it was first published and still does. J. W. Ivy, writing in the *Crisis* and representing the NAACP's high-minded attitudes toward black life, complained that Petry's portrayal of Harlem was exaggerated: "Harlem is not the seething cesspool of sluts, pimps, juvenile delinquents, and clucks pictured in this novel. There are normal and responsible people in the community but you would never suspect it from reading this book."[109] Nearly half a century later, Mary Helen Washington protested that Petry's novel "cuts off every avenue of triumph."[110] However, another black novelist, Gloria Naylor, who grew up in Harlem and has written extensively about life there, credited Petry for her honest depiction: "When I was coming up in Harlem in the '60s, we felt these things would change. We felt Harlem could be a springboard into greater opportunity, the way it had been for other immigrant groups. Now we look back and see that did not turn out to be the case; Harlem and places like it become holding tanks, if not prisons."[111] Ann Petry's *The Street* encodes a compelling vision, from an original perspective, of Harlem as "nowhere."[112] When *The Street* was reissued in 1992, Petry, at age eighty-four, still living in Old Saybrook, reflected on the unchanging destructiveness of life in Harlem: "It just saddens my heart so that if you added crack [to the Harlem of the 1930s], it would basically be the same story today. It's just so painful and frightening."[113]

In Abraham Rodriguez Jr.'s 1993 novel, *Spidertown*, this sense of life as "nowhere" extends out of Harlem and beyond the black community, into the devastating South Bronx of Puerto Ricans. "There is nothing out there," says Rodriguez, of the novel's South Bronx neighborhood—only crack houses, arson, and shoot-outs. "Some people see it as a bleak message, some people see it as a message of hope," he said. "For me it's my way of expressing my feelings about things. I'm not really saying anything about the community or the South Bronx, except that it's a lousy place to live."[114] Certainly Ann Petry would agree with Rodriguez's bleak vision of New York street life and his articulation of responsibility to portray it in art.

P{AULE MARSHALL AND GLORIA NAYLOR ARE CONTEM}porary novelists who build on the tradition of black women writers who portray New York City's destructive impact upon its black citizenry. Marshall, born in 1929 in Barbados, grew up in Brooklyn's Stuyvesant Heights (now Bedford-Stuyvesant) and studied at Hunter College. She published her first novel, an autobiographical recreation of her coming-of-age, *Brown Girl, Brownstones*, in 1959. Naylor, born in 1950, grew up in Harlem, graduated from Brooklyn College, and received an M.A. in African-American studies from Yale. Both Marshall and Naylor, after the fashion of Petry, create contemporary parables of black women whose lives are defined and whose fates are determined by significant places in New York City. The troubled "Harlem" of Fauset, Larsen, and Petry comes to characterize all sections of New York.

Of the two, Marshall's fiction is less allegorical, more realistic. *Brown Girl* opens with an arresting image of the City: "In the somnolent July afternoon the unbroken line of brownstone houses down the long Brooklyn street resembled an army massed at attention." The brownstones are joined in somber uniformity. Although each is in fact separate and has its own distinctive details, "they all shared the same brown monotony. All seemed doomed by the confusion in their design." The rowed houses turn their backs to the sun and enclose the lives within them: "Behind those grim facades, in those high rooms, life soared and ebbed."[115] Marshall's New York is a walled city.

Inside one of these brownstones lives a brown girl, young Selina Boyce, who is growing into full consciousness; she is particularly attentive to the rich oral tradition of storytelling passed along by her mother, Silla, a West Indian émigré. Her father, Deighton, is a lazy but loving man, while her mother is hard and driven. Silla wants Deighton to sell his beloved land in Barbados so that they can afford to buy their own Brooklyn brownstone. In the midst of the conflicts between her parents and their values, Selina must compose a self, make a life, and choose a world in which to live it—either in Brooklyn or Barbados. After years of contention, after the deportation of her father (brought about by her mother) and his subsequent death, Selina sets herself against her mother's willingness to sacrifice anything for American success, symbolized by property ownership. In the end, Selina decides to return to Barbados, to a more loving and less driven culture than the one that has ruined her family in New York City.

While the heroine's departure from the City in Petry's *The Street* was a clear symbolic defeat for the hopes of those in the black community who wished to find safety and success in New York, the heroine's departure in *Brown Girl* is a gesture (and the beginning of a journey) of symbolic affirmation. Mary Helen Washington, who criticized Petry for the bleak implications of her novel, celebrated Marshall's first work of fiction as "one of the most optimistic texts in Afro-American literature, for it assigns even to an oppressed people the power of conscious political choice: they are not victims."[116] However, though their visions differ, Petry and Marshall both identify the City as a destructive place from which young women of promise must escape to save their lives and restore their souls.

Gloria Naylor's first novel, *The Women of Brewster Place* (1982), tracks, as its title suggests, the relations between a place and its residents. Brewster Place is created after the Great War, a neighborhood designed by politicians to connect with a new boulevard. The boulevard, however, is never built, so Brewster Place is quite literally walled-off from the rest of the City. In Brewster Place, Naylor's characters find a home, but they also discover there is no easy way out. Naylor's second novel, *Linden Hills* (1985), describes a community of affluent, middle-class blacks who try to separate themselves not only from the white community, but also from the poor women of Brewster Place.[117] Both Brewster Place and Linden Hills are fictional places that derive their symbolic meanings from Naylor's experience in the City.

The Women of Brewster Place focuses upon a city block that has evolved from Irish to Italian to black; however, by the time it becomes black, Brewster Place is, in every sense of the word, a dead end. The women of Brewster Place lead lives of quiet desperation, mitigated by love: "They came, they went, grew up, and grew old beyond their years. Like an ebony phoenix, each in her own time and with her own season had a story."[118] Naylor interweaves the stories of several characters who show resilience and courage in the face of betrayals by callous men and by a racist society. As Barbara Christian has pointed out, women's nurturing of other women is central to Brewster Place, but such love provides no means of escape to a better life from this walled-in city-within-the-City.[119] Though black women's community is celebrated in a concluding block party, the buildings of Brewster Place are condemned and its citizens are forced to leave. However, the shaping spirit of that hard but vital place remains: "The colored daughters of Brewster" still "ebb and flow, ebb and flow, but never disappear. So Brewster Place still waits to die."[120] This is another way of saying that the experience of black life in the City, however daunting, lives on in the minds and in the art of another generation of black women writers—a metaphoric rather than an actual triumph of community.

Naylor's *Linden Hills* presents an even less salvific myth of urban black life. The fictional community is founded in the 1820s by Luther Nedeed, who is determined to show white America that blacks can be rich and successful. Linden Hills will become "a wad of spit—a beautiful, black wad of spit right in the white eye of America."[121] The price paid for Nedeed's dream of success, passed along through his successors for 150 years, is the community's submission to its leader's will; its isolation from the rest of the world, black and white; and its subordination of black women, personified by the line of Nedeed wives, who are dispensed with after they have borne a male heir. Naylor's pointed narrative centers on the imprisonment of Willa Prescott Nedeed, who is suspected of infidelity because her son does not sufficiently resemble the latest Luther Nedeed. This driven patriarch—like Faulkner's Thomas Sutpen in *Absalom, Absalom!*—brings about the death of his own son, thus ending his line. When Nedeed's house burns (another echo of Faulkner's novel), no one in the community helps to put out the fire, because no true community has ever been created. What is saved are the stories of the women whose lives have been sacrificed for bourgeois success.

The only other sustaining value to emerge from Linden Hills is reflected in the character of Melanie Browne. Rebelling against the class bias and the demeaning acquisitiveness of Linden Hills, she adopts an African name and goes to Brewster Place to try to help the women of that community gain power. However, in the end, both Brewster Place and Linden Hills are destroyed. Despite her compelling portraits of black women's love, Gloria Naylor offers no redemptive myths of black life in the City.

Certainly the history of that life is alive—still happening, as Faulkner put it—in Paule Marshall's *Praisesong for the Widow* (1983), a novel published twenty-four years after *Brown Girl*. In her first novel, a family from Barbados struggles with the American dream of success in New York City. In *Praisesong for the Widow*, a black woman struggles with the price of having attained that success.

The novel, set in 1977, centers upon Avey Johnson, a sixty-four-year-old widow in crisis, a woman adrift. Indeed, Avey is on a cruise in the Caribbean, aboard the *Bianca Pride*. Suddenly, suppressed memories of her passionate past overwhelm her—memories of how she and her husband, Jay, once danced to jazz, early in their marriage, in their Halsey Street apartment in Brooklyn. Dreams also pull her back to her Great-aunt Cuney, who called Avey "Avatara." In 1923, her aunt had taken ten-year-old Avatara to the Landing, on Tatem Island, Georgia, where the old woman told the girl the legend of the Ibos, a captured tribe who escaped from slavery by walking on water back home to Africa. "In instilling the story of the Ibos in her child's mind, the old woman had entrusted her with a mission she couldn't even name yet had felt duty-bound to fulfill. It had taken her years to rid herself of the notion."[122] That is, Avey, no longer Avatara, has abandoned this dream of escape from white America, and she has denied the mission imposed upon her by her great-aunt for American success. But such memories, desires, and obligations are not so easily put aside. Avey Johnson, cruising somewhere between Nicaragua and Grenada, finds her life welling up inside her, making her ill, "clogged" and "bloated," as if "a huge tumor had suddenly ballooned up to her center." Sitting in the Versailles Room of the *Bianca Pride*, eating rich desserts among wealthy whites, she feels invisible. She is unable to recognize herself in the mirror.[123]

On Grenada, after leaving the cruise ship, Avey feels similarly suffocated by the Miramar Royale Hotel, which she suddenly sees as an emblem of the success-driven culture for which her husband had sacrificed his life. Avey wanders away from the hotel and walks along the beach, where she fortuitously meets an old black man. He persuades her to join a group of "out-islanders," people from the nearby island of Carriacou who live and work in Grenada, rooted folks who return home once each year. During the crossing—a symbolic passage from white, commercial culture to the remnants of a vital black culture—Avey faints and dreams of her past, of her dead husband. On Halsey Street, Jay had held two menial jobs for twelve years, while he also studied accounting, until they could afford to move from Brooklyn to North White Plains. In the process he became grim and joyless, but also fiercely determined. Finally he became a CPA, and he had "his own office on Fulton Street with his name in large gold letters on the window and the house in North White Plains lay ahead."[124] However, Avey too late realizes, their success, measured by their move to a white, middle-class suburb, was bought at the cost of their black culture and their passion. In their Halsey Street apartment, she and Jay had danced to a recording of Coleman Hawkins saxophone solos and Jay had recited the poetry of Paul Laurence Dunbar before they made love. In North White Plains, however, Jay became Jerome, a grim man with clenched teeth, which is how he looked when he died.

On Carriacou, Avey is bathed—rebaptized—and she joins a dance that reminds her both of the dances she saw as a child on Tatem Island and the dances she and Jay shared on Halsey Street. Avey comes away from her immersion into black folk culture with a new sense of her identity and a new goal. She determines to become a missionary, like her Aunt Cuney, imparting the message of redemption through the acknowledgment of black culture. She decides to sell the house in North White Plains, to rebuild the house on Tatem Island, and to educate her grandchildren—by telling them all about the Ibos.

Paule Marshall's novel shows New York City's blacks caught in a double bind. They can accept their assigned, second-class status, but risk sinking into self-indulgence, as so many did along Halsey Street, or they can turn away from their culture as a means of getting ahead in white America, another route toward self-destruction. Avey finally rejects North White Plains just as she rejected the *Bianca Pride*. Though it is too late to save vital Jay, who became responsible Jerome (at the cost of his life), it is not too late for Avey to recover the Avatara who has been repressed within her. What is crucial to her salvation, as in so many literary myths of New York, is that she leave the City. New York City is no longer necessary for Marshall's heroines, who break free from its walls.[125]

MORE THAN ANY OTHER WRITERS, RALPH ELLISON AND James Baldwin made Harlem into a central city of the American imagination. Ellison, principally in *Invisible Man* (1952) but also in his essays, and Baldwin, principally in his essays from *Notes of a Native Son* (1955) but also in his fiction and plays, gave imaginative life to the black experience in Harlem. Ellison, born in 1914 in Oklahoma City, brought an outsider's perspective to Harlem; the hero of *Invisible Man* is a desperately naive young man from the rural South who comes to Harlem, where he is quickly disabused of his illusions and eventually turned into a latter-day version of Dostoyevsky's antihero. Baldwin, born in 1924 in Harlem, brought an insider's understanding to his native grounds; the hero of *Notes of a Native Son*, an autobiographical collection, is a savvy young man who yearns to escape the psychic and social vices that entrap so many like him. Both Ellison and Baldwin drew upon the literary heritage of the Harlem Renaissance and, specifically, upon Richard Wright, who provided a working model of the city as a psychic jail in his portrayal of Chicago in *Native Son*. But Ellison and

Baldwin also drew upon an array of literary exemplars selected from the wide tradition of Western letters, particularly upon Henry James. That is, neither Ellison nor Baldwin treated Harlem as a subject of merely regional interest, a way of adding local color. Both writers insisted that Harlem is part of the mainstream of American life; that black experience serves as an informing parable of the American dream; that African-Americans are, in all respects, representative modern men and women.

In the opening pages of Ellison's *Invisible Man*, the narrator establishes himself as not only "invisible," but also as an "underground man," for he lives beneath the streets of New York City, stealing power (1,369 lights) from Monopolated Light & Power. There he smokes reefers and listens to recordings of Louis Armstrong, who "made poetry out of being invisible." The novel's setting is quasi-allegorical, or symbolist-modernist, placing this estranged hero beyond the pale of the American community: "I live rent-free in a building rented strictly to whites, in a section of the basement that was shut off and forgotten during the nineteenth century." Monopolated Light & Power knows that "a hell of a lot of free current is disappearing somewhere into the jungle of Harlem," though the narrator does not "live in Harlem but in a border area." That is, the hero's borderline experience is to be understood as a metaphor, present and historical, for black-white relations in America. Ellison's idealistic hero can find no place for himself in either black or white America, though he promises (or threatens) to emerge from his underground confinement.

When "the invisible man"—no longer seen for himself but only in the images and associations that surround any black man—bumps into a white man on the streets of the City, the encounter has implications far larger than the immediate confrontation. When the white man looks arrogantly at him, "the invisible man" butts the white man's head and demands an apology; when no apology is offered, "the invisible man" knocks down the white man, kicks him, and nearly kills him with a knife: "It occurred to me that the man had not *seen* me, actually; that he, as far as he knew, was in the midst of a walking nightmare!" Indeed, neither man, black or white, can truly see the other; instead, each sees only his own worst nightmare. "The next day I saw his picture in the *Daily News*, beneath a caption that he had been 'mugged.' Poor fool, poor blind fool, I thought with sincere compassion, mugged by an invisible man!"[126] Since the unnamed black narrator has not been accepted as a man, not seen, he turns murderous. This confrontation stands as a central epiphany of race and place in *Invisible Man*.

Ralph Ellison first came to New York City during the summer of 1936, after his third year of study at Tuskegee. He intended, like the unnamed young man in his novel, to earn enough money to return to school. However, his plans quickly changed when he met Langston Hughes and Alain Locke outside a library near the 135th Street YMCA, where he was staying. Through Hughes, Ellison met Richard Wright, his literary idol. Wright accepted a review from Ellison for his magazine, *New Challenge*. By then Ellison "was hooked" on a literary career, so he decided to stay on in New York City. There he wrote *Invisible Man*, between 1945 and 1952. Yet Ellison never wished to be defined by Harlem: "I did *not* come to New York to live in Harlem." Rather, he sought "a wider world of opportunity. And, most of all, the excitement and impersonality of a great city. I wanted room in which to discover who I was."[127] For Ellison, as for his fictional hero, the trip North to New York City was a journey of discovery, however painful: "In my novel the narrator's development is one through blackness to light; that is, from ignorance to enlightenment: invisibility to visibility. He leaves the South and goes North; this, as you will notice in reading Negro folktales, is always the road to freedom—the movement upward. You have the same thing again when he leaves his underground cave for the open."[128]

Invisible Man is a novel that rose from many streets and sections of the City. It "preoccupied" Ellison "in various parts of New York City, including its crowded subways: in a converted 141st Street stable, in a one-room ground floor apartment on St. Nicholas Avenue and, most unexpectedly, in a suite otherwise occupied by jewelers located on the eighth floor of Number 608 Fifth Avenue." Thus a novel that plunges its hero and its readers to the lower depths of the City was composed, in part, in offices high above the streets. A novel that dramatizes a black man's alienation from white America was written, in part, within the citadel of white money and power. Such tensions and ambivalences helped to prepare Ellison to write *Invisible Man*. Moving back and forth between Harlem, where he lived, and midtown, where he worked, Ellison became something of an invisible man himself: "In retrospect it was as though writing about invisibility had rendered me either transparent or opaque and set me bouncing back and forth between the benighted provincialism of a small village and the benign disinterestedness of a great metropolis. Which, given the difficulty of gaining an authorial knowledge of this diverse society, was not a bad discipline for an American writer."[129]

Despite his movements about the City, Ellison has said that *Invisible Man* was largely written in Harlem, "where it drew much of its substance from the voices, idioms, folklore, traditions and political concerns of those whose racial and cultural origins I share." There he confronted the nation's "moral evasiveness" on the issue of race, with the race riot of 1943 (which he reported for the *New York Post*), the rise of Adam Clayton Powell, the efforts to desegregate stores along 125th Street, and various political protests. There he discovered that "the voice of invisibility issued deep from within our complex American underground."[130] There, combining jazzlike improvisations with his sense of the alienated state of black Americans, Ellison found his voice and articulated what may be the most powerful vision of black life in an American novel.[131]

Invisible Man is Ellison's high modernist epic of a young hero's quest for personal and racial identity. The novel traces his spiritual pilgrimage for self-realization and for the redemption of his people; it can be seen as an American *Portrait of the Artist as a Young Man*, for in each work a sensitive young man rises from a beleaguered citizenry to give voice, through his art, to his people's presence.

When Ellison's hero finds his way from the South to New York City, where he becomes a successful orator and an organizer for the Brotherhood (a satirical representation of the Communist Party), he recalls how one of his teachers had bent the description of James Joyce's alter ego, Stephen Dedalus, to the purposes of black identity: "Stephen's problem, like ours, was not actually of creating the uncreated conscience of his race, but of creating the *uncreated features of his face*."[132] Ellison's nascent artist figure tries, less successfully than Joyce's, to transcend the limitations of racial designation, to establish an original relationship with the universe, to shape an identity.

Ellison's narrator, idealistic and innocent, wins a college scholarship from his Southern town, though he is forced, along with other young black men, to participate in a battle royal while blindfolded, in a show to amuse the white men who have organized the funding. He is later expelled from the college by its manipulative president, Dr. Bledsoe—a parody of Booker T. Washington—for exposing one of the school's wealthiest white patrons to sordid examples of black low life. After being humiliated by his white benefactors and rejected by a hypocritical black educator, the young man, his illusions still intact, goes to Harlem to seek his fortune, thinking he can there redeem himself and go on to become a savior of his people.

"New York!" he is warned by a cynical veteran of the Great War before he leaves, "that's not a place, it's a dream."[133] When he does arrive in Harlem, he is overwhelmed, like so many before him, by the sight of so many black people: "This was really Harlem, and now all the stories which I had heard of the city-within-a-city leaped alive in my mind. The vet had been right: For me this was not a city of realities, but of dreams."[134]

As in dreams, messages may have a hidden meaning. On his first trip downtown, the young man goes to Wall Street, carrying what he thinks are letters of introduction from Dr. Bledsoe to prominent white businessmen. In fact, the letters betray the young man and warn the businessmen not to employ him. As in a dream, things are not what they seem in the City. Beyond the high-rise office's plate-glass windows, the Statue of Liberty looms, eerily indistinct in the mist. Back on street level, the young man encounters a cart-pushing, blues-singing black man, who tells him that "Harlem ain't nothing but a bear's den"; yet, paradoxically, he adds, "it's the best place in the world for you and me." Then the streetwise vendor assures him that "all it takes to get along in this man's town is a little shit, grit and mother-wit."[135] However, Ellison's hero learns that it takes much more.

The young man, having discovered his betrayal by Dr. Bledsoe, gets a job at Liberty Paints, on Long Island. For F. Scott Fitzgerald this was the landscape of rich glitter that symbolized the true glory and promise of American life. For Ellison's central character, Long Island becomes the site of true initiation into the horror of New York City. In the factory, he makes a mistake while mixing paints, so that what should have been "Optic White"—the "Right White" used to paint national monuments—takes on an unacceptable gray tinge. Then he fails to watch the pressure gauge on a boiler, which explodes. As punishment, Liberty Paints' officials have him committed for insanity. He is given shock treatments, after which he does not know his own name.[136] Thus in a few short days, he has been stripped of his illusions and his identity.

After his release from the factory hospital, his second entry into Harlem plunges him deep into a nightmare realm: "When I came out of the subway, Lenox Avenue seemed to career away from me at a drunken angle, and I focused upon the teetering scene with wild, infant's eyes, my head throbbing."[137] He finds a savior in Mary Rambo, who takes him in and gives him valuable advice: "Don't let this Harlem git you. I'm in New York but New York ain't in me, understand what I mean? Don't git corrupted."[138] However, Ellison's young hero can neither wake from the terrifying dream of New York nor so easily resist the challenges and the corruptions of the City.

After he speaks up in protest against the eviction of an old couple, former slaves, he finds himself drawn into the Brotherhood, an organization of white Communists whose members set out to exploit his passionate idealism for their own ends. After initiation into the Brotherhood, he is brought downtown to meetings and driven through the Park: "We were flashing through Central Park, now completely transformed by the snow. It was as though we had plunged suddenly into mid-country peace, yet I knew that here, somewhere close by in the night, there was a zoo with its dangerous animals. . . . And there was also the reservoir of dark water, all covered by snow and by night, by snow-fall and by night-fall, buried beneath black and white, gray mist and gray silence."[139] In this arresting description, the City, symbolized by the Park, is transformed into a dangerous jungle, a surface of stark black and white contrast with a hidden realm of gray mystery. Ellison uses color tropes as did Herman Melville in *Moby-Dick*: white hides evil; ambiguous gray colors all. Small wonder that Ellison's hero is wary, even paranoid.

The Brotherhood wants him to be the new Booker T. Washington, leading his people, and for a while he is happy to be just that—stirring crowds in Harlem, where he feels, finally, at home: "I am a new citizen of the country of your vision, a native of your fraternal land."[140] However, when he becomes the Brotherhood's chief spokesman for Harlem, his success is short-lived. Ras the Exhorter, a leader of the Black Nationalist Party, becomes his enemy. After being challenged again within the Brotherhood for careerism, the narrator is demoted and reassigned to lecture on racial aspects of the "woman question." He is also seduced by a wealthy white woman. Ellison's New York City then turns surreal.

A riot takes place at the climax of *Invisible Man*. The narrator's friend, Brother Clifton, is shot dead by a policeman. Ras the Exhorter, now Ras the Destroyer, appears on "a great black horse. . . . A figure more out of a dream than out of Harlem, than out of even this Harlem night, yet real, alive, alarming."[141] In disguise as Rinehart, a confidence man, Ellison's hero sees his whole life and quest as a joke. He finally rejects all of those who would enlist him in their causes: Communism, black nationalism, even opportunism. He throws a spear at Ras. Then he plunges down a manhole. His story has led to this realization: "I'm an invisible man and it placed me in a hole—or showed me the hole I was in, if you will—and I reluctantly accepted the fact."[142] Harlem, then, becomes a black hole in which Ellison's hero lays in wait, sucking power from the City, brooding and dangerous.

For Ellison, "the history of the American Negro is a most intimate part of American history. The novel satirizes those who would divide to conquer, from the Communist Party clone (The Brotherhood) to black nationalists. Through the very process of slavery came the building of the United States."[143] *Invisible Man* thus serves as a warning to those who refuse to acknowledge this American duality and racial interdependence. The novel's young hero transcends, in his mind if not in his experience, his racial and class visions of exclusivity, declaring, "Our fate is to become one, and yet many—This is not prophesy, but description."[144]

In an essay on identity and place, Ellison sees Harlem itself as an underground world: "To live in Harlem is to dwell in the very bowels of the city; it is to pass a labyrinthine existence among streets that explode monotonously skyward with the spires and crosses of churches and clutter under foot with garbage and decay. Harlem is a ruin"—and a nightmare. On the streets of Harlem, when asked "How are you?" often the reply will be "Oh, man, I'm *nowhere!*" For Ellison, "the phrase 'I'm nowhere' expresses the feeling borne in upon many Negroes that they have no stable, recognized place in society." As he was writing *Invisible Man*, Ellison discovered the perfect metaphor for Harlem in the underground wards of the Lafargue Psychiatric Clinic, which extended free psychiatric care to the citizens of Harlem. In the clinic's underground rooms, "a frustrated science goes to find its true object: the confused of mind who seek reality." Just the same can be said for Ralph Ellison's portrait of the artist as a tortured young black man. Fittingly, Ellison's essay on the shaping significance of place was titled "Harlem Is Nowhere."[145]

JAMES BALDWIN WAS BORN AT HARLEM HOSPITAL, IN August 1924, in the midst of the Harlem Renaissance. However, his stepfather, David Baldwin, a religious fanatic who hated all whites for their prejudices and most blacks for their sinfulness, kept his distance from both white and black culture. James Baldwin spent the first eighteen years of his life in Harlem, developing himself in various roles: the attentive eldest of nine children; the stepson of a bitter and stern patriarch; the loyal son of a loving mother; the brilliant, young Pentecostal preacher (surpassing his stepfather), first at the Mount Calvary of the Pentecostal Faith Church on Lenox Avenue, then at the Fireside Pentecostal Assembly on 136th and Fifth Avenue; and, most important, the black artist as a young man.

Between Lenox Avenue to the west, the Harlem River to the east, 135th Street to the north, and 130th Street to the South, James Baldwin came of age: "We never lived beyond these boundaries; this is where we grew up."[146] In those years Harlem was a mixed neighborhood full of the sounds and rituals of Germans, Greeks, Irish, Jews, and other immigrant groups. However, Harlem was a community set against itself, divided as much by money as by race or culture: "There were those who lived on Sugar Hill and there was the hollow, where we lived. There was a great divide between the black people on the Hill and us."[147] Yet Baldwin's Harlem, he discovered as a child, was sufficiently black to make downtown Manhattan seem like alien country: "When you go

downtown you discover that you are literally in a white world. . . . You know—
you know instinctively—that none of this is for you."[148] Harlem was for James
Baldwin—his lifelong psychic center, even when he hated it, even when he left
it behind.

Eventually all of New York City became James Baldwin's neighborhood. Accompanied by a solicitous white teacher, the young Baldwin saw Orson Welles's
production of *Macbeth*, set in Haiti with an all black cast, at Harlem's Lafayette
Theater. Farther from home, Baldwin discovered a hill in Central Park that became a new center for his world; from this hill he could look uptown, toward Harlem, and then gaze downtown, toward the Village—where he would someday
live—and beyond New York City to wider horizons. When Baldwin wrote about
this experience in his first novel, *Go Tell It on the Mountain*, his alter ego, John
Grimes, revels in the sense of power derived from seeing "the skyline of New
York" and imagining himself etched against it. From the hill's heights, John
"felt like a giant who might crumble this city with his anger; he felt like a tyrant
who might crush this city beneath his heel; he felt like a long-awaited conqueror
at whose feet flowers would be strewn, and before whom multitudes cried Ho-
sanna!" New York City for John Grimes, as for James Baldwin, stood as a symbolic moral landscape, across which a pilgrim either progressed or regressed.
John recalled how his preacher stepfather told him that "perdition sucked at the
feet" of the people who walked the City's streets. John and James would both
pursue a less censorious spiritual quest.

> Broadway: *the way that led to death* was *broad, and many could be
> found thereon; but narrow was the way that led to life eternal, and
> few there were who found it. But he did not long for the narrow way,
> where all his people walked; where the houses did not rise, piercing,
> as it seemed, the unchanging clouds, but huddled, flat, ignoble, close
> to the filthy ground, where the streets and the hallways and the rooms
> were dark, and where the unconquerable odor was of dust, and
> sweat, and urine, and homemade gin.*

His stepfather urged John to reject the broad way to perdition and, instead, to
choose the narrow path to the glories of salvation. However, for John, as for Baldwin, "these glories were unimaginable—but the city was real."[149] There, on the
streets of the City, these young men would discover themselves.

In 1936 Baldwin enrolled in Frederick Douglass Junior High, where he came under the influence of Countee Cullen, who taught French and served as literary advisor, inspiring dreams of foreign travel and literary glory. Studying under another teacher, Baldwin wrote an essay, "Harlem—Then and Now," published in the *Douglass Pilot*, which showed his increasing consciousness of place and its cultural complexities: "I wonder how many of us have ever stopped to think what Harlem was like two or three centuries ago? Or how it came to be as it is today?"[150] Here Baldwin precociously articulates his own literary mission: to bring to consciousness Harlem, in all of its aspects, as a model of black life and as a paradigm of the American experience.

At DeWitt Clinton High in the Bronx, where he encountered a diverse, though largely Jewish, student body (Irving Howe, author of *World of Our Fathers*, was one of many distinguished graduates), Baldwin was an academic star and wrote plays, stories, and poems—works that showed his debt to the dialect poems of Langston Hughes.[151] After high school graduation in 1941, Baldwin joined the workforce to help support his brothers and sisters. While laying track as a railroad hand in New Jersey in 1942, Baldwin experienced a maddening encounter with American racism, recorded in *Notes of a Native Son*.

Like Ellison, Baldwin traces the personal and social costs exacted when citizens of the same republic refuse to acknowledge each other's existence. The title essay of *Notes of a Native Son* opens in the Harlem of July 1943, at a moment of personal and public convergence—Baldwin has turned nineteen, his stepfather has just died, and Harlem is being torn apart by a race riot. The riot seems to confirm the elder Baldwin's apocalyptic vision, though James tries to reject his stepfather's bitterness and paranoia, particularly his hatred for white Americans. However, Jimmy, as he is called, learns firsthand that his stepfather's anger was not unfounded: "I learned in New Jersey that to be a Negro meant, precisely, that one was never looked at but was simply at the mercy of the reflexes the color of one's skin caused in other people." He, too, is an invisible man in white America. Though he has left Harlem, Baldwin cannot escape its lessons.

Like Ellison's violent encounter between his invisible man and a white stranger, young Baldwin is pulled into a confrontation with whites. After going to a film in Trenton, he and a white friend enter "the American Diner"—for Baldwin, as for Ellison, the use of heavy symbolism extends the significance of the confrontation—and Baldwin is turned away. He feels sudden, blind rage; that is, he suddenly becomes his father's son. Testing his limits, he pushes his way into a fashionable restaurant where, he well knows, no black is ever seated.

When a frightened white waitress tells him he will not be served, Baldwin turns murderous, wanting to choke her; instead, he picks up a half-full water mug and flings it at her. Then he runs, shocked at the danger to which he has exposed himself and horrified that he has been, like Ellison's furious man in the crowd or Wright's Bigger Thomas, ready to kill. As Baldwin says, "My life, my *real* life, was in danger, and not from anything other people might do but from the hatred I carried in my heart."[152] For both Ellison and Baldwin, the problematic heritage of Harlem was the burden of hatred: the realization that blacks were indeed invisible and the even more frightening recognition that racial prejudice dehumanizes the victim as well as victimizer. Indeed, blacks and whites, for Ellison and for Baldwin, in and beyond Harlem, were caught in a mutually murderous syndrome of prejudice and paranoia.

In the first sentence of his "Autobiographical Notes" in *Notes of a Native Son*, Baldwin defines himself in relation to Harlem: "I was born in Harlem thirty-one years ago."[153] In "The Harlem Ghetto," Baldwin sees Harlem as an unchanging place of "bitter expectancy," ever awaiting a hard winter. Blacks and whites, he notes, see different Harlems: "All of Harlem is pervaded by a sense of congestion, rather like the insistent, maddening, claustrophobic pounding in the skull that comes from trying to breathe in a very small room with all the windows shut. Yet the white man walking through Harlem is not at all likely to find it sinister or more wretched than any other slum."[154] The remainder of Baldwin's essay discusses the problematic relation between Harlem's blacks and Jews, an issue that emerged from his childhood experiences and nagged him until his death.

In *Nobody Knows My Name* (1961), his second collection of essays, Baldwin describes his escape from Harlem to Greenwich Village, then his move from the Village to Europe. In "Fifth Avenue, Uptown: A Letter from Harlem," he returns to the circumscribed world of his youth. He contemplates the hated housing projects in which blacks are trapped: "The pressure within the ghetto causes the ghetto walls to expand, and this expansion is always violent."[155]

In his operatic novel, *Another Country* (1962), Baldwin again returns to the City for defining parables of black life and American destiny. Right from the start, his hero, Rufus, is squeezed by the pressures of New York City: "He was facing Seventh Avenue, at Times Square," walking under huge signs that display the names of Broadway stars. "Beneath them Rufus walked, one of the fallen—for the weight of the city was murderous—one of those who had been crushed on the day, which was every day, these towers fell." Like Baldwin, Rufus has sought to escape from Harlem, only to discover that he carries it with

him: "He had fled, so he had thought, from the beat of Harlem, which was simply the beat of his own heart."[156] Rufus takes up with a white woman who loves
New York, but he remembers only urban disasters—how, for example, a child
had drowned in the Harlem River. As Rufus moves toward his inevitable suicide, by jumping off the George Washington Bridge, he is consumed by a horrific, un-Whitmanian vision of the people of the City: "At Fifty-ninth Street a
man came on board [the subway] and many rushed across the platform to the
waiting local. Many white people and many black people, chained together in
time and in space, and by history, and all of them in a hurry. In a hurry to get
away from each other, he thought, but we ain't ever going to make it. We been
fucked for fair."[157]

"Sonny's Blues," a story included in *Going to Meet the Man* (1965), may be
James Baldwin's definitive statement on the New York City experience. The
story is told from the point of view of a cautious, conventional narrator, a high
school algebra teacher who is in shock when he learns that his young brother,
Sonny, a jazz pianist, has been arrested for "peddling and using heroin." Sonny
and the narrator represent two impulses, Apollonian and Dionysian, each of
which is destructive without the other. Each brother must acknowledge the
other, but this test is more difficult for the repressed narrator than it is for the
risk-taking Sonny. Only after Gracie, his daughter, dies can the older brother
write to Sonny; only then can he begin to understand an alienation so great that
it can lead Sonny to heroin addiction.

The narrator had sought a haven for himself and his family from "the vivid,
killing streets of our childhood." But he comes to realize that "these streets
hadn't changed, though housing projects jutted up out of them now like rocks in
the middle of a boiling sea." Safety was the lost dream of childhood. He could
not protect his own daughter from death. Stripped, finally, of his illusions and
his sense of superiority, the narrator is finally ready to *hear* his brother's music.
When Sonny improvises on "Am I Blue," the narrator finally understands; jazz
carries the teacher into a place where he learns that the dead can return to give
comfort. Sonny's knowing art, the bitter lyricism of the blues, helps his brother
to *see*: "And I was yet aware that this was only a moment, that the world waited
outside, as hungry as a tiger, and that trouble stretched above us longer than the
sky."[158] In this story of Harlem, Baldwin shows a character moving toward enlightenment by expanding his consciousness of life's dark, destructive
elements.

James Baldwin's funeral in Harlem, in the Cathedral of St. John the Divine on December 8, 1987, was held a few blocks away from where he was born, sixty-three years before. Baldwin's passing, it might be said, marked the true end of the Harlem Renaissance. W. J. Weatherby's tribute expresses the nature of the relationship between this writer and his City.

> *He had departed from Harlem when he was eighteen never to return except for brief visits, but as a writer he never left. In book after book, including those he was working on the last year, he returned obsessively to the Harlem he had grown up in. . . . . He kept the faith—the Harlem test—in all the ways that mattered. For many white Americans even when they gave up listening, he remained the messenger with bad news right up to the end.*[159]

JAMES WELDON JOHNSON, WE RECALL, DECLARED "Harlem is not merely a Negro colony or community, it is a city within a city, the greatest Negro city in the world. It is not a slum or fringe, it is located in the heart of Manhattan and occupies one of the most beautiful and healthful sections of the city." In 1925, when those brave words were written—when the famous Civic Club dinner was held, when *The New Negro* was published—Harlem was developing its presence as a black metropolis and establishing the identity eloquently expressed in the works of the Harlem Renaissance. Writers invented original metaphors and told new tales to illustrate the central presence of African-American life and culture in the City and the nation. They composed a literature of intense expression, ambivalent attitudes, symbolic reach, and national implications. Their works shifted the angle of vision on the American dream from F. Scott Fitzgerald's downtown rooftops to Ralph Ellison's uptown underground cave.

However, this flowering of arts and letters was brief, collapsing early in the Great Depression, though its influence remains. In every sense of the word, Harlem came to seem a much *darker* place. This is evident in two works published in 1965, *The Autobiography of Malcolm X* and Claude Brown's *Manchild in the Promised Land*, books that describe the fatal attractions of the City for bright young men drawn into self-awareness and self-destructiveness in New York. Malcolm X would become, in his succinct summary of his own and the City's degeneration, "one of the most depraved parasitical hustlers among New York's eight million people—four million of whom work, and the other four million of whom live off them."[160] Of course, he also made himself over into a charismatic

African-American leader. But Malcolm X was shot and killed in the Audubon Ballroom, on 166th Street, in 1965; thereafter, he became mythologized as a sacrificial victim of conflicting versions of black identity.[161] In *Manchild in the Promised Land*, Claude Brown portrays a Harlem in which "there were too many people full of hate and bitterness crowded into a dirty, stinky, uncared-for closet-size section of a great city."[162] Harlem, in the literary imagination of its most gifted citizens and pilgrims, stands at the center of the City of Destruction.

NEW YORK CITY

IN THE THIRTIES

New York's Hard Times

In THE MID 1930s, DUST STORMS SWEPT ACROSS KANSAS, Nebraska, the Dakotas, and Oklahoma like the wrath of God; in the midst of the Great Depression, they dramatized human helplessness before overwhelming natural forces.[1] Ben Shahn, Walker Evans, and Dorothea Lang captured this condition in a series of striking black-and-white photographs; Woody Guthrie in song ("I ain't got no home in this world anymore"); John Steinbeck in fiction, *The Grapes of Wrath*; and John Ford in his film adaptation of that novel. In America's cities, examples of helplessness were even more evident, as its artists and writers demonstrated. The urban version of the dust storms were the bread line, the shantytowns called "Hoovervilles," the empty, ominous skyscrapers, and the sight of homeless, unemployed men selling apples on street corners for five cents apiece—images documented in hundreds of grainy photographs and newsreels.[2] As the American heartland suffered from natural disaster, economic failure became evident everywhere in the nation, most dramatically in New York City.

In October 1929, the failure of the stock market changed America. A headline in *Variety* for October 30, 1929, cried "WALL STREET LAYS AN EGG," placing the blame at the nation's financial center. By the middle of November, the market had dropped some 40 percent in value and it would fall farther.[3] Six months after the Crash, more than four million Americans were out of work. New York City, the nation's center of culture, business, and finance, was, more than ever, the symbolic American city during the Great Depression.

As New York City offered, in the Wall Street Crash, an image of national decline, so too, in the World's Fair, which opened on April 30, 1939, would it offer a symbol of American recovery. The Fair's theme, "Building the World of Tomorrow," and its centerpiece, the 700-foot-high Trylon and the 200-foot-wide Perisphere, both painted pure white, revived hope in the City and in the nation.[4] (Yet when the Fair closed in late 1940, World War II was under way in Europe and America was on the brink of entry.) Writing in 1938 about the upcoming Fair, the authors of *New York Panorama* were filled with optimism. They predicted that "the City of New York itself will be the smash hit of its own exposition. No vista at the fair will equal the fantastic splendor of the view from a returning Staten Island ferry, and none of its spectacles is likely to match Times Square. The Empire State Building will be something to write home about as the big brother of the trylon."[5] However, between the Crash and the Fair stretched long years of hard times in New York City.

Early in the Great Depression, several grand structures, conceived in the boom years of the 1920s, were completed. In 1930, the seventy-seven story Chrysler Building, at Forty-second Street and Lexington Avenue, was finished, becoming (for one year) the world's tallest building.[6] The Empire State Building, begun before the Crash and opened in 1931, reached higher: 102 stories, 1,250 feet. Rockefeller Center (including Radio City Music Hall and the RCA Building) was completed in 1932. Much anxiety surrounded such projects, for these soaring skyscrapers, containing so many empty offices, loomed in ironic contrast to the despairing lives on the streets below—even, for some, to the sky above. "There is nothing more poetic and terrible than the skyscrapers' battle with the heavens that cover them," wrote Spanish poet and playwright Federico García Lorca, who visited the City in 1929.[7] By 1932 the unemployed and homeless had erected shantytowns along Riverside Drive and had even moved into Central Park, where they built shacks and scavenged in garbage dumps.[8] Mike Gold, a young Communist, wrote about his night in a Hooverville in the *Daily Worker* in 1933: "The nation that year was covered with these miserable colonies of the men without jobs. Here it was in New York, too."[9]

Writers from all across America and from beyond the nation's shores—García Lorca, Gold, Henry Roth, Thomas Wolfe, John O'Hara, Nathaniel West, Clifford Odets, and others—responded to the new, dour mood of the City and tried to convey the full depth of the suffering they saw. Dramatic and denunciatory imagery dominated portrayals of the City in the literature of the 1930s. *Christ in Concrete* (1939), Pietro di Donato's overwrought novel of Italian-American alienation in the City, opens, for example, with an accident at a building site, a collapse that serves as a bold metaphor of capitalism's implosion. The construction workers are just beginning to realize what is happening to them: Suddenly "the bottom of their world gave way. The building shuddered violently, her supports burst with the crackling slap of wooden gunfire. The floor vomited upward. . . . Walls, floors, beams became whirling, solid, splintering waves crashing with detonations that ground man and material in bonds of death."[10] By the end of the novel, the young hero has turned against the economic system that killed his father. In *Christ in Concrete*, di Donato portrays New York as a wasteland, making of the City what Steinbeck, in *The Grapes of Wrath*, did of the countryside.

In the eyes of many writers of the day, foreign and domestic, New York was full of homeless wanderers and prostitutes. The City was a place where young men and women grew up abused and afraid, a land where battles between the possessors and the dispossessed flared, a doomed metropolis where buildings burst into flames, breaking up frantic parties. The streets of the City spewed misery. If the aesthetic and philosophical basis for many of this period's works was realism—an adaptation of narrative techniques and themes developed by Whitman, Howells, Crane, and Dreiser—the effect of many 1930s works was surreal, for the City was often portrayed as a living nightmare.

That, of course, was not the whole story line of New York in the 1930s. As we will see, writers responded to the City's infinite variety with an adventurous range of styles and attitudes. Many still saw the City as the only place to live for those who chose the writer's trade. As James T. Farrell, who came from Chicago to New York in 1927, said, "Ambitions were poured into this city." (Although Farrell also wondered what had happened to those ambitions: "Here is one of the main things I must develop, discover, correlate, and put down.")[11] Others, notably Damon Runyon, saw the City as a place of raffish charm—best captured in humorous dislocations that ignored true deprivations. Like generations of writers before them, some writers during the Great Depression—Mary McCarthy, for example—sought in the City opportunity for self-transformation, escape from parochialism, sexual and intellectual release, and the attainment of a new level of awareness they were not likely to discover anywhere else.

But the dominant images that appear in the literature of New York City during the 1930s were lurid, extravagant, and lethal in their implications. During this period, the metastory of New York told of promising young men and women who were coming of age, with the City serving as the site of their initiation. The young heroes of the novels, plays, and poems of the 1930s typically discover their limited powers to control their destinies. New York City was seen, even more than before, as an organism dictating the fate of those it surrounds. Above all, the representative figures of these works come to see economic victimization as the City's salient fact. Sexual exploitation, particularly of young women, was also depicted as a frequent occurrence in the New York of this era. These young men and women learn that the promises of American life have not been kept, that life elsewhere—typically in Europe, not back where they came from—might be better. They are unable to change things, but they wait in vain for someone to come who is able to redeem them and their City. As a result, the protagonists of many of these works have limited choices between political radicalization and alienation. Some works conclude in riots or demonstrations. Others end in the central character's death. In most cases, the works of this dark period in the life of the City climax in disillusionment.

Because the Great Depression was so pervasive and enduring, many writers of the 1930s turned away from the self-obsessiveness of the 1920s. They saw in their own and in their characters' tales patterns of larger significance that revealed the heart of the City, of the nation, of the human condition. In "The Crack-Up," published as three pieces in *Esquire* in 1936, F. Scott Fitzgerald made a moral and spiritual accounting that placed his life in the wider context of his age. His twenties, like the period of revelry and plenty known as the Jazz Age, passed in a blur of boozy success, but the thirties meant crack-up for Fitzgerald and for America. Fitzgerald came to the characteristically 1930s realization "that the natural state of the sentient adult is a qualified unhappiness." The ecstasy that he had frequently experienced a decade before, decided Fitzgerald, "was not the natural thing, but the unnatural—unnatural as the Boom; and my recent experience parallels the wave of despair that swept over the nation when the Boom was over."[12]

Many writers in these years played changes on Fitzgerald's realization that personal depletion paralleled national decay; that the party in America, which had been most avidly celebrated in New York City, was over; that it was time to put away childish things; that the Great Depression placed great demands upon their abilities as writers to come up with what William Butler Yeats called, in another context, "befitting emblems of adversity."[13]

It was "A low dishonest decade," wrote W. H. Auden in "September 1, 1939." Auden issued his judgment from "one of the dives/ On

Fifty-second Street," where he watched "the clever hopes expire" among those "faces along the bar."[14] Auden wrote this poem at the beginning of the Second World War, looking back on the City in the 1930s. García Lorca, looking upon the City for the first time at the end of the 1920s, anticipated Auden's vision in even more vivid imagery, establishing grotesque surrealism as a style appropriate to New York in the thirties.

Federico García Lorca arrived in New York City from Spain in June 1929 and stayed until March 1930. He saw the visit as "useful," for he was recovering from a failed love affair and escaping censorship in his homeland; however, he also found the visit depressing. He was "a lonely poet," writes Rafael Alberti, "lost amid docks and avenues and skyscrapers, returning in nostalgia and anguish to his little room at Columbia University."[15] Out of that lonely encounter came *Poet in New York* (1940), a posthumously published collection of poems expressing his contorted vision of the City. "His city," writes Peter Conrad, "is a body of diseased extremism, and his images are its lesions, because the surrealist image records the agonizing dissolution of forms."[16]

García Lorca's New York City is an abattoir. "New York is something awful, something monstrous," he told an interviewer. "I like to walk the streets, lost, but I recognize that New York is the world's great lie." It promised a freedom of expression, political and sexual, that it did not deliver.[17] Inspired by the poetic hubris of Hart Crane, García Lorca reached after striking images of nausea to characterize the City. His "dawn in New York," for example, is symbolized by a swarm of black pigeons "splashing in the putrid waters."[18] García Lorca again anticipated Auden in condemning the capitalist power structure of the City, particularly the oppression of its black citizens, whose natural vigor and rhythm had been "mechanized," he believed, by the culture of commerce. Lorca's heart's cry was unambiguous: "New York, mire,/ New York, wire and death."[19]

Auden and García Lorca were European poets who were horrified by New York City. Nathaniel West was a New York novelist who developed his own line of surreal and grotesque expression to portray the City.[20] Born Nathan Weinstein in New York City in 1903, West knew the City, from its uptown intellectuals to its downtown artists. After his graduation from Brown in 1924 and his father's death, West, as he renamed himself, became the assistant manager of the Kenmore Hotel, at East Twenty-third Street, in 1927, then o) the Sutton Hotel, at East Fifty-sixth Street. At both hotels West met (and often gave free rooms to) a number of important writers, among them Quentin Reynolds, Dashiell Hammett, Maxwell Bodenheim.[21]

In March 1929, West met a woman in a Village restaurant who wrote an advice column for the *Brooklyn Eagle* under an assumed name. She thought West's dinner companion, S. J. Perelman, might be able to get some comic use out of the letters she received from New York's outcasts, but it was West who recognized their pathos.[22] He was inspired to write *Miss Lonelyhearts* (1933), a novel of New Yorkers in the depths of economic and personal depression who seek advice to help them with their desperate lives from a newspaper man who calls himself "Miss Lonelyhearts." "The New York of Miss Lonelyhearts, heartache columnist for the *New York Post-Dispatch*, is a dismal landscape without relief," writes Robert A. Gates.[23] However, the novel's message was not limited to New York City.

Miss Lonelyhearts finds the letters he is assigned to answer "no longer funny." "Desperate," for example, who was born without a nose, asks, "Ought I commit suicide?"[24] The letters reinforce the narrator's view of the world as a place without coherence, meaning, or remission of pain. Though West's novel stands as another indictment of the cold, callous City, it is more. Miss Lonelyhearts' wanderings through the streets of the City only confirm his vision of cosmic alienation. Even the sky reflects a sick universe; it "looked as if it had been rubbed with a soiled eraser."[25] Around him skyscrapers "menaced the little park from all sides."[26] In West's universe, there is no escape anywhere. Even "in the deep shade" of the countryside, where he goes with a friend to flee urban horrors, "there was nothing but death—rotten leaves, gray and white fungi, and over everything a funereal hush."[27] After a brief respite in the country, Miss Lonelyhearts drives back into the City, through the Bronx slums, noticing that "crowds of people moved through the street with a dream-like violence."[28] This violence foreshadows his own grotesque, sacrificial death at the hands of a desperate, jealous, crippled man. New York City, for Nathaniel West, was an example of a universe gone awry.

So, too, was the New York City of Eugene O'Neill. O'Neill's *The Iceman Cometh* was not a protest play, but a dramatized meditation on the nature of man; revolution, his play implied, is just another illusion, for rescue from the human condition of suffering is impossible. His characters live in a world without meaning. Though *The Iceman Cometh* was not completed until 1940 (and not produced until 1946) and the play was set in 1912, it belongs in a study of works of the 1930s that characterize the soul of the City. Period concerns and techniques are reflected in the play's theme (the pathos of the human condition), manner of presentation (realistic set and dialogue), and tone (bitter).

The setting of *The Iceman Cometh* is based upon Jimmy-the-Priest's West Side bar and rooming house, which O'Neill frequented in his misspent youth. In this play the bar is called Harry Hope's, "a cheap gin mill of the five-cent whiskey, last-resort variety situated on the downtown West Side of New York," O'Neill explains.[29] O'Neill populates the bar with a vivid collection of social outcasts who, with time on their hands, spin fabulous excuses for their failures and articulate unrealistic expectations of rescue from their pathetic lives. Even Larry Slade, whose cynicism seems complete, has, like Harry Hope's other barflies, a hidden faith that he will be saved someday. As he tells the night bartender, "I'll be glad to pay up—tomorrow."[30]

While they drone about all that "tomorrow" will bring, the men in the bar await the annual visit of Hickey, a charismatic hardware salesman, who usually picks up their spirits with his bluster and his tall tales. However, when Hickey finally does arrive, he proceeds to strip the men at Harry Hope's of all their comforting self-justifications and their delusory hopes. Hickey believes that his friends will be better off without their illusions; he keeps reassuring them, "The one thing I want is to see you all happy before I go. . . . Can't you see there is no tomorrow now? You're rid of it forever!"[31] But his clearsightedness is revealed to be bankrupt, a rationalization, when he admits that he has killed his wife. The false Messiah turns out to be a murderer. Hickey's gospel is that life in the City, indeed, life anywhere, is unbearable. O'Neill places New York City at the dramatic center of this dark revelation.

T HE CITY IMPARTS DIFFERENT LESSONS TO ITS CITIZENS and does so in a variety of ways. One of the most striking tales of coming of age in the City from this period is Henry Roth's *Call it Sleep* (1934). Roth dramatizes the struggle of a displaced Jewish immigrant family living on the Lower East Side: Albert Schearl, his wife, Geya, and his son, David. David gets lost between the hostilities of his home and the terrors of the City, through whose streets he wanders in search of a self. The City is an alienating place for this Yiddish-speaking family. The City is also a brutal instructor, for example, when David learns about sexuality in "The Cellar" section of the novel. He discovers that the lessons of the City are hard to assimilate, impossible to escape, and dire. After a beating from his father, David runs away, and, overwrought, he inserts a metal dipper can into the trolley track on Tenth Street. Here the City imparts an electric shock upon David, a moment of transcendence. David seems to escape the closing walls of the City without invoking a political Messiah. The novel climaxes in a mixed chorus of urban voices that surround David. Elements of the City project their presence in surreal fashion: "The street paused. . . . While at the foot of Tenth Street, a quaking splendor dissolved the cobbles, the grimy structures, bleary stables, the dump-heap, river and sky into a single cymbal-clash of light."[32] As Alfred Kazin says, "with this novel we are in the city-world not of *Sister Carrie* but of James Joyce's *Ulysses*."[33] Art, for Roth, as it was for García Lorca and others, served as a refuge from the ravages of the City. But Roth's artistic commitment conflicted with his political commitment when he joined the Communist Party in 1933, so he fell silent for more than half a century.

Sixty years after publishing *Call It Sleep*, Henry Roth continued his saga of transformation in the first volume, *A Star Shines over Mt. Morris Park*, of a projected six-volume novel, *Mercy of a Rude Stream* (1994). In this work, David Schearl is called Ira Stigman, whose family moves from the Lower East Side to 119th Street, into "Jewish Harlem," where he is surrounded by Irish "goys" and where he feels doubly alienated. However, Roth's long-delayed second novel portrays a young man who survives the dislocations and traumas of the City to become a streetwise adolescent and who may grow up to become a writer capable of composing *Call It Sleep*. Henry Roth, at age eighty-seven, promises that the rest of his New York City epic, clearly a fictionalized autobiography about surviving in the City, will be completed.[34]

Mike Gold, born Irwin Granich (1893), was another native New Yorker who wrote about coming of age and hard times on the Lower East Side. Less modernist than Roth, Gold balanced his sentimental evocation of New York with political messages. Little shocked and less surprised Gold in New York, who loved the City, yet he too saw its horrific aspects. In *Jews Without Money* (1930), he wrote of the unfulfilled "hunger for country things" that he and his peers suffered: "New York is a devil's dream, the most urbanized city in the world. It is all geometry angles and stone. It is mythical, a city buried by a volcano. No grass is found in this petrified city, no big living trees, no flowers, no bird but the drab little lecherous sparrow, no soil, loam, earth; fresh earth to smell, earth to walk on, to roll on, and love like a woman. Just stone. It is the ruins of Pompeii, except that seven million animals full of earth-love must dwell in the dead lava streets."[35] Gold was converted to Communism at age nineteen when he was knocked down during a police charge on a crowd demonstrating in Union

Square. He eventually wrote for the *Masses*, the *Liberator*, and the *New Masses*, where he took over as editor from Max Eastman in 1928.

Gold promoted proletarian literature, literary expressions of sympathy for (sometimes by) "the disinherited," as Jack Conroy called oppressed workers in his 1933 novel.[36] "Proletarian literature will reflect the struggle of the workers in their fight for the world," wrote Gold in the *New Masses* in the 1930s.[37] But proletarian literature, as *Partisan Review* editor Philip Rahv has said, was also the literature of the Communist Party disguised as the literature of class.[38]

Despite Gold's ideology, *Jews Without Money* is more an evocative memoir than a political tract; only in the book's final words is the young Gold radicalized, while listening to "a man on an East Side soap-box" talk about poverty. The experience of growing up poor in New York City was so traumatizing for Gold that only a compensatory faith in the "Workers' Revolution" made him believe in the Messiah: "You will destroy the East Side when you come, and build there a garden for the human spirit."[39] As Malcolm Cowley put it in the title of a memoir of the 1930s, "the dream of the golden mountains," was political not religious for many young writers of his day. Like Gold, Cowley underwent "essentially a religious experience" in political terms. They looked for the collapse of New York, the City of Mammon, so that, said Cowley, "a City of Man would rise on the other side of the disaster."[40]

Many novels of the 1930s followed the pattern of Gold's memoir. For example, Albert Halper's *Union Square* (1933), a pro-Communist work, climaxes in a Union Square confrontation between a crowd of Communist demonstrators and the police, who are defending the bastions of capitalism.[41] A central symbol of Union Square for Halper was Klein's, a huge department store specializing in low-priced women's clothing, a cathedral of commerce where shoppers battle for bargains. Tatty shops and theaters surrounding Klein's amplify Halper's portrayal of capitalism's divisive effects on the City. For Halper the forces of good and evil are opposed in the street battle, echoing the symbolism of earlier fictional accounts of confrontations between police and demonstrators, for example, by Howells and Dreiser.

Daniel Fuchs's novels—*Summer in Williamsburg* (1934), *Homage to Blenholt* (1936), and *Low Company* (1937)—center on the Jewish immigrant communities in Brooklyn: Williamsburg and Coney Island. For Fuchs these urban ghettos are summed up in the image of the hangman's noose. His protagonists struggle but they do not escape these lethal landscapes.[42] Given the evidence of these narratives by Henry Roth, Mike Gold, and others, it is amazing that any bright young men and women survived to maturity in New York City in this era.

In SOME OF THE SIGNIFICANT PARABLES OF THE PERIOD, those who did survive childhood and adolescence in the City grew up to fight the system that ground them down. In his kinetic play *Waiting for Lefty* (1935), Clifford Odets effectively dramatized the political alienation and radicalization of the time and invited his audience to rise up against the forces of oppression.

Clifford Odets was born in Philadelphia in 1906, but his family moved to the Bronx when he was six; his plays drew upon the energy and verbal vigor of his working-class Jewish neighborhood. As a young actor in the road company of *Abie's Irish Rose*, Odets joined the Group Theater. In 1934 he briefly became a member of the Communist Party, but he left when he saw that it would compromise his art.

In *Waiting for Lefty*, Odets caught the mood of righteous anger that characterized New York City in the 1930s. Odets based this play on the New York City taxi strike of 1934; it is set as a union meeting in which cabbies debate a strike motion. Fatt, a union organizer, tries to keep his union members from striking, but they await Lefty Costello, a committeeman in whom they place their trust, to lead them. While they wait, Odets presents a series of scenes that serve to fill in the background of characters involved in the strike and to amplify its significance. Joe's wife, Edna, urges him to stand up against bullying cab company owners. Miller, a scientist who is forced to drive a cab, refuses a lucrative job for a chemical company that plans to develop poison gas. Florrie is urged by her brother not to marry Sid, a hack driver, until times get better. Clayton, a labor spy, is exposed by his brother. Dr. Benjamin is dismissed from his medical post because he is a Jew. When the play turns back to the strike meeting, a union member rises and criticizes Fatt. Don't wait for Lefty, he shouts. When it is announced that Lefty is dead—implying that the cabbies will have to lead themselves—the same critical union member begins the chant for a strike.

The play's opening performance in January 1935, at the old Civic Repertory Theater on Fourteenth Street, caused a sensation. A wave of acknowledgment went through the audience, recalls Harold Clurman, director of the Group Theater, where Odets's early plays were developed. "When the audience at the end of the play responded to the militant question from the stage: 'Well, what is the answer?' with a spontaneous roar of 'Strike! Strike!' it was something more than a tribute to the play's effectiveness, even than a testimony of the audience's hunger for constructive social action. It was the birth cry of the thirties. Our youth had found its voice."[43]

When members of the audience rose and cried "Strike!" they ceased to be an audience and became, instead, participants in the class struggle. Odets thus transformed artistic into political expression. He divided his New York into haves and have-nots, two nations at war, and he urged his viewers to decide which side they were on. "The play is one-sided in its outlook and is often questionable in terms of its logic; but in 1935 it spoke with a force which few playwrights have ever been able to attain and which Odets, as he became more artistically aware, was never to attain again."[44]

A month after *Waiting for Lefty* was produced, Odets succeeded again in *Awake and Sing!* This play focuses upon a family much like his own; the Bergers live in a crowded Bronx apartment, where they and their friends debate the meaning of the Depression. Young Ralph Berger, employing truisms of the day, wonders why success requires moral compromise, "why so much dirt must be cleared away before it is possible to 'get to first base.'"[45] However, Uncle Morty has done well in his clothing sweatshop by exploiting laborers, so he has no worries. On the other hand, Moe Axelrod, a small-time racketeer who lost a leg in the Great War, sees everything in America as a scam. At the end of the play, inspired by the death of his grandfather, Ralph, Odets's moral spokesman, declares that fighting for "nickels" has transformed houses and neighborhoods into places ruled by hatred: "We don't want life printed on dollar bills, Mom!"[46] The play, says Clurman, "was written out of the distress of the 1932 depression (not to mention Odets's whole youth)."[47]

Both *Waiting for Lefty* and *Awake and Sing!* end with characters' denouncing economic oppressors, and both plays urged their 1930s audience to do something about injustice. Though Odets's plays stirred no revolution on the streets of Manhattan, they did help to transform the American theater into an arena where attention would be paid to the victims of capitalism: the castoff laborers who had outlived their usefulness in the workplace but who still fought to survive in the City. Odets's play prepared the way for Arthur Miller's *Death of a Salesman*, perhaps the greatest drama about New York City.

THOMAS WOLFE OFFERS A PARTICULARLY INTERESTING case study of initial attraction to the City and eventual repulsion from it. A prose rhapsodist devoted to celebrations of his various, ever-transforming selves, Wolfe seemed well-suited to the mercurial extravagance of New York, just the place for his overweening ego, his adolescent rapturousness, and his rococo sensibility, which bounced from wonder to horror without pause. In the end, the City was too much for Thomas Wolfe, as it was for his fictional heroes. The City exacted too high a price for success—the loss of self. Its rich, beautiful women were too demanding and were finally alien to his nature. New York City existed, for Thomas Wolfe, to be courted, won, and finally, rejected as unworthy.

Wolfe first saw New York City in 1920, at age twenty; he was on his way from Asheville, North Carolina, to enter the English master's program at Harvard. At the time, he imagined New York as "the ecstatic Northern city" and added in his "Autobiographical Outline," that "no other city has ever given me anything to compare it with."[48] Eugene Gant, the hero of Wolfe's autobiographical novel, *Of Time and the River* (1935), is equally enchanted by the City: " 'Incredible! Oh, incredible! It moves, it pulses like a single living thing! It lives, it lives, with all its million faces'—and this is the way he always knew it was."[49] Gant soon sees, however, "men starving in the heart of a great plantation."[50]

Wolfe describes the City, through Gant's eyes, in characteristically extreme terms: "Around him, in the streets, again, as winter came, he heard a million words of hate and death: a million words of snarl and sneer and empty threat, of foul mistrust and lying slander."[51] By night Gant sees, luridly lit, "the pale and swarthy faces of a million rats of the flesh," while by day he sees, at the university, "the venomous faces of the rats of the spirit."[52] Yet Gant, like Poe's man of the crowd, is drawn inexorably into his fateful encounter, for what the City offers is the knowledge of good and evil.

Gant visits a friend from his Harvard days, Joel Pierce, at his family's mansion overlooking the upper Hudson River. There Gant tries to explain to Mrs. Pierce his restless walks through the City. At first he thinks he can tell her "about the city's dark and secret heart, and what lay buried in the dark and secret heart of all America," but he finds he cannot express himself.[53] He cannot adequately describe, for example, the thrill he gets from ascending the Brooklyn Bridge, "the bridge of power, life and joy, the bridge that was a span, a cry, an ecstasy—that was America"—or his disillusionment with the lives of New York's very rich.[54] The City strikes Gant speechless.

Gant—who, like Wolfe, has several teaching stints at New York University in the 1920s—witnesses the City's heartlessness in the sterile university and its perverse students. In Gant's world, the most deformed, yet the most resilient students are Jewish. Gant, for example, meets Abe Jones and his sister, Sylvia, whose body has been bent by life on the Lower East Side. Sylvia stands in Wolfe's mind as a model for Jewish women who suffer but survive, at the cost of their humanity. Gant realizes "that they had lived so long and grown so wise and crafty that their subtle, million-noted minds could do without and hold in dark contempt the clumsy imperfections of a fleshly evil." In Wolfe's bitter, anti-Semitic vision, the City kills the spirit and its citizens worship idols—"of which the most heroic was the gangster, the most sagacious was a pimp, the most witty was some Broadway clown."[55] In Thomas Wolfe's New York, only the rich and the cunning survive.

"For Wolfe, the City absorbs its citizens, leaving behind mere shells of former humanity. The outlines of the human physique are chiselled into hard angularity by the City's heartlessness," writes Robert A. Gates.[56] This is especially clear in one of Wolfe's most autobiographical stories, "No Door." In this tale a young writer visits a millionaire and his mistress in a penthouse near the East River. The writer wants to be a citizen of this world, but he can find "no door" through which to enter, much as Hurstwood could not enter that walled city of privilege.[57] Disappointed, Wolfe's writer returns to his flat in South Brooklyn. The flat is shaped like a pullman car: one long room with barred windows at each end; it is clammy, and it smells of the Gowanus Canal. Though he is hemmed in, when the writer hears the noise of his neighbors' argument, he is pleased to be there. Wolfe suggests that the apartment in Balcony Square, however dreary, stands far closer to the truth of the human condition than the millionaire's East River place, where the wealthy enclose themselves, cut off from contact with other New Yorkers.

In *The Web and the Rock* (1939), the Wolfian hero, now called George Webber, is still trying to break down "that great door, the huge, hinged, secret wall of life."[58] Briefly, he finds entry into New York's high society through his lover, Esther Jack, but then everything falls apart. Esther Jack's house stands on the West Side between West End Avenue and the river. Webber is fascinated by the luxury he discovers there: "Everything in the house seemed to have been put there to give joy and comfort to people." The big house holds the promise of American life, a place where "the belief in success and golden wealth touches everything."[59] However, George and Esther soon separate, and the hopes inspired by her great home fade. George had sought in the City what Esther represents—culture, sophistication, money, and sex—but he comes to realize that she, like the City, threatens to possess him, so he rejects them both.

Wolfe's definitive statement on New York City was framed in a short novel published in *Scribner's Magazine* (1939), *The Party at Jack's*, which was, in turn, incorporated into *You Can't Go Home Again* (1940).[60] The story continues the urban saga of George Webber, who renews his relations with Esther Jack. In heavy symbolism, Wolfe makes Mr. and Mrs. Jack's party, held exactly one week before the stock market crash of 1929, into a model of the decadent 1920s, the era of the great American binge and bust. Wolfe's satirical depiction of the party takes its tone from the anticapitalism of the 1930s.

The Jacks' "house" is in a large square building, with a central courtyard, which covers a City block. There representatives of all classes, guests and servants, gather for a party more opulent than any Gatsby threw. But George decides, once again, that he is through with Esther Jack and her way of life. "Could he as a novelist, as an artist, belong to this high world of privilege without taking upon himself the stultifying burden of that privilege?"[61] He decides, as did the writer in "No Door," that he cannot. Perhaps the party is described so fully by Wolfe—as other parties are in Edgar Allan Poe's "The Masque of the Red Death" and Tom Wolfe's *The Bonfire of the Vanities*—because the collective dance of death is a central conceit for many literary Jeremiahs of the City.

Retribution comes as a fire that stops the party at the Jacks' home, a fire that reveals and undermines the whole structure of invidious distinction upon which Wolfe's City is built. The wealthy run in panic from their no-longer-safe habitations. "Some of them felt, dimly, that they had been caught up in some mysterious and relentless force, and that they were being borne onward as unwitting of the power that ruled them as blind flies fastened to a revolving wheel."[62] Their social "inferiors" are stalled as the subway tunnels fill with water. The whole superstructure of society quivers; Esther even experiences a premonition of financial disaster when she worries about "faint tremors in the [stock] market."[63] While the fire is being put out, there is a brief moment of comradeship in the courtyard among the survivors, high and low; however, this is quickly forgotten when it is safe to go back inside. Thomas Wolfe makes his point inescapable: New York City, symbolized by the Jacks' house and party, is a city hanging on the edge of self-destruction—either by fire or by class warfare.

THOMAS WOLFE FOUND A SANCTUARY FROM NEW YORK City in Berlin in the 1930s. Henry Miller found his home-away-from-home in Paris. Miller was born in 1891 in Manhattan and was brought up in the Williamsburg and Bushwick sections of Brooklyn, though he became a wanderer as a young man and he set his most memorable works elsewhere. In 1935 Miller left his beloved Paris and returned to New York in pursuit of Anaïs Nin, who had left Miller and Paris in the company of the psychologist Otto Rank. When, after a few months, Nin decided to return to Paris, Miller did too, though he did not mention this in his long letter to a French friend, Emil Schnellock, a letter published as *Aller Retour New York*.[64] In this letter, a litany of his disenchantment with America, Miller saw all things in New York as inferior to those in Paris: "Everywhere it is drunkenness and vomiting, or breaking of windows and smashing heads. Twice recently I narrowly missed being cracked over the head. People walk the streets at night lit up and looking for trouble. They come on you unexpectedly and invite you to fight—for the fun of it! It must be the climate—*and the machine*. The machines are driving them screwy. Nothing is done by hand anymore."[65] Though politically indifferent, scorning both the have-nots and the rich, Miller, like Wolfe, saw New York City as the symbolic center of American corruption.

Miller was jealous and bitter about the reception of Wolfe's *Of Time and the River*, which was then being hailed as the great American novel, but he shared Wolfe's anti-Semitism: "All New York owned and run by pushing, grabbing Jews." Indeed, Miller outdid Wolfe in virulence: "The intellectuals are in my hair—and the artists and the communists and the Jews. New York is an aquarium—maybe I said this before—where there are nothing but hellbenders and lungfish and slimy, snag-toothed groupers and sharks with pilotfish aft and stern."[66]

Miller also assumed the persona of the walker in the City, but he never found what he was looking for: "And now, Joey, I'm going to tell you a little more about my lonely nights in New York, how I walk up and down Broadway, turning in and out of the side streets, looking into windows and doorways, wondering always when the miracle will happen, and if. And nothing ever happens."[67] Whatever the City valued, he decided, it was not art. In the Village, Miller went to the "'Poet's Corner,' a dingy Village rendezvous where the communist poets sat and chewed the fat over a cup of pale, greasy coffee. Here," he noted wryly, "is where America's great poems are made," and then sold on street corners (perhaps next to the apples) for ten cents each.[68]

Henry Miller's New York was a city of the lowest depths—"the poverty of New York is on a grand scale, as is everything else"—and disturbing heights.[69] Atop the Empire State Building, Miller could "see the humus of old buildings out of which this fantastic toy block world has been created. Looking down on the low roofs of the dingy red-brick buildings you might well imagine that New York was an island over which there flew endless flocks of obscene migratory birds. The whole city seems to be covered with bird lime."[70] In his brief, unhappy visit, Miller confirmed his anti-American and anti–New York City prejudices, finding exactly what he set out to discover: "Walking down Broadway I noticed how lousy the street was with whores."[71] For Henry Miller, even the prostitutes of Paris were more inspiring.

JOHN O'HARA WAS MORE INTERESTED IN THE SEXUAL PATH-
ology of New York as a means to measure the City's fall from grace. O'Hara's
Butterfield 8 (1935) was a *roman à clef* based upon the case of Starr Faithfull, a
twenty-five-year-old woman-about-town whose body was found washed up on
the shores of Long Island in June 1931. According to Matthew J. Bruccoli,
O'Hara's biographer, an "autopsy revealed that she had been drugged and that
she had sustained injuries before drowning."[72] Her adventurous life and ambiguous death—suicide? murder?—led to lurid press coverage. O'Hara, who had
known the victim slightly, read her sensational diaries, in which she said she
wished to end her "worthless, disorderly bore of an existence before I ruin anyone else's life."[73] O'Hara found in her life an opportunity to write a book about
the dissipated, self-destructive soul of the City.

Both in characterizations and in technique, John O'Hara structured *Butterfield 8* within the traditional boundaries of the New York novel. "Faced with
the choice of writing a panoramic novel in the manner of Dos Passos' *Manhattan
Transfer* or a book in which the characters represent types, as Dreiser's *Sister Carrie*, O'Hara . . . decided to try to combine the two approaches," suggests Frank
MacShane.[74] O'Hara too included a cross-section of the City, though—as the
novel's title, based upon a Manhattan telephone exchange, suggests—O'Hara
limited his cast to residents of the City's Gold Coast, and most of his novel's
scenes to the Upper East Side. Like Dreiser and Dos Passos before him, O'Hara
tried to represent the size, range, and variety of the City's population through
the use of scenic juxtapositions and narrative intersections; his novel constantly
shifts from one set of characters to another. Some critics, like MacShane, are disturbed by the fact that O'Hara left loose ends, failing to relate all the story lines.
However, all the novel's characters are related, in one way or another, to the wild
life and early death of Gloria Wandrous—"it's pronounced Wan-drous, pale
and wan."[75]

O'Hara tried to discourage any easy identification of Gloria with her times.
Editorial writers found "in Gloria a symbol of modern youth." But the novel's
narrator denies this. Gloria, born in Pittsburgh in 1899, was actually "corrupted"
(raped) by an older man at age eleven, before she came to the City, so she is not
wholly responsible for the loose life she leads in New York. Furthermore, New
York provides pressures that hasten her decline. She is seduced and passed
around a group of Yale men. "Because of the Yale boys she had an abortion, and
after that many benders."[76] She later picks up Weston Liggett, an East Side
snob and a married man, after another bender. He watches her die. After an encounter in which Liggett tells her she has ruined his marriage, Gloria either

jumps or is pushed from the boat she has taken to Massachusetts, trying to escape the City; she is sucked down to her death by the side wheel. Gloria's death thus recalls Bud's final fall in *Manhattan Transfer* and Hurstwood's lonely suicide in *Sister Carrie*. In O'Hara's tale yet another seeker comes to the City, grows disillusioned, and dies.

O'Hara's 1960 introduction to *Butterfield 8*, written for Modern Library but not published, makes it clear that the novel was quasi-autobiographical. O'Hara, too, had come to the City (from Pottsville, Pennsylvania, at age twenty-three, in 1928) with the attitude of "defenseless optimism. New York would take care of the newcomer." However, he soon learned that the City took care of newcomers in its own perverse way: "Within two years I was literally starving, by which I mean that for one three-day stretch I went without anything to eat." This "debasing and degrading" experience motivated O'Hara to succeed where others had failed: "Six years after I arrived in New York I was the author of a highly successful first novel [*Appointment in Samarra*] and was already at work on *Butterfield 8*, in which I was determined to make plain what I had seen."[77] What O'Hara saw—an oft-repeated tale—was the power of the City to chew up and spit out the lives not only of the poor and ordinary but also of the rich and beautiful. Like O'Hara, Gloria learns the harsh ways of the world in the City, but she cannot protect herself. Gloria is jaded by parties that she compares with Roman orgies: "[Though] Rome never saw parties like that. Rome didn't have electric light and champagne and the telephone, thirty-story apartment houses and the view of New York at night, saxophones and pianos. Here she was, just a girl on the town, but about the only thing she had missed was lions and Christians, and she supposed if she hung around long enough she'd have to see that."[78] O'Hara did see it all and he learned how to survive by telling, in plain and unsentimental prose, with cynical assurance and an eye for detail, tales that counted up the costs of success and the penalties for failure in the City.

MARY MCCARTHY SAW THE CITY AND DEFINED HER PLACE in it in far more positive terms. She discovered in New York personal liberation and the realization of her artistic ambitions. Her collection of stories, *The Company She Keeps* (1942), written at the end of the Great Depression, stands as one of the rare books of the era. While critical of the City and its citizens, her novel is characterized by its lively style, sustained by its wit, and concludes in optimism. *The Company She Keeps* is a coming-of-age-in-the-City novel that provides a positive portrait of the artist as a young woman. Yet Mary McCarthy's last look at New York City was full of regrets.

Mary Theresa McCarthy was born in 1912, in Seattle. She was orphaned as a child and raised by various relatives, as she recounted in *Memoirs of a Catholic Girlhood* (1957). She went to college at Vassar (class of 1933) and arrived in New York at age twenty-two, in 1934. In her 1992 foreword to McCarthy's *Intellectual Memoirs: New York 1936–1938*, Elizabeth Hardwick looked back in amazement at all that time had wrought since McCarthy first came to the City—a place that can "excite intensely or suddenly as if by electrical shock," in McCarthy's words.[79] This "very heaven" sense of discovery of New York was hard for McCarthy to recall and recreate—she died in 1989, at age seventy-seven—when she wrote this brief memoir during her final illness. For a record of her initial excitement over the City, we have to return to the opening pages of *The Group* (1963), a novel in which eight recent Vassar graduates gather, in June of 1933, in the Chapel of St. George's Church on Stuyvesant Square, to attend the wedding of one of their number: "They were in the throes of discovering New York, imagine it, when some of them had actually lived here all their lives."[80] The novel, however, ends in the funeral of another of their company, and any sense of New York's wonder has long since fled. When Mary McCarthy set out to "imagine it" in a memoir, her New York saga tracked a similar arc—from wondrous excitement over the possibilities of new life to world-weary resignation at its loss.

Intellectual Memoirs opens by establishing McCarthy's literary and political innocence. She recalls walking proudly down lower Broadway beside her first husband in a May Day parade in 1936, publicly affirming Stalinist Communism. Soon this young woman from Vassar walked into more complex and compromising positions. She learned, under Malcolm Cowley's supervision, to write slashing reviews at the *New Republic*, but she also learned to say the right things about favored authors. At "Jim" Farrell's apartment on Lexington Avenue, she became aware of the Stalin-Trotsky split in the ranks of American leftists; she joined the staff of the Trotskyite *Partisan Review*, and she became the lover of its coeditor, Philip Rahv. McCarthy moved to the Village and she practiced "free" love: "I realized one day that in twenty-four hours I had slept with three different men." Sexual and literary enlightenment combined in a scene in which McCarthy, Rahv, and Dwight Macdonald swam naked in a Connecticut stream, while arguing about Henry James. In this memoir, McCarthy is constructing a myth to account for her New York experiences, particularly when she personifies Rahv, her lover, as Good, and Edmund Wilson, her second husband, as Evil. *In-*

tellectual Memoirs concludes with her disillusionment during her honeymoon, when a drunken and paranoid Wilson accuses her brothers of being Stalinist agents who are out to get him. Her marriage, McCarthy concludes, "never recovered."[81] However, more than her marriage was damaged; for her, the bright, electric promise of New York was dimmed, though it burned enough for satiric recreation in McCarthy's fiction, the form Wilson urged her to pursue.

From 1939 to 1945, McCarthy and Wilson lived for long periods on Cape Cod (mostly in Wellfleet). She wrote her first story there, "Cruel and Barbarous Treatment," in a single sitting in 1938, and it was published in Robert Penn Warren's *Southern Review* in 1939. She then wrote more stories about the same protagonist, Margaret Sargent, a fictional version of herself.[82] Six other stories followed over the next few years until she had a book, *The Company She Keeps*. This work tracks the fortunes of a bright and ambitious but unfocused young woman who is trying to discover her place in the City. In "Cruel and Barbarous Treatment," she betrays her husband in an affair with a young man whom she eventually drops. In "Rouge's Gallery," Margaret works, as had McCarthy, for a dishonest art dealer whom she protects. In her private and public lives, Margaret learns the way of the world in New York.

The third story in *The Company She Keeps*, "The Man in the Brooks Brothers Shirt," caused a sensation. It was turned down by the *Southern Review* because it was too sexy, but it was published in the *Partisan Review* (summer 1941). In this story Margaret, by then a writer for a liberal journal who has grown somewhat bored with Manhattan life, gets drunk and has an affair with a much older and overweight businessman she meets on a westbound train. On the morning after lovemaking, she suffers embarrassments from her hangover and her disheveled clothes. Margaret tries to explain herself to herself and decides that this man, who represents everything her New York politics has taught her to scorn, has restored a sense of passion that she had mislaid in the City—"a feeling she had once had when, at twenty, she had come to New York and had her first article accepted by a liberal weekly, but which had slowly been rubbed away by four years of being on the inside of the world that had looked magic from Portland, Oregon."[83] She sees in this businessman a vigor she has long associated with the heartland of America. So many New York men are deficient that she is pleased when this man from the heartland choses her. Yet, Margaret knows that she, too, cannot go home again, so she returns to New York City and the affair ends. In a sense, McCarthy implies, the new woman can both love and leave this personification of traditional America.

Other stories focus further upon those deficient New York men, particularly upon an androgynous, vengeful host and a predatory, hypocritical Marxist. Because of the latter, in "Portrait of the Intellectual as a Yale Man," Margaret is fired from a Stalinist magazine because she is an outspoken Trotskyite. The final story, "Ghostly Father, I Confess," finds Margaret married to an architect who bullies her, so she consults a psychiatrist. But Margaret rejects the option of psychological adjustment to her sad situation; instead she celebrates her own contradictions. In *The Company She Keeps*, Mary McCarthy shows how one woman can survive the pressures—career, sex, politics, status—of the City and, in the process, grow up.

D AMON RUNYON CHOSE TO TURN HIS BACK ON THE DIRE 1930s and devote his literary efforts to memorializing the roaring 1920s. For Jimmy Breslin, a City newspaper columnist in the Runyon tradition, "Runyon invented the Broadway of *Guys and Dolls* and the Roaring Twenties, neither of which existed, but whose names and phrases became part of theater history and the American language."[84] In his biography, *A Life of Damon Runyon* (1991), Breslin grants that Runyon's life "gave off a reflection of more than three decades of the city of New York, and it has almost become the official record of the times. He practically invented at least two entire decades of his times, and he had everybody believing that his street, Broadway, actually existed. So much of it never happened." All of which is fine with Breslin, who, in his pugnacious City style, challenges anyone who might say it is not: "What do you care? What does anybody care? Go to any library and the illusion is there as fact."[85] Runyon's New York City, then, is a landscape of the mind.

In 1884 Damon Runyon was born in Manhattan—Manhattan, Kansas, last stand of the cowboy—a fact that colored his superficially cynical but essentially romantic vision of New York City. "The thing to remember about Runyon," notes Frank Rich, "is that he was born in Kansas and didn't reach Manhattan until he was 26. His love for his adopted town is the helpless romantic ardor of a pilgrim who finally found his Mecca."[86] Despite his cast of shady characters with vivid names, Runyon's City was safe, comic, and reassuring. Things turn out all right at the end of his stories—just as they had for his true predecessors, Horatio Alger and O. Henry, writers who showed Runyon how to turn tame tales of the City's eccentrics into a fortune through careful observations and judicious editing of the urban text.

"I am the sedentary champion of the City," Runyon once said. "In order to learn anything of importance, I must remain seated."[87] So, too, is the knowing narrator of Runyon's stories often a passive observer. He sits in a Broadway restaurant late at night, his eyes and ears alert to the passing show, seemingly without a past of his own, observing New York City's finest sharpies and fools, characters who speak an argot wholly invented by Runyon.

In Runyon's world, everything is *now*, in the present tense. In "Broadway Complex," for example, Runyon's narrator is in Mindy's, "enjoying a sturgeon sandwich, which is wonderful brain food," and listening to Ambrose Hammer, drama reviewer ("newspaper scribe"), tell of his troubles. Trouble inevitably catches up with Ambrose: "But of course if a guy is looking for trouble on Broadway along toward four o'clock in the morning, anybody will tell you that the right address is nowhere else but Mindy's, because at such an hour many citizens are gathered there, and are commencing to get a little cross wondering where they are going to make a scratch for tomorrow's operations, such as playing the horses." The trouble in this 1933 story—a typically absurd Runyon plot—involves a hired murderer who comes to believe he is Don Juan; as a result, he is able to win away a "beautiful" from a pompous actor.[88]

Runyon's Broadway stories are often variations on the same basic plot. In "Broadway Incident" (1941), the narrator dines at the Canary Club, listening to Ambrose Hammer talk about yet another "beautiful," one Hilda Hiffenbrowner, when Hammer is attacked by an irate playwright. (In "Broadway Complex" he is attacked by an irate actor.) After this attack, Hammer rumbas with Mrs. Brumby News, who tells him she is being pressured to kill her husband by women con artists who want to share in her inheritance. Things get even more tangled, but then, as usual, they clear rapidly, in a dozen pages. In "The Bloodhounds of Broadway" (1931), Runyon sets his tale in Mindy's at 4:00 A.M., where the narrator meets a man who is leading bloodhounds named Nip and Tuck. Soon the bloodhounds track a suspected murderer through the streets of the City and corner him in a house of prostitution, but then it turns out there was no murder after all. This, then, like most Runyon stories, is more about the chase than the prize, more about the telling than about what is told, and above all, more about Runyon's idea of the City than about New York as it was. Nearly half a decade after Runyon's death, when Frank Loesser's adaptation of *Guys and Dolls* was revived on Broadway, New York City found the will to believe once again in Damon Runyon's salvific vision.

Seen close up, American life during the Great Depression warranted the apocalyptic descriptions that many writers of the time employed to describe it. The Crash of 1929 and its devastating aftermath raised doubts about the viability of American democracy and called into question the promise of American life. Seen from a distance, however, the 1930s can be re-imagined as an interlude between the post–World War I boom of the 1920s and America's entry into World War II in 1941. Democracy was tested and survived; the American covenant was renewed. In 1939 and 1940, inside the World Fair's Perisphere, visitors saw a "brave new world," a planned city of the future, as the voice of radio commentator H. V. Kaltenborn described it.[89] In a sense, the Great Depression fostered such dreams of transcendence, dreams that would be realized in the chaotic expansiveness of America, in its cities, after World War II.

E. L. Doctorow's *World's Fair* (1985), a novel that appeared nearly half a century after the events it describes—a young man's coming of age in 1930s New York City—beautifully captures both the devastations and the hopes of that period. Looking back from a time when American cities, particularly New York, were under siege, Doctorow could, like Edith Wharton before him, see good in the old ways of the City.

"Almost all of Mr. Doctorow's novels have been, to some degree, documents of New York history, and one of his great strengths has been the richness of his descriptions of its cultural landscape, from turn-of-the-century New Rochelle and Manhattan in *Ragtime* to the Jewish Bronx of his 1930s childhood in *World's Fair*," writes Simon Schama.[90] Doctorow's 1994 novel, *The Waterworks*, which will be discussed in the final chapter, presents the City as a "post-bellum Gehenna," in the words of Schama, but *World's Fair* shows a City that, despite the dark days of the Depression, prepared young New Yorkers to emerge triumphant.

Like Doctorow, Edgar, the novel's hero, was born on Clinton Street, in the Lower East Side in 1931. At four he moves with his family to the Bronx, near Claremont Park, part of a Jewish migration within the City. Edgar's father works downtown, selling music at the Hippodrome Radio store in Times Square, while his mother tends to their home and family, fretting about money.

Edgar's world is circumscribed by his Bronx neighborhood, but for occasional beach afternoons at Far Rockaway or trips to the Polo Grounds to watch the Giants, about whom Edgar has little feeling. However, he assigns social value and local character to New York City's other two baseball teams. Edgar does not like the raffish Dodgers, known as the "Bums," but he does admire the elegant Yankees: "When things were going badly for them, they did not complain but bore down harder. They were civilized and had a naturally assured way about them. That was the true New York quality of spirit. Not bumhood."[91]

"I didn't think of the Bronx as a place where anything happened." But the wider world intrudes upon the safe and dull routine of his life when Edgar sees the German zeppelin, *Hindenburg*, fly low over the Bronx. Amazingly, "the *Hindenburg* was headed over Claremont Park now, toward Morris Avenue." Edgar realizes the fragility of all life when he hears on the radio that the *Hindenburg* has burned over Lakehurst, New Jersey, in 1937.[92]

After this, Edgar begins to imagine a world beyond the Bronx and wonders what his place will be in it. He enters an essay contest for boys sponsored by the New York World's Fair Corporation on the topic "The Typical American Boy." On the flyer announcing the contest rules appear the shadowy emblems of the Trylon and Perisphere: "They emerged in my mind as a message just for me, a secret summons, wordless, indelible." He is determined to enter and win, to "propose the essence of American boyhood." His essay begins: "The typical American boy is not fearful of Danger. He should be able to go out into the country and drink raw milk. Likewise, he should traverse the hills and valleys of the city. If he is Jewish he should say so."[93]

Edgar has his first chance to go beyond his narrow world when he is invited to attend the Fair with his friend Meg and her mother, Norma. At the General Motors Building they see the World of Tomorrow, which features the Futurama: a miniature city in which everything is planned, "just as if 174th Street and all the neighborhood around were packed into one giant building. . . . In the cities of the future, pedestrian bridges connected the buildings and highways were sunken on tracks below them. No one would get run over in this futuristic world. It all made sense, people didn't have to travel except to see the countryside; everything else, their schools, their jobs, were right where they lived." Through Edgar's amazed eyes, Doctorow offers a vision of an ordered, serene City, where no harm would come to its citizens.

> *At the Consolidated Edison exhibit, again everything was shrunk—it was a diorama of the entire city of New York, showing the life in the city from morning till night. We could see the whole city and across the Hudson River to Jersey, the Statue of Liberty in the harbor. We could see up in Westchester and Connecticut. I looked for my house in the Bronx, but I couldn't see it. Norma thought she saw Claremont Park. But below us were the great stone sky scrapers, the cars and buses in the streets, the subways and elevated trains, all of the working metrop-*

olis, all of it sparkling with life, and when afternoon came there was
even a thunderstorm, and all the lights of the buildings and streets
came up to deal with the darkness.[94]

After this noble vision Edgar learns that Norma works in the Amusement
Zone of the Fair as a swimmer, along with other young women, in a tank with a
grasping man dressed as an octopus. Norma's job is to wrestle with Oscar the
Amorous Octopus. When it gets dark, Edgar and Meg go off on their own, onto
the Parachute Jump. As they are raised up, Edgar witnesses a daunting sight of
the actual City: "I saw out over the world now, over the Fair. I saw Manhattan,
I saw clouds over the city lit from below by electric light. I grew dizzy." But as
he floats to the ground, Edgar hears a reassuring song, "The Sidewalks of New
York"; Meg presses against him for protection and he is pleased at his show of
courage.[95] Later, when he sees the "octopus" pull the bathing suits off Norma
and the other swimmers in their last performance of the day, Edgar realizes he
has seen everything he came to see at the Fair, and more.

Edgar wins honorable mention in the essay contest; as a result, he is granted
a free pass for himself and his family to the Fair and all its attractions for one day.
Then young Edgar becomes their guide to the Fair: "The minute we entered
the fairgrounds I felt at home. Everything was there just as I had left it. It was
even more amazing to see the second time." He leads his family into the Perisphere where a moving belt carries them over the "totally planned city of the future." They see the Time Capsule, which holds artifacts of their age. After they
view the Futurama, with its "splendid panoply of highways and horizons," Edgar's father suggests that it is just a pitch by General Motors for government support to build highways so the company will be able to sell its cars. Edgar laughs,
pleased to have this vision of an orderly urban future undercut by his father's
suggestion of commercial connivances.

At the Dodgem, Edgar and his older brother, Donald, ride a bumper car:
"Donald let me drive, his arm over my shoulders, as we spun about crashing and
banging into people and being bashed in return, everyone's head threatening to
fly off. Donald yelled over the din: '*This* is the Futurama!'" They end their day
at the Fun House and the Savoy, listening to the Jimmy Lunceford Band and
watching dancers jitterbug and dance the Big Apple: "Later it rained, and I remember seeing the fireworks go up in the black night and lighting the rain as if
some battle were being fought between the earth and the sky."[96]

In *World's Fair*, Doctorow presents a redemptive myth of coming of age in the
Great Depression and conflicting visions of the City's future: the orderly, safe,

sterile, commercially exploitative image of the future offered by the Futurama is set against the sometimes dangerous, but far more vital, sense of the City that emerges from Edgar's days at the Fair. At the end of *World's Fair*, Edgar makes his own time capsule—containing a Tom Mix decoder badge, his four-page biography of FDR, a harmonica, and other treasures—which he and a friend bury in Claremont Park. In a sense, a time capsule is just what E. L. Doctorow has created in this novel, capturing and preserving the City at its worst and best. *World's Fair* presents the City as a living presence with the power to shape its citizens, but also with the malleability to be reconfigured by their wills and imaginations.

In THE 1930s, THE DESTRUCTION OF NEW YORK CITY, LONG predicted by pessimists, seemed imminent. The stock market crashed; businesses closed; the unemployed and the desperate thronged the City's streets; even the well-off suffered. Many writers, in particular those who were already critical of capitalism, voiced bleak visions of the City's future, while others mourned great days gone by. Yet chaos did not come to New York. The resilient City not only survived, it celebrated itself and America's future in the World's Fair. As we have seen, at least some of its writers found a saving grace in New York City during the Great Depression.

NEW YORK CITY'S GOLDEN AGE

New York

After World War II

Nᴇᴡ Yᴏʀᴋ ʙᴇᴄᴀᴍᴇ ᴋɴᴏᴡɴ ᴀs ᴛʜᴇ Eᴍᴘɪʀᴇ Cɪᴛʏ ᴀꜰᴛᴇʀ World War II, a war in which nearly 900,000 New Yorkers served and more than 16,000 were killed.[1] When the United Nations decided in 1945 to locate its permanent headquarters there, the City's influence extended far beyond what it had been when New York was, a century and a half before, briefly the capital of the United States of America. (Erected on a seventeen-acre lot adjacent to the East River, replacing slaughterhouses, the UN Building was completed in 1954.) For those who arrived from devastated Europe, like Beverley Nichols, a visiting English novelist and journalist, New York seemed "the centre of the world."[2] New York had become a center of civilization—as, perhaps, Boston had been in the nineteenth century—"the supreme metropolis of the moment" in the words of another English writer, Cyril Connolly. For Connolly, New York presented "an unforgettable picture of what a city ought to be: that is, continuously insolent and alive."[3]

New York City was suddenly open to a stunning range of opportunities for personal expression, though some observers thought this golden age faded quickly. For travel journalist Jan Morris, New York had already reached its apogee in the spring of 1945, when the soldiers who had fought in Europe began to return. Looking back in *Manhattan '45* (1987), Morris recalled "a late epitome of a more youthful America," a City that "still worshiped gods, . . . a good and merry place." Then, inevitably, all changed: "Out of the delights of 1945 another city had emerged." For Morris the postwar City quickly lost the confidence it sported when New Yorkers walked down Fifth Avenue with "the boxer's truculence of Tom Buchanan."[4]

But most observers remained optimistic about the City and its prospects. Fiorello La Guardia, mayor from 1933 to 1945, vowed to create in New York "a new kind of city—more beautiful, healthful, and convenient; a more comfortable place to live, work, and play."[5] New arrivals from abroad and from other parts of the nation flooded the City to take advantage of this promise. (The City's African-American population rose from 150,000 in 1920, the era of the Harlem Renaissance, to nearly 750,000 by 1950, the first year of the decade that marked the struggle over civil rights.) At the same time, new prosperity, new roads, and new housing led to the loss of some 800,000 New Yorkers to the suburbs. Levittown, for example, offered its first 2,000 houses for sale twenty miles from Manhattan, in Nassau County, Long Island, in the spring of 1947, beginning what David Halberstam describes as "a massive migration from the cities, to the farmland that surrounded them."[6] William O'Dwyer, who was elected mayor in 1945, carried on La Guardia's pledge, but O'Dwyer was forced to retire, under a cloud of corruption accusations, after his reelection in 1949. In the 1950s, Mayor Robert F. Wagner, Jr., presided for three terms over the City's postwar boom, "the last era of good feeling New York would enjoy for some time," according to Oliver E. Allen.[7]

The period between 1947 and 1957 has also been called "the last golden age of baseball" in New York City. In only one of those eleven seasons (1948) did at least one New York team *not* compete in the World Series. The New York Yankees won nine American League championships and seven World Series—five of them in a row. The Brooklyn Dodgers won six National League championships and one World Series. The New York Giants won two National League championships and one World Series. As Harvey Fromer puts it, "throughout the long steamy summer nights and in the blaze of its days, from early spring to the winds of autumn, baseball dominated New York City. The deeds and the personalities of the Dodgers, the Giants, the Yankees transformed the huge metropolis into a small town of neighborhood rooting."[8] However, when, in the late 1950s, the Dodgers and the Giants moved to California and the Yankees lost their dominance, the days of summer drew to a close.

After World War II, new skyscrapers added massive glass surfaces to the City's skyline—Lever House in midtown and the Chase Manhattan Building downtown, for example. LeCorbusier, the acclaimed international architect, described New York in 1946 as "a vertical city," which troubled him: "It is a catastrophe with which a too hasty destiny has overwhelmed courageous and confident people, though a beautiful and worthy catastrophe."[9] Robert Moses— Mayor Wagner's park commissioner and construction coordinator, an imperial figure who became the City's "power broker"—oversaw the building of a major highway system that linked the City internally and externally, but at the cost of some long-standing neighborhoods, for example, in the South Bronx.[10] Museums expanded, as did the Museum of Modern Art; relocated to midtown, as did the Whitney Museum of American Art; or erected striking new structures, as did the Guggenheim Museum, which opened its circular building, designed by Frank Lloyd Wright, at Fifth Avenue and Eighty-eighth Street in 1959. Lincoln Center, a complex built in the West Sixties, became the home of the Metropolitan Opera and the New York City Ballet. New York City had become, as its artists and writers portrayed it in a range of striking expressions, a capital of the world. "The New York that O. Henry described forty years ago was an American city," wrote J. B. Priestly in 1947, "but today's glittering cosmopolis belongs to the world, if the world does not belong to it."[11]

This chapter focuses on the writers of New York City's golden age, the immediate postwar period, from several angles. This was a time when many writers left their homes and neighborhoods, casting off their naive selves, and journeyed to the City in search of transformation and self-knowledge. Therefore, it is important to discuss several examples of meaningful movement to Manhattan, as well as to note examples of those left behind, in the fiction of Lynne Sharon Schwartz, Betty Smith, Elizabeth Cullinan, Jimmy Breslin, Mary Gordon, and Anna Quindlen. Some writers saw the City's beauty as painfully transient: John Cheever and Irwin Shaw, for example. The New York intellectuals—a loose association of literary critics and political commentators who reached the peak of their long-standing influence in this period, including Irving Howe, Lionel Trilling, Alfred Kazin, and many more—sought to understand the City on a deeper level. In their own works and in the works of the playwrights, poets, and novelists they influenced and promoted—Arthur Miller, Saul Bellow, Isaac Bashevis Singer, Bernard Malamud, Norman Mailer, and others—the problematic character and purpose of the City were debated during these years. The *New Yorker*, a magazine that began to celebrate the City in the 1920s and prospers even today, had its best years in this period, when it was edited by William Shawn. Writers associated with the *New Yorker* produced evocative meditations on the City, most notably E. B. White and John Updike—writers who eventually left New York. While writers were, as ever, drawn to all parts of the City, Greenwich Village attracted yet another generation of young men and women— Michael Harrington, Dan Wakefield, Joan Didion, Frank O'Hara, Allen Ginsberg, for example—who sought all that it was reputed to offer by those predecessors who had made the Village legendary. As we have seen in a previous chapter, Ralph Ellison, James Baldwin, and other writers in these years were making Harlem into a national symbol of African-American experience in their compelling essays and novels. While many writers were discovering so much to value in the City, others, like J. D. Salinger and Sylvia Plath, were finding tarnish beneath its glitter. New York's golden age was marked by an array of literary expressions, ranging from celebrations to denunciations, in which the City played a central role in the lives of its residents and in the destiny of the nation.

THE LITERATURE WRITTEN IN OR DESCRIPTIVE OF THE City in this period stresses the themes of maturation—movement and realization—in stories, poems, and plays about the struggle to leave rural and suburban homes for life in Manhattan, about the exposure to a wider, enlightening, but often disturbing and sometimes dangerous, world. Journalist Pete Hamill grew up during World War II in Brooklyn, where he says one encountered "toughness and lyricism, along with their occasional merger. There [was] provincialism too, along with its twin, the romantic desire for escape and possibility."[12] These contradictory qualities are present in the literature of Brooklyn and other boroughs of New York of this period.

Lynne Sharon Schwartz's *Leaving Brooklyn* (1989), a novel in the form of a memoir about coming of age in Brooklyn in these years, can be read as an account of a representative New Yorker, her complex ethnic community, and their transcendence of provincialism. Schwartz's heroine, Audrey, the novel's central consciousness, encounters moral ambiguity where she least expects to find it— in her community and in her own heart.

In Schwartz's Brooklyn, parents try to shield their children from the experience and knowledge of evil, but Audrey craves to learn through suffering. In "the climactic conditions of postwar Brooklyn," writes the adult Audrey of her childhood years, there was "a presumption of state-of-nature innocence, an imaginative amnesia, and a disregard of evidence such as photographs of skeletal figures in striped pajamas clawing at barbed wire, of mushroom clouds and skinned bodies groping in ashes."[13] But young Audrey seeks out such images. Adult Audrey makes clear that her "Brooklyn" is more a place of the imagination than a geographic location: "The Brooklyn of my story is a state of mind or perception, the shadow field on which my good and bad eyes staged their struggle. . . . One can only live in it or flee."[14]

Audrey grows up in an out-of-focus world because one of her eyes is damaged—a condition that also serves as a metaphor for her refractory perceptions of Brooklyn. As narrator, she tries to bring into focus her lost Brooklyn: "Brooklyn on the eve of the war, a locus of customs and mythologies as arbitrary and rooted as in the Trobriand Islands or the great Aztec city of Teotihaucan where ritual sacrifices were performed monthly, the victims' blood coursing down the steps of the great Pyramid of the Sun. In comparison, my damage was minor."[15]

Young Audrey's "wandering eye" drives her to romantic dreams of transcendence: "The eye was of scant use in seeing what had to be seen in daily life in Brooklyn. It was made for another sort of vision."[16] With only her bad eye open, she can dissolve and recompose the world into a Seurat painting. With only her good eye open, she can see Brooklyn, as Emily Dickinson saw Amherst, "slant." With both eyes open, she can see the world in all of its doubleness: from glittering Manhattan to horrors beyond—the Holocaust and the atomic bomb.

Audrey's injured eye carries her out of Brooklyn's bounds when she goes, with her mother, to consult a Park Avenue doctor, in "mythic Manhattan, a mere river away, though it felt like another planet as we emerged into brilliant light."[17] He fits Audrey for painful lenses, which constrict her accustomed freedom to transform her world at will, merely by closing either eye. In a later visit she responds to the doctor's touch and—suddenly, shockingly—they have sex. Audrey is less amazed by this act than by his cool response after it: "Of all the ways I had dreamed the world outside Brooklyn to be, I had never conceived of its nonchalance."[18] There is, she discovers, far more in Manhattan than anyone dares dream in Brooklyn. In wondrous Manhattan she is transformed. At the doctor's office, Audrey willingly participates in actions—infidelity, anal sex, even blackmail—that shock her: "In his office I did the inconceivable."[19]

Having passed, she assumes, beyond the ken of innocent Brooklyn, Audrey comes to realize that there is in fact far more to Brooklyn than has met her eyes. For example, she is surprised to hear of several cases in which Brooklyn residents have lost their jobs because of their leftist convictions. (Truman Capote, who lived in Brooklyn at the time, noted the excitement surrounding the capture of Colonel Rudolf Abel, the Soviet secret agent, on Fulton Street.)[20] Then Audrey is amazed to hear her father complain that President Franklin D. Roosevelt had allowed millions to die in concentration camps and that the Pope did nothing to stop the genocide of Jews. Above all, Audrey is stunned to learn that there *is* passion in Brooklyn: "PASSION. Conflict. Thought. An ample scene for both my eyes. But only under cover of darkness, with the children safely unconscious."[21]

Audrey, cursed or blessed with her "double vision," leaves Brooklyn for Manhattan, where she eagerly enters a world where there are no clear moral choices. Only then can she see, or comprehend, the subtlety and complexity of the Brooklyn of her youth. In Brooklyn adults tried to protect children from an awareness of evil, while in Manhattan adults conspired to initiate children into evil, but both places knew the worst of human behavior. Having learned that lesson, Audrey is able to take possession of Brooklyn in her art, just as James Joyce, an exile in Zurich, is able to portray Dublin in his art of fiction: "I left Brooklyn. I leave still, every moment. For no matter how much I leave, it doesn't leave me."[22] Lynn Sharon Schwartz's Audrey, like many other of the City's initiates, develops what Henry James called an imagination of disaster and survives to write about it.

Other writers also chronicled life in New York's neighborhoods and featured characters who tried to escape. Betty Smith's popular novel, *A Tree Grows in Brooklyn* (1946), a model for many Brooklyn writers, portrays a limiting but finally a nurturing place.[23] Like her heroine, Francie Nolan, Smith was marked by the social stratifications and discriminations of Irish-American culture in the Williamsburg section of Brooklyn, a narrow world bounded by symbols and stereotypes—the kitchen table around which the family gathers and the Tammany Hall wardheeler whom the family turns to for help—but both she and Francie manage to transcend its limitations. Betty Smith's later novels, *Tomorrow Will Be Better* (1948) and *Maggie-Now* (1958), continue to map an escape from the loving but constricting world of the Brooklyn Irish.

Elizabeth Cullinan's beautifully realized novel, *House of Gold* (1970), portrays a similar Irish-American family, the Devlins, whose members try to live past the influence of their dying mother, Julia Devlin. She is an immigrant, a dominating matriarch who has reared her children with rigid Catholic values. She has pursued a vision of sanctity and success to her end—her death on a hot, summer evening in the Bronx. Julia has strived to be what she could not become: like the Virgin Mary, a queen in her House of Gold. Instead, Julia has controlled her own house and family, stifling her children's ambitions to lead independent lives. Julia's children can never find places for themselves in the world of compromise that exists beyond the shabby house in which they have been instilled with a sense of their own privilege and sacredness.[24]

Cullinan, born in 1933 to Irish-American parents, places her art within New York's Irish-American cultural milieu, where, as she has written in describing her early life in the City, "you were given a context to grow up in and that was supposed to be your identity. That's where you were. You were fortunate. You didn't need anything else."[25] Clearly Cullinan did need something else, for she went from Marymount College in Manhattan to the *New Yorker*, where she honed her art of fiction under the direction of William Maxwell. That is, Elizabeth Cullinan, like Betty Smith before her, wrote her way out of New York's Irish-American ghetto, though that world remains the subject of her exemplary fiction.

Cullinan's story "Commuting" incorporates a liberating vision of ethnic life in the City. Her narrator travels from her old neighborhood in the Bronx, where she has finished teaching at a college located in her old neighborhood (Fordham?), and she returns, by bus, to Manhattan, where she lives. "The result," notes Charles Fanning, "is a paradigm of chosen migration and a metaphor for ethnic consciousness in our time."[26] On upper Fifth Avenue the narrator recalls Harlem's successive occupants: middle-class Protestant families in the nineteenth century, Irish immigrants at the turn of the century, and African-Americans now. Passing through streets that "throb with menace," she arrives safely in Manhattan, where she finally relaxes; "I've reenacted, in spirit, the journey that has given my life its substance and shape, color and brightness. I've escaped."[27] The story reveals the "doubleness of ethnic consciousness" that grounds writers who possess the will and the ability to move beyond their old neighborhoods in the boroughs and discover new lives in midtown.[28]

In his journalism and in several works of fiction, Jimmy Breslin has described his native Queens as a vital, sometimes brutal, often comic place that its residents find hard to leave. Breslin, born in Queens in 1930, left and became a legendary man-about-town. He ran unsuccessfully for the city council in 1969, the same year that Norman Mailer lost his race for mayor. ("VOTE THE RASCALS IN" was the Mailer-Breslin campaign slogan.)[29] Breslin became a columnist for the *New York Herald Tribune*, the *Journal American*, and other City newspapers. He wrote a biography of his journalistic model, Damon Runyon, and includes Runyonesque types (Fat Thomas, a bookie; Jerry the Rooster, a shoplifter; and Marvin the Torch, an arsonist, for example) in his columns. However, Breslin has invented, in his fiction, a far more desperate and deterministic New York than Runyon's City of charming hoods and hookers. In *World without End, Amen* (1973), for example, Breslin's central character, Dermot Davey, *comes out of St. Monica's Parish in Jamaica, in Queens, in New York City. He was living now in Holy Child Parish, in Richmond Hill, in Queens, in New York City. Richmond Hill is only twenty-five minutes from Manhattan. But everybody in Queens always thinks of Manhattan as another place. The people say, "I'm going to the city," or, "I'm going to New York." Queens begins at the East River, directly across the water from Midtown Manhattan. In Manhattan, you have the United Nations building on the water, sun exploding on the windows, sprinklers throwing water on the lawns and gardens. Directly across the river from the United Nations is the Pepsi-Cola plant in Long Island City, in Queens, its red neon sign bare and ugly in the daylight, eerie at night in the smoke rising around it.*[30]

Davey is not only defined but destroyed by his place as an outer-borough Irish-American. Though sensitive as a lad, he becomes a regional type: an alcoholic cop and an abusive husband. On a trip to Ireland he meets the doom he seeks.

Breslin's *Forsaking All Others* (1982) explores the killing streets of New York, but extends out of Queens to the South Bronx and reaches beyond the Irish-American community. In his fictional exploration of the limitations imposed by New York's code of ethnic loyalty and the price exacted for tribal betrayal, Breslin offers star-crossed lovers: Nicki Mariani, daughter of a Mafia don and wife of an imprisoned Mafia soldier, falls in love with Maximo, a Puerto Rican lawyer whose friend, Teenager, is trying to take over the Mafia's drug business. Personal passions and turf wars combine in an explosion of blood.[31] Ethnic strife fuels urban apocalypse in Breslin's New York City.

Table Money (1986), set in Queens, is the tale of another doomed Irish-American, Owney Morrison—Vietnam veteran, alcoholic, a "sandhog" (a tunnel-digger), and a wife-abuser. The title refers to the ritual in which Irish-American men cash their paychecks in barrooms, drink their fill, then go home and toss what money is left onto their kitchen tables; their wives pick up this table money and learn to make do with less than their family needs. However, in *Table Money*, Owney's wife, Dolores, rebels, changes her own life through education, and helps Owney to change his. Breslin grants some of his characters the will to leave home and overcome ethnic, territorial, and cultural limitations.[32]

Mary Gordon's narrative of Irish-American family life, *The Other Side* (1990), stands as an exception to this pattern in which young people of promise find ways out of their constricting neighborhoods. Gordon, born in 1949, grew up Catholic (though not Irish) on Long Island; her first novel, *Final Payments* (1978), concerns a young woman who belatedly escapes her cultural chains. Isabel Moore cares for her ill father, a dominating patriarch, for eleven years, limiting her life to his house in Queens. After he dies, Isabel struggles to transcend the sexual guilt that is part of her religious and family heritage and determines to become a new woman. A similar emergence is portrayed in Gordon's *The Company of Women* (1981). In that novel, heroine Felicitas Taylor breaks out of the bell jar of Catholic thought and culture; finally, she too braves the world on her own. In these works Gordon—like Smith, Cullinan, and Breslin—portrays the fraying bonds that tie women to the old ways in New York's ethnic neighborhoods.

However, in *The Other Side*, Gordon stresses all that may be lost in the transition. Another dying matriarch, Ellen MacNamara, reflects upon "the net of kinship" that spreads around her. Inside the net "there is a place for everyone, she thinks, but not all places are equal and not everyone is happy in his place."[33] Indeed, no one is happy in the doomed MacNamara clan. Though Vincent and Ellen have been married for sixty-six years, have raised two children, and have many grandchildren, they look back and wonder what has been the point of it all: "For sixty-three years, they have lived in one house, 128 Linden Street, Queens Village, ten miles from the center of Manhattan. . . . They crossed the ocean to the place, America, that had been called at home 'the other side.' "[34] This side of the Atlantic became the wrong side for the MacNamara family and, by Gordon's extension, for many Irish immigrants. In America Vincent has dug subway tunnels and Ellen has tried and failed, like other Irish women before her, to control a family that has broken away from its religious and cultural heritage and broken apart. At the end of his day, Vincent wishes he had stayed in Cork. Here the MacNamara clan faces only depletion, disintegration, and death. *The Other Side* is a depressing parable of the Irish-American journey from somewhere (Ireland) to nowhere (New York City).

Mary Gordon is not alone among Irish-American writers and analysts to ask if life in a New York City borough is better than the life in Ireland that they, or their ancestors, left behind. Many Irish-American writings about the City are marked by a tone of bitterness over discriminations they have encountered and a sense of emptiness over the success they have achieved. As poet Terence Winch jauntily puts it, "We put out the fires and controlled city hall,/ We started with nothing and wound up with it all."[35] However, in gaining the world's *all*, some wonder if Irish-Americans have sacrificed their identity. "Has the actual as well as the literary Irish-American trek from ghetto to suburbs been a passage from someplace to no place?" asks cultural historian Lawrence J. McCaffrey in *Textures of Irish America*.[36]

Certainly in J. P. Donleavy's eerie story *A Fairy Tale of New York* (1961), the City is a disillusioning experience for Cornelius Christian, whose Irish wife dies on board ship as they sail from Ireland to New York, his native city. As Charles Fanning notes, "like Famine immigrants, Christian runs a gauntlet of crass, money-grubbing American sharpers."[37] In this story the hopeful journey to the New World is transformed into a funeral procession for Donleavy, who was born in Brooklyn in 1926, became an expatriate, and made himself over into an Irish country gentleman. For Donleavy, New York—that is, America—has become a nightmare, "a land of lies . . . vulgarity, obscenity and money. A country of sick hearts and bodies." Cornelius experiences a series of mad adventures and survives in "the great sad cathedral that is New York City."[38]

Though most writers who focused on life in the City and its ethnic neighborhoods before, during, and after World War II were optimistic, some, as we have seen, portrayed disillusionment and disappointment. Either way, these writers saw their fictionalized versions of their own and their neighbors' experiences of coming of age in the City's boroughs as "object lessons" about life in America. *New York Times* columnist Anna Quindlen uses this phrase as the title of a novel about a slightly later time in New York's story. Her heroine, Maggie Scanlan, is growing up in Kenwood, a small town near the Bronx border, in the early 1960s. Both her Italian and her Irish grandfathers are still living, so Maggie, a child of suburbia, is heir to two ethnic traditions. Maggie feels divided, pulled between old and new worlds: "When she thought of herself and of her family, and of the town in which they lived, she thought of them torn in two—as they were before and as they were afterward, as though there had been a great rift in the earth of their existence, separating one piece of ground from the other."[39] Yet, like so many others in this genre of urban ethnic transitions, Maggie makes her way between and beyond these divisions and emerges the richer for it. For Quindlen and other writers, the boroughs contain the City's secret history and prepare those who will shape its future.

SOME WRITERS WHO FOUND SUCCESS IN THE CITY wondered whether the game was worth the candle. Looking back on his career in the preface to his collected *Stories* (1978), John Cheever evoked the wistful atmosphere of Manhattan's lost glories: "These stories seem at times to be stories of a long-lost world when the city of New York was filled with a river light, when you heard Benny Goodman quartets from the radio in the corner stationery store, and when almost everybody wore a hat." Yet his stories reach beyond ephemeral period details: "The constants that I look for in this sometimes dated paraphernalia are of a love of light and a determination to trace some moral chain of being."[40] Cheever's New York, then, is a landscape of youthful drama, lost felicities, and enduring moral implications.

Characters typically come into Manhattan for work and romance in Cheever's stories; then they catch the 5:48 commuter train back to one of his invented suburbs, Shady Hill or Proxmire Manor, where they drink gin, grow depressed, and ponder their next escapes. In Bullet Park, a suburban development from which Cheever drew the title of his 1969 novel, upscale residents find no haven from urban terrors. "In Cheever's world," writes Robert A. Gates, "there is no absolute difference between these two environments, only an imagined, mythical difference supported by suburban cliches."[41] Madness and other dangers regularly arrive from the City, like the commuter trains, to tear away the illusion of safety that blankets the suburbs—as in "The Five-Forty-Eight," a story in which a jilted secretary pursues her former boss and lover to Shady Hill, where she threatens him with a gun and forces him to lie with his face in the dirt before she walks away.

John Cheever was born in 1912, in Quincy, Massachusetts, and he always viewed New York City with an eye conditioned by his New England Puritan background. Disenchantment with Broadway in particular and New York City in general is reflected in a Cheever story of the postwar period, "O City of Broken Dreams." This simple tale of disillusionment begins when a Broadway producer offers a contract to a small-town author who has written a play based on one of his neighbors in Wentworth, Indiana. On the basis of this offer, Evarts Malloy sells all he has in Wentworth, then brings his wife and daughter to New York. At first, as the Malloys walk along brightly lit Broadway, the City appears to meet their high expectations: "The tall buildings in the east were lighted and seemed to burn, as if fire had fallen onto their dark shapes. The air was full of music, and the light was brighter than day. They drifted with the crowd for hours."[42] The shows at Radio City Music Hall and the meals at the Broadway Automat fill the Malloys with delight.

However, Malloy makes the mistake of getting caught up in a contractual disagreement between the producer and an agent. The producer retaliates by bringing the Wentworth man upon whom the play is based to Manhattan to sue Malloy. All hope of a production of his play is lost. At the end of the story, the Malloys are seen aboard another train, heading west, either back to Indiana or all the way to California, to pursue their dreams in Hollywood. What remains intact, as the title indicates, is Cheever's realization that New York City retains the power to entice and to extinguish the bright hopes of Americans.

John Cheever had his own theatrical hopes deflated in the City. Cheever, his wife, and two other couples rented a large townhouse on East Ninety-second Street in the fall of 1944; this experiment in communal living lasted only until the spring of 1945, when the Cheevers moved to East Fifty-ninth Street, but the townhouse supplied Cheever with "funny funny pieces" for the *New Yorker* and the subject of a play.[43] However, Cheever's *Town House* closed after twelve performances in September 1948.

Cheever lived in Manhattan, on and off, from the early 1930s to the early 1950s, when he and his family moved to the suburbs, first to nearby Westchester County, then up the Hudson to Ossining. The stories that he sets in the City are filled with mystery and danger. In "The Enormous Radio," for example, Jim and Irene Westcott, a couple noteworthy only in their averageness, live near but not, as they desire, on Sutton Place. Their latent anxieties emerge when Jim brings home a magic radio on which they can listen in on the shocking private conversations of their neighbors: "She overheard demonstrations of indigestion, carnal love, abysmal vanity, faith, and despair. Irene's life was nearly as simple and sheltered as it appeared to be, and the forthright and sometimes brutal language that came from the loudspeaker that morning astonished and troubled her."[44] Though they have the radio fixed so that they can no longer hear others' secrets, their own secret passions emerge. Jim complains about money, accuses his wife of vile deeds (stealing, abortion), and their marriage fails.

"The Season of Divorce" also focuses on an apparently conventional middle-class couple, living "in a walk-up in the East Fifties" sometime during World War II. The narrator tells us that his wife, Ethel, is being pursued by a casual acquaintance, Dr. Trencher. At first the narrator dismisses Dr. Trencher's obsession as one of those brief connections so common in New York City: "The city is full of accidental revelation, half-heard cries for help, and strangers who will tell you everything at the first suspicion of sympathy." The City is also full of omens. On Lexington Avenue, the troubled couple watch bombers heading for the sea: "It seemed the ebb of the year—an evil day for gastritis, sinus, and respiratory disease—and remembering other winters, the markings of the light convinced me that it was the season of divorce." Acknowledging her own empty life and her husband's indifference, Ethel feels sympathy for the passionate Dr. Trencher, who brings her roses. She wonders what difference it would make if she chose to go off with him. Though she does not do so and Dr. Trencher eventually leaves her alone, this Manhattan couple has no place to go but down.[45] Or to Cheever's suburbs, where they, or other couples like them, will try and fail to insulate themselves from terrors they first encounter in the City.

In Cheever's notorious journals—published posthumously, they reveal his alcoholism, his family turmoil, and his secret struggle with homosexuality—New York appears in all of its contradictions. In a brooding entry for December 1949, he walks along Fifth Avenue in an actual and symbolic mist: "The light in the sky is somber, there is brume in the air. The dead city trees of Central Park are massed like a thicket in the sombre light. In the brume the long double track of street lamps seems yellow. This appears to be a city of the Enlightenment—like Paris or London at the turn of the century; the irreducible evidence of man's inventiveness; progress."[46]

Despite its prosperous shine, Cheever's New York was a lonely place, with undertones of tension. On Christmas Eve 1952, as he recorded it, Cheever took his son to the skating rink in Central Park, where he hugged the boy with a sudden rush of love. Around him circled New Yorkers on holiday, but to Cheever "whole neighborhoods seemed desolate and forsaken and I felt myself sad and alone."[47] A few months later he walked along Madison Avenue and noted the surroundings with a heightened sense of place: "The tense atmosphere of an economic and a sexual content. Barring the admiration that follows pretty women, there is a good deal of tension—true ignorance—in the scrutiny New Yorkers give one another. There is not much gentility or trust in the looks on Madison Avenue."[48] However, New York remained the city of sexual energy, a place that aroused Cheever, as he revealed in a 1959 entry: "At 11 A.M. on the corner of Park Avenue and Thirty-sixth Street a tart gives me the eye."[49]

By 1971 the City's magic, though not its sluttish appeal, had eluded Cheever: "What has happened to this place where I used so happily to pound the sidewalks? Where has my city gone, where shall I look for it?"[50] He admitted to himself that he was more attracted to a row of young men fondling themselves at the urinals in Grand Central Station than he was to the string music played in the Palm Court. If the Cheever suburbs were awash in the sorrows of gin and the burdens of family life, his City was the place to release inhibitions, to throw off his sense of duty, to put away adult things, and to become, once again, a greedy, dreamy adolescent, bent on satisfying every sense. For John Cheever, New York City was a place of infinite possibilities, rare beauties, and dangerous promises, but in the end, it was also a place of pervasive sadness, of loss, and a fitting subject for his plaintive, elegant prose songs.

Irwin Shaw also evoked a City of transient beauty. Shaw, born in Brooklyn in

1913, began his long career by writing pacifist plays for leftist theater groups in the 1930s (*Bury the Dead*, 1936) and ended it by writing popular novels that were adapted for Hollywood and television films.

Shaw's New York stories are characterized by a special concern for the pervasive mystery and faded romance of the City. In "Noises in the City," Weatherby, an architect who works for a firm that erects glass-box buildings, encounters in a bar an old acquaintance who is drinking heavily; it is gradually revealed to Weatherby that his drinking companion is waiting to hear that the man who raped and murdered his wife has been executed. When Weatherby finally leaves the bar, gets home, and climbs into bed with his wife, he composes an urban prayer: "God deliver us from accident . . . and make us understand the true nature of the noises arising from the city around us."[51] For Shaw the case history reveals the vulnerability, derangement, and impermanence of the City, just as the stories in Joyce's *Dubliners* suggest a state of paralysis in that city.

Shaw's characters are also driven to interpret the sights of the City as emblems of their own desires, as does a man in "The Girls in Their Summer Dresses." Shaw sets Michael and his wife, Frances, on the streets of the City—those avenues of promise and betrayal: "Fifth Avenue was shining in the sun when they left the Brevoort and started walking toward Washington Square." Michael and Frances seem close and loving on this bright November Sunday in the glistening City. But New York is no Eden, for on its streets lurks an imp of the perverse, which will destroy their marriage. Michael cannot stop staring in appreciation at every beautiful woman he passes, and Frances does not like it. They argue, and he admits, "One of the things that I like best about New York is the battalion of women" it offers to admiring eyes. "When I think of New York I think of all the girls, . . . the young girls at the football games, with the red cheeks, and when the warm weather comes, the girls in their summer dresses." Both Frances and Michael know that the day will soon come when he will do more than admire the City's passing beauties from a distance.[52] Within a few blocks, the City, for this apparently happy couple, modulates from a romantic setting to the landscape of loss.

The City is also a place of regret for a character in Shaw's "Search through the Streets of the City." Paul runs into Harriet, an old love who is now married and pregnant, on Twelfth Street. They walk together, past old haunts from the days of their romance. The farther they walk, the further back Paul goes in his memory of their relationship, until he confesses how much he misses her: "I walk along Fifth Avenue and every time I pass St. Patrick's I half look up to see if you're passing." Harriet insists she doesn't remember their time together, though her tears suggest otherwise, and she rushes away from Paul. "He watched her cab go down Fifth Avenue until it turned. Then he turned the other way and started walking, thinking, I must move away from this neighborhood. I've lived here long enough."[53] Irwin Shaw's New York, like John Cheever's City, provides elusive, unrecoverable flashes of beauty and truth to those who search through its streets for their lost loves, their next loves, and their own misplaced sense of purpose.

THE SAGA OF THE NEW YORK INTELLECTUALS—A GROUP OF purposeful writers defined by their relations to the *Partisan Review* and driven by their passion for radicalism in the arts and politics—follows an arc over three decades: ascent from humble origins, eventual national acknowledgment, then diffusion and decline. "The New York intellectuals," writes Morris Dickstein, "were probably the closest thing America had to a Russian or French intelligentsia, a group of deracinated writers in rebellion against their social origins, passionate about ideas, marginal to political and economic power yet subtly influencing the mind and character of future generations."[54] They drew upon the City's cultural resources, and in turn, they gave the City a standing it had lacked in the world's intellectual community.[55]

These bright young men and women who composed the New York intellectuals emerged during the 1930s, frequently, though not exclusively, from the Jewish neighborhoods of New York's outer boroughs. Diana Trilling, one of their number, explains this in *The Beginning of the Journey* (1993), a memoir of her writing career and her marriage to Lionel Trilling, perhaps the most important writer among them:

> We casually speak of the intellectual life of New York City in the mid-twentieth century as New York Jewish intellectual life. This is not because it lacked distinguished practitioners who were not Jews but because so many of its influential figures were Jews, not only self-conscious but self-advertised Jews whose parents had come to this country from East Europe to escape religious and political oppression. These first-generation Americans were importantly concentrated in New York City and they gave its tone of significant contention to the intellectual life of America for several decades.[56]

The New York intellectuals have influenced critics and thinkers, if not often policymakers, for half a century, shaping a line of continuity from the 1930s to the 1980s, as have the journals they published, from the *Partisan Review* to the *New York Review of Books*. They placed literary works and political issues in broad national and international contexts. They insisted that the assumptions behind and the implications beyond judgments be explored. They fostered the life of the mind and the importance of the word more than any group in America since the Puritans. In Irving Howe's description of this group, of which he was a prominent member, they were anti-Communists, radicals—though *Commentary*, under the editorship of Norman Podhoretz, turned neoconservative in political and cultural concerns—and they were characterized by their ideology: "They revel in polemics; they strive self-consciously to be 'brilliant'; and by birth or osmosis, they are Jews."[57]

Initially, they were defined by their relations to Communism in politics and modernism in the arts. (*Partisan Review* began under the sponsorship of the John Reed Club, which, in turn, was supported by the Communist Party. In 1936, *Partisan Review* editors Philip Rahv and William Phillips suspended publication, broke with the Communists, and in 1937, brought out the new *Partisan Review*—a journal that was radical in the arts and politics, but independent of party affiliation, though it remained sympathetic to Leon Trotsky as well as to the artistic avant-garde.) In the late 1940s and 1950s, the New York intellectuals muted some of their political commitments, becoming more broadly social in their criticism and more literary in their expression.

They were in New York City, but not entirely of it. Instead of constituting a community, they were a fractious "family." Indeed, they were, in Podhoretz's words, a "Jewish family," with all the tangled ties, buried or expressed affections, and rivalries that that phrase implies.[58] "These were people who by virtue of their tastes, ideas, and general concerns found themselves stuck with one another against the rest of the world whether they liked it or not (and most did not), preoccupied with one another to the point of obsession, and intense in their attachments and hostilities as only a family is capable of being."[59]

Their story begins in American ghettos: Jewish neighborhoods from which they sought escape. As Clement Greenberg puts it, "Again and again they describe escapes or, better, flights from the restriction or squalor of the Brooklyns and Bronxes to the wide open world."[60] Writing provided them with wings—the means of transcendence. For example, Irving Howe was born in the East Bronx in 1920, in a neighborhood of Jewish immigrants, "a self-contained little world, lacking the cultural vivacity that had brightened the Lower East Side of Manhattan a decade or two earlier but otherwise, in custom and value, not very different." The Howe family grocery store went out of business in 1930, and Irving's father became a peddler. This condition of reduced expectations, combined with an attack of scarlet fever at age thirteen, drove young Howe inward, made him bookish. He also became an active socialist at DeWitt Clinton High School in the northwest Bronx.

After World War II, Howe began to publish literary pieces in *Commentary* and found work at Dwight Macdonald's short-lived monthly, *Politics*. Howe attacked *Partisan Review* for its postwar retreat from Marxism and was surprised when its editor, Philip Rahv, invited him to contribute essays. Howe felt he had crossed over into a brave new world: "When I began publishing my little pieces in *Partisan Review*, I swelled with a secret pride, feeling I had made my way into the best literary magazine in America. It seemed I was stepping into 'another world,' a community bright with freedom, bravura, and intimate exchange."[61]

In Irving Howe's vision, New York is a city of extremes: "It was New York as both imperial city and center of action, the powerhouse of capitalism and the crucible of socialism."[62] The City became his mythic center, the site of his personal and political maturation: "This New York also shaded off into myth, but usefully, for that was how some of us needed to see the city: enemy of philistines, antithesis of hayseed, proudly internationalist in vision. So it was, a little."

Howe's New York was an attractive place for a man who promoted Leon Trotsky in politics and high literary modernists in literature. Yet his City held many dangers and foreshadowed more to come: "The New York we knew was not just a vital metropolis brimming with politics and confusion; it was also brutal and ugly. . . . New York was frightening, not in the way it later became, as a place of violence and crime, but as a social vortex into which you might be dragged down, forever beyond rescue."[63]

Howe's New York belonged to the sons and the daughters of immigrants in ways that it never did to their parents. His City was a hive of political activity and was unified by the culture of the word. Irving Howe's memoir, *Margin of Hope* (1982), is amplified by what might be called his large "family" history of Jewish immigration, *World of Our Fathers* (1976). At his death, at age seventy-two, in 1993, the *New Yorker* fairly described Howe as a most distinguished member of the group he helped to define: "He was the most energetic, the hardest-working, arguably the most independent and idealistic, certainly the most authentic."[64] Indeed, it was Howe who came up with the term "New York intellectuals."

As the story of Howe and others illustrates, many of the New York intellectuals journeyed into downtown Manhattan to write for *Partisan Review*, the central clearinghouse and vetting-station in political and cultural matters from the late

1930s to the 1960s. (the *New Republic*, *Commentary*, *Dissent*, and other journals also drew upon this group of writers.) Philip Rahv and William Phillips declared that the *Review* would "bring about a rapprochement between the radical tradition on the one hand and the tradition of modern literature on the other."[65] Thus revolutionary modernism defined the focus of the *Partisan Review* mind.

Lionel Trilling, who personified this mind, was born and grew up in the City; he, too, studied at DeWitt Clinton High School; then he studied at Columbia University, where he began his distinguished teaching career in 1932. But Trilling blended the passions and styles of many sections of the City. In 1929 he had moved into a Greenwich Village apartment; there he watched the comings and goings of Edmund Wilson, who lived across the street. For Trilling, Wilson's presence in the Village was enough "to validate its present dignity, to suggest that what the Village stood for in American life was not wholly a matter of history."[66] Wilson, an essayist, a political radical, and an advocate of European literary modernism, served as a model for Trilling and for other members of the New York intellectuals who sought to transform themselves and their world.

Perhaps Wilson also provided the observant Trilling with an example of detached participation in his milieu. Daniel Aaron says that Wilson, in the Village in that era, "became as bohemian as he ever would be. He conquered his sexual inhibitions, drank excessively, mingled with types he had seldom encountered at Princeton, yet retained his reserve and kept himself at a distance from the undisciplined revelers."[67] Trilling, though no reveler, would also serve as an elegant, somewhat detached presence in this world of passionately held opinions. When *Partisan Review* held the symposium "The Situation in American Writing" in the summer and fall of 1939, Trilling wrote out his credo: "My own literary interest—and I suppose that in a writer this is an allegiance—is in the tradition of humanistic thought and in the intellectual middle class which believes that it continues this tradition."[68] He might have been speaking for the other members of the New York intellectuals who had escaped their ethnic neighborhoods, and who sought as well to transcend the parochialism of the City and the provincialism of American culture to find their places in "the tradition of humanistic thought."

Trilling's fascination with Wilson also demonstrates the link between the Village bohemians of the 1920s and the *Partisan Review* radicals of the 1930s and beyond. In both eras, young Americans turned their eyes to Europe for inspiration and validation.[69] As Podhoretz puts it, "When the family spoke of itself or was spoken of as 'alienated,' the reference might be to any number of things, but the deepest thing of all was this: *They did not feel that they belonged to America or that*

America belonged to them."[70] According to Delmore Schwartz, "New York was not really an American city—it was 'the last outpost of Europe' on these shores—and the intellectual life does not fit in with our native American habits. I think there is something to be said for this point of view."[71]

Lionel Trilling established a presence for the "family" at Columbia, where he taught until his death in 1975. High-minded, respectable, and rational, Trilling spoke for and to what he called the liberal imagination. "The job of criticism," wrote Trilling, "would seem to be, then, to recall liberalism to its first essential imagination of variousness and possibility, which implies the awareness of complexity and difficulty."[72] In his only novel, *The Middle of the Journey* (1947), Trilling looked back to the 1930s era of ideological disputation; to do so, he removed his characters to the idyllic countryside of Crannock, Connecticut, perhaps implying that such matters could not be adequately addressed in Manhattan. His protagonist, John Laskell, who is recovering from scarlet fever, seeks a new life in the country, but he discovers, as do many characters in Cheever's stories, that the ideological and emotional tensions of the City have followed him.

Trilling saw his best hopes for a liberal consensus fade in 1968, when students struck against Columbia—more family divisions—police brutally attacked the student strikers, and the New York intellectuals divided, making passionate verbal attacks upon each other.[73] By the 1970s, as Alexander Bloom notes, Trilling, though held in high esteem, presided over a fractured, depleted community: "He had become a New York intellectual of widespread influence, not the representative of an influential community of New York Intellectuals."[74]

The *Partisan Review* world, for editor and essayist William Barrett, was cut off from the rest of Manhattan. Though "cosmopolitan in its ideas, [it] was a sealed-off circle and it seemed to transpire largely below Fourteenth Street. 'Midtown' was for us the name of an alien territory, the haunt of the middlebrows and philistines of the cultural world."[75] However, some New York intellectuals—Alfred Kazin, Irving Howe, Dwight Macdonald, for example—found employment and literary purpose in midtown, working for Henry Luce at *Fortune* or *Time*. Eventually the New York intellectuals moved up—uptown from the Village, up the economic and power scale, and up in their own sense of authority and importance.

These changes are dramatized in Alfred Kazin's three-volume memoir—*A Walker in the City* (1951), *Starting Out in the Thirties* (1965), and *New York Jew* (1978)—an account of his rise from a Jewish neighborhood to a place of prominence as an American literary critic and an example of the move by many members of this group from critical commentary to creative, usually autobiographical, writing. In his tribute, Dickstein says that Kazin, "in three passionate, turbulent volumes of memoirs" showed himself "as a writer, not just a commentator on other people's books."[76]

New York Jew opens in 1942, when, during "one dreamlike week" in his twenty-seventh year, Kazin saw his first book published (*On Native Grounds*, a study of American literature and society); became an editor of the *New Republic*; and, with his first wife, moved into an apartment on Twenty-fourth Street and Lexington Avenue. Alfred Kazin, who had been born and bred in East Brooklyn, in Brownsville, had "arrived." He had never lived in Manhattan, so his literary successes became his "personal deliverance" from the life and mind of the ghetto. Throughout his first weeks in the City, he moved "in a dizzy exaltation mixed with the direst suspicion of what might happen next."[77]

On Native Grounds had been researched in the open reading room of the New York Public Library. Between 1938 and 1942, Kazin had crossed Fifth Avenue and passed under the inscription over the main door: "BUT ABOVE ALL THINGS TRUTH BEARETH AWAY THE VICTORY." There he had rooted himself in the tradition of American letters, absorbing authority and power from his surroundings: "Even the spacious twin reading rooms, each two blocks long, gave me a sense of the powerful amenity that I craved for my own life, a world of American power in which my own people had moved about as strangers."[78] The City would provide Kazin with other settings from which he would draw authority.

By the 1940s, the *New Republic* had also moved uptown, from its original location on West Twenty-first Street to the midtown center of corporate power at Forty-ninth Street and Madison Avenue. When he went to work for Henry Luce, writing for *Fortune*, Kazin worked his way even closer to this hub of power. Luce exulted in "the American Century"—his term for the theory that America must accept the fact of its own preeminence—and he saw its center as the Time-Life Building in Rockefeller Center. Kazin absorbed Luce's charisma and assertiveness into his own character and prose: "It was impossible in that office, overlooking the heaped-up splendor of New York, to feel oneself less than brilliant. It was from working in that building that I knew why every sentence in *Time* had to strike like a rapier, shine like steel."[79]

Though Kazin had been nurtured in socialism, he and Luce, a bully missionary for capitalism, shared a similar vision of the City: "New York in 1943 was the beacon, the world city of freedom, openness, hope." European intellectuals escaped Fascist Europe and they found a new life in Manhattan. Yet Kazin's City was never as provincial as Luce's. "My 'world city' was never more full of talent, brains, buried treasure. Delmore Schwartz was right. Europe was still the biggest thing in North America."[80]

Still, Kazin never ceased to appreciate the wonder of New York. Though he would complain that F. Scott Fitzgerald had viewed the City through the awed eyes of a midwestern tourist, Kazin admits that he, too, "was still a tourist in midtown, Rockefeller Center, Greenwich Village." As a result, City places held for him boundless promise, particularly the Village, which was, in his mind's eye, suffused in culture and sexuality. There even "the purple, red, and green lights flashing into the street were a promise of wickedness"; there literary voices resounded: "No one from Indiana ever felt the freedom of the Village as much as I did—I who had never lived in it, who could never walk down Eighth Street without expecting that one of the many girls in ballet slippers that year would skip into my life."[81]

Perhaps not surprisingly, one young woman did, and soon Kazin was tortured over his opportunity to begin an affair that he knew would end his marriage. At the same time, his elevated location in the Time-Life Building gave Kazin delusions of grandeur, and he describes being poised on the brink of damnation through infidelity: "Looking out at my window, I knew that I had been brought to the top of the mountain and shown the kingdom of this world—there was nothing to do but to do it." New York's beauty and power enticed him to leap into transforming experience and awful awareness. "The gruffness of the stone," Kazin notes, staring down at Fifth Avenue, "the sharpness of the view, the steely white brilliance of the cold New York spires around me made me dizzy. I was falling through the air, rushing to my doom."[82] More prosaically, Kazin phoned the young artist from the Village and learned to live with the ways of the world in the City.

Indeed, this story line was oft-repeated in Kazin's life, as a new young love replaced the old; each time the City lent drama and danger to his brief encounters. After World War II, returning to Brooklyn Heights from an evening with the exotic Louise, "in her chic little walk-up on Fifty-fifth off Fifth," Kazin was struck anew by the grandeur and potential destructiveness of the City: "The tritest word for the city was 'unbelievable.' Its beauty rested on nothing but power, was dramatic, unashamed, flinging against the sky, like a circus act, one crazy 'death-defying' show after another."[83] The City, for Kazin, represented what the English Romantic poets called the Sublime.

Kazin saw his fate inextricably interwoven into the destiny of the City. Small wonder that he labored long to write a "wildly ranging book on all of New York" and came to compose a memoir of his youth titled *A Walker in the City*. In that book, written after his second divorce, Kazin describes himself as a young man from a Yiddish-speaking home who suffered from a stammer, and who, as a result, sought his true voice in the English language and his true home in American literature.[84] As he reiterated in *New York Jew*; "he became a walking pilgrim, quick to sniff the New York ozone as the many exciting worlds of which literature is made."[85] For Kazin, New York City stood as the grand backdrop to his passionate quest for his authentic self and for possession of his idea of America.

Kazin concludes *New York Jew* with a scene that combines, characteristically, impressions drawn from literature and life. High up in a library at Park Avenue and Sixty-ninth Street, he confers with a young West Indian woman on the intricacies of William Butler Yeats's "Sailing to Byzantium." Though Kazin does not say so, the student, with her halting English, seems an echo of his stammering, younger self; she, too, is a representative of a generation of strangers who search for their America. Kazin ends his memoir with a vivid sense of his own and his City's transformation:

> *I feel I am dreaming aloud as I look at the rooftops, at the sky, at the massed white skyline of New York. The view just across the rooftops is as charged as the indented black words on the white page. The mass and pressure of the bulging skyline are wild. New York is wild and Yeats is wild. How wonderful and funny it can be, this late October afternoon, to be going over Yeats word for word and line by line against the screech of millions all over the city. Even in its "last days," the secret of New York is raw power, mass and volume, money and power.*[86]

William Barrett, in his memoir, *The Truants* (1983), looks back on the world of the New York intellectuals with far less enthusiasm than does Kazin. Barrett grew up in a Catholic family, in the Bronx, but he was initiated into the New York intellectuals' world during his studies at City College in the 1930s. After World War II, he was enlisted by his friend Delmore Schwartz to do editorial work and write essays (notably on existentialism) for *Partisan Review*. For Barrett the New York intellectuals of his generation were "truants" because they pursued ideas that detached them from the common concerns of life. Though the *Review* group lived in New York, Barrett charged, their minds were elsewhere: on European politics and art or in some empyrean realm of imagination. Barrett's truant intellectual "goes in search of original and sweeping ideas, and in the process may conveniently forget the humbling conditions of his own existence."[87]

The writer who most strongly asserted the primacy of European culture, Delmore Schwartz, died a broken alcoholic in 1966; he served as a model of blighted promise for Barrett, who invoked Wordsworth for Schwartz's epitaph and, in a way, for the entire group of New York intellectuals: "We poets in our youth begin in gladness,/ But thereof come in the end despondency and madness."[88]

Schwartz, a "New York boy," was first buoyed by great expectations, but he grew disillusioned after the Crash, which destroyed his family's fortunes: He "fell with the market that October day,/ In New America in 1929!"[89] Schwartz's most notable story, "In Dreams Begin Responsibility," was published in the first *Partisan Review* in 1937, when he was twenty-four. It is a brilliant but bleak tale in which Schwartz begs his parents not to marry and have children. The story became a self-fulfilling prophesy for Schwartz, who died of a heart attack, alone in a cheap hotel. His rapid literary rise and dramatic fall exemplified the success and foreshadowed the decline of the whole New York intellectual community.

A series of strains loosened the group's family ties after World War II. By the 1950s, Podhoretz suggests, the *Partisan Review* group resembled "nothing so much as a bad marriage being held together for the sake of the child."[90] Ironically, Podhoretz—who helped Paul Goodman get *Growing Up Absurd* (1960) published—became one of the "prodigal sons," in Alexander Bloom's phrase, in this increasingly dysfunctional family. Podhoretz grants its "disintegration" in the third (that is, his) generation of New York intellectuals, but he blames "the inexorable process of acculturation," not their ideological differences.[91] Whatever the cause, by the 1970s the New York intellectuals were a family only in memory, a family without a future, indeed, a family whose members were leaving their home in the City.

As early as the 1950s, academic appointments were breaking up the gang. First Irving Howe and then Philip Rahv went off to teach at Brandeis, outside Boston. In 1963 *Partisan Review* itself did what would once have been unthinkable, moving out of the City, to Rutgers, in New Brunswick, New Jersey, where William Phillips joined the faculty. Later, the journal, along with Phillips, moved again, to Boston, where it is housed at Boston University.

Political differences, always a part of the community, further strained relations in this period. The Rosenberg and Hiss cases, along with the McCarthy investigations of fellow travelers, caused many crises of convictions. Sidney

Hook, Norman Podhoretz, and other former radicals turned sharply conservative. Dispersal and disputation broke down what unity was left among those Harold Rosenberg called "the herd of independent minds." The generation of intellectuals who were born after 1940 found their true home in academe, argues Russell Jacoby in *The Last Intellectuals*. As a result, most notably in the 1950s, they abandoned the freelance journalism and City-living of previous generations of intellectuals.[92]

The City grew too expensive to support its long-standing bohemia.[93] Robert Moses carried forward the Eisenhower era's emphasis upon road building, which led to the expansion of suburbia, a phenomenon that depleted the resources of the cities. In the mid 1950s, Moses even tried to push a major highway across lower Manhattan, through Washington Square Park. Jane Jacobs, with the help of others, successfully opposed this destruction of a valuable urban neighborhood, and was inspired by the experience to write *The Death and Life of Great American Cities*.[94] Gentrification revitalized a few neighborhoods, but that was balanced by the collapse of many more in an increasingly stratified City.

Ambitions added to the fragmentation of the New York intellectuals in the 1960s. In *Making It* (1967), an autobiography written when he was thirty-seven, Norman Podhoretz wrote: "One of the longest journeys in the world is the journey from Brooklyn to Manhattan—or at least from certain neighborhoods in Brooklyn to certain parts of Manhattan." Podhoretz made that journey from Jewish Brooklyn, via Columbia and Cambridge, to literary New York, where he became the editor in 1960 of *Commentary*, a journal whose influence during the 1960s reached far beyond the Jewish community.[95] In *Making It*, Podhoretz traces the intellectual and social ascent that carried him into another country, a Manhattan world of cocktail parties and intellectual discourse far from his native Brooklyn. In his journey, Podhoretz claims to have discovered that ambition "seems to be replacing erotic lust as the prime dirty little secret of the well-educated American soul."[96] Certainly Podhoretz found his center of literary ambition in Manhattan. In time he encountered, as well, some cold shoulders from his old friends in the intellectual community when he supported America's involvement in Vietnam and blamed the antiwar movement for that country's condition.[97]

The New York intellectual community can be seen as a phenomenon undermined by its own success. Their achievement, in the end, was not in political discourse—all those fine discriminations between the positions of Lenin, Stalin, and Trotsky that fixed their attention for so long. Their achievement can better be seen in a kind of criticism that fused literary and cultural concerns, like Alfred Kazin's *On Native Grounds* and Lionel Trilling's *The Liberal Imagination*.

Perhaps their most achieved work appears in a number of striking memoirs, books that acknowledge the shaping presence of the City. For many New York intellectuals, reverie replaced radicalism in the 1970s and 1980s. So many memoirs appeared—by Alfred Kazin, Irving Howe, Lionel Abel, William Phillips, Sidney Hook, William Barrett, Elizabeth Hardwick, Mary McCarthy, and Diana Trilling—that Morris Dickstein said, "In the twilight of their existence as a recognizable group, the New York intellectuals threatened to be taken up as an American Bloomsbury, more famous for their witty sallies and outlandish personalities than for anything they wrote."[98] These autobiographical statements recount the quest these young men and women undertook when they made that long trek, that significant passage—often across the Brooklyn Bridge—from their Jewish immigrant ghetto to the wider world offered by Manhattan.

Diana Trilling concludes her memoir with the death of Lionel Trilling and a lament for the world they had known, "the intellectual culture of this country," which "no longer exists." A noble way of life and thought—at home in America's quintessential city, but looking far beyond America's borders for inspiration and achieving an intellectual authority that transcended its New York identity—was gone: "The New York intellectuals had their moment in history and it has passed. Theirs was uniquely the age of criticism. Their criticism went everywhere. They had no gods, no protectorates or sacred constituencies. They were a small, geographically concentrated group, but if they did nothing else, they kept the general culture of the country in balance."[99]

THE NEW YORK INTELLECTUALS CELEBRATED THOSE writers of drama and fiction who presented New York City as a center of crisis—personal and public, economic and moral—in works of art that built upon the tradition of European modernism. Arthur Miller, Saul Bellow, Isaac Bashevis Singer, Bernard Malamud, Norman Mailer, and others helped to give New York a particularly Jewish intellectual emphasis; at the same time, the central characters of their works are offered as representative men and women of the Republic. Indeed, in part through the influence of their works, marginality (of race, class, ethnicity, and culture) becomes the most informing experience of New York literature.

Arthur Miller's *Death of a Salesman*, first produced in New York in early 1949, describes the tragic life of Willy Loman, whose name, Miller explains, implies "a terror-stricken man calling into the void for help that will never come."[100] Willy is "tired to death" after years of selling an unnamed product for the Wagner Company, which no longer values him. Loman and his family live in a borough of New York City, in a neighborhood that is closing in upon its residents. "The street is lined with cars," Willy complains to his wife, Linda. "There's not a breath of fresh air in the neighborhood. The grass don't grow any more, you can't raise a carrot in the back yard. They should've had a law against apartment houses. Remember those two beautiful elm trees out there? When I and Biff hung the swing between them?" Linda underlines Miller's point in her reply: "Yeah, like being a million miles from the city."[101] For Miller, born in New York in 1915, the City exemplifies pernicious elements in American life. Yet the City is the site of dramatic conflict and tragic realization for Miller's trapped characters.

The sterile life of the City, where nothing grows, and the reductive values of a salesman's life—"Business is definitely business," says Willy to the callow young man who is firing him—lead Willy to conclude that he is worth more to his family dead than alive.[102] His son, Biff, hates and blames the City for their condition: "We don't belong in this nuthouse of a city! We should be mixing cement on some open plain, or—carpenters. A carpenter is allowed to whistle."[103] Willy has never built anything enduring. Even his house, as called for in Miller's set description, is semi-transparent, an insubstantial place where characters pass through imaginary walls, as though they are drifting in a dream. Indeed, New York City in *Death of a Salesman* is a dreamscape. The best that can be said for Willy, who commits suicide before the play's end, is stated at his funeral by his neighbor, Charley: "A salesman has got to dream, boy. It comes with the territory."[104] However, given the waste and pathos of Willy Loman's life, that territory, located on the outskirts of New York City, is a lifeless desert.

Though Saul Bellow was born in Canada in 1915 and was reared in Chicago, he became the chief fictional voice of the New York *Partisan Review* circle—in Maxwell Geismar's phrase, the "novelist of the intellectuals."[105] Alfred Kazin also notes that "more than anyone else, Bellow connected one novel after another with a representative Jew in order to represent Jewish experience itself." But Bellow's works reach beyond his Jewish intellectual base. From Augie March to Herzog, Bellow's heroes became even larger figures—postwar America's representative men—an opinion supported by the award of the Nobel Prize for Literature to Bellow in 1976.[106]

First "discovered" by Philip Rahv in Chicago in the 1930s, Bellow published

"Two Morning Monologues" in *Partisan Review* in 1941, then contributed five more stories to that journal during the next ten years. Bellow became, in Podhoretz's words, "the family's White Hope, as it were, in fiction."[107] Bellow's heroes possess what might be called the definitive urban intellectual style—self-conscious, culturally allusive, combative, anxious, and probing.

Bellow's heart of America is big-shouldered Chicago. "Chicago with its gigantesque outer life contained the whole problem of poetry and the inner life in America," reflects Charlie Citrine, narrator of *Humboldt's Gift* (1975). In Chicago "you could look into such things through a sort of fresh-water transparency."[108] In New York City, however, Bellow's heroes are more likely to look into such things through a glass darkly. Yet they travel to New York to learn more about the inner life of America and to find their places in it. Citrine, for example, comes from Wisconsin to New York to meet a famous, troubled poet, Von Humboldt Fleisher, a character based upon Delmore Schwartz. Fleisher's *Harlequin Ballads*, published in the 1930s, echoes Schwartz's poems of that period. Both Fleisher and Schwartz die young, self-destructive, and disconsolate in Manhattan, their early promise unrealized. In Bellow's fiction, too, New York can be a lethal experience, a killer of the poetic spirit.

Bellow—like other Chicago novelists before him, most notably Theodore Dreiser and James T. Farrell—came to New York to seek his literary fortune. First in *Dangling Man* (1944), a novel about the existential dread of a man awaiting his draft call-up, and then in *The Victim* (1947), Bellow established a knowing, urban voice for postwar American fiction. "The air of having lived, of experiencing the big city in every pore, of being on the spot, is the great thing about Bellow's fiction," says Kazin.[109]

Bellow's *The Victim* is an allegory of sorts, set in New York City, in which a hero finds himself in an Inferno but seeks release into Purgatorio.[110] The landscape of Manhattan is far more surreal and romantic than that of Bellow's hog-butcher Chicago: "On some nights New York is as hot as Bangkok. The whole continent seems to have moved from its place and slid nearer the equator."[111] The City is the realm of moral ambiguity, a place "where Jew and Gentile form a symbiotic relationship in which the Jew becomes the keeper of the social torch, by way of Gentile blackmail of him," in an analysis of this novel by Frederick R. Karl.[112] In *The Victim*, Asa Leventhal is hounded by Kirby Allbee, though it is Allbee who feels victimized and it is Leventhal who experiences guilt at Allbee's misfortune. Though the novel has the cosmopolitan feel of European fiction— invoking the "double" figure out of Dostoyevsky and Conrad—it also owes much to New York writers Poe and Melville. From the moment when Leventhal nearly misses his stop on the Third Avenue train, he feels pursued, another potential victim, like Poe's man of the crowd. The responsibility Leventhal feels for Allbee, who lost his job at the trade magazine where Leventhal still works, reminds us of the concerned lawyer who employed Bartleby in Melville's story of mid-nineteenth-century urban office life. In both cases, the reputed victims, Bartleby and Allbee, insist that attention be paid to the common humanity that binds them to their ostensible victimizers. Yet both "victims" may be urban con men. Thus are the City's airs polluted with deceits.

On his way to Staten Island, Leventhal contemplates the eerie City: "The towers on the shore rose up in huge blocks, scorched, smoky, gray, and bare white where the sun was direct upon them." For Leventhal the light appears yellow, "like the slit of the eye of a wild animal, say a lion, something inhuman that didn't care about anything human and yet was implanted in every human being too." The whole land-and-seascape takes on this surreal aspect: "The Jersey shore, yellow, tawny, and flat, appeared on the right. The Statue of Liberty rose and traveled backward again; in the trembling air, it was black, a twist of black that stood up like smoke."[113] Similarly, the promise of liberty recedes in the New York of *The Victim*.

In *Seize the Day* (1956) Bellow studies a day in the life of a dispossessed and ineffective man who holds onto redeeming values despite his destructive urban environment. Tommy Wilhelm's threatening, horrific New York (Upper West Side) constitutes "the most living, throbbing character" in the novella, suggests Kazin.[114] Tommy, an unemployed salesman, divorced and nearly broke, is making one final push to get his life together. Like Willy Loman, he is a pastoral romantic and wants to escape from the City's prison walls and bottom line. He tells his father, a fellow resident of the Hotel Gloriana on upper Broadway, "I can't take city life any more, and I miss the country. There's too much push here for me."[115] Indeed, New York is Bellow's modern wasteland. When Tommy and his deceiver Tamkin—who persuades him to invest his last savings in lard rather than winter rye—emerge from the Gloriana onto Broadway, on their way to get disastrous market reports, they encounter an atmosphere that is "not clear but throbbing through the dust and fumes, a false air of gas visible at eye-level as it spurted from the bursting buses. From old habit, Wilhelm turned up the collar of his jacket."[116] This gesture, however, does not protect him. Lard falls and Tommy fails.

Yet Bellow, nothing if not dialectical, also shows the City as a test of faith in democracy, a test Tommy passes when he recalls a moment of Whitman-like love he once felt for his fellow New Yorkers in the subway tunnel under Times

Square. Tommy's epiphany is embedded in the ordinary events of life in New York: "The idea of this larger body had been planted in him a few days ago beneath Times Square, where he had gone downtown to pick up tickets for the baseball game on Saturday (a double header at the Polo Grounds)." There, deep under the City's streets, "all of a sudden, unsought, a general love for all these imperfect and lurid-looking people burst out in Wilhelm's breast. He loved them."[117] However, Tommy's capacity to love and his affirmation of human dignity count for little in the survival-of-the-fittest atmosphere of the City. At the end of this determining day, rejected by his cold father and duped out of his money by the scheming Tamkin, Tommy moves through the gassy air of Broadway, toward a revelation: "The traffic seemed to come down Broadway out of the sky, where the hot spokes of the sun rolled from the south. Hot, stony odors rose from the subway grating in the street."[118] In the novel's final scene, Tommy stumbles into a funeral parlor and cries with abandon for the death of a stranger, perhaps for the death of the City. Bystanders are puzzled and unmoved by his grief, for they, true New Yorkers all, do not want to acknowledge, as does Tommy, their common humanity.

In *Mr. Sammler's Planet* (1969), Arthur Sammler, a man in his seventies, mixes his Holocaust-era memories with his responses to the contemporary horrors of the City. In Sammler's eyes, the City's women are wanton, its students are crude and ignorant, its streets are dangerous. Sammler dwells on the Upper West Side, in a room with a view of the City's various displays. "Brownstones, balustrades, bay windows, wrought-iron," suggest "bourgeois solidity" to him. To the east he sees "a soft asphalt belly rising, in which lay steaming sewer navels," in this sleeping giant of a City. Westward, across the Hudson, he contemplates an electric sign, flashing out the word "SPRY." "But," he ruefully acknowledges to himself, "he was half blind."[119] However, he is not so blind that he cannot attend to the perverse art of the black pickpocket who robs passengers on a bus that Sammler regularly rides. His wallet is stolen by the pickpocket, who then stalks him to his apartment, flaunting his huge penis before the old man as a warning to stay silent about the crime. Though terrified, Sammler admires the bravura of this obscene act. In *The Victim*, it is difficult to tell the victim from the victimizer, the dancer from the dance; however, in the *danse macabre* of Sammler's New York, the lines are clear. Culture and civility are under threat from a new, predatory urban violence and vulgarity.

Though Sammler dwells in an upper story of his apartment house, he too is something of an underground man, a survivor in a hostile environment. An Oxford graduate, Sammler knew Bloomsbury culture in the 1920s before he experienced persecution from Nazis in the 1930s; he has survived all that to test himself against the terrors of New York in the 1960s. "You must train yourself," he reflected. "You had to be strong enough not to be terrified by local effects of metamorphosis, to live with disintegration, with crazy streets, filthy nightmares, monstrosities come to life, addicts, drunkards, and perverts celebrating their despair openly in midtown." It is not at all clear that Arthur Sammler, who stands for the best in modern Western culture, can endure the assaults, physical and psychic, of contemporary New York City: "Daily at five or six A.M. Mr. Sammler woke up in Manhattan and tried to get a handle on the situation. He didn't think he could."[120]

In "New York: World-Famous Impossibility," a 1970 essay that echoes some of the complaints made about New York by Henry James in 1904, Bellow tries to define the character of the City. "New York is stirring, insupportable, agitated, ungovernable, demonic." It is a city that has lost its claim to being the artistic center of American culture; it has become, instead, "the business center of American culture, the amusement center, the excitement center, the anxiety center." New York, which once celebrated its theater, has itself become "the theater of the nation," a place whose continuous performance of outrages and vulgarities outsiders never tire of watching. Bellow, it seems, has given up on New York, for he warns people away from the City: "Those who wish to *feel* its depth had better be careful. For fifteen years I lived in and with New York. I now reside in Chicago."[121]

Isaac Bashevis Singer, who won the Nobel Prize for Literature in 1978, may have served Bellow as a partial model for Arthur Sammler, for Singer, too, escaped European fascism and carried Old World culture (Jewish, modernist) to the New World. Singer came to America from Warsaw in 1935, when he was thirty-one. In New York City, where he continued to write his fiction in Yiddish, publishing in the *Jewish Daily Forward*, he expressed the Yiddish-American cultural tradition previously articulated by Abraham Cahan. In 1953 Singer's audience was dramatically expanded when Saul Bellow translated a Singer story, "Gimpel the Fool," for *Partisan Review*.

New York for Singer, as it was for Bellow, was concentrated in the Upper West Side. For Singer, however, this was a more benign territory, perhaps because he lived there most of his life and saw it as a refuge from the European totalitarianism that overran his beloved Warsaw. Indeed, New York's Upper West Side—with its Yiddish voices and flavors, its cafeterias, coffee and pastry shops, and crowds along Broadway—reminded Singer of the Warsaw of his youth. Singer would walk the City, some 120 blocks a day, before returning to his rent-controlled apartment in the massive, Renaissance-style Belcord, located at Eighty-sixth Street and Broadway, where he wrote with a view of the streets. "On Broadway," said Singer's neighbor, "he could see images of those characters that he often wrote about."[122]

In *Enemies, a Love Story* (1972), Singer's best work of fiction, the setting is a Jewish community in Brooklyn, just after World War II. There, Herman Broder, a Holocaust survivor, is still wary. As he walks along Stillwell Avenue, "his eye sought hiding places in case the Nazis were to come to New York." However, he reassures himself that he is in a land of safety and plenty: "The richness of color, the abundance, the freedom—cheap and shoddy as everything was—surprised Herman each time he saw it."[123] New York City, he thought, was a place of freedom and opportunity. But Herman learns that this freedom does not release him from the past. Already pulled between two wives, fellow émigrés, he is confronted by his first wife, whom he thought had died in one of the death camps. Singer's America, as defined by his highly textured New York City, is no land of innocence; instead it is a place where freedom from oppression allows one the chance to choose a morally responsible course of action, if that can be discerned.

Bernard Malamud's *The Assistant* (1957) looks back on Depression-era Jewish New York, which he knew from first-hand experience. (Malamud was born in Brooklyn in 1914; he earned degrees at City College and Columbia during the Depression.) Yet *The Assistant*, with its surreal feel and post-Holocaust emphasis upon the Jew as moral exemplar, is clearly a postwar work. Malamud uses a Jewish immigrant's run-down grocery store as a central symbol of the City as wasteland. As Frederick R. Karl suggests, "the neighborhood seems hooded or veiled, hardly alive, the city a Kafkan necropolis."[124] Malamud's City contracts to the size of Morris Bober's mean and narrow store, which has been suffering a slow decline for twenty-one years. Bober is a latter-day Job, suffering the inexplicable and unrelieved afflictions of humanity: "He recalled the bad times he had lived through, but now times were worse than in the past; now they were impossible. . . . When he had first bought the grocery it was all right for the neighborhood; it had got worse as the neighborhood had." Though he has worked sixteen hours a day, he is "close to bankruptcy, his patience torn."[125] So, on one level, the novel, like Miller's *Death of a Salesman*, is a realistic narrative of diminishing expectations and disillusionment with the mocking promise of success and personal transformation offered by the City.

On another level, the store, the neighborhood, and the City in *The Assistant* dissolve into a symbolic moral landscape, a terrain where one's faith, capacity, and character are tested. After Morris is robbed and beaten, he hires Frankie Alpine, a young man who asks to work in the store. The reader is aware, though Morris is not, that Frankie is one of those who assaulted Morris. Frankie is at first driven by guilt, then by lust for Morris's daughter, and finally by his goal to transform himself into Morris—to become another Jew whose nobility is confirmed through suffering. After Morris dies, Frankie becomes the caretaker of the miserable store. He even has himself circumcised: "The pain enraged and inspired him. After Passover he became a Jew."[126] In *The Assistant*, the marginal, persecuted New York Jew becomes Everyman and the alienated urban man becomes a Jew.

Malamud's *The Tenants* (1971) focuses upon the troubled City of the 1960s by posing a stark contrast between two writers: Lesser, a white Jew, and Spearmint, a black revolutionary. They share an abandoned building in the City, read each other's works, and debate the art and purpose of fiction. Lesser urges detachment and formal control, while Spearmint stresses passionate involvement, whatever it costs the form of his work. Each writer becomes the other's nemesis. Each seduces the other's woman and destroys the other's work. The confrontation between these two cultural and aesthetic traditions results in a kind of personal apocalypse for each man. Lesser conveys an especially bitter view of New York and their place in it: "Ah, this live earth, this sceptered isle on a silver sea, this Thirty-first Street and Third Avenue. This forsaken house."[127] This forsaken city, Malamud implies, either fosters the death of art or promotes an art that portrays death.

Norman Mailer's New York is low, mean, and dirty. Though Mailer, born in New Jersey in 1923, was reared in Brooklyn, where he still makes his home, Mailer's City is a threatening place of dangerous encounters that liberate dark political and sexual impulses. After he graduated from Harvard in 1943, Mailer became a rifleman in an infantry unit, serving in the South Pacific. Thereafter, war became Mailer's central metaphor. "A good war, like anything else which is good, offers the possibility that further effort will produce a determinable effect upon chaos, evil and waste," writes Mailer in *The Armies of the Night* (1968).[128] New York exemplifies warfare—between his characters, and between his characters and their country.

New York is a place of persecution in Mailer's *Barbary Shore* (1951), a novel set in a Brooklyn rooming house. The novel's protagonist and narrator, Michael Lovett, is a veteran who lost his memory during the war. He is determined to become a successful novelist, but he gets stalled by his involvement in political and sexual intrigues. This static novel presents case histories of derangement: the strange tales of Lovett's randy landlady and his conspiratorial fellow boarders.

The action of the novel revolves around a mysterious man, McLeod, who is killed because he possesses an unrevealed secret, which he passes along to Lovett, who escapes with it. Mailer's deliberately disconnected novel, full of devious and depraved characters, illustrates McLeod's contention that "the deterioration continues until we are faced with mankind in barbary."[129] Mailer would come to see *Barbary Shore*, a novel with "high fevers," as a work possessing "a kind of insane insight into the psychic mysteries of Stalinists, secret policemen, narcissists, children, Lesbians, hysterics, revolutionaries—it has the air which for me is the air of our time, authority and nihilism stalking one another in the orgiastic hollow of this century."[130]

Advertisements for Myself (1959)—a collection carrying the definitive Mailer title, theme, and format—contains essays, columns, letters, interviews, bits of fictional works-in-progress, and two tables of contents; these are stitched together by italicized passages of autobiography. In *Advertisements* Mailer sets form against chaos, in manner and matter.[131] In *Advertisements* Mailer is also often at war with himself, especially in "The Homosexual Villain," an essay in which he reveals and tries to surmount his prejudice against homosexuals, or in "The White Negro," an essay that draws upon white stereotypes of blacks to define the "hipster" as a "white Negro." (James Baldwin pointed out Mailer's limited angle of vision on the subject: "I am a black boy from the Harlem streets, and Norman is a middle-class Jew." Baldwin also rejected the role of "walking phallic symbol" implied by Mailer.)[132]

Mailer's volatile persona is the only unifying point of *Advertisements*, a book he describes, in one of its sections, as a "biography of a style." *Advertisements* is Whitman-like in its vaunting of self and style, but, far more than Whitman ever did, Norman Mailer celebrates his uncertainty of purpose.[133] "To write about myself is to send my style through a circus of variations and postures, a fireworks of virtuosity designed to achieve . . . I do not even know what."[134] In its improvisatory style, fragmentary arrangement, and often brutal content, *Advertisements* is Mailer's quintessential New York City book.

As writer, resident, and personality, Mailer made himself into a representative man of the City: marginal, combative, garrulous, at times brilliant, often witty, frequently vulgar, and defiantly wrong-headed. In his *Village Voice* essays, in his many appearances on television and on public platforms, in his political campaigns, in his occasional roles as director and actor on stage and in his own films, he became a one-man band: the novelist, the polemicist, the anthologist, the publicist all in one. Norman Mailer took every advantage of the opportunities for self-promotion presented by the City. He became famous for his barroom fights, his polemics, even for stabbing his wife, in 1960. (Charges were not pressed.) That year he also ran for mayor of the City on the Existential ticket. In 1969, Mailer tried again, running for mayor in the Democratic primary, advocating New York City's secession from the state. He set out, in the words of Gloria Steinem, to "turn this big excessive city on its ear," but Mailer's aggressive, crowd-baiting campaign style put off many voters, and in the end, he finished fourth out of five candidates.[135] Norman Mailer, self-created hipster and self-designated prophet, would have to exert his powers in less direct ways.

Mailer's "The Time of Her Time," a story included in *Advertisements*, is set in a huge Village loft and celebrates "hipster" sexuality: brutal and vengeful violation. In the deeds and words of Sergius O'Shaugnessy, a character Mailer uses several times as a spokesman for subversive views, New York City is characterized by sexual vengeance against a woman and by the sight of six-year-olds who dig through the morning's garbage:

> *They were the defilers of the garbage, knights of the ordure, and here, in this provincial capital Manhattan, at the southern tip of the island, with the overhead girders of the Manhattan and Brooklyn bridges the only noble structures for a mile of tenement jungle, yes here the barbarians ate their young, and any type who reached the age of six without being altogether mangled by father, mother, family or friends, was a pint of iron man, so tough, so ferocious, so sharp in the teeth that the wildest alley cat would have surrendered a freshly caught rat rather than contest the meal.*[136]

In *Advertisements*, Mailer presents himself as just such "a pint of iron man"—a man hardened by the City's cruel lessons.

In *An American Dream* (1965), Mailer's protagonist, Stephen Rojack—combat veteran, Congressman, professor of existential psychology—wars with the world by killing his unfaithful wife. After he has sex with their maid, he plunges into the most dangerous parts of the City, testing his courage in Harlem, where he fights a black man. Rojack is a deranged rebel against the American establishment, represented by his wealthy, influential wife and their Park Lane apartment. He deliberately plunges into the lower depths of the City, but when he decides he wants "to be free of magic, the tongue of the Devil, the Dread of the Lord," he leaves New York.[137] "Sometimes I think there's a buried maniac who runs the mind of the city," thinks Rojack.[138] Many of Mailer's works try to come to terms with this dark, controlling mind, and Norman Mailer exemplifies the City's new barbarism.

APPEALING TO A MORE GENTEEL SIDE OF THE CITY'S sensibility, the *New Yorker* was a magazine designed, said founder Harold Ross, for "caviar sophisticates."[139] E. B. White helped to define the "Talk of the Town" genre, beginning in 1926, accepting the magazine's persona of urbane observation, embodied in the detached "we" of the narrative voice: "We are writing this in bed," begins a White essay in 1951.[140] John Updike, who contributed to the "Talk of the Town" section in the 1950s, asked, "Who, after all, could that indefatigable, fascinated, perpetually peripatetic 'we' be but a collection of dazzled farm boys?" Thus the *New Yorker* "we" was a self-ironic mask, a pose of knowingness for recently arrived rubes who were still agog in Gotham and a literary voice aimed at restless souls who were still trapped elsewhere. The *New Yorker* was a magazine designed for those who dreamed of freedom and romance in the City.

When William Shawn took over its editorship in 1952, the *New Yorker* extended its circle of concern and the reach of its voice. Without sacrificing its sense of style, Shawn brought a new level of seriousness to the magazine. For example, while serving as managing editor, Shawn committed the magazine to publishing an entire issue devoted to John Hersey's "Hiroshima" in 1946. As full editor, "Shawn changed *The New Yorker* from a smarty-pants parish tip sheet into a journal that altered our experience instead of just posturing in front of it," wrote John Leonard in 1975.[141] The magazine also became, noted Joseph Epstein, "even more of a writer's magazine than it was before."[142] Shawn relied upon the talents of E. B. White, Edmund Wilson, A. J. Liebling, and Joseph Mitchell to sustain the magazine's knowing tone, light style, and diverse interests.[143] The *New Yorker* also featured works by Truman Capote, James Baldwin, Rachel Carson, and Hannah Arendt. Shawn published some of the best short fiction of his day—by John Cheever, J. D. Salinger, Donald Barthelme, and John Updike. In tribute to Shawn, after his death in December 1992, Updike wrote, "His adamancy of taste had been hardened in a buried moral fiber, and his *New Yorker* was a realm from which many types of unseemliness were excluded. But his exclusionary sword had an edge of venturesomeness as well: the magazine's fiction became more avant-garde and its nonfiction more mandarin under his guidance."[144]

For two of the magazine's most eloquent writers, E. B. White and John Updike, the experience of the City was brief and remained intermittent; each eventually abandoned New York (though not the *New Yorker*) for a life in New England. Each writer reflected his ambivalence toward the City in his "Talk of the Town" contributions.

In the spring of 1955 White, on the eve of one of his departures from the City, paused to note its transient magic: "The two moments when New York seems most desirable, when the splendor falls all round about and the city looks like a girl with leaves in her hair, are just as you are leaving and must say goodbye, and just as you return and can say hello." (By implication, then, New York is far less desirable during the periods when one actually lives in the City!) White was particularly struck by the wonders of urban place just before he took leave of the City. During the hot night, he could glimpse stars through the branches of trees, and in that moment "we somehow tasted New York on our tongue in a great, overpowering draught, and felt that to sail away from so intoxicating a place would be unbearable, even for a brief spell."[145] Of course, White, who helped to shape the magazine's collective voice, did eventually leave, for a farmhouse in Maine. But not before he celebrated the City in one of its greatest tributes, "Here Is New York." In this 1949 essay White—who was born in Mount Vernon in 1899—praises the City for its inclusiveness: "New York is the concentrate of art and commerce and sport and religion and entertainment and finance, bringing to a single compact arena the gladiator, the evangelist, the promoter, the actor, the trader, and the merchant." Then he praises the City for its concentration: "The city is like poetry: it compresses all life, all races and breeds, into a small island and adds music and the accompaniment of internal engines." Even the City's soaring skyscraper becomes the object of White's admiration: "It is to the nation what the white church spire is to the village—the visible symbol of aspiration and faith, the white plume saying the way is up." Why, then, would a man who so loves New York leave it? White hints at an answer at the end of his essay when he talks about the City's vulnerability to destruction: "The intimation of mortality is part of New York now: in the sound of jets overhead, in the black headlines of the latest edition."[146]

As John Updike notes in *Self-Consciousness: Memoirs* (1989), he remains ever-grateful for his experience in New York, at the *New Yorker*, which transformed him from a dazzled Pennsylvania farm-boy into a writer: "While I can now almost glimpse something a bit too trusting in the serene sense of artistic well-being, of virtual invulnerability, that being published in the *New Yorker* gave me for over thirty years, the self who looked up into the empyrean of print from that dusty farm in Pennsylvania with its outhouse and coal-oil stove is not so remote from me that I can still think it anything less than wonderful to have become a writer."[147]

In 1962, the thirty-year-old Updike, writing in the assured voice of the *New Yorker*, described walking along Fifth Avenue during a spring rain: "The scene seemed squeezed so tight that it yielded the essence of granite, the very idea of the city." After the rain, Updike was drawn to the light on the face of St. Patrick's Cathedral and to Rockefeller Center, across the street: "We hastened toward the omen, but by the time we reached the site the sunshine had faded. Yet, looking up through the skeleton globe upheld by the grimacing Atlas, we saw beyond the metal framework what was, patchy blue and scudding gray, indisputably sky."[148] As White left the intoxications of Manhattan for Maine, so too did Updike abandon the elusive omens of the City, though not his extensive contributions to the *New Yorker*, for Massachusetts in the 1950s.

The City is a place where some of Updike's characters are threatened, as is James, the central consciousness in an early Updike story, "A Gift from the City." James has a safe professional "perch" as a package designer in an office "twenty-two stories above Park Avenue," and he shares a fine apartment with his wife, Liz, some forty blocks south, on Tenth Street, near Fifth Avenue. Yet his life in the City is a mix of anxiety and apprehension as he moves between his safety zones of work and home: "As the months passed harmlessly, James's suspicion increased that the city itself, with its steep Babylonian surfaces, its black noon shadows, its godless millions, was poised to strike." The plot of the story centers on a black man who wheedles money from Liz and James, but the true subject of the story is James's unshakable conviction, despite the good fortune that has befallen him, that the City is dangerous.[149]

In 1994, some four decades after John Updike found success in New York, he was still musing on the meaning of the City in a poem, "New York City." He finds in it a "Pandemonium," a "hell" that "holds sacred crevices where lone/ lost spirits preen and call their pit a throne."[150]

Dawn Powell and Truman Capote recorded in their fiction a City full of evanescent fun. They wrote of outcasts from mainstream America, characters, like themselves, who came to New York to give full reign to their eccentricities and become writers. However, both of these stylish and satiric writers also caught an undercurrent of loss and regret on the streets of Manhattan. "New York is not the same city it was, being now overrun with Americans," said Dawn Powell in 1947.[151] Powell died in 1965, her work out of print, and Capote died in 1984, his early promise having sputtered out in gossipy fiction—an unfinished novel titled *Answered Prayers*.

In Powell's New York novels, the City plays "a pervasive role," notes Gore Vidal, whose efforts helped to bring Powell's works back into print.[152] This is especially true in *The Golden Spur*, her 1962 novel, which tells the familiar story of a naive young man in the City. Jonathan comes from Silver City, Ohio, to Manhattan, in 1956, in search of his true father. (Jonathan's mother had been in the City in the 1920s, but she returned to Silver City, pregnant.) This slight, witty novel, which tracks the footloose and generally merry lives of City characters, is notable for the intensity of its hero's response to the City. On arrival, Jonathan is as awed by Manhattan as his mother had been. Even when he witnesses, on his first day on the streets, the demolition of Wanamaker's, a major department store, Jonathan is irrepressibly optimistic, for "The Golden Spur," the bar-restaurant where his mother used to meet her lover, still stands, offering Jonathan entry into his land of Oz: "He breathed deep of the heady New York air, that delirious narcotic of ancient sewer dust, gasoline fumes, roasting coffee beans, and the harsh smell of sea that intoxicates inland nostrils. Then he pushed open the door."[153] On the other side, Jonathan eventually finds what he has come to the City for. The City takes away with one hand, but it gives back with the other: "Jonathan recognized New York as home. . . . Within a month he knew more of New York than he had ever known about the whole state of Ohio."[154] So, too, did Dawn Powell trade in what she knew of Ohio—where she was born, in Mount Gilead, in 1897—for what she learned of New York's literary circles and cafe society.

Powell arrived in the City in 1917 and remained until her death in 1965. She wrote of its brittle beauties and disillusionments in *Turn, Magic Wheel* (1936), a novel that shifts nervously from one group of New Yorkers to another. All of the many characters in this novel are buoyed by wary expectations, expressed in Powell's lyrical evocations: "The five o'clock people swept through the city hungrily, they covered the sun, drowned the city noises with their million tiny bells, their five o'clock faces looked eagerly toward Brooklyn, Astoria, the Bronx, Big Date Tonight."[155] Most of her characters are disappointed in the ways their lives turn out in the City, but Powell celebrates their freedom to choose their destinies. "New York City [is] the only place where people with nothing behind them but their wits can be and do everything," she wrote in 1931 to a friend who was back in Ohio. "Every place else but New York, you have to hide all your low beginnings and pretend everybody in the family is white and can read and write and play the harp. What I mean, friend, is that you can be yourself here and it's the only place where being genuine will absolutely get you anywhere you want."[156]

Truman Capote was born in New Orleans in 1924, but he came to New York as soon as he could. He became a copy boy at the *New Yorker* in 1942. In a 1946 essay, Capote called the City a living "myth":

> *This island, floating in river water like a diamond iceberg, call it New York, name it whatever you like; the name hardly matters because, entering from the greater reality of elsewhere, one is only in search of the city, a place to hide, to lose or discover oneself, to make a dream wherein you prove that perhaps after all you are not an ugly duckling, but wonderful, and worthy of love, as you thought sitting on the stoop where the Fords went by; as you thought planning your search for the city.*[157]

By 1947, with his success in publishing *Other Voices, Other Rooms*, a story collection, Capote was the toast of the town. In a novella, *Breakfast at Tiffany's* (1958), an immensely popular and critical success, Capote celebrated his adopted city by telling the story of another talented misfit who finds a true home in New York. Holly Golightly arrives (from Tulip, Texas), eager to have a good time. Sustained by her faith that nothing bad will ever happen to her in Tiffany's—and protected by the St. Christopher medal that the narrator, her friend, has purchased for her at the expensive jewelry store—Holly becomes a legend for her ability to survive men and dangerous adventures, even when she becomes involved with drug smugglers, has to leave the country, and disappears.[158] Holly represents Capote's ideal of spontaneous expression and fulfillment; only in New York City, he implies, are such things possible.

Truman Capote had large ambitions for his last work, *Answered Prayers*, published posthumously in 1987. He wanted to do for New York society, which had become his milieu, what Proust had done for Parisian society: "I want to say, 'Here. This is American high society in the second half of the twentieth century. This book is about you, it's about me, it's about them, it's about everybody.'"[159] But Capote's overwriting, combined with his ambivalence about the swells he portrayed and his own self-destructiveness, ensured the novel's failure. Perhaps its best moment occurs early on, when the narrator—P. B. Jones, a hustler who is writing from the sixth floor of the YMCA—recalls the youthful promise that the City once held out for him: "I was eighteen, it was October, and I've always remembered the October glitter of Manhattan as my bus approached across the stinking New Jersey marshes. As Thomas Wolfe, a once-admired and now-forgotten idol, might have written: Oh, what promise those windows held!— cold and fiery in the rippling shine of a tumbling autumn sun. Since then I've fallen in love with many cities, but only an orgasm lasting an hour could surpass the bliss of my first year in New York. Unfortunately, I decided to marry."[160]

Capote, of course, never married, but the early bliss of Manhattan faded for him as well. Diminished by drugs and alcohol, he died in an East Side glass tower, his ambitious New York City book unfinished.

THE PILGRIMS OF THE POSTWAR PERIOD, MEMBERS OF THE so-called silent generation who wrote so much, came on the scene to recreate their sense of Manhattan, particularly of Greenwich Village, as a wonderland. When she arrived in Washington Square in 1946, to attend Washington Square College, Cynthia Ozick—the future essayist and novelist was then seventeen years old—felt her "life was luminously new." Washington Square meant Henry James, who once lived nearby, and W. H. Auden and Marianne Moore, who then lived in the neighborhood. Washington Square meant Greenwich Village, where "Edna St. Vincent Millay has sent the music of her name (her best, perhaps her only, poem) into these bohemian streets: bohemia, the honey pot of poets."[161] In *Fragments of the Century* (1973), speaking for many others like him, commentator Michael Harrington recalled the moment when he "arrived one fall afternoon in 1949, put down my bags and went out to find Greenwich Village," which was filled with other "voluntary exiles from the middle class."[162]

No New York City writer took more delight in removing himself from the middle class than Frank O'Hara. Richard Poirier suggests that O'Hara was "almost evangelically convinced by the Manhattan of the '50s and early '60s that America had become the most culturally exciting place in the world." Taking his cue from Walt Whitman, his "great predecessor," O'Hara expressed his conviction that "New York is everywhere like Paris!" For all that, says Poirier, "O'Hara in New York is the story of an emotionally reckless man, wasteful of affection as well as anger."[163]

Born and reared in Grafton, Massachusetts, O'Hara did not discover himself as a writer until he found himself in Manhattan in 1951. "Over the next fifteen years," writes Joan Acocella, "until his death, at age forty, he became the city's most representative poet" and a central presence in the New York art world. "In one of New York's most splendid moments—some would say its last splendid moment—O'Hara was for many Manhattanites a symbol of the city and a kind of paradigm of the phenomenon that [E. B.] White has described, the person who becomes himself, or his most interesting self, by moving to New York."[164] O'Hara worked as curator and critic at the Museum of Modern Art, advancing the Abstract Expressionists, or as Robert Motherwell would deem them, the New York school of painters. O'Hara—along with John Ashbery, James Schuyler, and Kenneth Koch—was a central member of what was called the New York school of poets. Midtown Manhattan and Fire Island, a resort community on Long Island, defined the limits of O'Hara's world.

Frank O'Hara's poetry came on the run; it is topical, prosaic, witty, and seemingly spontaneous. For example, once on his lunch hour he wrote a poem that begins, "It's my lunch hour." This poem takes him through Times Square, where he finds occasions of beauty in advertisements: "The sign blows smoke over my head, and higher/ the waterfall pours lightly."[165] Indeed, O'Hara seemed to love everything about the City. "I love this hairy city," he wrote. "New York/ greater than the Rocky Mountains."[166] As Helen Vendler says, "O'Hara follows Walt Whitman and William Carlos Williams in writing urban pastoral, but neither Whitman nor Williams took the pleasure in the city that O'Hara did."[167] In one of his most anthologized poems, "A True Account of Talking to the Sun at Fire Island," O'Hara has the sun chide him for his urban passions: "I know you love Manhattan, but/ you ought to look up more often."[168] However, things ended badly and quickly for O'Hara. He grew alcoholic, his poetic inspiration dried up, and finally he died in an absurdist accident—run down by a jeep at 2:00 A.M.—on Fire Island.

John Ashbery describes New York as "a logarithm/ Of other cities," a place "alive with flirtations, shuttlings."[169] However, even when he praises New York, as he does in "The Friendly City," Ashbery often includes a subtext of reservation. He concludes this ambiguous poem by giving the City only a tepid affirmation: It "will probably stay around," despite those "who are even now clogging its approaches,/ giving the place a bad name."[170] But of all the New York poets of his era, as Geoff Ward points out, Frank O'Hara best captures and celebrates the City in his poetry. "He is made up of bits of it; and it is only through such poetry that people in the future will think that life in New York City in the fifties and sixties must have been good."[171]

Dan Wakefield's *New York in the Fifties* also reveals Greenwich Village as a place of wonder—a city of words, romance, and personal transformation, a place worthy of recreation in his meditation of *temps perdu*. According to Alfred Kazin, by the 1950s, Wakefield's era, the Village had reached its peak and was in decline as an artistic and literary center. By 1956, "the older and more 'successful' writers became, the easier they found it to depart from the Village."[172] Though the idea of the Village as a place where like-minded outcasts and exiles from American towns could gather was fast fading, it still held promise for the youth of the Eisenhower age who were in search of love and literature. Certainly it did for Dan Wakefield, who was born in 1932, reared in Indianapolis, and educated at Columbia University.

Wakefield's account, published forty years after his initial encounter with New York in 1952, is an evocative rendering of a city that retains its power to stir imaginations and to elicit revelations. Wakefield's remembrance pays tribute to an era—framed by the end of the postwar recovery period and the time when the so-called baby-boom generation began to dominate American culture—which he believes was the best of times for the City. Further, Wakefield articulates many of the central experiences and myths that have given New York its power, for better or worse, as a symbol of national and personal transformation.

Wakefield's personal map of New York led him from Columbia in 1955 to apartments on the Upper West Side: "On to what would be home in Greenwich Village (appropriate antithesis of what the midwest means by 'home'), until I said goodbye to New York in 1963."[173] More than a personal memoir, his is a generational biography, composed after the fashion of those written by Malcolm Cowley about his literary generation: the midwesterners who became émigrés to New York and Paris after the Great War. As Cowley called his touchstone book *Exile's Return*, Wakefield might have titled his *Internal Émigrés*, for he, too, describes a generation made up of those who left home—many, like him, from the Midwest, but others from other parts of the nation, or even from New York City boroughs beyond Manhattan—in order to "'find themselves' in the pulsing heart of the hip new world's hot center, with the ghosts of the recent past as a guide."[174] They drew a new family heritage from Cowley's generation of writers: Fitzgerald, Hemingway, Millay, Cummings, a lineage wed to the word, bonded in booze, and fired by ambition. For Wakefield's generation, however, psychoanalysis replaced politics—"the dream of the golden mountains" that enticed Cowley and others of his generation in the 1930s—as a means by which to seek salvation. But members of both generations were committed to personal freedom (of public expression and sexual action) and driven by the dream of success.[175] For Wakefield's generation, as for Cowley's, leaving home for New York City was their way of sailing to Byzantium.

In 1992, nearly three decades after he left the City, Wakefield moved back to Greenwich Village. As he wrote in a *Times* essay, "Writers are always coming to New York and, even when they leave, coming back to it." New York is their "source, for this is the mecca of books, magazines, newspapers, words, stories, language, the place where The Word is not only written, but is honored, packaged, proclaimed and . . . inspired."[176] Despite all of its problems, New York City, for Dan Wakefield and others, is still America's cultural capital. In the 1950s "New York had no real rival for youth who wanted to be at the creative— and creating—center of the American dream."[177] Indeed, in Dan Wakefield's memoir, New York stands as something of a dream—at once a memory, an evocation, an inspiration, an invention. It is his testimony of unyielding faith in New York as a redemptive City.

Joan Didion, a contemporary of Dan Wakefield, in her essay "Goodbye to All That" (1967), offers a somewhat different narrative and analysis of her initial encounters with New York, a record of her sentimental education in the City of broken dreams. Didion first came to New York in 1955, as a guest editor at *Mademoiselle* during the summer of her junior year in college, when she was twenty-one; later she won a *Vogue* literary contest and returned to the City. Her attitudes toward New York were shaped by popular myths. As a young woman, Didion said, "[I was] programmed by all the movies I had ever seen and all the songs I had ever heard sung and all the stories I had ever read about New York" and its effects upon the life of one who comes to the City, which "informed me that it would never be quite the same again. In fact it never was."

During her first days in Manhattan, Didion thought only of her home in California: "[All I could do] was talk long-distance to the boy I already knew I would never marry in the spring. I would stay in New York, I told him, just six months, and I could see the Brooklyn Bridge from my window. As it turned out the bridge was the Triborough, and I stayed eight years." New York, then, existed as a myth of expectation and intimidation before it became an instructive experience for this "native daughter" from California; the City moved her from innocence to jaded awareness. Nevertheless, well into her eight-year stay, Didion retained a romantic attachment to the City; she refused to accept it as "real." For those who arrive from far away American places, she said, "New York was no mere city. It was instead a romantic notion, the mysterious nexus of all love and money and power, the shining and perishable dream itself. To think of 'living' there was to reduce the miraculous to the mundane; one does not 'live' at

Xanadu." It was not until she was twenty-eight, by which time she had learned much about the devious ways of the City, that Didion realized that "it is distinctly possible to stay too long at the Fair." New York, for Didion, was a proper place in which to be young and naive; but when she grew up, her education completed, she married and left for Los Angeles, where she and her husband wrote films in a place that most Americans believe to be the real Xanadu—Hollywood.[178]

Life in New York in the 1950s and 1960s is also portrayed as problematic in the poetry of Allen Ginsberg, though he took the City-affirming Walt Whitman as his model. "What thoughts I have of you tonight, Walt Whitman, for I walked down the sidestreets under the trees with a headache self-conscious looking for the full moon," Ginsberg once wrote.[179] However, that sentence comes from a poem titled "A Supermarket in California," not from a poem about the City. Though Ginsberg, born in Newark in 1926, was shaped by his experiences in the City, his poetic realization was in California. The obscenity trial for Ginsberg's *Howl and Other Poems* (1956) also took place in San Francisco, where the poem was published. Even when Ginsberg celebrates New York, as he does in "Walking New York Part II," a 1968 poem in which he catalogs urban details (towers, voices, odors), he concludes on an anxious note: "Where is my comfort, where's heart-ease,/ Where are tears of joy" in "Stuyvesant Town"?[180]

Greenwich Village was key to the development of Ginsberg's persona and poetic style. He discovered the Village in 1943 when he was a freshman at Columbia, where he eventually studied under Lionel Trilling. In the Village, Ginsberg met William Burroughs, Jack Kerouac, Gregory Corso, and others who initiated the "Beat Generation" movement—young writers, experimenting with sex, drugs, and writing styles, who challenged middle-class values. They drank and talked at the San Remo, a bar on MacDougal Street, where they encountered noted poets and painters. Ginsberg called his group the "subterraneans." Kerouac picked up the term for a novel about the group, though he set it in San Francisco.[181]

In the mid 1950s, Ginsberg spent time in California. After a long absence, he returned to the City, specifically to Greenwich Village, late in 1958. Ginsberg was struck anew—as Henry James had been long before him—by the height and the power of the City: "Look back over my shoulder, 7th Avenue, battlements of window office buildings shouldering together high, under a cloud, tall as the sky."[182]

Ginsberg's return may also have been dictated by a desire to reconnect with his parents' past, for Louis and Naomi Ginsberg had settled in the Village after emigrating from Russia, before he was born. Allen absorbed his parents' socialism and passion for poetry. As a tribute on his return to the Village, he set out to give poetic shape to the story of his mother, who died in 1956. "Strange now to think of you, gone without corsets & eyes, while I walk on the sunny pavement of Greenwich Village," wrote Ginsberg in "Kaddish" (1959).[183] Another side of the City is evoked by Ginsberg in "Mugging," a poem based on an experience on East Tenth Street; muggers knocked Ginsberg down, stole seventy dollars and credit cards, but left "10,000 dollars full of poetry" behind, thus revealing the reductive, mercenary values of the City.[184] Yet Ginsberg has made New York City his home, living in one or another walk-up apartment on the Lower East Side, for the past thirty years.[185] Like Dan Wakefield, Allen Ginsberg continues to celebrate the City.

The City, of course, no matter how bad it gets, is always a site for poetic meditation. James Merrill, for example, who was born in the City in 1926, recalls the lost world of his grandmother's New York in "164 East 72nd Street" and in "An Urban Convalescence." Merrill wonders at how quickly things pass in the City. New York, ever razing and building, tests his powers of mind and memory: "Let me try to recall/ What building stood here. Was there a building at all?"[186]

In "Letter to N.Y.," the far-traveled Elizabeth Bishop expresses homesickness for the plays and other pleasures of the City, so she asks a friend who lives in the City to tell her "what you are doing and where you are going."[187] Just after graduating from Vassar in 1934, Bishop came to the City. She learned to write—in part from copying lyrical poems in the New York Public Library—and came under the tutelage of Marianne Moore. Bishop also fell under the sway of the City: "I think that it is in the city alone, maybe New York alone, that one gets in this country these sudden intuitions into the *whole* of contemporaneity. . . . You catch it coming toward you like a ball, more compressed and acute than any work of 'modern art.' "[188] However, as David Kalstone points out, when Bishop translates her impressions of the City into poetry, her "excitement seems transposed into an equally wondering but more sinister key."[189]

Bishop's "Love Lies Sleeping" concludes with the image of a distinctly sinister man, lying in bed, open-eyed, contemplating a City that is "distorted and revealed,/ if he sees at all."[190] However, it is in "The Man-Moth"—a poem, argues Kalstone, based upon Bishop's impression of a dead-looking woman she saw on a subway, a poem whose title is derived from a newspaper misprint ("man-moth" for "mammoth")—that the poet reveals the reduced human condition in New York. The antihero of this poem is a sad figure whose attempts to escape his underground entrapment are futile, a figure who rides the subway, "facing the wrong way," immobilized, dead in the eyes, caught like a moth.[191]

J. D. Salinger's *The Catcher in the Rye* (1951), which caught the inchoate aspirations and the tentative alienations of 1950s youth, is a novel of grim revelations about the City in which Salinger was born. Like Sylvia Plath's *The Bell Jar* (1971), it tells an old story and makes a familiar point: New York City provides a haven for escapees from repressive and conformist America; New York titillates and instructs, but sooner or later it also destroys.

In *The Catcher in the Rye*, sixteen-year-old Holden Caufield leaves Pencey Prep, where he is flunking out, and returns to New York, where his family lives. Holden's weekend on his own in the City offers instances of light and grace (the nuns he talks with in Grand Central Station, for example), but mostly it is an extended night journey to bitter awareness of the adult world's moral failure, its inability to provide answers to his questions. Holden never does find out what he most wants to know: where Central Park's ducks go in the winter. Nor does he find out where *he* will go—what he will become when and if he grows up—since Holden cannot, like Huck Finn, light out for the territories. Instead, Holden tells his tale from the confines of a sanitorium, under psychiatric care. No one in the City, which has no fields of rye, rescues Holden before he falls off the edge. After his brief stay in the City, Holden becomes another dangling man.

Holden brings his own moral ambivalence and hesitancies to the City. From his room in the Edmont Hotel, he is amazed by the "perverts" he can see in other hotel rooms from his window—a man dressed as a woman, a couple spitting drinks at each other—but he admits "that kind of junk is sort of fascinating to watch, even if you don't want to be in it."[192] This confused young voyeur wanders the City, dances at the Lavender Room, watches a show at Radio City Music Hall, and listens to jazz at Ernie's, in the Village—all of which depresses him. So he walks forty-one blocks back to his hotel, where he has a painful encounter with a young prostitute, incongruously named Sunny. Underneath his knowing, New York ways and wise-guy attitudes, Holden is vulnerable: "New York's terrible when somebody laughs on the street very late at night. You can hear it for miles. It makes you so lonesome and depressed."[193] In a City of millions, Salinger's sad young man feels all alone.

Holden is drawn to the City's "adults only" offerings, but he is wary of the maturation they require. At the Biltmore Hotel he watches the pretty girls, but he gets depressed when he thinks that they will inevitably grow up and marry "jerks." At the reassuringly unchanged exhibits of the Museum of Natural History, Holden recalls his boyhood visits and decides that all things should stay the same, though he realizes that both he and the City must change. He goes ice skating at Rockefeller Center with his friend, Sally, but he grows enraged when she refuses to run off with him to Vermont. After drinks with a pretentious young man at the Wicker Bar of the Seton Hotel, Holden's loneliness makes him cry. Memories of his dead brother, Allie, haunt him. Holden's City is crowded with memories of lost innocence.

Holden goes home briefly, to his family's East Side apartment, to see his sister, Phoebe, the only person he loves; then he seeks consolation from Mr. Antolini, a former teacher who lives with his rich wife on Sutton Place. When Holden, sleeping on their sofa, wakes in the night and discovers Mr. Antolini patting his head, the young man runs away from what he presumes to be more urban perversion. In Grand Central, Holden reconsiders, weighs the adult and urban worlds he knows, and comes close to accepting his own maturity, but he is unready to become another "phony" (morally compromised) adult. New York City for Holden is what Bellow calls some of his tough-guy characters—a reality instructor—but Holden recoils from such reality. He decides to run away, to head west—to go "on the road," as would Jack Kerouac later in the decade—and to become a hermit.

At the zoo in Central Park, Holden meets Phoebe, who wants to run away with him. When Phoebe rides the carousel to the tune "Smoke Gets in Your Eyes," Holden fears she might fall off, but he realizes he cannot protect her and must trust her to take care of herself. This makes him briefly happy. But, in his final words to the reader, Holden admits he "got sick and all" and had to be hospitalized. The City dramatizes and clarifies Holden's crisis—maturity means the acceptance of his own and others' failures—but it also breaks him. Perhaps not surprisingly, J. D. Salinger left Manhattan and did become something of a hermit in idyllic Vermont.

While Holden Caufield ends up in a sanatorium after his weekend in Manhattan, Esther Greenwood, the autobiographical heroine of Sylvia Plath's *The Bell Jar*, attempts suicide after her brief encounter with the City. Plath grew up outside Boston and was awarded a scholarship to Smith College (class of 1954) in

Northampton, Massachusetts. In 1952, she won a guest editorship at *Mademoi-selle* ("the magazine for smart young women"). Her disastrous visit to Manhattan for four weeks in June 1953 contributed to her breakdown, during which, after receiving shock treatments, she first attempted suicide. The City lifted her, provided excitement, offered hard lessons in the ways of the world, and gave her material for her novel, but then it shattered her.

At first Plath strained to express the rapture she thought she should be feeling about coming to New York in her gushy notebook account of her days as a "Smith Cinderella" in the City: "Working—hatted & heeled—in *Mlle's* aircon-ditioned Madison Ave. offices. . . . Fantastic, fabulous, and all other inade-quate adjectives go to describe the four gala and chaotic-weeks I worked as guest managing Ed . . . living in luxury at the Barbizon, I edited, met celebrities, was feted and feasted by a galaxy of UN delegates, simultaneous interpreters & artists."[194]

In truth, Plath was overwhelmed by the pressures surrounding her meetings with celebrated writers: Marianne Moore, Elizabeth Bowen, and Richard Wil-bur. During Plath's stay, she and the other young guest editors had to dress in matching outfits and carry themselves with dignity while they posed during photo sessions designed to show off the season's styles in campus wear. *Made-moiselle* even got Plath to write fashion copy for a picture of twenty identically dressed guest editors—garbed in matching caps, shirts, and tartan skirts—who are grinning, holding hands, and shaping themselves, like latter-day Busby Berklee dancing girls, into a star-shaped pattern. "We're stargazers this season," wrote Plath, "bewitched by an atmosphere of evening blue. Foremost in the fashion constellation we spot *Mlle's* own tartan, the astronomic versatility of sweaters, and men, men, men—we've even taken the shirts off their backs!"[195]

Soon, however, New York sickened Sylvia Plath. She suffered ptomaine poi-soning at an advertising agency's luncheon, and she was nearly raped by a Peru-vian delegate to the UN at a Forest Hills tennis club dance. In a fit of rage and an act of symbolic appropriateness, Plath threw her clothes out of the window of the Barbizon Hotel. She then seized on the execution of Julius and Ethel Ro-senberg, also in June, as further evidence that the times, personal and public, were out of joint.[196]

The Bell Jar, Plath's slightly fictionalized account of her journey of discovery in Gotham, opens on an ominous note that links Esther Greenwood's anxieties with the Rosenberg executions and the derangements of New York City: "It was a queer, sultry summer, the summer they electrocuted the Rosenbergs, and I didn't know what I was doing in New York." Esther's City, like Holden's, remains a lost, pastoral dream. "New York was bad enough. By nine in the morning the fake country-wet freshness that somehow seeped in overnight evaporated like the tail end of a sweet dream."[197] Salinger provided the model for Plath's narrative persona—the sensitive, innocent youth with a brittle veneer who is crushed by the City's hard lessons.

Esther, like Holden, is hungry for experience, which means she has to come to New York, but then, like Holden, she is sickened by all that the City forces her to ingest. For *The Bell Jar*, Plath converted the Barbizon into the Amazon Hotel and made *Mademoiselle* into *Ladies' Day*, underlining the feminist implications of Esther's exploitations, which Plath felt so intensely during her stay: "I was supposed to be having the time of my life," says Esther, bitterly, for her effort to fulfill the American dream of success and freedom by coming to Manhattan becomes a nightmare from which she barely (and only briefly) escapes.[198]

NEW YORK'S ERA OF GOLD SEEMS TO HAVE COME AND GONE in a flash. Writers of the postwar period responded to the City's variety of experiences. For some of those, like Dan Wakefield, who came on the scene in the 1950s, the City has remained a source of literary inspiration and a refuge from middle-class America. For others, like J. D. Salinger and Sylvia Plath, New York presented an illusion of success that masked its latent destructiveness. For others, like John Cheever and Irwin Shaw, the City was a receding image of felicity. During this period of prosperity, urban and national, the New York intellectuals, many of whom were critical of American capitalism and culture, reexamined and debated their values, wrote their best work, and watched many of their "family" leave the City. The writers advanced by the New York intellectuals, from Arthur Miller to Norman Mailer, helped define the character and tone of postwar literature in works that were frequently critical of New York. The *New Yorker*, which found much to celebrate in postwar New York, flourished, along with its circle of writers, though some of them also grew disenchanted with the City and moved away. Writers like Lynne Sharon Schwartz and Mary Gordon tell the stories of New Yorkers' lives in the boroughs and neighborhoods, recreating the City's myth of transformation and transcendence.

With wide eyes and high hearts, young men and women leave their families and their familiar neighborhoods to travel to the impersonal and various City. There they are free to choose their friends, compose their identities, and mold their destinies—within the limits imposed upon them by the City. They move from provincial innocence to urban awareness, from expectation to experience.

The City offers them the freedom to know the world: its social stratifications, its romance, its money, its injustices, its delights, its griefs. Above all, the City offers these young men and women a chance to write, a great subject to write about, and the opportunity to publish what they have written. Almost always, however, the once golden City grows tarnished in their eyes. Many of them, having learned resilience, start over in the City. Many of them leave in disappointment; they are soon replaced by newcomers who are ready to embark on the great adventure. Even those who do leave, however, will return to the City, if not in person then in memories that are, as we have seen, often shaped into worthy works of art.

B R I G H T N E S S

F A L L S

Contemporary New York

New York City, which has long reflected the state of the nation, has fallen on troubled times. During the 1980s and 1990s, New York has grown dirtier, more dangerous, more expensive, and far more aggressive in its tone and manner. "New Yorkers are not polite," notes Calvin Trillin, with understatement and some detectable pride.[1] More important, New York is characterized by street violence, illegal drugs, racial and ethnic tensions, homelessness, and pessimism among its residents over its future.[2] Midtown development contrasts with neighborhood deterioration. "Outsider groups," who have traditionally found a home in the City, are driven away.[3] Increasingly, the City is populated by the rich and the poor.[4]

The decline of the city, as emblem and actuality, is eroding the nation's stated commitment to life, liberty, and the pursuit of happiness. For it is the gritty city, particularly New York City, rather than the fabled New England village, that represents the true test of American democracy, the place where "aliens"—the huddled masses from across the Atlantic and the internal émigrés from the heart of the country—have arrived with great expectations, and it is the city that has transformed them into committed members of the body politic. What is in danger of being lost is not only our collective faith in the transformative powers of New York City, which once held out such promise to so many of the world's "wretched refuse," but also our capacity to believe in a redemptive national future.

"The hatred of cities is the fear of freedom," writes Lewis H. Lapham, editor of *Harper's Magazine*. "The fear is contagious, and as larger numbers of people come to perceive the city as a barren waste, the more profitable their disillusion becomes to dealers in guns and to political factions that would destroy not only New York and Chicago but also the idea of the city."[5] It is just that, the diminishing idea of the city as a place of promise and freedom, that lies between the lines of works that take modern New York City as their setting.

New York City, always open for reconstruction, is now particularly available for reconsideration. Though clearly in decline as a center of civilization and culture, the City remains vibrant, ready for inscriptions of significance in which we may read the state of the nation. That is, the City offers a range of images so various in their implications—from the heights of the World Trade Center to the depths of the South Bronx, from the elegantly appointed Frick Museum to tatty, midtown peep shows, from the Park to a thousand drug-cribs—that observers can make of it what they will. If cities are mouths, said Frank Lloyd Wright, then New York City is the biggest mouth of all. "It devours food, people, ideas, freedom, bellowing its head off between bites," writes Herbert Muschamp. "Gobble, gobble, gobble, demand attention, toot the horn."[6] To circumscribe, if not devour the City, writers too must raise their voices. Some writers still shout in praise of the City, but many more utter laments.

Works about the character and destiny of the City published in the final decades of the twentieth century have become increasingly nostalgic and apocalyptic in their visions. A sense of loss permeates the pages of many books about New York and other American cities. In *Los Angeles: Capital of the Third World* (1991), for example, David Rieff twits his fellow New Yorkers for holding onto a conception of cultural importance that has gone with the wind: "To hear New Yorkers talk, one might think that they still live in the city of Dorothy Parker, Edmund Wilson, the Jewish intelligentsia of the forties and fifties, and the international art world." For Rieff, indeed for many, the show is all but over for New York City. "The lesson of New York's decline was that the curtain comes down just as surely on historical periods as it does on individual lives."[7] In literature about the City, we live in an era of curtain calls, reminiscences, dire predictions, and faint hopes.

In his *New York Intellect* (1987), Thomas Bender celebrates the sustained achievements of New York's intellectual life, but he also calls attention to "the persistent pattern of retreat and the chronic pattern of movements falling short of democratic aspirations. What has eluded New York City—and still eludes it—is the creation of a vital public culture, harmoniously integrating civic, literary, and academic elements."[8] What is also under threat is the American ideal of democratic polity.

As we shall see from an examination of recent works about the City and its character, writers have shown a growing awareness of economic, ethnic, racial, and gender differences among New Yorkers, but these distinctions are usually portrayed as exacerbations that contribute to urban alienation, rather than as causes for celebration, as they were for Walt Whitman. The voices in these recent works have become distraught, at times even deranged. The imagery that evokes the City, hyperbolic from the first, has become increasingly extravagant and threatening. The stories, or informing narrative structures, of these works have developed into clear parables of destruction for the characters involved and, by extension, for the nation. Finally, the sense of place that emerges from these works has become toxic. At the same time, paradoxically, some writers can still find in the City signs of redemption.

THE STORIES THROUGH WHICH WE KNOW THE CITY ARE being revised to take account of its precarious state, as evidenced in the autobiographical reconsiderations of life in the City of Lewis Mumford and Elizabeth Hardwick. Mumford, a distinguished urban analyst, lived long enough to see his ideal vision of the American city dissolve and his beloved Manhattan, the embodiment of that ideal, decline and fall from grace. Hardwick, a distinguished literary critic, has lived long enough to reconsider her celebratory assessment of the City.

Lewis Mumford articulated his urban ideal in *The Culture of Cities* (1938): "The city is the form and symbol of an integrated social relationship: it is the seat of the temple, the market, the hall of justice, the academy of learning. Here is where human experience is transformed into viable signs, symbols, patterns of conduct, systems of order."[9] Mumford stressed the goals of unity, cohesion, and coherence: for him the city should compose, out of its diverse residents and elements, one living and nurturing organism. Yet New York City, as he saw it, fell apart.

Born in Flushing, Queens, in 1895, Mumford, who called himself "a child of the city," grew up on Manhattan's Upper West Side, in a "typical New York brownstone." Eventually all of the City became his landscape of discovery; he took to its streets like an explorer; the port of New York stood as his frontier. His

City was an expanded village.[10] "Not merely was I a city boy but a New Yorker, indeed a son of Manhattan, who looked upon specimens from all other cities as provincial—especially Brooklynites," he confessed in *Sketches from Life* (1982). Despite its problems, deriving from vast inequities of wealth, the New York of Mumford's youth offered "a moral stability and security," which, by the 1970s, when the City nearly went bankrupt, was long gone. In the early 1980s, near the end of his long life, Mumford looked back on his old City with regret and contemplated its future with despair: "More than once lately in New York I have felt as Petrarch reports himself feeling in the fourteenth century, when he compared the desolate, wolfish, robber-infested Provence of his maturity, in the wake of the Black Plague, with the safe, prosperous region of his youth."[11]

Mumford's memoir recounts his development from his youth before World War I, to his coming of age as one of America's most influential cultural critics between the wars, then to his adult sense that he had become a "displaced person," almost an invisible man in modern, plague-ridden Manhattan: "The city I once knew so intimately has been wrecked; most of what remains will soon vanish; and therewith scattered fragments of my own life will disappear in the rubble that is carried away."[12]

Deconstruction of the City's once-fabled image of cultural primacy also occurs in Elizabeth Hardwick's reexamination of the City. More than a third of a century ago, Hardwick and Robert Lowell, then married, returned to New York from Boston; she celebrated their two-hundred-mile sea-change in "Boston: The Lost Ideal" (1959): "In Boston there is an utter absence of that wild electric beauty of New York, of the marvelous, excited rush of people in taxicabs at twilight, of the great Avenues and Streets, the restaurants, theaters, bars, hotels, delicatessens, shops."[13] In her later assessment, the City comes under radical revision. In "New York City: Crash Course" (1991), she wonders why people still come to New York: "Once here, a lingering infection seems to set in and the streets are filled with complaints and whines of the hypochondriac who will not budge, will not face a fertile pasture." Images of disease, plague, and infection characterize her postmodern New York: "Here it is, that's all, the place itself, shadowy, ever promising and ever withholding, a bad mother, queen of the double bind . . . Nevertheless." *Nevertheless*, the words of Walt Whitman cannot be dismissed: "Give me faces and streets—give me these phantoms incessant and endless along the trottoirs!"[14] Hardwick invokes Whitman's noble lines, but she offers only ignoble examples of muggers, addicts, derelicts, and beggars, who today patrol the City's trottoirs alongside the well-heeled. Elizabeth Hardwick's "crash course" on New York is an instructive document on a city trapped in a downward spiral.

T HE FADING REMNANTS OF OLD NEW YORK SOCIETY AND the pushy presence of the City's new rich have been held up to scorn for their willingness to sacrifice manners and morals for power and money. Louis Auchincloss's fiction, for example, satirizes New York City's East Side cultural aristocracy. Born in 1917, Auchincloss was like Edith Wharton part of the New York high society that he takes as his subject. In *The House of Five Talents* (1960), Auchincloss traces the decline of an old New York family that resembles his own. His *Portrait in Brownstone* (1962) chronicles the Denisons—who are based upon his grandmother's family, which once ruled Fifty-third Street—from the death of Victoria to the 1950s.[15] Both novels show once-grand families of old New York who are barely surviving; they are in the grip of fierce matriarchs and they feel left behind in the City.

In *Tales of Manhattan* (1964), Auchincloss includes one story, "The Landmarker," in which the protagonist depends upon the City's hidden treasures for his identity. Lefferts, running out of his inherited money, finds himself gradually losing his social standing. As his dinner invitations decline, Lefferts spends his time revisiting corners of New York that hold memories of better days for himself and for the City. Examining the gothic gates of Greenwood Cemetery in Brooklyn, Lefferts thinks, "It was as if he and the old by-passed city had found each other in a golden twilight." He does not even mind when he discovers that New York's landmark treasures have been hidden away or encroached upon by new excrescences. After all, "what was he but a sober, four-story brownstone facade, with gothic arches and an iron grille, such as one might find in Hicks Street over at Brooklyn Heights?"[16]

Auchincloss, a lawyer, gained entry into the world of business through his work for various Wall Street law firms. As in the social fiction of his mentor, Henry James, in Auchincloss's novels of manners the protocols of public life mask fierce social and financial ambitions.[17] Auchincloss documents, as he titled a 1968 novel, "a world of profit"—closed, competitive, and costly.[18] In another aptly titled, early work, *A Law for the Lion* (1953), a bullying lawyer spies on his unfaithful wife; then he sues for divorce and custody of their children—all life is reduced to a struggle for power. His daughters recoil from his dominance and return to their mother, who finds a way to survive outside the New York City jungle. In *The Great World and Timothy Colt* (1956), an idealistic young man is tempted and nearly destroyed by the fast-and-loose ways of his Wall Street law firm.

Auchincloss shows the City slipping from bad to worse. In *Diary of a Yuppie* (1986), he tracks the ruthless rise of another unprincipled Wall Street lawyer, Robert Service, age thirty-two, whose specialty is corporate takeovers. The novel, a first-person narrative, is a document of self-incrimination, for Service openly admits to his hunger for success and his inner emptiness: "Partnership has been my sole ambition—you might even call it my obsession—throughout eight years of driving work, including most weekday nights and many weekends. And what do I feel, now that triumph is nigh? Very little."[19] Making it in Manhattan numbs the soul. However, Service's lack of principles carry him far in the 1980s era of greed, which found its center in the financial markets of New York City. Auchincloss's fictional range is narrow, spanning the territory between Wall Street law offices and East Side drawing rooms, but his eye is sharply focused on the empty manners and lax morals evident in the contemporary City's glass towers and elegant brownstones.

OTHER NOVELISTS—PAUL AUSTER AND IVAN GOLD, FOR example—see the City as increasingly surreal, like Kafka's Prague. Gold was born in the City in 1931, reared on the Lower East Side, and educated at Columbia. He writes mock-epic sagas of exuberant antiheroes who yield to the City's many temptations, yet survive to write about it. Auster was born in Newark in 1947, reared in New Jersey, and also studied at Columbia. Living at Park Slope and writing cryptic parables of haunted urban characters, he has been called "the Brooklyn symbolist."[20]

Paul Auster brings an arch postmodernism—self-ironic, parodic, yet obsessed with matters of form—to his refractory vision of New York City in *The New York Trilogy*, which includes *City of Glass* (1985), *Ghosts* (1986), and *The Locked Room* (1986). These strange, inward-looking novels represent the City as a mysterious labyrinth. *City of Glass* turns on an incident of mistaken identity. In 1980 Auster kept receiving phone calls asking for the Pinkerton Agency; after repeated denials, Auster, mixing fictional impersonation into his life, said it was. In *City of Glass* a writer named Quinn—he writes under the name "William Wilson" in tribute to a Poe story in which a man kills his double—receives repeated calls from a man asking for Paul Auster, of the Auster Detective Agency. On a whim, Quinn finally identifies himself as Auster, and the strangeness begins. Quinn searches through the maze of the City for its elusive meaning: "New York was an inexhaustible space, endless steps, and no matter how far he walked, no matter how well he came to know its neighborhood and streets, it always left him with the feeling of being lost."[21] "Each of these short, elegant books [in *The New York Trilogy*] turns on a search of some kind—all of them feature detectives, missing persons, mistaken identities," explains critic Sven Birkerts. Auster uses the urban detective genre to reveal "that all existence is, at root, a stalking of clues to the self, and to the true relation of that self to everything that is Other."[22]

In Auster's 1987 novel, *In the Country of Last Things*, a young woman arrives by boat at an unnamed city. She is searching for her lost brother, but she has all she can do to survive the dislocations and terrors of the city: "The city is a place of worst fears. All municipal order has broken down. Gangs terrorize and pillage." Soon she becomes a scavenger with nothing left but her own capacity for charity.[23] Auster's City of Glass is a hall of mirrors—cold, empty, and infinitely self-reflexive.

In his autobiographical fiction, Ivan Gold has also left a record of an insider's sense of "the fantastic city . . . where he would live again one day, the city he had not stopped living in yet."[24] He writes tales of failure and recovery centered in the City. In *Sick Friends* (1969), writer and teacher Jason Sams suffers self-destructive responses to his friends, his women, and his urban adventures. By *Sams in a Dry Season* (1990), Jason has moved to Boston, but he has also fallen close to the bottom of the barrel, or rather, nearly reached the bottom of his glass. At age forty-three, having lost his teaching job in Boston, Jason deems it "high time to return to the literary wars," so he travels home again, to New York, where he meets with his agent and tries to squeeze more money from his publishers—an advance for a book he knows he cannot write.[25]

In *Sams in a Dry Season*, Gold writes a tale of two cities in the 1970s, Boston and New York City, each a symbolic site, representing a distinct stage of his life and a different state of his being. Sams, who came of age in the City, finds himself banished and blocked in Boston, so he seeks renewal through his quest for mislaid promise in New York. Yet, back again, he finds himself disoriented by the City's constant changes. Along Madison Avenue, for example, Sams feels like a "hick . . . craning for a better look at New York City's newest skyscrapers, measuring these relaxed giants against the self-conscious pair back 'home,'" in Boston.[26] But Boston is straining to become New York by erecting its own skyscrapers. Where, then, is Jason Sams's true home?

Gold's novel tracks Sams's lurching movements around the City, charts his heavy drinking, and portrays his grief-filled encounters with friends, family, and abandoned hopes. He watches his life flash before him in an inventory of steps mistaken, comic pratfalls, blunders, and betrayals. Rebuffed by his publisher and his agent, Sams drinks all the booze that he can buy and steal. He reels through a family funeral; he offends old friends and he makes new enemies— from the East Village to Queens. Then, with no evident exit, his life suddenly turns toward the light. He quits New York, where the wild things are, and he returns to his family, to Boston, where he enters Alcoholics Anonymous and eventually resumes his writing. Gold's New York City is the last stop on the way down, the site of revelation, and the bottom from which his fictional protagonist begins to pick himself up.

As we have seen in other chapters, Jewish and Irish literary voices—ethnic counterpoints in the City's raucous chorus—have been eloquently registered in the City, which has provided both groups with opportunities to realize the American dream. The classic dilemma of assimilation articulated in works by members of these groups—Americanization at the price of ethnic self-identification—is evident as well in the literature of other ethnic groups. Jaime Manrique's *Latin Moon in Manhattan* (1992), for example, portrays the City as a new El Dorado, particularly in the novel's lyrical opening:

> *After it leaves Manhattan, the number seven train becomes an elevated, and crosses a landscape of abandoned railroad tracks, dilapidated buildings and, later, a conglomerate of ugly factories that blow serpentine plumes of gaudy poisonous smoke. As the train journeys deeper into Queens, the Manhattan skyscrapers in the distance resemble monuments of an enchanted place—ancient Baghdad, or even the Land of Oz. The sun, setting behind the towers of the World Trade Center, burnishes the sky with a warm orange glow and the windows of the towers look like gold-leafed entrances to huge hives bursting with honey.*

The novel tracks the picaresque adventures of Santiago Martinez, a failed poet who leaves Queens to settle in Times Square, which he thinks of as "a foreign country."[27] Manrique evokes the rich street life of Latino Manhattan, which survives amid pathos and tragedy: Santiago's cat dies, his friends get caught up in cocaine traffic, and his childhood companion dies of AIDS—the City's contemporary plague.

In Oscar Hijuelos's spirited novel, *The Mambo Kings Play Songs of Love* (1989), Cuban émigrés' dreams of success in New York City come to nothing. In 1949 two young musicians, the Castillo brothers, come from Havana to play mambo music in the dance halls of the City. They briefly become known as the Mambo Kings and even appear on an episode of the *I Love Lucy* television show. The novel is dominated by the remembrances of Cesar Castillo, an old, disappointed alcoholic, who in 1980 sits alone with his bottle and his memories in the Hotel Splendor, on 125th Street and Lenox Avenue. Not only his own life but all of New York City has fallen apart since the Mambo Kings recorded their songs in 1954:

> *Everything was different then: 125th Street was jumping with clubs, there was less violence, there were fewer beggars, more mutual respect between people; he could take a late-night stroll from the apartment on La Salle Street, head down Broadway, cut east on 110th Street to Central Park, and then walk along its twisting paths and across the little bridges over streams and rocks, enjoying the scent of the woods and nature's beauty without a worry. He'd make his way to the Park Palace Ballroom on East 110th Street to hear Machito or Tito Puentes, find musician friends at the bar, chase women, dance. Back then, you could walk through that park wearing your best clothes and a nice expensive watch without someone coming up behind you and pressing a knife against your neck. Man, those days were gone forever.* [28]

In the Hotel Splendor, the last of the Mambo Kings sings a swan song for himself and for his adopted City. Oscar Hijuelos joins the ranks of writers, from Henry James to Lewis Mumford, who compose nostalgic testimonies to the City's great days gone.

THE CHANGING MOOD OF THE CITY CAN BE SEEN EVEN at the *New Yorker*. William Shawn, after twenty-six years as editor, was replaced by former Random House editor Robert Gottlieb in 1987, two years after the magazine was sold to S. I. Newhouse Jr.'s publishing empire. The *New Yorker* grew more liberal in its language and in its portrayal of sexual issues. Gottlieb was replaced in late 1992 by Tina Brown, an English editor who made her reputation at *Vanity Fair*; she radically altered the format and style of the magazine. The cover of her first issue implied that the magazine would show more flash and try to reach a new audience. A watercolor and ink drawing by Edward Sorel portrays a punkish young man, wearing leather and sporting a fuchsia mohawk cut, lounging in the seat of a horse-drawn carriage, being driven through Central Park, arrayed in autumn colors, by a noticeably nervous driver. Brown dropped the "we" from the "Talk of the Town" section—as though in open admission that the *New Yorker* could no longer presume to speak to and for New Yorkers in one inclusive, assured voice. Older readers would have to make room, as does that cabby on Edward Sorel's cover, for new styles of expression. Joseph Epstein, editor of the *American Scholar*, knew what to expect, so he said his farewell: "Eustace Tilley, . . . sensing the game is up, sheds a single, shimmering, poignant tear."[29]

The new *New Yorker* seemed to parody Epstein's gloomy expectations. The annual anniversary cover of the magazine had long featured a drawing by Rea Irvin of Eustace Tilley, a top-hatted Regency dandy who stared through his monocle, contemplating a butterfly. As a sign of the *New Yorker*'s new direction and, perhaps, a reflection of the manners of the day, in February 1994 the magazine cover, drawn by Robert Crumb, parodied the long-standing Tilley cover by featuring Elvis Tilley, a scruffy-looking teenager, wearing an earring and his baseball hat turned backward, standing amid other drifters and misfits; instead of musing on a butterfly, Elvis is squinting at a handbill for a triple-X-rated sex shop in Times Square.[30] The new *New Yorker* has wittily caught the contemporary character of the city.

TOM WOLFE'S *THE BONFIRE OF THE VANITIES* (1987) stands as the most illustrative and telling work on the City since Washington Irving's *History of New York*. New York literature, begun in whimsical burlesque with Irving, has moved to bitter satire with Wolfe. In the process, New York has been reconfigured: from a pretentious small town to a lethal metropolis.

Tom Wolfe followed *The Bonfire of the Vanities* with a 1989 "manifesto," an essay advancing the central importance of "the new social novel," particularly the New York City novel.[31] "To me the idea of writing a novel about this astonishing metropolis, a big novel, cramming as much of New York City between covers as you could, was the most tempting, the most challenging, and the most obvious idea an American writer could possibly have."[32] Wolfe complains that too many

American writers, pursuing surreal chimeras, have turned away from the Balzacian task of serving as a secretary to society; his manifesto celebrates the vibrant tradition of the city novel.

Tom Wolfe runs his antihero in *The Bonfire of the Vanities* like a rat through a maze of City streets, to see how far he gets and to measure how much he can take. Sherman McCoy, age thirty-eight, seems at first one of the City's most favored sons. Yet he cannot manage to support himself and his family on his yearly income of $1,000,000, most of which gets spent before it is earned. Wolfe enjoys cataloging all that McCoy possesses: a WASP lineage, a Yale degree, a beautiful wife and daughter, a gorgeous mistress named Maria, a fourteen-room Park Avenue co-op, which he bought for $2,600,000 ($1,800,000 borrowed) and on which he owes "$21,000 a month in principal and interest, with a million dollar balloon payment due in two years."[33] McCoy imagines himself a "Master of the Universe," but Wolfe shows that his protagonist is a fool of fortune, a man whose story reveals much about contemporary New York, "a city boiling over with racial and ethnic hostilities and burning with the itch to Grab It Now."[34] Indeed, New York City itself is the central concern of Wolfe's urban epic, rather than his characters, who, for all their self-importance, are mere pieces of flotsam, adrift upon "the rousing sound of the greed storm."[35]

The novel opens with a raucous scene in which Mayor Goldberg is shouted down by citizens of Harlem. The mayor wonders who owns the City. How naive, he thinks, are rich Manhattan co-op owners who think themselves insulated from third world New York, which surrounds their opulent enclaves.

Sherman McCoy, one of those wealthy and deluded New Yorkers, while driving over the Triborough Bridge, appreciates the view of what he thinks of as his Manhattan, "the Rome, the Paris, the London of the twentieth century, the city of ambition, the dense magnetic rock, the irresistible destination of all those who insist on being *where things are happening*—and he was among the victors!"[36] But Sherman is forced to face the other side of the City, the wasteland, and to confront its dispossessed. On his way home from Kennedy Airport with Maria in his $48,000 Mercedes, Sherman takes a wrong turn and, terrified, suddenly finds that they are driving through the ravaged South Bronx: "*Astonishing.* Utterly empty, a vast open terrain. Block after block—how many?—six? eight? a dozen?—entire blocks of the city without a building left standing. . . . Here and there were traces of rubble and slag. The earth looked like concrete, except that it rolled down this way . . . and up that way . . . the hills and dales of the Bronx . . . reduced to asphalt, concrete, and cinders . . . in a ghastly yellow gloaming."[37] On a ramp leading back to the expressway, his car is blocked by barrels and they are approached by two black youths. Sherman and Maria panic. When he gets out of the car, she takes the wheel and runs down one of the young men before she and Sherman drive off to "White Manhattan."[38] Out of this ambiguous encounter comes Wolfe's version of *An American Tragedy*.

However, Tom Wolfe echoes F. Scott Fitzgerald more than Theodore Dreiser. In *The Bonfire of the Vanities*, as in *The Great Gatsby*, a woman drives the opulent car of her wealthy lover into the dangerous territory of another class, just outside Manhattan. In the valley of ashes, each woman strikes down one of the dispossessed. In each case the man takes the blame for the hit-and-run and is punished for the crime—though Gatsby's motives are noble, while Sherman only wants to keep his affair with Maria a secret. Though both authors include similar incidents to show the callousness of the rich, Fitzgerald treats the event as tragedy, for Gatsby is killed by the victim's husband. Wolfe treats it as farce, for McCoy is offered up as a sacrificial victim (more useful alive than dead) by those who exploit him for their political and career advantages. Mayor Goldberg, for example, playing for votes, delights in putting "the Wasp to the wall."[39]

A Bronx district attorney, up for reelection, spends most of his days prosecuting blacks; therefore, he too needs the publicity and the votes that will come from convicting a rich white man. An assistant district attorney in the Bronx is "tired of watching *other people* lead . . . The Life," so to advance his career, he also goes after Sherman.[40] A corrupt black minister exploits the hit-and-run case to gain money and power through his manipulations of the media. An alcoholic reporter for a scandal sheet finds his career transformed when the minister indirectly uses him to run stories against McCoy. Sherman McCoy, then, becomes enmeshed in the slow but inexorable system of Dickensian "justice" of New York City.

Surprisingly, McCoy gradually shucks off his acquired affectations of class and culture; as he gets ground up, he grows more genuine. In losing everything, McCoy gains new insight into his environment and composes a more authentic self; knowledge of the way things actually work in the City becomes his only power. At the end of the novel, after he has been stripped of all his emblems of authority, Sherman is tough, ready to stand up for himself, though still held in the bizarre world of jail and courts—symbolized by the Bronx County Building, the Bleak House of New York City, an elaborate "island fortress of the Power, of the white people" where one heard "a *Rigoletto* from the sewer, from the rancid gullet of the Bronx!"[41]

Wolfe's satirical art depends upon stereotypes and caricatures, evident in his description of a posh East Side dinner party, where all the men are rich and old, but the women fall into two types: the thin, older women, "starved to perfection," and the "so-called Lemon Tarts," or younger women "who were the second, third, and fourth wives or live-in girlfriends of men over forty or fifty or sixty (or seventy), the sort of women men refer to, quite without thinking, as *girls*."[42]

At this dinner party for the *nouveau beau monde*, whose values have set up Sherman McCoy for his fall, Lord Buffing, a British poet who has AIDS and is dying, tells the assembled guests about a story by Poe in which party guests dance with Death: "They are bound together, and they whirl about one another, endlessly, particles in a doomed atom—and what else could the Red Death be but some final stimulation, the *ne plus ultra*? So Poe was kind enough to write the ending for us more than a hundred years ago."[43] *The Bonfire of the Vanities*, then, is also Wolfe's camp version of Poe's "The Masque of the Red Death."

Wolfe clearly rejects the myth of New York as a melting pot. His City is a warring camp in which power and prestige are fought over by manipulators and the mob. Wolfe's mock-heroic style—designed to level his characters' pretensions—exposes New Yorkers from all boroughs, classes, races, and ethnic backgrounds as greedy and self-seeking: "*Make it now!* That motto burned in every heart like myocarditis."[44] Wolfe defends himself against the charge of negative stereotyping and blatant prejudice by saying that it would have been wrong to portray New Yorkers in the heroic mode. "I felt this was a book about vanity in New York in an age of money fever," he told an interviewer. "In fact, those who triumph in an age like that are seldom what we usually consider heroic and admirable characters."[45] But Wolfe's *The Bonfire of the Vanities* revives a literary tradition of disdain for the masses and their leaders, a genre established by Irving, Cooper, Strong, and many more writers who recorded their anxieties over expressions and manipulations of the popular will in New York City.

Tom Wolfe has not, as he implies, been alone in this genre; in the hangover aftermath of the 1980s boom-and-bust cycle, several young writers have also taken the City's dire straits as their primary fictional concern: notably Richard Price in *Clockers* (1992), Bret Easton Ellis in *American Psycho* (1991), and Jay McInerney in *Brightness Falls* (1992). These writers represent a range of urban characters and settings, but each of their protagonists yields to contemporary corruptions offered by the City.

What Tom Wolfe does for midtown, Richard Price does for New York's boroughs and beyond. In his novels, Price shows the dark side of the brief lives of those who are confined to the Bronx—a violent world baptized in blood loyalties and confirmed in bloodletting. Price grew up in a Bronx housing project, but he escaped this urban ghetto by studying at Cornell. His literary enablement also came in part through his reading of the fiction of another boroughs naturalist, Hugh Selby Jr.'s *Last Exit to Brooklyn* (1964). Selby's collection takes its title from a sign on the Gowanus Expressway, which appears just before the entrance to the Battery Tunnel. That exit leads to a wasteland of docks, abandoned factories, bars, slums, and housing projects, structures left for the down-and-out of the City. In "Landsend," for example, Selby juxtaposes, in Dos Passos fashion, choral and individual responses to this end zone: "The sun rose behind the Gowanus Parkway lighting the oil filmed water of the Gowanus Canal and the red bricks of the Project."[46] However, little light shines on those who "live" in Selby's New York.

"In 'Last Exit' I saw, in print, a neighborhood similar to my own, voices I'd been hearing all my life," writes Price. "I experienced the music of the projects, and it was *good*, it was literature, and apart from the more intense scenes of sex, drugs and bloodshed, 'I BEEN DERE.' I loved it."[47] Thus, once he was out of the projects, Price returned, imaginatively, to treat them in his harsh stories about life in the boroughs.

In *The Wanderers* (1974), Price portrays a teenage gang of the 1960s—roaming the edge of maturity and civility: "There he was in Big Playground. Richie Gennaro. Seventeen. High Warlord of the Wanderers. Surrounded by the Warlords of the Rays, Pharaohs, and the Executioners."[48] These "wanderers" prove to be as confined to their assigned place as were the Chicago corner-boys in James T. Farrell's *Studs Lonigan*.

In *Bloodbrothers* (1976), young Stony DeCoco, who lives with his family in Co-op City, a sterile high-rise housing project, is in conflict. Will he be able to escape his binding family ties by doing what he wants to do (working with hospitalized children) or will he stay tied down by family expectations (construction work)? Finally, Three-Fingered Annette, a prostitute, shows Sonny that there is another world, and he escapes the projects.[49]

In *Clockers* (1992), another young man, a black drug dealer named Strike, escapes the even darker world of Dempsy, an imaginary city located at the New Jersey end of the Holland Tunnel. Life for the young residents of Dempsy is so constricted that they go to New York City for release. One day Strike and a boy he is recruiting into the drug business drive into New York: "The trip to New York took only thirty minutes, and as they flew around the glazed fluorescent curves of the Holland Tunnel, a false promise of daylight around each bend" drew them on. On the New York side, Strike takes out his twenty-five caliber pistol and says, "New York, New York, city of dreams, sometimes it ain't *all* what it seems."[50] In another New York scene, Buddha Hat, an assassin, brings Strike to a Times Square showing of the pornographic film in which Buddha Hat lost his virginity. On their way back to Dempsy, the two young men pause on the New Jersey side of the Hudson, "staring out at the shut-down New York skyline"; they talk about the few years they think they have left to live, and they try to decide which would be the best spot on their bodies to take a quick, fatal gunshot.[51]

Rocco Klein, a Dempsy cop who lives in Manhattan, likes and understands Strike, for they share the same dark vision: "Rocco looked out the bedroom window at their nighttime view of the bridges leading into the southern tip of Manhattan. Underlit by the city, the sky was an eerie muddy purple."[52] With Rocco's help, Strike escapes the destructive world of Dempsy–New York City.

No ONE ESCAPES IN BRET EASTON ELLIS'S HORRIFYING novel about the contemporary City, *American Psycho*, which opens with epigraphs from Dostoyevsky (on the social representativeness of the perverse narrator of *Notes from Underground*); from Miss Manners (on society's need for manners, for "if we followed every impulse, we'd be killing one another"); and from the Talking Heads (a rock group, which sings of things falling apart with nobody paying much attention). Together these epigraphs suggest that the novel's narrator, Patrick Bateman, will show how far America has come from any common assumption of civility.

Bateman, twenty-six years old, leads a double life. He is at once a Wall Street high-finance hustler (he works at Pierce & Pierce, an aptly named brokerage firm) and a serial murderer who kills for the fun of it. Bateman's acts of violence are inflicted upon the City's most vulnerable citizens: women, the homeless, children, and animals. His inability to feel any responsibility or regret and his numbing materialism are offered as evidence that things have indeed fallen apart. At its best, Ellis's novel is his way of making Americans pay attention to a derangement at the heart of our culture—to the madness loose in our cities. At its worst, redundant and lurid, the novel is yet another example of that derangement.

Patrick Bateman's account of his night journeys through sex and violence in New York City are also offered by Ellis as evidence of the "end of the 1980s," as a chapter is titled. By the time of *American Psycho*'s publication, this era of acquisitiveness and conspicuous consumption seemed long gone. However, though Ellis was a latecomer to the genre of cautionary tales about the immoral selfishness and brutality of our times—a tale set, of course, in America's Gomorrah—he outdoes all his predecessors.

"If you can make it there, you can make it anywhere," sing the Vegas crooners about New York, "the city that never sleeps." Patrick Bateman seldom sleeps, and he makes it there with a new level of callous violence. Indeed, the sensibilities of many, in the literary community and outside it, were offended by the novel. For example, *American Psycho* was called "misogynist garbage" by Tammy Bruce, the president of the Los Angeles Chapter of the National Organization for Women, a group that called for a boycott of the novel.[53]

Even Norman Mailer was shocked, which came as a surprise, for the author of *An American Dream* (1965) may have provided the literary model for *American Psycho*: "I cannot recall a piece of fiction by an American writer which depicts so odious a ruling class—worse, a young ruling class of Wall Street princelings ready, presumably, by the next century to manage the mighty if surrealistic levers of our economy. Nowhere in American literature can one point to an inhumanity of the moneyed upon the afflicted equal to [some of the scenes in Ellis's novel]."[54] Mailer finally came down against *American Psycho*, for all of its author's talent and all of the novel's hyperbolic brilliance, because Ellis made a banality of his murderer's evil.

Patrick Bateman lives in a City in which the rich and poor, the sane and insane, inhabit completely different worlds. The word "FEAR" is "sprayed in red graffiti on the side of a McDonald's on Fourth and Seventh," where two handsome and affluent young men, leaving their work day on Wall Street, hail a cab on the opening page of *American Psycho*. During their cab ride, one of these men-on-the-make scans the newspaper and reports on the daily record of urban horrors:

> *Strangled models, babies thrown from tenement rooftops, kids*
> *killed in the subway, a Communist rally, Mafia boss wiped out,*
> *Nazis . . . baseball players with AIDS, more Mafia shit, gridlock,*
> *the homeless, various maniacs, faggots dropping like flies in the*
> *streets, surrogate mothers, the cancellation of a soap opera, kids*
> *who broke into a zoo and tortured and burned various animals*
> *alive, more Nazis . . . and the joke is, the punch line is, it's all in*
> *this city—nowhere else, just here, it sucks, whoa wait, more Nazis,*

> *gridlock, gridlock, baby-sellers, black-market babies, AIDS babies,*
> *baby junkies, building collapses on baby, maniac baby, gridlock,*
> *bridge collapses . . .* [55]

This seemingly limitless catalog of urban diseases and afflictions—which makes no distinctions between the serious and the silly, recounted by a young man who is not even the sociopathic antihero of the novel—serves as Ellis's reference point for the reader. *Then* the reader is presented with the loathsome activities of Patrick Bateman, who gets away with murder; *then* the reader is trapped inside the permutations of horror he inflicts upon the innocent and vulnerable citizens of Ellis's City of the Dead.

JAY MCINERNEY'S *BRIGHTNESS FALLS* (1992) IS A NOVEL framed as an elegy for the loss of innocence during the 1980s, the failed promises of American life, and the fading image of New York City. McInerney's representative young Americans, born in Eisenhower's 1950s, came of age in the sinister years of Nixon and Watergate; buoyed by Reagan-era delusions of grandeur, they participate in its compromises and they suffer its consequences. The novel, centering on three gifted, witty, and intelligent young characters (a writer, a publisher, and a broker), is more than a pattern of interlocking narratives of private failures. It is also a novel about the shattering of the American dream—money, success, power, beauty—at the time of the Iran-Contra scandal and the stock market collapse of 1987. The novel, fittingly, is set in the vital center of this economic "action," New York City.

McInerney's title comes from a poem by Thomas Nashe, "A Litany in Time of Plague" (1600). The Nashe poem is read at a memorial service held at St. Mark's-in-the-Bowery for a gifted young writer, Jeff Pierce, who has died of AIDS-related pneumonia. In this novel, as in Nashe's poem, "the plague full swift goes by" and "brightness falls from the air." Corrine Calloway, Jeff's friend and the conscience of the novel, at first does not understand the trope, but then she suddenly gets it—"she could picture it clearly: brightness and beauty and youth falling like snow out of the sky all around them, gold dust falling to the streets and washing away in the rain outside the church, down the gutters into the sea."[56] In *Brightness Falls*, Jay McInerney recreates in the early 1990s the same sense of lost innocence that F. Scott Fitzgerald articulated in the mid 1920s in *The Great Gatsby*.[57] Clearly it was Fitzgerald who scored the melody line to which some New York novelists still write their lyrics.

Russell and Corrine Calloway, both age thirty-one, are five years married in

1987. Their marriage seems blessed, "a safe haven in a city that murdered marriages." In Manhattan they live in a one-bedroom rental on the East Side, with a view from their terrace of the City to the south. He works in publishing and she is a stockbroker. All is well until they are both pulled into the updraft of expectations in New York in the early 1980s, a mood well caught in McInerney's Fitzgeraldian prose, which combines evocation and irony:

> *After nearly collapsing in bankruptcy during the seventies, their adoptive city had experienced a gold rush of sorts; prospecting with computers and telephones, financial miners had discovered fat veins of money coursing beneath the cliffs and canyons of the southern tip of Manhattan. As geological and meteorological forces conspire to deposit diamonds at the tip of one continent and to expose gold at the edge of another, so a variety of manmade conditions intersected more or less at the beginning of the new decade to create a newly rich class based in New York, with a radical new scale of financial well-being. The electronic buzz of fast money hummed beneath the wired streets, affecting all the inhabitants, making some of them crazy with lust and ambition, others angrily impoverished, and making the comfortable majority feel poorer. Late at night, Russell or Corrine would sometimes hear that buzz—in between the sirens and the alarms and the car horns—worrying vaguely, clinging to the very edge of the credit limits on their charge cards.*[58]

McInerney sets his tale in the larger context of the City's history. Wall Street, he notes, marks the northern boundary of New Amsterdam, where in the seventeenth century a log wall stood, over which settlers threw their garbage. Corrine is oblivious to all this repressed history, "not really seeing the towering temples to Mammon as she walked toward the one in which she toiled, reading her paper in the available light that found its way to the canyon floor." Yet she realizes that the rising Dow Jones is crazy. Investors are building "castles in the air."[59] However, Russell, her impetuous and ambitious husband, is eager to storm the turrets.

Life grows precarious for the Calloways when Russell attempts a hostile takeover of Corbin, Dean and Company, the old publishing house for which he works as an editor. (The company, built during the commercial and literary idealism of 1920s New York, is shattered during the speculative madness of 1980s New York.) Russell is encouraged in his scheme by Victor Propp, a novelist who exploits the system for ever-larger bids on his long-unproduced novel: "I feel that we in this insane city are living in an era in which anything can happen. Do you remember what Nick Carraway said as he was driving into Manhattan in Gatsby's big car and the skyline of the city came into view over the Queensboro Bridge? As they cross into the city, Nick says, 'Anything can happen now that we've slid over this bridge . . . anything at all.' "[60]

Strange things do happen in *Brightness Falls*. For example, newspapers report that a rogue leopard, panther, or tiger is wandering the streets, attacking citizens. ("Wild Cat Terrorizes City," headlines the *Post*.)[61] Near the end of the novel, Corrine, who volunteers at a soup kitchen on the Lower East Side, gets caught up in a raid on a shantytown ("Reagantown"), when the police try to remove the homeless to make way for the developers: "Corrine envisioned the violence spreading and consuming the entire city."[62] Then she sees that the "terrifying" cat is actually a terrified ocelot who is standing helpless in an empty lot, an animal threatened by the murderous City. In New York City the worst, it sometimes seems, has already happened.

Corrine has a premonition of further disaster: "Lately it seemed to her that the horsemen of the apocalypse were saddling up, that something was coming to rip huge holes in the gaudy stage sets of Ronald McDonald Reaganland."[63] Russell, however, thinks the music will never stop. "Partying is such sweet sorrow," Russell jokes to Corrine, not realizing the full implications of what he says.[64] Russel overextends and, inevitably, the soaring stock market crashes. His takeover effort is blocked; after Corrine learns of his affair with a merger specialist, the Calloway marriage goes bust. All falls down. The center has not held, Russell realizes, in exile in Los Angeles: "Years before, he'd moved to New York believing himself to be penetrating to the center of the world, and all of the time he lived there the illusion of a center had held: the sense of there always being a door behind which further mysteries were available, a ballroom at the top of the sky from which the irresistible music wafted, a secret power source from which the mad energy of the metropolis emanated. But Los Angeles had no discernible center and was also without edges and corners."[65]

The New York City of *Brightness Falls* is hollow at the core. At one point Jeff and Russell walk along Great Jones Street—an ominous sign they pass says "DANGER HOLLOW SIDEWALK"—looking for the baths that they hope are still there: "Buildings disappeared overnight in the city, like black rhinos from the African savanna. In the morning only a smoking pile of brick and mortar would be left, the skin and bones; the next day a Pasta Fasta or a Younique Boutique."[66] Indeed, by the end of the novel the old bathhouse is gone, its site converted to yet another club for young partygoers. Old, established businesses fail, replaced by trendy, fly-by-night shops; at every level New York is strip-mined for quick profits.

Even more will be lost. Jeff, the writer who is convinced, like Fitzgerald before him, of life's insupportable sadness, has his vision confirmed when he learns he has AIDS; the Calloways find themselves "alone in the world, shivering at the dark threshold"—the final words of the novel.[67] In McInerney's New York the lights are dimming.

THOUGH IN THE IMAGINATION OF MANY OF ITS WRITERS brightness may have fallen from the skies over New York, it still attracts literary astrologers and cartographers who fix their positions, chart their destinations, and debate the course and purpose of the City. The New York literature of the early 1990s either looks to the past for parallels to the contemporary City or examines its current condition for portents of its future. In *Banished Children of Eve* (1994), Peter Quinn recounts the shocking facts of the New York draft riots of 1863 and assesses their implications, then and now. In *The Waterworks* (1994), E. L. Doctorow returns to the gaslight era of New York, which Doctorow holds up "as a mirror in which we are meant to see our own time and manner."[68] In *New York Days* (1993), Willie Morris, former editor of *Harper's*, writes about the lost glory of the City's near past. Sarah Schulman's novel of postmodern New York, *People in Trouble* (1990), carries readers through a refractive looking-glass to gaze with new eyes on the City's outrage, tragedy, humor, and saving grace. Taken together, these works eloquently sum up a sense of New York City at the end of the century.

Banished Children of Eve is a novel built around the deadliest riot in American history—when, for four days in July 1863, poor New Yorkers, most of them Irish-Americans, rose up in protest against the Draft Act that had been signed into law that spring and against working conditions that put them in competition with African-Americans. The Draft Act allowed a draftee either to hire a substitute or to buy his way out for $300, an amount equal to a working man's annual wages. Thus, suggests Peter Quinn, what happened on the streets of the City "was a race riot because class and race in America have always been intertwined, but it was also class warfare."[69] More than one hundred people, most of them blacks, were killed, and Federal forces, weary from the battle at Gettysburg, had to be called in to quell the riot.

Quinn dramatizes these events through the eyes of many onlookers: Jimmy Dunne, a streetwise hustler; Eliza, an African-American actress; her lover, Jack

Mulcahey, a man who escaped Ireland's famine and found his precarious place in New York's minstrel shows; Charles Bedford, a stockbroker; and his immigrant servant girl, Margaret O'Driscoll. Stephen C. Foster, America's foremost balladeer, drifts through the novel, a drunken and desperate man who has given away the songs that haunt him, songs that serve as a refrain in the novel. Foster was ignored, he believed, because "New York had too much of its own music. It couldn't carry one tune. It would drown a single song, smother it. New York gave you freedom, indulged tastes and vices that could get you hanged somewhere else, but at a price. Silence. An inability to concentrate. And when you could no longer pay that price, what then?"[70] This, then, is another novel both about the misfortunes of New Yorkers and the uncertain destiny of the City.

Quinn gives voice to the Irish-American poor who were driven by discrimination and desperate conditions to commit brutal acts that strengthened long-standing prejudices against them. This novel, finally, is a gesture of reconciliation for all the immigrant "banished children of Eve." Its last words, fittingly enough, come from Walt Whitman: "Each belongs here or anywhere as much as the welloff . . . just as much as you,/ Each has his or her place in the procession."[71] Quinn also offers a novel that, in the words of reporter Francis X. Clines, "is ripe with prefiguring," for the City of 1863 was, like the City of 1994, marked by the diseased, the homeless, street children, and the addicted.[72] Yet Peter Quinn—a native of the Bronx who lives in the Park Slope section of Brooklyn—is optimistic about the City: "New York is doing a lot of things, but it's not dying." The City recovered from its devastating draft riots and will, he believes, recover again. "It does absorb people. You don't have progress unless there's turmoil."[73]

There is much turmoil in E. L. Doctorow's *The Waterworks*, a vision of the City, as one reviewer described it, as "a gaslight necropolis."[74] Doctorow's novel is set in 1871, when Boss Tweed's ring, which had long controlled the City, was in the process of being exposed and destroyed, but it refers, as well, to the era of urban disintegration in which the novel was written. Today's New York, like yesterday's, Doctorow implies, represents self-consuming corruption, a city in which the very rich seek to live longer by sucking life out of the young.

The Gilded Age City only seems a very heaven in romantic retrospection, the novel's narrator, a jaded newspaper editor, ironically notes. "O my Manhattan!" McIlvaine declares, contemplating postwar changes in his City: the building of the Brooklyn Bridge, the heavy commercial traffic on land and water, the new telegraph, and the busy stock exchange. His City is rife with dramatic contrasts: "As a people we practiced excess. Excess in everything—pleasure, gaudy display, endless toil, and death." Fires rage through the City, burning up evidence of its past: "So it was a pungent air we breathed—we rose in the morning and threw open the shutters, inhaled our draft of the sulfurous stuff, and our blood was roused to churning ambition. Almost a million people called New York home, everyone securing his needs in a state of cheerful degeneracy."[75] McIlvaine, narrating events long past, invites us, reading him far in the future, to see ourselves in his story: The New York of 1871 "stands to your New York City today as some panoramic negative print, inverted in its lights and shadows . . . its seasons turned around . . . a companion city of the other side."[76] Doctorow also intends his novel about the City's postwar predators and dispossessed to stand as a corrective to narrow representations of the period in previous works of fiction. "I realized I was writing about everyone Edith Wharton had left out," said Doctorow.[77]

The Waterworks' central symbol—the Croton Holding Reservoir, a massive structure with walls twenty-five feet thick and forty-four feet high, located at Fifth Avenue and Forty-second Street—represents an ignored font of absolution at the heart of a City determined to pursue perversions. In this novel, which ranges from romance in its evocation of mystery to realism in its descriptions of urban miseries, Doctorow subsumes many previous literary approaches and attitudes toward the City. In the macabre sighting of the recently dead, speeding past in a horse-drawn omnibus, we hear Poe; in McIlvaine's despairing vision of his doomed City, we hear Melville.[78] *The Waterworks*, then, is something of a summing-up, a hail-and-farewell to the nostalgic notion of old New York City and a song of mourning for its future.

Doctorow's plot focuses on the death, disappearance, and eerie reappearance of millionaire Augustus Pemberton, followed by the permanent disappearance of his son, Martin, a journalist. McIlvaine, along with Edmund Donne, New York's only honest police captain, conducts a search that takes them to the City's dark inner sanctums. They discover, among other horrors, that a Doctor Sartorius has been conducting grotesque medical experiments, extracting blood and bone marrow from the City's cast-off children, for the purpose of extending, through injections of these fluids, the lives of aged millionaires.

McIlvaine denounces the City and wishes that it might dissolve into the beautiful and uncorrupted landscape it once must have been: "I have dreamt sometimes . . . I, a street rat in my soul, dream even now . . . that if it were possible to lift this littered, paved Manhattan from the earth . . . and all its torn and dripping pipes and conduits and tunnels and tracks and cables—all of it, like a scab from new skin underneath—how seedlings would sprout, and freshets bubble up, and brush and grasses would grow over the rolling hills." Soon, if McIl-vaine had his way, the City he knew would be gone; in its place would rise again "the lean, religious Indians of the bounteous earth, who lived without money or lasting architecture."[79] Then the City that Doctorow and the rest of us have come to know would never have been. F. Scott Fitzgerald memorialized the City's promise in an arresting image, the fresh green breast of a new world that flowered for Dutch sailor's eyes; Doctorow turns that trope inside out, dissolving the actual City in his imagination. "I fervently wished there were no buildings of any kind on this island. I envisioned the first Dutch sailors giving up on the place as a mosquito-infested swamp, and returning in their longboats to their ship."[80]

Lost promise is also the theme of Willie Morris's *New York Days*, a chronicle of his brief time of wine and roses in the City during the 1960s and 1970s. "I came to the city and it changed my life. I was exalted by it, exulted in it." So begins Morris's memoir of his dramatic rise and sudden fall in New York, the city H. L. Mencken once dismissed as a "third-rate Babylon." Morris, however, has never seen that "ineluctable town, sinew and fabric, of youth and dreams," as anything less than a romantic (though a near fatal) attraction.[81]

In 1967, at the age of thirty-two, Morris became the youngest editor-in-chief in the 117-year history of *Harper's Magazine*; then, in 1971, after making *Harper's* the most influential magazine in the country, he was fired. In *New York Days*, Morris tries to come to terms with all that happened to him, his magazine, his adopted city, and his nation. *New York Days* stands as the latest and one of the best examples of a familiar American saga: yet again a young man from the provinces (Yazoo, Mississippi), on a wave of early successes—Morris was educated at the University of Texas, where he became editor of the *Daily Texan*, and at Oxford University, where he went as a Rhodes Scholar—comes to the Big Cave, as Morris calls it, where he is lifted beyond his wildest expectations and, after the good times, has a great fall.

When Morris had made it in Manhattan, he let down his guard: "I began to feel that the city enveloped me, protected me, required more of me." But New York and *Harper's* turned on him. New York "tested who you are, in the deepest and most contorted way."[82] Thus, Morris's journey from Yazoo ballfields to Manhattan penthouses and then home again to exile in Mississippi is another tale in which the heady wine of success has a bitter aftertaste. At the end of his New York days, Morris found himself divorced, out of work, and hung over.

Still, it was fun while it lasted. Partying, drinking, and dining with some of the foremost American magazine writers, this good old boy from the South was at play in the fields of the lords and ladies of Gotham. Morris hired David Halberstam, Larry King, Gay Talese, John Corry, Marshall Frady, and Midge Decter to his staff. Contributions came in from William Styron, Joan Didion, and, above all, Norman Mailer. Indeed, for better or worse, Morris on occasion gave the magazine over to the riotous, rhetorical excursions of Mailer: his "Steps of the Pentagon" took up a whole issue in March 1968, and "Prisoner of Sex" appeared in the March 1971 issue, Morris's last. Morris had sought to create "a truly *national* magazine," but *Harper's* owners, the Cowles family of Minneapolis, accused him of editing it for an urban, leftist, intellectual audience. There may have been some truth to their charge, but it is also clear that the Cowles family did not recognize that Willie Morris was the finest editor of *Harper's* since William Dean Howells shaped American literature in its pages.

Morris still appreciates what the City once offered him, but that early enthusiasm has been tempered by his knowledge of the City today: "The glittering intoxication of the New York days, all their playfulness and gratification and drama, existed in moments for me in emotional counterpoise with other vestigial aspects of it. Some natives say the seeds of the future decline of the giant metropolis were being implanted even then in the Sixties."[83] *New York Days* thus concludes with a chilling scene. When Morris returns for a visit in 1992, he finds the City uglier, dirtier, and more dangerous, and most of the landmarks by which he once defined himself are gone: *Harper's* offices have abandoned the building in which he had free reign; even the Empire Chinese Restaurant, where he used to drink, talk with authors, and edit manuscripts, has been boarded up. In his final pages, it becomes clear that we are reading a somewhat muffled account of Willie Morris's own and his adopted City's crack-up: "I had come to New York with a heart full of stars and hopes, and to have gone so high so fast, then down in a moment, was more than I had ever bargained for, as if I had somehow lost my reason for existing."[84] Willie Morris, revisiting the haunts of his personal morality play in 1992, wanders the streets of the City, searching for his own lost self. He finally realizes that New York City not only knocks down its buildings; it also consumes its citizens. The only way he can ever recover his days of heady success will be in words—in the pages of a book: "I came to the city as a stranger, and although I became a New Yorker, I left it finally as a stranger, too."[85]

Sarah Schulman's *People in Trouble* brings to the familiar story of urban crisis a new emphasis, fresh details, and a surprisingly optimistic twist. Set in the New York of the late 1980s, this novel focuses upon an era when the City's inequities and miseries were dramatically evident in its streets. The effect of the AIDS epidemic upon all New Yorkers had become increasingly apparent. The growing number of street people, from the homeless to drug dealers, could not be ignored. At the same time, the City was booming with showy buildings, businesses catering to moneyed New Yorkers, and other signs of the glittering presence of the rich and famous. It was the best of times for a few and the worst of times for many in New York. "It was the beginning of the end of the world but not everyone noticed it right away. Some people were dying. Some people were busy. Some people were cleaning their houses while the war movie played on television."[86] New York City, in Sarah Schulman's observation, has become a neon-lit necropolis.

In the foreground of this novel, three young people try to find themselves, work out their relations, and make their ways through the outrages they encounter daily in the City. When Peter, who works as a theater lighting technician, walks the streets, he goes out of his way to avoid a fight between two young black men—a turf war between crack dealers, Peter assumes. *We New Yorkers always have something else to fear*, he told himself, turning up University Place. *First it was herpes, this year it's crossfire.*"[87] Peter's wife, Kate, an artist, is less fearful of the City: "[She] feared the consequences of chaos but was comfortable with fragments, when they were freely chosen."[88] Kate's lover, Molly, who barely supports herself as a theater cashier, fears little for her own safety or success, but she worries about the fate of the City. Public disorder makes private happiness difficult. "Here we are trying to have a run-of-the-mill illicit lesbian love affair," Molly tells Kate, "and all around us people are dying and asking for money." Most residents and tourists refuse to acknowledge the desperate and dying. "Thousands of people are dropping dead and no one cares," says Molly. "People won't do anything until it affects them."[89]

This urban "death camp" is ruled by the wealthy and powerful, like developer Ronald Horne, a man who is running for mayor on the platform that the AIDS-infected should be quarantined on barge internment camps. Horne is the builder of Downtown City, a landfill complex that extends into the East River, a "company town" for investment bankers.[90] He is also the owner of Ronald Horne's Castle, an ostentatious midtown hotel that encloses, among other showy oddities, a transplanted tropical rain forest featuring a moat. Guests can look down on live crocodiles and "feel like authentic [colonial] aristocracy instead of the robber barons that they really [are]."[91] The jewel in Horne's crown is the Taj McHorne, a new office and condominium complex on the site of the old Public Library—also the former site of the City's waterworks.

While Kate, Molly, and Peter are trying to sort out their tangled love lives, conditions in the City worsen. Hospital death watches and funerals for AIDS victims become routine. Stinking subway stations fill with the homeless, beggars patrol the streets in alarming numbers, and goods stolen by drug addicts are sold openly on the street. Yet the victims in this postmodern plague era do not remain passive. In particular, AIDS-infected men, organized under the name Justice (based upon the actual organization ACT UP), demonstrate publicly for medical treatment, for government support, and for public recognition. These men—each wearing a black T-shirt with a pink triangle and the word "Justice" across his chest—occupy the restaurant and lobby of Ronald Horne's Castle, protesting the eviction notices sent by the developer to homosexual men who are living in Horne-owned buildings. Justice, joined by Fury, a radical lesbian group, begins a campaign to redistribute the City's wealth by charging items on stolen company credit card numbers. Fur coats purchased at Bergdorf's go to residents of women's shelters, for example. At a meeting, a Justice member, nicknamed Cardinal Spellman because he wears a scarlet cape and a red velvet hat, testifies "that charging the hell out of New York City with no intention to pay is a fabulous way to work out your anger."[92] This novel catches the élan of destruction, perhaps, like graffiti, a new urban art form.

Schulman's central characters are forced to make choices. Peter, weary of Kate's bisexual infidelity, finds a new lover in Shelly, who is "beautiful and New York sexy, ethnic."[93] Molly, also weary of sharing Kate, finds a new lover in Sam, "a Girl of the Golden West. She was a memory from another time," when America seemed more innocent.[94] Kate, too, chooses a new life when a Justice demonstration at the dedication ceremony for Horne's Taj McHorne results in a riot, during which Horne is killed. Kate may have accidentally caused a fire through her choice of combustible materials for the art installation she set up at the complex's health club, a fire that "enveloped the billionaire developer in a flaming collage," according to a television news report.[95] Using her art as a weapon, Kate becomes engaged in the new struggle for power and life. In Sarah Schulman's disturbing but somehow reassuring vision of life and death in contemporary New York, no matter how many plagues and predators prey upon it, the City has the resources and its citizens possess the will to call up forces of opposition and affirmation.

NEW YORK CITY BEGAN AS A SETTLEMENT AT THE LOWER tip of Manhattan—a concentration of people, culture, money, and power in a small space—and gradually expanded to become the cosmopolis it is today. The literature that evokes and evaluates the City, from Washington Irving's mock-heroic history to E. L. Doctorow's elegiac recreation, also stresses the concentration and expansion of forces in New York. The presence of the City—its height, its reach, its grasp—has been a constant source of wonder for its writers. The position of the City as a gateway between Europe and the United States has long been noted. (Los Angeles, the capital of the third world, has become our new gateway city.) The pressures of New York have lent the City's literature a rare intensity. The tests, personal and public, imposed by the City upon its residents, new and old, have made it America's most interesting and revealing city for writers. The purpose of the City is always under examination and reconsideration. As we have seen, New York City, more than any other American city, has long challenged the nation's democratic commitment, its word, and its will; so, too, does the City, with its history of literary achievements, dare its artists to live up to their full potential.

Writers have helped to establish New York City as the symbolic center of American life. In New York's literature, as in its life, the men and women of the New World face unique opportunities and pressures. Writers have long celebrated the City as a site of personal and public liberation, but New York has also been faulted for betraying its promises. The literature of urban disillusionment, as we have seen, is large and various. However, the City, as we have also seen, offers compensations—in knowledge, wisdom, and maturity—to those it disappoints. For many, New York City, no matter how bad it gets, is an infinitely renewable feast for the imagination.

With its range of attractions and repulsions, New York pulls writers in many directions, creating states of anxiety and ambivalence that serve them well when they turn their sights onto the City. John Steinbeck, for example, arrived in Manhattan from California in 1925, when he was twenty-three, and he never forgot the impact the City had upon him. He tried to resist the magnetic attraction of the "monstrous" City, but found himself unable to do so. Soon, to his surprise, he "had become a New Yorker." Looking back on this initiation nearly thirty years later, Steinbeck decided that New York could "destroy a man," but it could not bore him, particularly if he wished to be a writer. He summed up the lesson he drew from this experience, emphasizing the City's gift of ambivalence: "New York is an ugly city, a dirty city. Its climate is a scandal, its politics are used to frighten children, its traffic is madness, its competition is murderous. But there is one thing about it—once you have lived in New York and it has become your home, no place else is good enough."[96] A generation later, Jay McInerney makes a similarly mixed judgment: "New York has always been too rich, too poor, too tall, too fast, too big, too loud, too dangerous. It is a city of excesses. And I can't seem to live anywhere else. Even at this late date, as the American Empire slouches into decline, New York seems to me to be the exact center of the world."[97]

In 1992, the Writers' Guild of America, East, asked a number of its members to contribute brief essays on the theme "Why I Write in New York" and received a range of interesting answers. Some write in the City simply because that is where they have lived for so long or because they do not want to move their heavy typewriters. One screenwriter, Alfred Uhry, goes against the grain of expectations and praises New York for being "user friendly to me and my work." His "New York is navigable. New York is up front. New York makes sense." Some stay in the City, reasonably enough, because it remains the center of what Malcolm Cowley called the writer's trade, but others offer more idiosyncratic and revealing reasons. Charles H. Fuller, a screenwriter, suggests that the air of the City must be addictive—"some combination of pollution, chestnut smoke, and Summer subway riders had poisoned the air," which immobilizes him. Author and screenwriter Eleanor Bergstein offers the most searching reasons for remaining in the City where she was born: "I write in New York because it holds me to a standard in finding my material." All around her, every day, her creative imagination is challenged when she encounters in New York the voices and visions of the American scene. When she is away, she dreams of the City, but her dreams never encompass its mystery: "One might say I dream of a different New York. I would say that if I dreamed of the violent crowded New York we all know, I'd awake so full of impressions and longing it would obliterate whatever daily life I was experiencing in whatever non–New York place I was."[98]

In the spring of 1992, several of the City's and the nation's most distinguished poets gathered in the Cathedral of St. John the Divine to pay tribute to Walt Whitman, the poet who boldly claimed "this is the city and I am one of the citizens," on the one hundredth anniversary of his death, and to read sections from Whitman's *Leaves of Grass*.[99] Allen Ginsberg was among those who read from Whitman, and the Cathedral Singers sang works based upon Whitman's texts. In "I Love Old Whitman So," Ginsberg, that most Whitmanian of contemporary poets, had already tipped "the hat on my skull/ to the old soldier, old sailor, old writer, old homosexual, old Christ poet journeyman,/ inspired in middle age to chaunt Eternity in Manhattan."[100] In honoring Whitman, these poets also celebrated the City in which Whitman wrote. Through literature they, like so many writers who came before them, help all of us to appreciate the power and promise of New York City.

N O T E S

Preface

1. Nelson W. Aldridge Jr., "Notes of a Native Son," *Boston Globe*, March 22, 1992, 68–69; Saul Bellow, *Mr. Sammler's Planet*, in *Bartlett's Familiar Quotations*; 16th ed., ed. Justin Kaplan (Boston: Little, Brown, 1992), 738.

2. David Halberstam, *Summer of '49* (New York: William Morrow, 1989).

3. F. Scott Fitzgerald, *The Great Gatsby* (1925; New York: Charles Scribner's Sons, 1980), 182.

4. Thomas Bender, *New York Intellect: A History of Intellectual Life in New York City, from 1750 to the Beginnings of Our Own Time* (New York: Alfred A. Knopf, 1987), 55.

5. Oliver E. Allen, *New York, New York: A History of the World's Most Exhilarating and Challenging City* (New York: Atheneum, 1990), 2.

6. Alan Trachtenberg, "The American Scene: Versions of the City," *Massachusetts Review* 8, no. 2 (Spring 1967): 295.

7. Witold Rybezynski, "The Mystery of Cities," *New York Review of Books*, July 15, 1993, 13.

8. Mario Cuomo, *The New York Idea: An Experiment in Democracy* (New York: Crown Publishers, 1994), xiii.

9. Emma Lazarus, *The New Colossus: Inscription for the Statue of Liberty, New York Harbor* (1883), in *Bartlett's Familiar Quotations*, 558.

10. Alfred Kazin, "New York from Melville to Mailer," *Partisan Review* 47, no. 1 (1981): 91.

1. Cited in the Works Progress Administration (WPA) Federal Writers' Project, *New York Panorama: A Companion to the Guide to New York City* (1938; New York: Pantheon Books, 1984), 15.

2. A. J. Liebling, "The Sea in the City," in *Back Where I Came From* (San Francisco: North Point Press, 1990), 25.

3. Oliver E. Allen, *New York, New York: A History of the World's Most Exhilarating and Challenging City* (New York: Atheneum, 1990), 4.

4. Milton M. Klein, "Shaping the American Tradition: The Microcosm of Colonial New York," *New York History* 59 (1978): 174; cited in Allen, *New York, New York*, 2.

5. Elihu Hubbard Smith, *The Diary of Elihu Hubbard Smith (1771–1798)*, ed. James E. Cronin (Philadelphia: American Philosophical Society, 1973), 299; cited in Thomas Bender, *New York Intellect: A History of Intellectual Life in New York City, from 1750 to the Beginnings of Our Own Time* (New York: Alfred A. Knopf, 1987), 34.

6. Cited in Bayrd Still, *Mirror for Gotham: New York as Seen by Contemporaries from Dutch Days to the Present* (New York: New York University Press, 1956), 10.

7. Cited in ibid., 23.

8. Sarah Kemble Knight, *The Journal of Madame Knight*, ed. George P. Winship (Boston, 1920); cited in *The Norton Anthology of American Literature*, 3d ed., ed. Nina Baym et al. (New York: W. W. Norton, 1989), 1: 258–60.

9. Bender, *New York Intellect*, 11.

10. Van Wyck Brooks, *The World of Washington Irving* (New York: E. P. Dutton, 1944), 28.

11. Cited in Still, *Mirror for Gotham*, 27.

12. Cited in ibid., 34–35.

13. Morton and Lucia White, *The Intellectual versus the City: From Thomas Jefferson to Frank Lloyd Wright* (Cambridge: Harvard University Press and MIT Press, 1962), 14.

14. Allen, *New York, New York*, 88–89.

15. Bender, *New York Intellect*, 55.

16. Cited in Still, *Mirror for Gotham*, 55.

17. Stuart M. Blumin, introduction to *New York by Gas-Light and Other Urban Sketches by George G. Foster*, ed. Stuart M. Blumin (Berkeley: University of California Press, 1990), 3.

18. Henry Adams, *The United States in 1800* (Ithaca: Cornell University Press, 1962), 80–81.

19. Ibid., 81.

20. "Trading-Post to Cosmopolis," in WPA Federal Writers' Project, *New York Panorama*, 35–80.

21. Cited in Arthur M. Schlesinger Jr., *The Disuniting of America: Reflections on a Multicultural Society* (n.p.: Whittle Books, 1991), 1–2.

22. Cited in ibid., 6; Morton and Lucia White, *The Intellectual versus the City*, 24.

23. Cited in Schlesinger, *Disuniting*, 6. *The Melting-Pot*, Israel Zangwill's 1908 play

about a Jewish immigrant who wants to write a symphony in praise of America, would dramatize this point. See chapter 2.

24. Arthur M. Schlesinger Jr. suggests that the bonding faith in a transcendent idea of "America" is today in danger of being lost in an atmosphere of group disputation. "The rising cult of ethnicity [is] a symptom of decreasing confidence in the American future," writes Schlesinger. The new "cult" of ethnicity "threatens to become a counterrevolution against the original theory of America as 'one people,' a common culture, a single nation" (*Disuniting*, 16–17).

25. Cited in Josh Barbanel, "Some Signs of Hope Glint from New York's Clouds," *New York Times*, July 30, 1991, 1.

26. Alexis de Tocqueville, *Democracy in America*, ed. Philips Bradley (New York: Vintage Books, 1945), 1:299–300.

27. Ibid., 2:78.

28. Cited in Still, *Mirror for Gotham*, 121–22.

29. Charles Dickens, *American Notes for General Circulation* (1842; New York: Penguin Books, 1972), 127, 128.

30. Dickens, *American Notes*, 141. For Dickens, Peter Conrad suggests, "the prisons and asylums he visits during the tour described in *American Notes* are morbid refuges where characters protect a deranged and dangerous individuality which their bland, uniform society won't tolerate" (*The Art of the City: Views and Versions of New York* [New York: Oxford University Press, 1984], 48).

31. Perry Miller, *The Raven and the Whale: The War of Words and Wits in the Era of Poe and Melville* (New York: Harcourt, Brace and World, 1956), 97–98.

32. Dickens, *American Notes*, 136.

33. Ibid., 141.

34. Peter Conrad, *Imagining America* (New York: Avon Books, 1980), 59.

35. Blumin, *New York by Gas-Light*, 5.

36. Anthony Trollope, *North America*, ed. Donald Smalley and Bradford Allen Booth (New York: Da Capo Press, 1951), 191.

37. Ibid., 193.

38. Ibid., 194.

39. Ibid., 203.

40. Ibid., 206.

41. Ibid., 215–16.

42. Allen, *New York, New York*, 96.

43. Bender, *New York Intellect*, 41.

44. Sidney Smith, *Edinburgh Review* 33 (January 1820): 79.

45. WPA Federal Writers' Project, *New York Panorama*, 164.

46. Cleanth Brooks, R. W. B. Lewis, and Robert Penn Warren, eds., *American Literature: The Makers and the Making* (New York: St. Martin's Press, 1973), 1:233.

47. Washington Irving, *Salmagundi; or, The Whim-Whams and Opinions of Launcelot Langstaff, Esq. & Others*, in *Washington Irving: History, Tales, and Sketches*, ed. Bruce I. Granger et al. (New York: Library of America, 1983), 49.

48. Ibid., 143.

49. Bender, *New York Intellect*, 133.

50. Geoffrey Moorehouse, *Imperial City: The Rise and Rise of New York* (New York: Sceptre, 1989), 337.

51. Conrad, *Art of the City*, 4.

52. F. Scott Fitzgerald, *The Great Gatsby* (1925; New York: Charles Scribner's Sons, 1980), 182.

53. Washington Irving, *A History of New York, from the Beginning of the World to the End of the Dutch Dynasty by Diedrich Knickerbocker*, in *Washington Irving: History, Tales, and Sketches*, 444–46.

54. Ibid., 446.

55. Fitzgerald, *Gatsby*, 182.

56. Irving, *History of New York*, 450.

57. Ibid., 729.

58. Conrad, *Art of the City*, 5.

59. William Cullen Bryant, "Hymn of the City," in Brooks, Lewis, and Warren, *American Literature*, 1:219.

60. Cited in Marius Bewley, "James Fenimore Cooper, William Cullen Bryant," in *Major American Writers*, vol. 1, ed. Perry Miller (New York: Harcourt, Brace and World, 1962), 281.

61. James Fenimore Cooper, *Home as Found* (1838; New York: Capricorn Books, 1961), 108–9.

62. Miller, *The Raven and the Whale*, 82.

63. Ralph Waldo Emerson, "The American Scholar," in *Essays and Lectures*, ed. Joel Porte (New York: Library of America, 1983), 70.

64. Miller, *The Raven and the Whale*, 512.

65. Bender, *New York Intellect*, 151.

66. Cited in Miller, *The Raven and the Whale*, 110.

67. Cited in ibid., 85.

68. Cited in ibid., 78.

69. Leon Howard, *Herman Melville: A Biography* (Berkeley: University of California Press, 1951), 4–5.

70. Herman Melville, *Moby-Dick; or, The Whale* (New York: Hendricks House, 1962), 1–2.

71. Lewis Mumford, *Herman Melville* (New York: Literary Guild of America, 1929), 326–27.

72. Cited in Susan Edmiston and Linda D. Cirino, *Literary New York: A History and Guide* (n.p.: Peregrine Smith Books, 1991), 148.

73. WPA Federal Writers' Project, *New York Panorama*, 166.

74. Herman Melville, "Hawthorne and His Mosses," in *The Shock of Recognition: The Development of Literature in the United States Recorded by the Men Who Made It*, ed. Edmund Wilson (New York: Farrar, Straus and Cudahy, 1955), 197.

75. Ibid., 187.

76. Herman Melville, *Pierre; or, The Ambiguities* (New York: Hendricks House, 1962), 13.

77. Ibid., 283.

78. Ibid., 424.

79. Herman Melville, "Bartleby," in *Billy Budd and Other Stories* (New York: Penguin Books, 1986), 5.

80. Ibid., 13. Egbert S. Oliver, editor of the Hendricks House edition of *Piazza Tales*, suggests the Bartleby-Thoreau connection: Herman Melville, *Piazza Tales* (New York: Hendricks House, 1962), 229.

81. Melville, "Bartleby," 23.

82. Miller, *The Raven and the Whale*, 306–11; David S. Reynolds, *Beneath the American Renaissance: The Subversive Imagination in the Age of Emerson and Melville* (Cambridge: Harvard University Press, 1989), 292–93.

83. Herman Melville: "The House-Top," in *Herman Melville*, ed. R. W. B. Lewis (New York: Dell Publishing, 1962), 324–25. See, too, Alfred Kazin, *A Writer's America: Landscape in Literature* (New York: Alfred A. Knopf, 1988), 158–61.

84. Justin Kaplan, *Walt Whitman* (New York: Simon and Schuster, 1980), 61.

85. Whitman, *Specimen Days*, in *Walt Whitman: Complete Poetry and Collected Prose*, ed. Justin Kaplan (New York: Library of America, 1982), 695.

86. Ibid., 698.

87. Cited in Kaplan, *Walt Whitman*, 113.

88. Whitman, *Specimen Days*, 701.

89. Cited in Henry M. Christman, ed., *Walt Whitman's New York: From Manhattan to Montauk* (New York: New Amsterdam Books, 1963), 3–7.

90. Cited in ibid., 23.

91. Cited in ibid., 20.

92. Ralph Waldo Emerson to Walt Whitman, in Whitman's *Complete Poetry and Collected Prose*.

93. William Dean Howells, for example, is dubbed an "ambivalent urbanite" in the Whites' *The Intellectual versus the City*, 95.

94. Walt Whitman, *Leaves of Grass* (1891–92 ed.), in *Complete Poetry and Collected Prose*, 210. "Walt Whitman has been called the great poet of the democratic masses, with good reason. He believed the masses to be the foundation and proof of the political experiment called American democracy" (Donald Pease, *Visionary Compacts: American Renaissance Writings in Cultural Context* [Madison: University of Wisconsin Press, 1987], 108). Pease follows the argument set down by Roy Harvey Pearce, in *Historicism Once More* (Princeton: Princeton University Press, 1969).

95. Whitman "openly celebrates his divinity and insists that his listeners are equally worthy of celebration" (G. Thomas Couser, *American Autobiography: The Prophetic Mode* [Amherst: University of Massachusetts Press, 1979], 85).

96. Walt Whitman, *Leaves of Grass*, 5, 176.

97. Conrad, *Art of the City*, 8.

98. Cited in David S. Reynolds, "Of Me I Sing: Whitman in His Time," *New York Times Book Review*, October 4, 1992, 27.

99. Walt Whitman, *Specimen Days*, 703.

100. Cited in Conrad, *Art of the City*, 15.

101. WPA Federal Writers' Project, *The WPA Guide to New York City: A Comprehensive Guide to the Five Boroughs of the Metropolis—Manhattan, Brooklyn, the Bronx, Queens, and Richmond—Prepared by the Federal Writers' Project of the Works Progress Administration in New York City* (1939; New York: Pantheon Books, 1982), 308.

102. Christman, *Walt Whitman's New York*, x–xi.

103. Whitman, *Specimen Days*, 823.

104. Cited in Kaplan, *Walt Whitman*, 66.

105. Cited in Conrad, *Art of the City*, 16.

106. Walt Whitman, *First Annex: Sands at Seventy*, in *Complete Poetry and Collected Prose*, 613.

107. Whitman, *Leaves of Grass*, 414.

108. D. H. Lawrence, *Studies in Classic American Literature*, in Wilson, *The Shock of Recognition*, 912.

109. Cited in Kaplan, *Walt Whitman*, 107.

110. Whitman, "Crossing Brooklyn Ferry," in *Complete Poetry and Collected Prose*, 307–13.

111. Lawrence, *Studies*, 1072–77.

112. Cited in Kaplan, *Walt Whitman*, 318.

113. Cited in Kazin, *Writer's America*, 162.

114. James L. Machor argues that Whitman, in his poetry, made the City over into a version of himself, into what Whitman called his "aesthetic personality." His persona, Walt Whitman, "shapes urban materials into an amalgam of city and nature"—into "pastoral cities." Machor is right to insist that the world represented in Whitman's "Crossing Brooklyn Ferry" is "not Manhattan and Brooklyn of 1856 but a mythic urban middle landscape existing outside time and space by dint of the poet's power as time meddler" (*Pastoral Cities: Urban Ideals and the Symbolic Landscape of America* [Madison: University of Wisconsin Press, 1987], 180).

115. Kaplan, *Walt Whitman*, 70–73.

116. Ibid., 110–11.

117. Cited in ibid., 174–75.

118. Whitman, *Specimen Days*, 823.

119. Whitman, "Mannahatta," in *Complete Poetry and Collected Prose*, 586.

120. Whitman, *Democratic Vistas*, in ibid., 937.

121. Ibid., 937–38.

122. Ibid., 993.

123. Ibid., 988.

124. Ibid., 989–90.

125. Cited in Conrad, *Art of the City*, 8.

126. Herman Melville, "Hawthorne and His Mosses," in Wilson, *The Shock of Recognition*, 195.

127. Walt Whitman, "City of Orgies," in *Complete Poetry and Collected Prose*, 279.

1. The Great Barbecue was Vernon L. Parrington's name for the era. See Justin D. Kaplan, introduction to Mark Twain and Charles Dudley Warner, *The Gilded Age: A Tale of Today* (New York: Trident Press, 1964), vi.

2. Sam Roberts, "The Outer Boroughs Come Closer to the Inner Circle," *New York Times*, June 9, 1991, E6.

3. Thomas Bender, *New York Intellect: A History of Intellectual Life in New York City, from 1750 to the Beginnings of Our Own Time* (New York: Alfred A. Knopf, 1987), 62.

4. Philip Hone and George Templeton Strong, *The Hone and Strong Diaries of Old Manhattan*, ed. Louis Auchincloss (New York: Abbeville Press, 1989), 132.

5. Alan Trachtenberg, *The Incorporation of America: Culture and Society in the Gilded Age* (New York: Hill and Wang, 1982), 118.

6. Hone and Strong, *Diaries*, 54.

7. Ibid., 111.

8. Ibid., 171–72.

9. Trachtenberg, *Incorporation of America*, 112.

10. Hone and Strong, *Diaries*, 181.

11. Ibid., 138–39.

12. Ibid., 139.

13. Ibid., 158.

14. Ibid., 267.

15. William Dean Howells, "First Impressions of Literary New York," in *Literary Friends and Acquaintances: A Personal Retrospect of American Authorship*, ed. David F. Hiatt and Edwin H. Cady (1900; Bloomington: Indiana University Press, 1968), 63.

16. Ibid., 67–68.

17. Ibid., 69.

18. Cited in Peter Conrad, *The Art of the City: Views and Versions of New York* (New York: Oxford University Press, 1984), 39.

19. William Dean Howells, *Their Wedding Journey* (1872; New York: Fawcett Publications, 1960), 13.

20. Ibid., 26–27.

21. Cited in Kenneth S. Lynn, *William Dean Howells: An American Life* (New York: Harcourt Brace Jovanovich, 1971), 284.

22. William Dean Howells, "New York as a Literary Centre," in *Criticism and Fiction, by William Dean Howells [and] The Responsibilities of the Novelist, by Frank Norris* (New York: Hill and Wang, 1967), 231. Howells may have been echoing Hamlin Garland, that son of the Middle Border, who argued that New York's literary eminence was buoyed by the talents it drew from other regions. In *Crumbling Idols*, Garland held that "it is not so much a victory of New York over Boston, it is the rising to literary power of the whole nation. New York is but the trumpet through which the whole nation is at last speaking." But New York was likely to lose its ascendancy, just as Boston had: "New York, like Boston, is too near London. It is no longer America." See Hamlin Garland, *Crumbling Idols: Twelve Es-*

says on Art Dealing Chiefly with Literature, Painting, and the Drama, ed. Jane Johnson (Cambridge: Belknap Press of Harvard University Press, 1960), 117–19.

23. Howells's 1888 letter to T. S. Perry cited in Kermit Vanderbilt, *The Achievement of William Dean Howells* (Princeton: Princeton University Press, 1968), 160.

24. Henry James, entry of October 31, 1895, in *The Notebooks of Henry James*, ed. F. O. Matthiessen and Kenneth B. Murdock (1947; New York: Oxford University Press, 1962), 226.

25. Henry James to William Dean Howells, February 19, 1912, on the occasion of his 75th birthday, in *The Selected Letters of Henry James*, ed. Leon Edel (Garden City, N.Y., 1960), 161.

26. Alfred Kazin, *On Native Grounds: An Interpretation of Modern American Prose Literature* (1942; New York: Doubleday, 1956), 1.

27. Howells, *Literary Friends and Acquaintances*, 101–2.

28. William Dean Howells, "A Call for Realism," in *The Rise of Silas Lapham: An Authorized Text, Composition and Backgrounds, Contemporary Responses, Criticism*, ed. Don L. Cook (New York: W. W. Norton, 1982), 500.

29. Works Progress Administration (WPA) Federal Writers' Project, *New York Panorama: A Companion to the Guide to New York City* (1938; New York: Pantheon Books, 1984), 168.

30. William Dean Howells, *A Hazard of New Fortunes* (Garden City, N.Y.: Doubleday, n.d.), 12.

31. Vanderbilt, *The Achievement of William Dean Howells*, 160.

32. Howells, *Hazard of New Fortunes*, 20.

33. Ibid., 22.

34. Ibid., 48.

35. Ibid., 56–61.

36. Robert Underwood Johnson, associate editor of the *Century*, cited in Larzer Ziff, *The American 1890s: Life and Times of a Lost Generation* (New York: Viking Press, 1966), 40.

37. Howells, *Hazard of New Fortunes*, 270–71.

38. Ibid., 77.

39. Ibid., 140.

40. Ibid., 364.

41. Ziff, *The American 1890s*, 39.

42. Howells, *Hazard of New Fortunes*, 386–87.

43. Ibid., 261.

44. "Too often Howells contrived devices—chance encounters, changes of heart, sacrificial acts—to ensure a relatively benign outcome, if not exactly a happy ending, then at least a morally pleasing one. Thus, Howells resorted often to 'romance' to preserve the moral assurances of his 'realism.' Resorting to romance, Howells conceded, without acknowledgement, the fundament of illusion on which his realism rested: the illusion and romance of 'America' itself" (Trachtenberg, *Incorporation of America*, 192).

45. William Dean Howells, *A Traveler from Altruria* (1894; New York: Sagamore Press, 1957), 187.

46. William Dean Howells, *Through the Eye of the Needle: A Romance* (New York, 1907), 3.

47. William Dean Howells, "An East-Side Ramble," from *Impressions and Experiences* (New York, 1896), in *American Thought and Writing: The 1890's*, ed. Donald Pizer (Boston: Houghton Mifflin, 1972), 254.

48. Ibid., 256.

49. Ibid., 258–61.

50. Henry James to Charles Eliot Norton, January 16, 1871, in *The Letters of Henry James*, vol. 1, ed. Percy Lubbock (New York: Charles Scribner's Sons, 1920), 30–31.

51. William Dean Howells, *Life in Letters of William Dean Howells*, vol. 2, ed. Mildred Howells (Garden City, N.Y.: Doubleday, Doran, 1928), 172–73.

52. Leon Edel, *Henry James: The Untried Years, 1843–1870* (London: Rupert Hart-Davis, 1953), 41–42.

53. Henry James, *Autobiography: A Small Boy and Others, Notes of a Son and Brother, The Middle Years*, ed. Frederick W. Dupee (Princeton: Princeton University Press, 1983), 16.

54. Ibid., 38.

55. Ibid., 6.

56. Ibid., 25–27.

57. Ibid., 28.

58. Morton and Lucia White, *The Intellectual versus the City: From Thomas Jefferson to Frank Lloyd Wright* (Cambridge: Harvard University Press and MIT Press, 1962), 75.

59. Edith Wharton, *A Backward Glance* (1934; New York: Charles Scribner's Sons, 1964), 176.

60. Conrad, *Art of the City*, 23.

61. "It's a complex fate, being an American, and one of the responsibilities it entails is fighting against a superstitious valuation of Europe" (Henry James to Charles Eliot Norton, February 4, 1872, in *Henry James Letters*, vol. 1, ed. Leon Edel [Cambridge: Belknap Press of Harvard University Press, 1974], 274).

62. James, *Notebooks*, 12–13.

63. Henry James, *Washington Square* (1880; New York: Vintage Books/Library of America, 1990), 4.

64. Ibid., 15.

65. Ibid.

66. Ibid., 26.

67. Ibid., 173.

68. Cited in Peter Buitenhuis, *The Grasping Imagination: The American Writings of Henry James* (Toronto: University of Toronto Press, 1970), 127–28.

69. Charles R. Anderson, notes to Henry James, *The Bostonians* (1886; New York: Viking Penguin, 1984), 436.

70. James, *The Bostonians*, 196.

71. Ibid., 319.

72. Richard S. Lyons is right in saying that "the true subject of *The American Scene* is the imaginative effort of James to give shape and meaning to the raw experience of his

renewed confrontation with America" ("'In Supreme Command': The Crisis of the Imagination in James's *The American Scene*," *New England Quarterly* 55, no. 4, [December 1982]: 517–18). As is Leon Edel, who suggests, "He cared for the 'terrible town,' cared for it deeply, as one born in it; and it therefore hurt him all the more that man could create so blindly and so crudely the foundations of inevitable 'blight.' " (*Henry James: The Master, 1901–1916* [Philadelphia: J. B. Lippincott, 1972], 291).

73. Henry James, *The American Scene* (1907; Bloomington: Indiana University Press, 1968), 1.

74. Henry Adams, *The Education of Henry Adams: An Autobiography* (Boston: Houghton Mifflin, 1918), 499.

75. Brendan Gill calls attention to James's "racy description of his native city: he compares it, with evident relish, to a whore" ("The Sky Line: The Death of the Skyscraper?" *New Yorker*, March 4, 1991, 90).

76. James, *American Scene*, 1–2.

77. Ibid., 5.

78. Cited in Leon Edel, notes to James, *American Scene*, 472.

79. James, *American Scene*, 74–75.

80. Ibid., 74–75.

81. "Erecting buildings is a version of narrative, an accretion of storeys which resembles the telling of stories," (Conrad, *Art of the City*, 39).

82. Vincent Scully, *Architecture: The Natural and the Manmade* (New York: St. Martin's Press, 1991); cited in Brendan Gill, "The Art of Seeing," *New Yorker*, December 30, 1991, 94.

83. James, *American Scene*, 83.

84. Luc Sante, *Low Life: Lures and Snares of Old New York* (New York: Farrar, Straus, Giroux, 1991), 39.

85. Cited in Edel, *The Master*, 288.

86. James, *American Scene*, 75.

87. Ibid., 75.

88. Ibid., 76.

89. Gill, "The Sky Line," 91. In 1916, the looming presence of the Equitable Building, which cast Trinity in its shadow, led New York to pass a zoning ordinance that required setbacks at specified intervals.

90. Ibid.

91. James, *American Scene*, 77.

92. Ibid., 85.

93. Ibid., 86.

94. Ibid., 117.

95. Ibid., 139.

96. James was impressed by the process by which immigrants were absorbed, the "machinery" of the City which brings about "the 'ethnic' synthesis," in "the cauldron of the 'American' character." See Arthur M. Schlesinger Jr., *The Disuniting of America: Reflections on a Multicultural Society* (n.p.: Whittle Books, 1991), 10–11; James, *American Scene*, 120–21, 208.

97. James's image of the City as a "cauldron" is cited in Schlesinger, *Disuniting*, 11.

98. James, *American Scene*, 87.

99. Ibid., 88, 90.

100. Ibid., 91.

101. Ibid., 159.

102. Ibid., 162, 171.

103. Ibid., 191.

104. Ibid., 176.

105. Conrad, *Art of the City*, 37.

106. James, *American Scene*, 190.

107. Ibid., 94.

108. Oliver E. Allen, *New York, New York* (New York: Atheneum, 1990), 318.

109. James, *American Scene*, 100.

110. Ibid., 103.

111. Ibid., 105.

112. Cited in Edel, *The Master*, 324.

113. James to Charles Scribner's Sons, July 30, 1905, in *Henry James Letters*, vol. 4, ed. Leon Edel (Cambridge: Belknap Press of Harvard University Press, 1984), 368.

114. Cited in Edel, *The Master*, 312.

115. Henry James, "The Jolly Corner," in *Tales of Henry James*, ed. Christof Wegelin (New York: W. W. Norton, 1984), 314, 316.

116. Ibid., 335.

117. Ibid., 318.

118. Cited in Edel, *The Master*, 312.

119. Henry James, "Crapy Cornelia," in *The Cage and Other Stories* (Harmondsworth: Penguin Books, 1972), 192.

120. Ibid., 195.

121. Ibid., 206.

122. Henry James, "A Round of Visits," in *The American Novels and Stories of Henry James*, ed. F. O. Matthiessen (New York: Alfred A. Knopf, 1964), 844.

123. Ibid., 844.

124. Ibid., 847.

125. Henry James, *The Ambassadors* (1903; New York: W. W. Norton, 1964), 344.

126. Wharton, *A Backward Glance*, 5.

127. Ibid., 2–3.

128. Ibid., 7–21.

129. Ibid., 55.

130. Cynthia Griffin Wolff, preface to Edith Wharton's *The Touchstone* (1900; New York: Harper Perennial, 1991), 16.

131. Wharton, *A Backward Glance*, 107.

132. "*The Decoration of Houses* is a paying off of scores against the physical surroundings Edith had grown up in and perhaps against her mother as their creator" (R. W. B. Lewis, *Edith Wharton: A Biography* [New York: Harper and Row, 1975], 78–79).

133. Wharton, *A Backward Glance*, 124.

134. Henry James to Edith Wharton, August 17, 1902, in *Henry James Letters*, 4: 235–36.

135. Wharton, *A Backward Glance*, 206–7.

136. Lewis, *Edith Wharton*, 155.

137. Cynthia Griffin Wolff, *A Feast of Words: The Triumph of Edith Wharton* (New York: Oxford University Press, 1977), 136.

138. *The Letters of Edith Wharton*, ed. R. W. B. Lewis and Nancy Lewis (New York: Charles Scribner's Sons, 1988), 99.

139. Louis Auchincloss, *Pioneers and Caretakers: A Study of Nine American Women Novelists* (New York: Dell Publishing, 1965), 26.

140. Edith Wharton, *The House of Mirth* (1905), in *The House of Mirth: Authoritative Text Backgrounds and Contexts Criticism*, ed. Elizabeth Ammons (New York: W. W. Norton, 1990), 5.

141. Ibid., 7.

142. Ibid., 45.

143. Ibid., 23.

144. Referred to in Michael Frank's, "The New York that Wharton Turned into Art," a report on a display on Wharton's New York City at the National Academy of Design (*New York Times*, June 3, 1994, C1–16). Frank suggests that Wharton's talent "enabled her, ultimately, to make Old New York the subject instead of the object of her life."

145. Edith Wharton, "Bunner Sisters," in *Xingu and Other Stories* (New York: Charles Scribner's Sons, 1916), 309.

146. Ibid., 320.

147. Lewis, *Edith Wharton*, 67.

148. Edith Wharton, *The Custom of the Country*, in *Edith Wharton: Novels*, ed. R. W. B. Lewis (New York: Library of America, 1985), 669.

149. Ibid., 633.

150. Ibid., 933.

151. Ibid., 1012.

152. "No character Edith Wharton ever invented more closely resembles that bird of prey by which James, Sturgis, and others so often, and only half-jokingly, portrayed Edith herself. Undine Spragg is, so to say, a dark Angel of Devastation: Edith Wharton's anti-self; and like all anti-selves, a figure that explains much about its opposite" (Lewis, *Edith Wharton*, 350).

153. Wharton, *Custom of the Country*, 639.

154. Cited in Lewis, *Edith Wharton*, 423–24.

155. "I am saying that there seems to be one dominating form of modern understanding; that it is essentially ironic; and that it originates largely in the application of mind and memory to the events of the Great War" (Paul Fussell, *The Great War and Modern Memory* [New York: Oxford University Press, 1975], 35).

156. Lewis, *Edith Wharton*, 424.

157. Edith Wharton, *The Age of Innocence* (1920; New York: Charles Scribner's Sons, 1970), 347.

158. Ibid., 3.

159. Ibid., 45.

160. Ibid., 46.

161. Ibid., 15.

162. Ibid., 18.

163. Ibid., 77.

164. Ibid., 288–90.

165. Ibid., 349.

166. Ibid., 347.

167. Wolff, *A Feast of Words*, 333.

168. Edith Wharton, *Old New York*, in *Edith Wharton: Novellas and Other Writings* (New York: Library of America, 1990), 324.

169. Ibid., 332.

170. Ibid., 365.

Fin de Siècle New York City

1. Cited in Bayrd Still, *Mirror for Gotham: New York as Seen by Contemporaries from Dutch Days to the Present* (New York: New York University Press, 1956), 207–8.

2. Ibid., 213.

3. Luc Sante, *Low Life: Lures and Snares of Old New York* (New York: Farrar, Straus, Giroux, 1991), 11.

4. Oliver E. Allen, *New York, New York: A History of the World's Most Exhilarating and Challenging City* (New York: Atheneum, 1990), 213.

5. Edith Wharton, *The Age of Innocence* (1920; New York: Charles Scribner's Sons, 1970), 13.

6. James Davison Hunter, *Culture Wars: The Struggle to Define America* (New York: Basic Books, 1991), 70.

7. Allen, *New York, New York*, 232.

8. Cited in Works Progress Administration (WPA) Federal Writers' Project, *New York Panorama: A Companion to the Guide to New York City* (1938; New York: Pantheon Books, 1984), 171.

9. William Coyle, introduction to Horatio Alger Jr., *Adrift in New York and The World before Him* (New York: Odyssey Press, 1966), v–xvii.

10. Carl Bode, introduction to Horatio Alger Jr., *Ragged Dick and Struggling Upward* (New York: Viking Penguin, 1985), xv.

11. James H. Pickering, ed., *The City in American Literature*, (New York: Harper & Row, 1977), 59.

12. Alan Trachtenberg, *The Incorporation of America: Culture and Society in the Gilded Age* (New York: Hill and Wang, 1982), 105–7.

13. Norman Podhoretz, *Making It* (New York: Random House, 1967), xiii.

14. Horatio Alger Jr., *Ragged Dick; or, Street Life in New York* (1868), in *Struggling Upward and Other Works* (New York: Bonanza Books, 1945), 155, 162.

15. Ibid., 175.

16. Ibid., 280.

17. Ibid., 4–5.

18. Alger, *Adrift in New York*, 144.

19. Sante, *Low Life*, 311.

20. O. Henry, *The Four Million* (New York: A. L. Burt Company, 1906); *The Voice of the City: Further Stories of the Four Million* (New York: Doubleday, Page, 1914).

21. O. Henry, "The Pride of the Cities," in *The Best of O. Henry*, ed. Richard E. Nichols (Philadelphia: Running Press, 1978), 37.

22. O. Henry, *Four Million*, preface.

23. C. Alphonso Smith, *O. Henry Biography* (Garden City, N. Y., 1916), 173; cited in Eugene Current-Garcia, *O. Henry* (New York: Twayne Publishers, 1965), 37.

24. Peter Conrad, *The Art of the City: Views and Versions of New York* (New York: Oxford University Press, 1984), 62.

25. Ibid., 57.

26. Current-Garcia, *O. Henry*, 98.

27. Cited in Susan Edmiston and Linda D. Cirino, *Literary New York: A History and Guide* (n.p.: Peregrine Smith Books, 1991), 168.

28. O. Henry, "The Defeat of the City," in *The Best of O. Henry*, 31.

29. O. Henry, "The Green Door," in ibid., 71.

30. O. Henry, "The City of Dreadful Night," in ibid., 107.

31. O. Henry, "The Duel," in *Strictly Business: More Stories of the Four Million* (1910; New York: Doubleday, Page, 1914), 294–301.

32. Nathan Glazer and Daniel Patrick Moynihan, *Beyond the Melting Pot: The Negroes, Puerto Ricans, Jews, Italians, and Irish of New York City* (Cambridge: MIT Press and Harvard University Press, 1963), 138–39.

33. "Jews," in *Harvard Encyclopedia of American Ethnic Groups*, ed. Stephan Thernstrom (Cambridge: Belknap Press of Harvard University Press, 1980), 583–84.

34. Jules Chametzky, *From the Ghetto: The Fiction of Abraham Cahan* (Amherst: University of Massachusetts Press, 1977), 66–67.

35. Ibid., 57.

36. Abraham Cahan, *Yekl and The Imported Bridegroom and Other Stories of the New York Ghetto*, ed. Bernard G. Richards (New York: Dover Publications, 1970), 5.

37. Ibid., 2n.

38. Ibid., 6.

39. Ibid., 13.

40. Ibid., 14.

41. Irving Howe, *World of Our Fathers* (New York: Simon and Schuster, 1976), 525.

42. Cahan, *Yekl*, 73.

43. Howe, *World of Our Fathers*, 525.

44. Chametzky, *From the Ghetto*, 65.

45. Abraham Cahan, *The Rise of David Levinsky* (n.p.: Grosset and Dunlap, 1917), 3.

46. Chametzky, *From the Ghetto*, 127.

47. Andrew Carnegie, *The Gospel of Wealth and Other Timely Essays*, ed. Edward C. Kirkland (Cambridge: Belknap Press of Harvard University Press, 1962).

48. Cahan, *David Levinsky*, 3.

49. Chametzky, *From the Ghetto*, 143.

50. Cahan, *David Levinsky*, 88.

51. Ibid., 516.

52. Ibid., 529–30.

53. Cited in Howe, *World of Our Fathers*, 269.

54. Cited in Vivian Gornick, introduction to Anzia Yezierska, *How I Found America: Collected Stories of Anzia Yezierska* (New York: Persea Books, 1991), viii.

55. Anzia Yezierska, *Bread Givers* (1925; New York: Persea Books, 1975), 22.

56. Anzia Yezierska, "How I Found America," in *How I Found America*, 127.

57. Anzia Yezierska, *Red Ribbon on a White Horse* (1950; New York: Persea Books, 1981), 220; Louise Levitas Henriksen, *Anzia Yezierska: A Writer's Life* (New Brunswick, N. J.: Rutgers University Press, 1988), 273–75.

58. Charles A. Madison, preface to Jacob A. Riis, *How the Other Half Lives: Studies among the Tenements of New York* (1901; New York: Dover Publications, 1971), vi.

59. "As a one-man band of social reform, Riis altered the outlook of the whole City, and eventually the nation" (Sante, *Low Life*, 34).

60. Riis, *How the Other Half Lives*, 5.

61. Ibid., 49.

62. Ibid., 165.

63. Jacob Riis, *The Children of the Poor* (New York: Charles Scribner's Sons, 1892), 4–7.

64. "*Maggie* was less the result of Crane's experiments than their cause" (Christopher Benfy, *The Double Life of Stephen Crane: A Biography* [New York: Alfred A. Knopf, 1992], 61).

65. Stephen Crane, "An Experiment in Misery" (1894), in *American Thought and Writing: The 1890's*, ed. Donald Pizer (Boston: Houghton Mifflin, 1972), 272–81.

66. Conrad, *Art of the City*, 51.

67. Stephen Crane, "The Men in the Storm" (1894), in Pizer, *American Thought and Writing*, 282–87.

68. Daniel Aaron, "Howells' 'Maggie,'" *New England Quarterly* 38 (March 1965): 85–90.

69. Stephen Crane, *Maggie: A Girl of the Streets (a Story of New York)*, ed. Thomas A. Gullason (1893; New York: W. W. Norton, 1979), 3.

70. Hamlin Garland, "An Ambitious French Novel and a Modest American Story," cited in Gullason edition of *Maggie*, 144.

71. Crane, *Maggie*, 26–28.

72. William Dean Howells to Cora Crane, July 29, 1900, in Pizer, *American Thought and Writing*, 58–59.

73. William D. Griffin, *The Book of Irish Americans* (New York: Times Books, 1990), 326–27.

74. Bob Calahan, "The Leader of Our Clan," in *The Big Book of American Irish Culture* (New York: Viking Penguin, 1987), 14.

75. Cited in Griffin, *Irish Americans*, 327.

76. A. J. Liebling, *Back Where I Came From* (San Francisco: North Point Press, 1990), 16–17.

77. James Cagney and Studs Terkel, "It's All in the Scheme," in Calahan, *Big Book of American Irish Culture*, 236.

78. Finley Peter Dunne, *Mr. Dooley Remembers: The Informal Memoirs of Finley Peter Dunne*, ed. Philip Dunne (Boston: Atlantic Monthly Press, 1963), 307.

79. Edith Wharton, *A Backward Glance* (1934; New York: Charles Scribner's Sons, 1964), 178.

80. Cited in Charles Fanning, ed., *The Exiles of Erin: Nineteenth-Century Irish-American Fiction* (Notre Dame: University of Notre Dame Press, 1987), 109.

81. Charles Fanning, *The Irish Voice in America: Irish-American Fiction from the 1760s to the 1980s* (Lexington: University of Kentucky Press, 1990), 114–40.

82. James W. Sullivan, "Slob Murphy," in Fanning, *Exiles of Erin*, 207–22.

83. Glazer and Moynihan, *Beyond the Melting Pot*, 217.

84. "The power of the Irish boss grew with the development of the city. New spatial divisions created neighborhoods that could be exploited politically, the most prominent being the Irish. The personal reciprocal relationships on which the power of the political machine was based and the respect for seniority and service that characterized the hierarchical power structure harked back to rural Ireland" (*Harvard Encyclopedia of American Ethnic Groups*, 535).

85. Grace, Smith, and Walker were called the "Trinity" by Moynihan, *Beyond the Melting Pot*, 218–21.

86. Allen, *New York, New York*, 170–72.

87. Still, *Mirror for Gotham*, 212.

88. Allen, *New York, New York*, 180.

89. Cited in Arthur Mann, introduction to William L. Riordan, *Plunkitt of Tammany Hall: A Series of Very Plain Tales on Very Practical Politics Delivered by Ex-Senator George Washington Plunkitt, The Tammany Philosopher, from his Rostrum — the New York County Courthouse Bootblack Stand* (1905; New York: E. P. Dutton, 1963), xix.

90. Apart from improving their own condition, "the Irish didn't know what to do with power once they got it," argues Moynihan, and Mann accuses Tammany's leaders of failing to "envision a more just and more beautiful city than the mean and ugly neighborhoods in which they grew to manhood" (ibid., vii–xxii).

91. Riordan, *Plunkitt*, xxiii.

92. Ibid., 3.

93. Ibid., 41.

94. Ibid., 68.

95. Glazer and Moynihan, *Beyond the Melting Pot*, 27.

96. James Weldon Johnson, *Black Manhattan* (1930; New York: Da Capo Press, 1991), 3–4.

97. Cited in Sondra Kathryn Wilson, introduction to Johnson, *Black Manhattan*, xv–xvi.

98. Cited in ibid., xv.

99. Tin Pan Alley began along West Twenty-eighth Street, where sheet music pub-

lishers were located, and then moved uptown, following the relocation of theaters—from Tony Pastor's vaudeville house in Union Square to Broadway's fabled Forty-second Street. See Philip Furia, *The Poets of Tin Pan Alley: A History of America's Great Lyricists* (New York: Oxford University Press, 1990), 19.

100. Cited in ibid., 27.

101. James Weldon Johnson, *The Autobiography of an Ex-Colored Man* (1912; New York: Penguin Books, 1990), 65–66.

102. Ibid., 76.

103. Ibid., 144.

104. Ibid., 149.

105. Nat Huggins, *Harlem Renaissance* (New York: Oxford University Press, 1971), 145.

106. Gerald Early, introduction to Countee Cullen, *My Soul's High Song: The Collected Writings of Countee Cullen, Voice of the Harlem Renaissance* (New York: Anchor Books, 1991), 33.

107. James Weldon Johnson, introduction to *The Book of Negro Poetry* (New York: Harcourt, Brace and World, 1931), 9, 41.

108. Cited in Johnson, *Black Manhattan*, 265.

109. Ibid., 267, 271.

110. Ibid., 281–84.

111. Huggins, *Harlem Renaissance*, 4; David Levering Lewis, *When Harlem Was in Vogue* (New York: Oxford University Press, 1982), 246–47.

112. Theodore Dreiser, "Reflections," in *Theodore Dreiser: A Selection of Uncollected Prose*, ed. Donald Pizer (Detroit: Wayne State University Press, 1977), 56 (*Ev'ry Month* 2 [May 1896]: 6).

113. Theodore Dreiser, "The Real Howells," in *Uncollected Prose*, 143 (*Ainslee's* 5 [March 1900]: 137–42; and *Americana* 36 [April 1943]: 275–82).

114. Cited in Edmiston and Cirino, *Literary New York*, 66.

115. Cited in Richard Lingeman, *Theodore Dreiser*, vol. 1 (New York: G. P. Putnam's Sons, 1986), 217, 223.

116. Cited in W. A. Swanberg, *Dreiser* (New York: Charles Scribner's Sons, 1965), 59.

117. Lingeman, *Theodore Dreiser*, 1:139–41.

118. Conrad, *Art of the City*, 178.

119. *The "Genius"* is "the archetypal Dreiser story: the young man from the provinces, illusioned and naive, who escapes a dull Middle Western village and dreams, miraculously, of Beauty" and sexual fulfillment; he arrives in the City, where he is both fulfilled and disillusioned (Richard Lingeman, *Theodore Dreiser*, vol. 2 [New York: G. P. Putnam's Sons, 1990], 123).

120. Dreiser, *Uncollected Prose*, 72.

121. Lingeman, *Theodore Dreiser*, 1:150.

122. Dreiser, *Uncollected Prose*, 166.

123. Lingeman, *Theodore Dreiser*, 1:166.

124. Theodore Dreiser, "Reflections," in *Uncollected Prose*, 68–69 (*Ev'ry Month* 2 [June 1896]: 5–6).

125. Theodore Dreiser, "Reflections," in ibid., 97 (*Ev'ry Month* 3 [October 1896]: 6–7).

126. Theodore Dreiser, "Reflections," in ibid., 110 (*Ev'ry Month* 3 [February 1897]: 4–5).

127. Theodore Dreiser, "Curious Shifts of the Poor," in ibid., 140 (*Demorest's* 36 [November 1899]: 22–26). Dreiser later inserted much of this essay, as chapters 45–47, into *Sister Carrie*.

128. Cited in Morton and Lucia White, *The Intellectual versus the City: From Thomas Jefferson to Frank Lloyd Wright* (Cambridge: Harvard University Press and MIT Press, 1962), 136.

129. Theodore Dreiser, *Sister Carrie*, ed. Neda M. Westlake (Philadelphia: University of Pennsylvania Press, 1981), 339.

130. Theodore Dreiser, "The Loneliness of the City," in *Uncollected Prose*, 157 (*Tom Watson's Magazine* 2 [October 1905]: 474–75).

131. Swanberg, *Dreiser*, 104–8.

132. Dreiser, *Sister Carrie*, 320.

133. Ibid., 493.

134. Ibid., 304–5.

135. Ibid., 499. To comply with his publisher's requests, Dreiser changed the original ending, which concluded with Hurstwood's suicide, and put in an up-beat exhortation to Carrie, which has now been relocated to end of chapter 49 in the University of Pennsylvania edition.

136. Cited in Lingeman, *Theodore Dreiser*, 1:180.

137. As the Whites argue in *The Intellectual versus the City*, 124–38.

Flappers and Philosophers

1. F. Scott Fitzgerald, *The Great Gatsby* (1925; Charles Scribner's Sons, 1980), 12.

2. Paul Rosenfeld, *Port of New York* (1924; Urbana: University of Illinois Press, 1961), 292–93.

3. Oliver E. Allen, *New York, New York: A History of the World's Most Exhilarating and Challenging City* (New York: Atheneum, 1990), 258.

4. Cited in Robert A. Gates, *The New York Vision: Interpretations of New York City in the American Novel* (Lanham, Md.: University Press of America, 1987), 65; Bayrd Still, *Mirror for Gotham: New York as Seen by Contemporaries from Dutch Days to the Present* (New York: New York University Press, 1956), 277.

5. Gates, *New York Vision*, 67.

6. Allen, *New York, New York*, 260.

7. Malcolm Cowley, *Exile's Return: A Literary Odyssey of the 1920s* (1934; New York: Penguin Books, 1979), 60–61.

8. F. Scott Fitzgerald, "Notebooks," in *The Crack-Up*, ed. Edmund Wilson (1945; New York: New Directions, 1956), 108.

9. Cited in Malcolm Cowley's introduction to F. Scott Fitzgerald, *The Stories of F. Scott Fitzgerald* (New York: Charles Scribner's Sons, 1951), viii.

10. Cited in Andrew Turnbull, *Scott Fitzgerald* (New York: Charles Scribner's Sons, 1962), 92.

11. Cited in Arthur Mizener, *The Far Side of Paradise: A Biography of F. Scott Fitzgerald*, 2d ed. (Boston: Houghton Mifflin, 1965), 86.

12. F. Scott Fitzgerald, "My Lost City," in *The Crack-Up*, 25.

13. Opened in 1907, added to in 1921, the Plaza, as Paul Goldberger says, "was built for a remarkable site—behind an open square and adjacent to a corner of Central Park, and it commands this double-fronted urban site as a great chateau commands a rural vista." Along with Grand Central Terminal and the Empire State Building, the Plaza is famous, beloved, and it "has kept its integrity" as a symbol of New York (*The City Observed: New York* [New York Vintage Books, 1979], 178).

14. Fitzgerald, "My Lost City," 26.

15. Charles Fanning, *The Irish Voice in America: Irish-American Fiction from the 1760s to the 1980s* (Lexington: University of Kentucky Press, 1990), 248.

16. Edmund Wilson, *A Prelude: Landscapes, Characters, and Conversations from the Earlier Years of My Life* (New York: Farrar, Straus and Giroux, 1967), 106.

17. Turnbull, *Scott Fitzgerald*, 131.

18. F. Scott Fitzgerald, *This Side of Paradise* (New York: Dell Publishing, 1920), 8.

19. Ibid., 32.

20. Ibid., 20.

21. F. Scott Fitzgerald, "May Day," in *Stories of F. Scott Fitzgerald*, 126.

22. Cited in Mizener, *Far Side of Paradise*, 127.

23. A fall chronicled meticulously in Jeffrey Meyers, *Scott Fitzgerald: A Biography* (New York: HarperCollins, 1994).

24. F. Scott Fitzgerald, "Echoes of the Jazz Age," in *The Crack-Up*, 22.

25. Cited in Mizener, *Far Side of Paradise*, 152.

26. Peter Conrad shrewdly sees the elevator as Fitzgerald's fitting emblem of the City. See *The Art of the City: Views and Versions of New York* (New York: Oxford University Press, 1984), 195.

27. F. Scott Fitzgerald, *The Beautiful and Damned* (1922; New York: Charles Scribner's Sons, 1950), 405.

28. Turnbull, *Scott Fitzgerald*, 142.

29. Fitzgerald, *Gatsby*, 8.

30. Ibid., 4.

31. Ibid., 23.

32. Ibid., 28–34.

33. Ibid., 57.

34. Ibid., 81.

35. Ibid., 118.

36. Ibid., 136–37.

37. Ibid., 177.

38. Ibid., 182.

39. Fitzgerald, "My Lost City," 29–30.

40. Fitzgerald, "Echoes of the Jazz Age," 23. In "My Lost City," Fitzgerald recalls encountering "Bunny," Edmund Wilson, in New York, walking with a cane. Fitzgerald, then still an undergraduate at Princeton, realized that Wilson had become a New Yorker and was possessed of "the Metropolitan spirit." At the time Fitzgerald's heart still belonged to the Midwest, where his "girl" resided—"a fact which kept the warm center of the world out there, so I thought of New York as essentially cynical and heartless." However, having lost his girl, he now "wanted a man's world, and this sight of Bunny made me see New York as just that." Bunny's apartment became Fitzgerald's third symbol of New York: "The gentle playing of an oboe mingled with city noises from the street outside, which penetrated into the room with difficulty through great barricades of books; only the crisp tearing open of invitations by one man was a discordant note." However, Fitzgerald never attained the serenity that this symbol implied ("My Lost City," 25).

41. F. Scott Fitzgerald, "How to Live on $36,000 a Year," in *Afternoon of an Author: A Selection of Uncollected Stories and Essays,* ed. Arthur Mizener (New York: Charles Scribner's Sons, 1955), 88.

42. Fitzgerald, "Echoes of the Jazz Age," 13.

43. Fitzgerald, "My Lost City," 27–28.

44. Ibid., 28–29. Fitzgerald "is an author one should read when young," argues John Updike: "To readers past first bloom, his earnest reconstructions of adolescent and collegiate maneuvers of self-advancement may seem a bit archeological, and his insistence upon the moonlit mood of romantic—that is, early sexual—attraction a bit arrested" ("This Side of Coherence," *New Yorker*, June 27/July 4, 1994, 191).

45. Fitzgerald, "My Lost City," 30–31.

46. Ibid., 32. "Scott Fitzgerald is always described as a representative figure of the 1920s, but the point has to be made that he represented the new generation of ambitious college men rising in the business world much more than he did the writers. He earned more money than other serious writers of his generation, lived far beyond their means—as well as living beyond his own—and paid a bigger price in remorse and suffering for his mistakes. Like the others, he followed his own path through life, and yet when all the paths are seen from a distance they seem to be interwoven into a larger pattern of exile (if only in spirit) and return from exile, of alienation and regeneration" (Cowley, *Exile's Return*, 292).

47. Alfred Kazin, "New York from Melville to Mailer," *Partisan Review* 42, no. 1 (1981): 93.

48. Philip Fisher, *Hard Facts: Setting and Form in the American Novel* (New York: Oxford University Press, 1985), 134.

49. Fitzgerald, *Gatsby*, 28.

50. F. Scott Fitzgerald, "Undated Letters," in *The Crack-Up*, 305.

51. John Dos Passos, *The Best Times: An Informal Memoir* (New York: New American Library, 1966), 127–30.

52. Dos Passos, *The Best Times*, 86. "The eugenic ideality of Whitman produces in Dos Passos people whose lack of individuality isn't a boon of democracy, where, as in Whit-

man's New York, all men are comradely look-alikes, but a function of economic determinism" (Conrad, *Art of the City*, 186).

53. Cited in Townsend Ludington, *John Dos Passos: A Twentieth-Century Odyssey* (New York: E. P. Dutton, 1980), 14.

54. Cited in John H. Wrenn, *John Dos Passos* (New York: Twayne Publishers, 1961), 24.

55. Cited in Cleanth Brooks, R. W. B. Lewis, and Robert Penn Warren, eds., *American Literature: The Makers and the Making* (New York, St. Martin's Press, 1973), 2:2440.

56. Cited in Ludington, *John Dos Passos*, 119.

57. Cited in Ibid., 200–201.

58. John Dos Passos to John Howard Lawson, September 12, 1920, in *The Fourteenth Chronicle: Letters and Diaries of John Dos Passos*, ed. Townsend Ludington (Boston: Gambit, 1973), 299.

59. John Dos Passos to Robert Hillyer, November 1920, in ibid., 302.

60. John Dos Passos to Robert Hillyer, Spring (?) 1925, in ibid., 361.

61. Dos Passos, *The Best Times*, 132.

62. John Dos Passos, *U.S.A.* (Boston: Houghton Mifflin, 1960), v.

63. Cited in Townsend Ludington, "John Dos Passos and Nathaniel West: Satirists of the American Scene," in *American Literature*, vol. 9, ed. Boris Ford (New York: Penguin Books, 1988), 441.

64. "As much as anything, New York—to him a symbol of 1920s America, the land of the big money—solidified his instincts to be a chronicler and a satirist even before he became the overt political rebel he was by the late 1920s" (Ludington, *John Dos Passos*, 200).

65. Ibid., 122–23.

66. Dos Passos, *The Best Times*, 136.

67. Cited in Daniel Aaron, *Writers on the Left* (1961; New York: Avon Books, 1965), 116.

68. John Dos Passos, *Most Likely to Succeed* (1954; Boston: Houghton Mifflin, 1966); 41.

69. Cited in Brooks, Lewis, Warren, *American Literature*, 2:2441.

70. Ludington, *John Dos Passos*, 224–28.

71. John Dos Passos, *Manhattan Transfer* (1925; Boston: Houghton Mifflin, 1953), 12.

72. Ibid., 4–5.

73. Ibid., 24–25.

74. Ibid., 43.

75. Ibid., 65.

76. Ibid., 125.

77. Ibid., 37–39.

78. Ibid., 220.

79. Ibid., 119–21.

80. Cited in Robert Gorham Davis, *John Dos Passos* (Minneapolis: University of Minnesota Press, 1962), 18–19.

81. Dos Passos, *Manhattan Transfer*, 365–66.

82. Ibid., 404.

83. Gates, *New York Vision*, 88.

84. "It is as if a wave passed over Manhattan, carrying three or four characters across the island and picking up half-a-dozen others whom it abandons successively as it picks up still others in its path." Constant scene-shifting fixes characters in their fates. They are less characters than "a succession of reactions to stimuli" in a chaotic world (Charles Child Walcutt, *American Literary Naturalism: A Divided Stream* [Minneapolis: University of Minnesota Press, 1956], 281).

85. Cited in Ludington, "John Dos Passos and Nathaniel West," 443–44.

86. Conrad, *Art of the City*, 186.

87. Sinclair Lewis, *John Dos Passos' Manhattan Transfer* (New York: Harper and Brothers, 1926), 12–13.

88. Cited in Ludington, *John Dos Passos*, 245.

89. Edmund Wilson, "Dos Passos and the Social Revolution," in *The Shores of Light: A Literary Chronicle of the Twenties and Thirties* (New York: Farrar, Straus and Young, 1952), 431.

90. Cited in Ludington, *John Dos Passos*, 229.

91. Dos Passos, *U.S.A.*, 83.

92. Ibid., 413.

93. Daniel Aaron, "Disturbers of the Peace: Radicals in Greenwich Village, 1920–1930," in *Greenwich Village: Culture and Counterculture*, ed. Rick Beard and Leslie Cohen Berlowitz (New Brunswick, N.J.: Rutgers University Press, 1993), 236.

94. Edmund Wilson, *I Thought of Daisy* (1929; New York: Penguin Books, 1963), 45, 47.

95. Liz Heron, "Women Writing the City," in *City Women*, ed. Liz Heron (Boston: Beacon Press, 1993), 7.

96. Djuna Barnes, "Greenwich Village as It Is," in ibid., 32.

97. Cited in Aaron, *Writers on the Left*, 92.

98. Edna St. Vincent Millay, "First Fig," in *The Norton Anthology of Modern Poetry*, ed. Richard Ellmann and Robert O'Clair (New York: W. W. Norton, 1973), 492.

99. Cited in Susan Edmiston and Linda D. Cirino, *Literary New York: A History and Guide* (n.p.: Peregrine Smith Books, 1991), 71.

100. Edna St. Vincent Millay, "Recuerdo," in *Norton Anthology of Modern Poetry*, 492.

101. Leon Edel, "A Portrait of Edmund Wilson," in Edmund Wilson, *The Twenties: From Notebooks and Diaries of the Period*, ed. Leon Edel (New York: Farrar, Straus and Giroux, 1975), 5.

102. Edmund Wilson, "Edna St. Vincent Millay," in *The Portable Edmund Wilson*, ed. Lewis M. Dabney (New York: Penguin Books, 1983), 73, 108.

103. Wilson, *A Prelude*, 157.

104. Wilson, "Burlesque Show," in *Shores of Light*, 281.

105. Sherman Paul, *Edmund Wilson: A Study of Literary Vocation in Our Time* (Urbana: University of Illinois Press, 1965), 3.

106. Wilson, *The Twenties*, 23.

107. Wilson, *A Prelude*, 158.

108. Wilson, *The Twenties*, 287–88.

109. Edmund Wilson, "F. Scott Fitzgerald," in *Shores of Light*, 30.

110. Wilson, *The Twenties*, 74.

111. Cited in Lewis M. Dabney's introduction to Wilson, *The Portable Edmund Wilson*, xviii.

112. Edmund Wilson, "Greenwich Village in the Early Twenties," in *Shores of Light*, 81.

113. Aaron, "Disturbers of the Peace," 239.

114. Wilson, *The Twenties*, 301–12.

115. Edmund Wilson, "On This Site Will Be Erected," in *The American Earthquake: A Documentary of the Twenties and Thirties* (1958; Garden City, N.Y.: Anchor Books, 1964), 15–18.

116. Edmund Wilson, "The Crushing of Washington Square," in ibid., 94.

117. Edmund Wilson, "The Stieglitz Exhibition," in ibid., 101–2.

118. Edmund Wilson, "May First: The Empire State Building; Life on the Passaic River," in ibid., 293–95.

119. Edmund Wilson, "The Author at Sixty," in *The Portable Edmund Wilson*, 20.

120. Edmund Wilson, *The Fifties: From Notebooks and Diaries of the Period*, ed. Leon Edel (New York: Farrar, Straus and Giroux, 1986), 217.

121. Diana Trilling's position is discussed in Paul, *Edmund Wilson*, 156–57. Even Wilson's reflections on European Communism derived from his New York experiences. In 1932, while "walking in the streets in New York somewhere in those East Fifties, I think," he came up with the idea of writing *To the Finland Station* (Wilson, *The Thirties: From Notebooks and Diaries of the Period*, ed. Leon Edel [New York: Farrar, Straus and Giroux, 1980], 298).

122. Wilson, *I Thought of Daisy*, 7.

123. Ibid., 34.

124. Ibid., 212.

125. Edmund Wilson, "The Princess with the Golden Hair," in *Memoirs of Hecate County* (London: Hogarth Press, 1986), 312–13.

126. John Updike, afterword to Wilson, *Memoirs of Hecate County*, 453.

127. Edgar Allan Poe, "The Masque of the Red Death," in *Edgar Allan Poe: Poetry and Tales*, ed. Patrick F. Quinn (New York: Library of America, 1984), 488.

128. William H. Pritchard, *Lives of the Modern Poets* (New York: Oxford University Press, 1980), 237.

129. Crane's Whitman stood as a symbol of life and his Poe as a symbol of death, his biographer, John Unterecker, notes. However, as Unterecker continues, in Crane's dialectical, mystical, unifying vision, "Whitman contains Poe and Poe, Whitman. Whitman and Poe, light and dark, joy and pain, life and death must—in Crane's scheme of things—finally both coexist and interpenetrate" ("The Architecture of *The Bridge*," in *The Merrill Studies in The Bridge*, ed. David R. Clark [Columbus, Ohio: Charles E. Merrill Publishing, 1970], 102).

130. Cited in Conrad, *Art of the City*, 227.

131. John Unterecker, *Voyager: A Life of Hart Crane* (New York: Farrar, Straus and Giroux, 1969), 626.

132. Mystery surrounded this act, as it surrounds much of Crane's poetry, but his suicide took the shape of an informing parable for Waldo Frank, one of Crane's best friends and advisors. "Hart Crane fought death in Mexico," stated Frank in 1957. "He wanted to escape. But as his boat turned toward what seemed to him the modern chaos of New York, there was the sea. And he could not resist it" (foreword to Hart Crane, *The Bridge*, ed. Waldo Frank [1933; Garden City, N.Y.: Doubleday Anchor Books, 1958], xv).

133. Malcolm Cowley, *A Second Flowering: Works and Days of the Lost Generation* (New York: Viking Press, 1973), 194.

134. Edgar Allan Poe, "The City in the Sea," in *Edgar Allan Poe: Poetry and Tales*, 67.

135. Crane, "Modern Poetry," in Frank edition of *The Bridge*, 181–83.

136. Cited in Brooks, Lewis, Warren, *American Literature*, 2:2206.

137. Cited in Alan Trachtenberg, "The Shadow of a Myth," in Clark, *The Merrill Studies in The Bridge*, 113–14.

138. Cited in Alan Trachtenberg, *Brooklyn Bridge: Fact and Symbol*, 2d ed. (Chicago: University of Chicago Press, 1979), 168.

139. Cited in David R. Clark's preface to *The Merrill Studies in The Bridge*, vi–vii.

140. Cited in Trachtenberg, "The Shadow of a Myth," 125.

141. Warner Berthoff notes that Crane's poems do not have a narrative structure, but are, instead, lyrical, "precisely and beautifully figured." Cited in Pritchard, *Lives of the Modern Poets*, 248.

142. Trachtenberg, "The Shadow of a Myth," 1117–18.

143. Crane, *The Bridge*, 3–4.

144. Ibid., 12.

145. Ibid., 35.

146. Trachtenberg, "The Shadow of a Myth," 120.

147. Crane, *The Bridge*, 54–58.

148. Pritchard, *Lives of the Modern Poets*, 254–56.

149. Trachtenberg, discussing the legends of Atlantis and Cathay, invoked by Crane, reminds us that in *Timaeus* and *Critias* Plato portrayed Atlantis as a land founded by Poseidon that had grown lustful and, as a result, was punished for its sins and its pride by earthquakes and floods, destroyed in a day. This legend qualifies the optimism of the Cathay legend—the new land Columbus sought. See Trachtenberg, "The Shadow of a Myth," 130.

150. Crane, *The Bridge*, 62.

151. Alan Williamson, "Hart Crane," in *Voices and Visions: The Poet in America*, ed. Helen Vendler (New York: Random House, 1987), 333.

152. Cited in Pritchard, *Lives of the Modern Poets*, 260.

153. James Thurber, *The Years with Ross* (New York: Grosset and Dunlap, 1959), 21.

154. Cited in David Gates, "A Lover of the Long Shot," *Newsweek*, December 21, 1992, 53.

155. Brendan Gill, *Here at the New Yorker* (New York: Random House, 1975), 394.

156. Cited in Edmiston and Cirino, *Literary New York*, 199.

157. Caryn James, "At Wits' End: Algonquinites in Hollywood," *New York Times*, January 8, 1993, C1.

158. Cited in Edmiston and Cirino, *Literary New York*, 196.

159. Cited in Brendan Gill's introduction to Dorothy Parker, *The Portable Dorothy Parker* (New York: Penguin Books, 1976), xvii.

160. Cited in ibid., xxvii.

161. Mizener, *Far Side of Paradise*, 336.

162. Helen Vendler, *Part of Nature, Part of Us: Modern American Poets* (Cambridge: Harvard University Press, 1980), 59.

163. Edmiston and Cirino, *Literary New York*, 79–81.

164. Marianne Moore, "The Steeple-Jack," in *Norton Anthology of Modern Poetry*, 424–26.

165. Richard Ellmann and Robert O'Clair, "Marianne Moore (1887–1972)," in *Norton Anthology of Modern Poetry*, 418–20.

166. Marianne Moore, "New York," in *The Harper American Literature*, 2d ed., ed. Donald McQuade et al. (New York: Harper Collins, 1993), 2:1363–64.

Black Metropolis

1. Cited in David Levering Lewis, "W. E. B. Du Bois," in *The Portable Harlem Renaissance Reader*, ed. David Levering Lewis (New York: Viking Penguin, 1994), 3.

2. Malcolm X, *The Autobiography of Malcolm X*, with the assistance of Alex Haley (1965; New York: Grove Press, 1965), 81–83.

3. Nathan Huggins, *Harlem Renaissance* (1971; New York: Oxford University Press, 1973), 47.

4. "Men like James Weldon Johnson and Alain Locke expected some race genius to appear who would transform that source into *high* culture" (ibid., 10).

5. Lewis, introduction to *Portable Harlem Renaissance*, xlii.

6. William L. Andrews, introduction to *Classic Fiction of the Harlem Renaissance*, ed. William L. Andrews (New York: Oxford University Press, 1994), 4.

7. Huggins, *Harlem Renaissance*, 6, 32.

8. Bernard W. Bell, *The Afro-American Novel and Its Tradition* (Amherst: University of Massachusetts Press, 1987), 93.

9. Langston Hughes, *The Big Sea*, in *The Langston Hughes Reader* (New York: George Braziller, 1958), 368.

10. Lewis, introduction to *Portable Harlem Renaissance*, xvii–xviii.

11. James Weldon Johnson, *Black Manhattan* (1930; New York: Da Capo Press, 1991), 160–63.

12. Cited in the title of David Levering Lewis's study of the Harlem Renaissance, *When Harlem Was in Vogue* (New York: Oxford University Press, 1981).

13. Hughes, *The Big Sea*, 85.

14. Charles S. Johnson, "The Negro Renaissance and Its Significance," in Lewis, *Portable Harlem Renaissance*, 212.

15. Paul Laurence Dunbar, "Harriet Beecher Stowe" and "The Poet," in *The Black Poets*, ed. Dudley Randall (1971; New York: Bantam Books, 1988), 47, 52.

16. Paul Laurence Dunbar, *The Sport of the Gods*, in *The African-American Novel in the Age of Reaction: Three Classics*, ed. William L. Andrews (1902; New York: Mentor, 1992), 507–8.

17. Bone refers to Thomas Nelson Page, author of *Ole Virginia* (1887), and other white southern writers who glorified plantation life and damned city life in works published after the Civil War. See Robert A. Bone, *The Negro Novel in America*, rev. ed. (New Haven: Yale University Press, 1968), 42.

18. Dunbar, *Sport of the Gods*, 586.

19. Ibid., 510.

20. Ibid., 567.

21. Lewis, *Harlem in Vogue*, 3.

22. W. E. B. Du Bois, "Returning Soldiers," in Lewis, *Portable Harlem Renaissance*, 5.

23. Huggins, *Harlem Renaissance*, 24.

24. Henry Louis Gates Jr., "*Jazz*," in *Toni Morrison: Critical Perspectives Past and Present*, ed. Henry Louis Gates Jr. and K. A. Appiah (New York: Amistad Press, 1993), 53.

25. Toni Morrison, *Jazz* (New York: Alfred A. Knopf, 1992), 9.

26. Ibid., 7.

27. Ibid., 8.

28. Ibid., 2.

29. Ibid., 33.

30. Ibid., 67.

31. Ann Hulbert argues that Morrison's novel is engaged in "what looks like the ultimate mission of self-sabotage: she is questioning a black writer's efforts to penetrate the heart of a black world" ("Romance and Race," *New Republic*, May 18, 1992, 43–48).

32. Morrison, *Jazz*, 220.

33. Gates, "*Jazz*," 55. In a series of lectures delivered at Harvard, Toni Morrison attacks the nation's literary establishment and its canon for racism. She indicts other writers for failure of imagination in their portrayals of black America. *Jazz* represents her efforts to explore the mysteries of Harlem. See Toni Morrison, *Playing in the Dark: Whiteness and the Literary Imagination* (Cambridge: Harvard University Press, 1992).

34. Cited in Bell, *The Afro-American Novel*, 107.

35. Deborah McDowell, "Regulating Midwives," introduction to Jessie Redmon Fauset, *Plum Bun: A Novel without a Moral* (1928; Boston: Beacon Press, 1990), xxiii.

36. Fauset, *Plum Bun*, 96–98.

37. Cited in McDowell, "Regulating Midwives," x–xi.

38. Cited in Lewis, *Harlem in Vogue*, xv–xvi.

39. Cited in ibid., 93–94.

40. Ibid., 149–51.

41. For the Harlem Renaissance, "*The New Negro* is its definitive text, its Bible" (Arnold Rampersad, introduction to *The New Negro: Voices of the Harlem Renaissance*, ed. Alain Locke [1925; New York: Atheneum, 1992], ix).

42. Cited in Huggins, *Harlem Renaissance*, 58.

43. Alain Locke, foreword to *The New Negro*, xxv, xxvii.

44. Alain Locke, "The New Negro," in *The New Negro*, 6–7.

45. Rudolph Fisher, "The City of Refuge," in ibid., 57–59.

46. J. A. Rogers, "Jazz at Home," in ibid., 224.

47. Langston Hughes, "Jazzonia," in ibid., 226.

48. Charles S. Johnson, "The New Frontage on American Life," in ibid., 279, 285.

49. Editorial, *Messenger*, July 1923, 757. Quoted in Ernest Allen Jr., "The New Negro: Explorations in Identity and Social Consciousness, 1910–1922," in *1915, the Cultural Moment: The New Politics, the New Woman, the New Psychology, the New Art, and the New Theater in America*, ed. Adele Heller and Lois Rudnick (New Brunswick, N.J.: Rutgers University Press, 1991), 51.

50. Elise Johnson McDougald, "The Task of the Negro Womanhood," in *The New Negro*, 369.

51. Hughes, *The Big Sea*, 84.

52. Cited in Paul Witcover, *Zora Neale Hurston* (Los Angeles: Melrose Square, 1991), 78–79.

53. "Hurston's role in the esthetics of the Harlem Renaissance became part of the artistic politics of Locke, Du Bois and the New Negro; she helped lead the revolt of the young artist against 'propaganda' by interesting them in the 'pure art' created by the black masses" (Robert E. Hemenway, *Zora Neale Hurston: A Literary Biography* [Urbana: University of Illinois Press, 1980], 39).

54. As Robert Hemenway points out, *The New Negro* was published by a major white publisher, Albert and Charles Boni, but *Fire!!* was financed by its contributors (ibid., 45).

55. Ibid., 56.

56. Bell, *Afro-American Novel*, 96–97.

57. Darwin T. Turner, introduction to Jean Toomer, *Cane* (1923; New York: Liveright, 1975), xx.

58. David Levering Lewis, "Biographical Notes," in *Portable Harlem Renaissance*, 750–51.

59. Nella Larsen, *Quicksand and Passing* (New Brunswick, N.J.: Rutgers University Press, 1986), 46.

60. Lewis, *Harlem in Vogue*, 232.

61. Nella Larsen, *Passing* (1928; New York: Collier Books, 1971).

62. Bell, *Afro-American Novel*, 112.

63. Michael G. Cooke, *Afro-American Literature in the Twentieth Century: The Achievement of Intimacy* (New Haven: Yale University Press, 1984), 67.

64. James Weldon Johnson, "Harlem: The Cultural Capital," in Locke, *The New Negro*, 301, 310–11.

65. Claude McKay, review of *Shuffle Along*, *Liberator* 4 (December 1921): 24–26; cited in Wayne F. Cooper, foreword to Claude McKay, *Home to Harlem* (1928; Boston: Northeastern University Press, 1987), ix–xxvii.

66. Claude McKay, *Home to Harlem* (1928; New York: Cardinal, 1965), 141.

67. William L. Andrews, "Claude McKay," in *Classic Fiction of the Harlem Renaissance*, 101; Claude McKay, "If We Must Die," in Brooks, Lewis, Warren, *American Literature*, 2:2711.

68. Claude McKay, "Harlem Runs Wild," in Lewis, *Portable Harlem Renaissance*, 191.

69. Cited in Lewis, *Harlem in Vogue*, 55.

70. Claude McKay, *A Long Way from Home*, in Lewis, *Portable Harlem Renaissance*, 161.

71. Lewis, *Harlem in Vogue*, 56.

72. McKay, *Home to Harlem*, 10, 25–26.

73. Andrews, *Classic Fiction of the Harlem Renaissance*, 103.

74. Ibid., 104.

75. Claude McKay, "The White City," in Randall, *The Black Poets*, 61.

76. Cited in Countee Cullen, *My Soul's High Song: The Collected Writings of Countee Cullen, Voice of the Harlem Renaissance*, ed. Gerald Early (New York: Anchor Books, 1991), 23.

77. Gerald Early, who edited Cullen's poems for the 1991 collection, sees Cullen's artistic manifesto, expressed in *Caroling Dusk* (1927), an anthology of black poetry, as "nothing more than a variation of the bourgeois manifestoes of James Weldon Johnson and Alain Locke," a line which held that "racial consciousness leads, ironically, to racelessness or to a world where color will be depoliticized" (Gerald Early, introduction to Cullen, *My Soul's High Song*, 40–41).

78. Ibid., 3–4.

79. David Levering Lewis, "Countee Cullen," in *Portable Harlem Renaissance*, 242.

80. Countee Cullen, "Heritage," in *My Soul's High Song*, 104–8.

81. Countee Cullen, "The Litany of the Dark People," in ibid., 147.

82. Countee Cullen, *One Way to Heaven*, in ibid., 351.

83. Lewis, "Countee Cullen," in *Portable Harlem Renaissance*, 676.

84. Huggins, *Harlem Renaissance*, 191.

85. Bone, *The Negro Novel in America*, 93.

86. Hughes, *The Big Sea*, 233–38.

87. Wallace Thurman, "*Harlem*: A Forum of Negro Life," in Lewis, *Portable Harlem Renaissance*, 631.

88. Wallace Thurman, *The Blacker the Berry . . . : A Novel of Negro Life* (1929; New York: Collier Books, 1970), 3.

89. Ibid., 192.

90. Ibid., 223.

91. Amritjit Singh, foreword to Wallace Thurman, *Infants of the Spring* (1932; Boston: Northeastern University Press, 1992), xiv.

92. Thurman, *Infants*, 226–45.

93. Ibid., 284.

94. Cited in Huggins, *Harlem Renaissance*, 24.

95. Langston Hughes, "I Too," in Locke, *The New Negro*, 145.

96. Hughes, *The Big Sea*, 379.

97. Cited in William L. Andrews, "Langston Hughes," in *Classic Fiction of the Harlem Renaissance*, 364.

98. Langston Hughes, "The Negro Artist and the Racial Mountain," *Nation* 122 (June 23, 1926): 692–94.

99. Huggins, *Harlem Renaissance*, 129–36.

100. Langston Hughes, "Slaves on the Block," in *The Ways of White Folks* (1934; New York: Vintage Books, 1990), 19–31.

101. Langston Hughes, "Passing," in *The Langston Hughes Reader*, 115–16.

102. Huggins, *Harlem Renaissance*, 302–3.

103. Ann Petry, *The Street* (1946; Boston: Beacon Press, 1985), 1–2.

104. Cited in Anita Diamant, "A Vision of the Street," *Boston Globe Magazine*, February 2, 1992, 16.

105. Cited in Esther B. Fein, "An Author's Look at 1940's Harlem Is Being Reissued," *New York Times*, January 8, 1992, C13.

106. Cited in Bone, *The Negro Novel in America*, 180.

107. Petry, *The Street*, 229.

108. Ibid., 435.

109. Cited in Diamant, "Vision," 25.

110. Cited in ibid., 25.

111. Cited in ibid., 25.

112. Some critics complain that Petry imposes an outsider's point of view on the City. Mary Helen Washington argues that the novel's bleakness "comes from the fact that it was written very much from the outside" (cited in ibid., 25). "In *The Street* [Petry] explores New York from an Old Saybrook point of view" (Bone, *The Negro Novel in America*, 181). However, these critics do not explain why an outsider's perspective on the City is less valid than that of an insider.

113. Cited in Fein, "An Author's Look," C13.

114. Cited in Ian Fisher, "Chronicler of Bleak Truths in South Bronx," *New York Times*, August 9, 1993, B3.

115. Paule Marshall, *Brown Girl, Brownstones* (1959; Old Westbury, N.Y.: Feminist Press, 1981), 3.

116. Mary Helen Washington, afterword to Petry, *Brown Girl*, 322.

117. Gloria Naylor, *Linden Hills* (1985; New York: Penguin Books, 1986).

118. Gloria Naylor, *The Women of Brewster Place* (1982; New York: Penguin Books, 1983), 5.

119. Barbara Christian, "Gloria Naylor's Geography," *Reading Black, Reading Feminist*, ed. Henry Louis Gates Jr. (New York: Meridian, 1990), 363–66.

120. Naylor, *Brewster Place*, 192.

121. Naylor, *Linden Hills*, 9.

122. Paule Marshall, *Praisesong for the Widow* (New York: E. P. Dutton, 1984), 42.

123. Ibid., 52.

124. Ibid., 121.

125. This point is emphasized in *Daughters*, a novel in which yet another disillusioned black woman leaves soul-numbing New York City for renewal in yet another Caribbean island. Paule Marshall, *Daughters* (New York: Penguin Books, 1992).

126. Ralph Ellison, *Invisible Man* (1952; New York: Vintage Books, 1972), 4–8.

127. James Thompson, Lennox Raphael, and Steve Cannon, "A Very Stern Discipline: An Interview with Ralph Ellison," in Ellison's *Going to the Territory* (New York:

Vintage Books, 1987), 290; cited in Susan Edmiston and Linda D. Cirino, *Literary New York: A History and Guide* (n.p.: Peregrine Smith Books, 1991), 299–300.

128. Ralph Ellison, "The Art of Fiction: An Interview," in *Shadow and Act* (New York: Random House, 1964), 173.

129. Ralph Ellison, introduction to *Invisible Man*, vii–viii.

130. Ellison, ibid., v–xx.

131. In a poll conducted by *Book Week*, *Invisible Man* was voted "the most distinguished single work" published in America between 1945 and 1965. Noted in Bell, *The Afro-American Novel*, 194.

132. Ellison, *Invisible Man*, 345–46.

133. Ibid., 150.

134. Ibid., 157.

135. Ibid., 171–72.

136. Ibid., 192–244.

137. Ibid., 245.

138. Ibid., 249. This construction, which reflects so much ambivalence by African-Americans about life in New York, is found elsewhere in the literature of the City. For example, a railroad porter in the 1930s told the Federal Writers' Project, "I'm in New York, but New York ain't in me" (cited in Aaron Siskind, *Harlem Photographs, 1932–1940* [Washington: Smithsonian Institute Press, 1990], 54).

139. Ellison, *Invisible Man*, 292.

140. Ibid., 338.

141. Ibid., 544.

142. Ibid., 559.

143. Ellison, "The Art of Fiction," 172.

144. Ellison, *Invisible Man*, 564.

145. Ralph Ellison, "Harlem Is Nowhere," in *Shadow and Act*, 294–302.

146. James Baldwin, "Fifth Avenue, Uptown: A Letter from Harlem," in *Nobody Knows My Name: More Notes of a Native Son* (New York: Dial Press, 1961), 57; cited in W. J. Weatherby, *James Baldwin: Artist on Fire* (New York: Laurel, 1989), 6.

147. Cited in ibid., 13.

148. James Campbell, *Talking at the Gates: A Life of James Baldwin* (New York: Viking Press, 1991), 5–6.

149. James Baldwin, *Go Tell It on the Mountain* (New York: Universal Library, 1953), 35–37.

150. Cited in Campbell, *Talking*, 14.

151. Countee Cullen, Richard Avedon, George Cukor, Douglas Fairbanks Sr., Burt Lancaster, Richard Rodgers, Fats Waller, Paddy Chayefsky, Neil Simon, and Richard Hofstadter are a few of De Witt Clinton's graduates. See David Leeming, *James Baldwin: A Biography* (New York: Alfred A. Knopf, 1994), 26.

152. James Baldwin, "Notes of a Native Son," in *Notes of a Native Son* (1955; Boston: Beacon Press, 1983), 85–98.

153. James Baldwin, "Autobiographical Notes," in ibid., 3.

154. James Baldwin, "The Harlem Ghetto," in ibid., 57.

155. Baldwin, "Fifth Avenue, Uptown," 68.

156. James Baldwin, *Another Country* (New York: Dell Publishing, 1962), 12.

157. Ibid., 77.

158. James Baldwin, "Sonny's Blues," in *Going to Meet the Man* (1965; New York: Laurel, 1988), 86–122.

159. Weatherby, *James Baldwin*, 4.

160. Malcolm X, *Autobiography*, 75.

161. Edmiston and Cirino, *Literary New York*, 304.

162. Claude Brown, *Manchild in the Promised Land* (New York: Penguin Books, 1965), viii.

New York City in the Thirties

1. Robert Goldston, *The Great Depression: The United States in the Thirties* (New York: Fawcett Publications, 1968), 195.

2. The apple seller became a symbol of the Great Depression after the International Apple Shippers' Association sold their oversupply on credit to the unemployed, who then resold these apples on city street corners throughout the nation (Frederick Lewis Allen, *Since Yesterday: The 1930s in America, September 3, 1929–September 3, 1939* [New York: Perennial, 1972], 24). "Thus appeared the shivering, ragged apple sellers in American cities," notes Robert Goldston. "Standing over pitiful wooden crates of apples, they silently beseeched the more fortunate passerby to buy an apple—for a nickel, but perhaps for more, if the buyer was charitable" (*Depression*, 51).

3. Goldston, *Depression*, 42.

4. Stanley Applebaum, introduction to *The New York World's Fair 1939/1940 in 155 Photographs by Richard Wurts and Others* (New York: Dover Publications, 1977), ix–xviii.

5. Works Progress Administration (WPA) Federal Writers' Project, *New York Panorama: A Companion to the WPA Guide to New York City* (1938; New York: Pantheon Books, 1984), 486.

6. Oliver E. Allen, *New York, New York: A History of the World's Most Exhilarating and Challenging City* (New York: Atheneum, 1990), 265.

7. Federico García Lorca, "Lecture: A Poet in New York," in *Poet in New York*, trans. Greg Simon and Steven F. White, vol. 1 of *The Poetical Works of Federico García Lorca*, ed. Christopher Maurer (1940; New York: Farrar, Straus, Giroux, 1988), 185.

8. Goldston, *Depression*, 62.

9. Mike Gold, "Night in a Hooverville," in *Mike Gold: A Literary Anthology*, ed. Michael Folsom (New York: International Publishers, 1972), 216.

10. Pietro di Donato, *Christ in Concrete* (1939; New York: Signet Books, 1993), 14.

11. Cited in Alan M. Wald, *James T. Farrell: The Revolutionary Socialist Years* (New York: New York University Press, 1978), 110–11. In *My Days of Anger* (1943), Danny O'Neill escaped lethal Chicago for New York City, and in *Bernard Clare* (1946) Farrell wrote a full-blown account—closely paralleling his own experiences—of a young writer's arrival, trials, and disenchantments in the City.

12. F. Scott Fitzgerald, "The Crack-Up," *Esquire*, February 1992, 80 (originally published in *Esquire* in February, March, and April, 1936).

13. William Butler Yeats, "Meditations in Time of Civil War," in *W. B. Yeats: The Poems*, ed. Richard J. Finneran (New York: Macmillan Publishing, 1983), 202.

14. W. H. Auden, "September 1, 1939," in *Years of Protest: A Collection of American Writings of the 1930s*, ed. Jack Salzman with Barry Wallenstein (New York: Pegasus, 1967), 226–28.

15. Cited in Christopher Maurer, introduction to García Lorca, *Poet in New York*, xii.

16. Peter Conrad, *The Art of the City: Views and Versions of New York* (New York: Oxford University Press, 1984), 143.

17. Cited in Maurer, introduction to García Lorca, *Poet in New York*, xix.

18. García Lorca, *Poet in New York*, 11.

19. Ibid., 155–63.

20. Jay Martin, *Nathaniel West: The Art of His Life* (New York: Farrar, Straus and Giroux, 1970), 113.

21. Susan Edmiston and Linda D. Cirino, *Literary New York: A History and Guide* (n.p.: Peregrine Smith Books, 1991), 158.

22. Martin, *Nathaniel West*, 110.

23. Robert A. Gates, *The New York Vision: Interpretations of New York City in the American Novel* (Landham, Md.: University Press of America, 1987), 111.

24. Nathaniel West, *Miss Lonelyhearts and The Day of the Locust* (1933; New York: New Directions, 1962), 169–71.

25. Ibid., 174.

26. Ibid., 205.

27. Ibid., 219.

28. Ibid., 220.

29. Eugene O'Neill, *The Iceman Cometh*, in *Eugene O'Neill: Complete Plays, 1932–1943* (New York: Library of America, 1988), 563.

30. Ibid., 569.

31. Ibid., 689.

32. Henry Roth, *Call It Sleep* (1934; New York: Noonday Press, 1991), 419.

33. Alfred Kazin, introduction to Roth, *Call It Sleep*, xiii.

34. Henry Roth, *Mercy of a Rude Stream*, vol. 1, *A Star Shines over Mt. Morris Park* (New York: St. Martin's Press, 1994).

35. Michael Gold, *Jews Without Money* (1930; New York: Avon Books, 1965), 25.

36. Jack Conroy, *The Disinherited* (New York: Hill and Wang, 1933).

37. Mike Gold, "Proletarian Realism," in *Mike Gold: A Literary Anthology*, 205.

38. Alfred Kazin, *On Native Grounds: An Interpretation of Modern American Prose Masters* (1942; Garden City, N.Y.: Doubleday Anchor Books, 1956), 293.

39. Gold, *Jews*, 224.

40. Malcolm Cowley, *The Dream of the Golden Mountains: Remembering the 1930s* (New York: Viking Press, 1980), xii.

41. Joan Zlotnick, *Portrait of an American City: The Novelists' New York* (Port Washington, N.Y.: Kennikat Press, 1982), 145–47.

42. Ibid., 149–51.

43. Harold Clurman, *The Fervent Years: The Story of the Group Theater and the Thirties* (New York: Hill and Wang, 1957), 138–39; Clifford Odets, *Waiting for Lefty*, in *Six Plays of Clifford Odets* (New York: Modern Library, 1963), 5–31.

44. R. Baird Shuman, *Clifford Odets* (New York: Twain Publishers, 1962), 55.

45. Clifford Odets, *Awake and Sing!* in *Famous American Plays of the 1930s*, selected by Harold Clurman (New York: Dell Publishing, 1959), 22.

46. Ibid., 87.

47. Clurman, *Fervent Years*, 139.

48. Cited in Andrew Turnbull, *Thomas Wolfe* (New York: Charles Scribner's Sons, 1967), 44–45.

49. Thomas Wolfe, *Of Time and the River: A Legend of Man's Hunger in His Youth* (New York: Charles Scribner's Sons, 1935), 419.

50. Ibid., 479.

51. Ibid., 421.

52. Ibid., 422.

53. Ibid., 533.

54. Ibid., 536.

55. Ibid., 499.

56. Gates, *New York Vision*, 105.

57. Thomas Wolfe, "No Door: A Story of Time and the Wanderer," in *The Short Novels of Thomas Wolfe*, ed. C. Hugh Holman (New York: Charles Scribner's Sons, 1961), 161.

58. Thomas Wolfe, *The Web and the Rock* (New York: Charles Scribner's Sons, 1939), 86.

59. Ibid., 363–64.

60. Thomas Wolfe, "The Party at Jack's," *Scribner's Magazine* 105 (May 1939): 14; and *You Can't Go Home Again* (New York: Grosset and Dunlap, 1940), 230–54.

61. Wolfe, *Can't Go Home*, 249.

62. Ibid., 284.

63. Ibid., 294.

64. George Wickes, introduction to Henry Miller, *Aller Retour New York* (New York: New Directions, 1991), vii–xi.

65. Miller, *Aller Retour*, 2–3.

66. Ibid., 16.

67. Ibid., 5.

68. Ibid., 13.

69. Ibid., 15.

70. Ibid., 27.

71. Ibid., 30.

72. Matthew J. Bruccoli, *The O'Hara Concern: A Biography of John O'Hara* (New York: Random House, 1975), 123.

73. Cited in Frank MacShane, *The Life of John O'Hara* (New York: E. P. Dutton, 1980), 77.

74. Ibid., 76.

75. John O'Hara, *Butterfield 8* (New York: Harcourt, Brace, 1935), 144.

76. Ibid., 143.

77. Cited in Bruccoli, *O'Hara Concern*, 124–25.

78. O'Hara, *Butterfield 8*, 268–69.

79. Cited in Elizabeth Hardwick, foreword to Mary McCarthy, *Intellectual Memoirs: New York, 1936–1938* (New York: Harcourt Brace Jovanovich, 1992).

80. Mary McCarthy, *The Group* (New York: New American Library, 1964), 7.

81. McCarthy, *Intellectual Memoirs*, 62, 114.

82. "In *The Company She Keeps*, Mary McCarthy creates a self-portrait to carry the unbearable burden of being, in this instance, a little crazy, so that in 'real life' the subject appears indisputably sane, which is to say, *right*" (Carol Brightman, *Writing Dangerously: Mary McCarthy and Her World* [San Diego: Harcourt Brace, 1992], 238). Margaret Sargent "is a heroine with a background similar to McCarthy's own. The stories are autobiographical, and they include likenesses of several New Yorkers she knew" (Carol Gelderman, *Mary McCarthy: A Life* [New York: St. Martin's Press, 1988], 100).

83. Mary McCarthy, *The Company She Keeps* (San Diego: Harcourt Brace Jovanovich, 1942), 89.

84. Cited in William Kennedy, introduction to *Guys and Dolls: The Stories of Damon Runyon* (New York: Penguin Books, 1992), xii.

85. Jimmy Breslin, *A Life of Damon Runyon* (New York: Ticknor and Fields, 1991), 4.

86. Frank Rich, "Runyon's New York Lives Anew," *New York Times*, April 15, 1992, C15.

87. Cited in Ian Hamilton, "Whangity-Whang-Whang," *London Review of Books*, May 28, 1992, 19.

88. Damon Runyon, "Broadway Complex," in *Guys and Dolls: The Stories of Damon Runyon*, 1–13.

89. E. L. Doctorow, *World's Fair* (New York: Random House, 1985), 281–82.

90. Simon Schama, "New York, Gaslight Necropolis," *New York Times Book Review*, June 19, 1994, 1.

91. Doctorow, *World's Fair*, 273.

92. Ibid., 154, 157.

93. Ibid., 235–44.

94. Ibid., 253–54.

95. Ibid., 266.

96. Ibid., 281–85.

New York City's Golden Age

1. Oliver E. Allen, *New York, New York: A History of the World's Most Exhilarating and Challenging City* (New York: Atheneum, 1990), 283.

2. Cited in Bayrd Still, *Mirror for Gotham: New York as Seen by Contemporaries from Dutch Days to the Present* (New York: New York University Press, 1956), 340.

3. Cited in Gerald Clarke, *Capote: A Biography* (New York: Ballantine Books, 1988), 133.

4. Jan Morris, *Manhattan '45* (New York: Oxford University Press, 1987), 269–71.

5. Cited in Still, *Mirror for Gotham*, 314.

6. Robert A. Gates, *The New York Vision: Interpretations of New York City in the American Novel* (Landham, Md.: University Press of America, 1987), 122–24. "Starting in 1950 and continuing for the next thirty years, eighteen of the nation's twenty-five top cities lost population. At the same time, the suburbs gained 60 million people" (David Halberstam, *The Fifties* [New York: Villard Books, 1993], 142).

7. Allen, *New York, New York*, 286.

8. Harvey Fromer, *New York City Baseball, 1947–1957: The Last Golden Age* (1980; San Diego: Harcourt Brace Jovanovich, 1992), 32.

9. Cited in Still, *Mirror for Gotham*, 334.

10. "The city in which the shaping by his hand is most evident is New York, Titan of cities, colossal synthesis of urban hope and urban despair. . . . Robert Moses shaped New York" (Robert A. Caro, *The Power Broker: Robert Moses and the Fall of New York* [New York: Vintage Books, 1975], 5).

11. Cited in Still, *Mirror for Gotham*, 315.

12. Pete Hamill, introduction to *The Brooklyn Reader: Thirty Writers Celebrate America's Favorite Borough*, ed. Andrea Wyatt Sexton and Alice Leccese Powers (New York: Harmony Books, 1994), xiv. See, too, Pete Hamill, *A Drinking Life: A Memoir* (Boston: Little, Brown, 1994).

13. Lynne Sharon Schwartz, *Leaving Brooklyn* (Boston: Houghton Mifflin, 1989), 13.

14. Ibid., 16.

15. Ibid., 1.

16. Ibid., 4.

17. Ibid., 62.

18. Ibid., 77.

19. Ibid., 83.

20. Truman Capote, "A House on the Heights," in *Selected Writings of Truman Capote* (New York: Modern Library, 1959), 450.

21. Schwartz, *Leaving Brooklyn*, 144.

22. Ibid., 145.

23. Betty Smith, *A Tree Grows in Brooklyn* (New York: Harper, 1943).

24. Elizabeth Cullinan, *House of Gold* (Boston: Houghton Mifflin, 1970).

25. Cited in Daniel J. Casey and Robert E. Rhodes, eds., *Modern Irish-American Fiction: A Reader* (Syracuse: Syracuse University Press, 1989), 217.

26. Charles Fanning, "Ethnic Persistence and Liberating Doubleness: New York Irish Writing Since the Sixties" (manuscript, 1993), 33.

27. Cited in Ibid.

28. Ibid.

29. Joe Flaherty, *Managing Mailer* (New York: Coward-McCann, 1970).

30. Jimmy Breslin, *World without End, Amen*, in Casey and Rhodes, *Modern Irish-American Fiction*, 197.

31. Jimmy Breslin, *Forsaking All Others* (New York: Simon and Schuster, 1982).

32. Jimmy Breslin, *Table Money* (New York: Penguin Books, 1987).

33. Mary Gordon, *The Other Side* (New York: Penguin Books, 1990), 8.

34. Ibid., 5.

35. Terence Winch, *Irish Musicians/American Friends* (Minneapolis: Coffee House Press, 1985); cited in Charles Fanning, "Ethnic Persistence."

36. Lawrence J. McCaffrey, *Textures of Irish America* (Syracuse: Syracuse University Press, 1992), 176.

37. Fanning, "Ethnic Persistence."

38. J. P. Donleavy, "An Expatriate Looks at America," *Atlantic Monthly*, December 1976, cited in Casey and Rhodes, *Modern Irish-American Fiction*, 148; J. P. Donleavy, *A Fairy Tale of New York* (New York: Atlantic Monthly Press, 1961), cover copy.

39. Anna Quindlen, *Object Lessons* (New York: Ivy Books, 1991), 1–2.

40. John Cheever, preface to *The Stories of John Cheever* (New York: Alfred A. Knopf, 1978), xvii.

41. Gates, *New York Vision*, 139.

42. John Cheever, "O City of Broken Dreams," in *Stories*, 45.

43. Scott Donaldson, *John Cheever: A Biography* (New York: Random House, 1988), 105–6.

44. John Cheever, "The Enormous Radio," in *Stories*, 37.

45. John Cheever, "The Season of Divorce," in *Stories*, 137–46.

46. John Cheever, *The Journals of John Cheever* (New York: Alfred A. Knopf, 1991), 21.

47. Ibid., 28.

48. Ibid., 34.

49. Ibid., 98.

50. Ibid., 281.

51. Irwin Shaw, "Noises in the City," in *Short Stories: Five Decades* (New York: Delacorte, 1984), 303.

52. Irwin Shaw, "The Girls in Their Summer Dresses," in *Short Stories*, 62–75.

53. Irwin Shaw, "Search through the Streets of the City," in *Short Stories*, 69–75.

54. Morris Dickstein, *Double Agent: The Critic and Society* (New York: Oxford University Press, 1992), 92.

55. Yet Thomas Bender charges the New York intellectuals with ignoring "the culture of the eye and the ear" and with provincialism (*New York Intellect: A History of Intellectual Life in New York City, from 1750 to the Beginning of Our Own Time* [New York: Alfred A. Knopf, 1987], 340–42).

56. Diana Trilling, *The Beginning of the Journey: The Marriage of Diana and Lionel Trilling* (New York: Harcourt Brace, 1993), 81.

57. Irving Howe, "The New York Intellectuals," *Decline of the New* (New York: Horizon Press, 1970), 212.

58. Cited in Alexander Bloom, *Prodigal Sons: The New York Intellectuals and Their World* (New York: Oxford University Press, 1986), 4. For Bloom the extended Jewish "family" was doomed to disintegration from the moment when their parents arrived in America:

"They were young, Jewish, urban intellectuals whose radical politics became bound up with an assimilationist momentum begun when their parents left Europe" (ibid.).

59. Norman Podhoretz, *Making It* (New York: Random House, 1967), 109–10.

60. Cited in Bloom, *Prodigal Sons*, 27.

61. Irving Howe, *A Margin of Hope: An Intellectual Autobiography* (San Diego: Harcourt Brace Jovanovich, 1982), 119.

62. Ibid., 2–7.

63. Ibid., 25–26.

64. "Comment," *New Yorker*, May 17, 1993, 4.

65. Cited in Bloom, *Prodigal Sons*, 84.

66. Cited in ibid., 80.

67. Daniel Aaron, "Disturbers of the Peace," in *Greenwich Village: Culture and Counterculture*, ed. Rick Beard and Leslie Cohen Berlowitz (New Brunswick, N.J.: Rutgers University Press, 1993), 238.

68. Cited in Trilling, *Beginning of the Journey*, 314.

69. A point also made by Podhoretz, *Making It*, 112.

70. Ibid., 116–17.

71. Cited in William Barrett, *The Truants: Adventures among the Intellectuals* (Garden City, N.Y.: Anchor Books, 1983), 58.

72. Lionel Trilling, *The Liberal Imagination* (1950; New York: Doubleday Anchor Books, 1957), xii.

73. Diana Trilling, "On the Steps of Low Library," in *We Must March My Darlings: A Critical Decade* (New York: Harcourt Brace Jovanovich, 1973), 77–153.

74. Bloom, *Prodigal Sons*, 385.

75. Barrett, *The Truants*, 111.

76. Dickstein, *Double Agent*, 106.

77. Alfred Kazin, *New York Jew* (New York: Alfred A. Knopf, 1978), 3.

78. Ibid., 5–7.

79. Ibid., 73.

80. Ibid., 59–60.

81. Ibid., 71.

82. Ibid., 74.

83. Ibid., 152.

84. Alfred Kazin, *A Walker in the City* (1951; New York: Grove Press, 1958). Kazin advances that persona through the great Depression in *Starting Out in the Thirties* (Boston: Atlantic Monthly Press/Little, Brown, 1965).

85. Kazin, *New York Jew*, 209–10.

86. Ibid., 293–95.

87. Barrett, *The Truants*, 13.

88. William Wordsworth, "Resolution and Independence," cited in ibid., 6.

89. Cited in Bloom, *Prodigal Sons*, 77.

90. Cited in ibid., 375.

91. Podhoretz, *Making It*, 109.

92. Russell Jacoby, *The Last Intellectuals: American Culture in the Age of Academe* (New York: Basic Books, 1987), 16.

93. Ibid., 21.

94. Ibid., 42.

95. Podhoretz, *Making It*, 3.

96. Ibid., xvii.

97. Norman Podhoretz, *Why We Were in Vietnam* (New York: Simon and Schuster, 1982), 205.

98. Dickstein, *Double Agent*, 92.

99. Trilling, *Beginning of the Journey*, 420.

100. Arthur Miller, *Timebends: A Life* (New York: Grove Press, 1987), 179.

101. Arthur Miller, *Death of a Salesman* (1949; New York: Penguin Books, 1976), 17.

102. Ibid., 80.

103. Ibid., 61.

104. Ibid., 138.

105. Maxwell Geismar, "Novelists of the Intellectuals," *American Moderns: From Rebellion to Conformity* (New York: Hill and Wang), 210–24.

106. Alfred Kazin, *Bright Book of Life: American Novelists from Hemingway to Mailer* (Boston: Little, Brown, 1973), 128. After the Nobel Prize award, John Leonard, in the *New York Times*, wrote, "If Saul Bellow didn't exist, someone exactly like him would have had to have been invented, just after the Second World War by New York intellectuals, in a backroom at *Partisan Review*" (cited in Bloom, *Prodigal Sons*, 290).

107. Cited in ibid., 291.

108. Saul Bellow, *Humboldt's Gift* (New York: Viking Press, 1975), 9.

109. Kazin, *Bright Book*, 129.

110. Frederick R. Karl, *American Fictions, 1940–1980: A Comprehensive History and Critical Evaluation* (New York: Harper and Row, 1983), 118.

111. Saul Bellow, *The Victim* (1947; New York: Penguin Books, 1988), 1.

112. Karl, *American Fictions*, 506.

113. Bellow, *The Victim*, 44–45.

114. Kazin, *Bright Book*, 129.

115. Saul Bellow, *Seize the Day* (1956; New York: Penguin Books, 1974), 44.

116. Ibid., 74.

117. Ibid., 84.

118. Ibid., 101.

119. Saul Bellow, *Mr. Sammler's Planet* (1970; New York: Penguin Books, 1977), 9.

120. Ibid., 74.

121. Saul Bellow, "New York: World-Famous Impossibility," in *It All Adds Up: From the Dim Past to the Uncertain Future* (New York: Viking Press, 1994), 216–20.

122. Joseph Berger, "I. B. Singer's New York: Fading, Yes, but Still Here," *New York Times*, July 26, 1991, A1.

123. Isaac Bashevis Singer, *Enemies, a Love Story* (1972; New York: Fawcett Publications, 1973), 20–21.

124. Karl, *American Fictions*, 242.

125. Bernard Malamud, *The Assistant* (1957; New York: Avon Books, 1980), 10.

126. Malamud, *The Assistant*, 297.

127. Bernard Malamud, *The Tenants* (New York: Farrar, Straus and Giroux, 1971), 5.

128. Cited in Richard Poirier, *Mailer* (London: Fontana Books, 1972), 14.

129. Norman Mailer, *Barbary Shore* (New York: Holt, Rinehart and Winston, 1951); cited in Tony Tanner, *City of Words: American Fiction, 1950–1970* (New York: Harper and Row, 1971), 351.

130. Norman Mailer, *Advertisements for Myself* (1959; New York: Signet Books, 1960), 86.

131. "Form in general—now I let you in on the secret—is the record of a war," Mailer tells an interviewer (cited in Poirier, *Mailer*, 20). Poirier is sympathetic to Mailer's experiments in formlessness.

132. James Baldwin, "The Black Boy Looks at the White Boy," in *Nobody Knows My Name: More Notes of a Native Son* (New York: Dial Press, 1961), 216–17.

133. "If not exactly a Song of Myself, nevertheless *Advertisements* remains Mailer at his most Whitmanian" (Harold Bloom, introduction to *Norman Mailer: Modern Critical Views* (New York: Chelsea House, 1986), 2.

134. Mailer, *Advertisements for Myself*, 15.

135. Cited in Carl Rollyson, *The Lives of Norman Mailer: A Biography* (New York: Paragon House, 1991), 229.

136. Mailer, "The Time of Her Time," in *Advertisements*, 429.

137. Norman Mailer, *An American Dream* (New York: Henry Holt, 1965), 255.

138. Ibid., 82.

139. James D. Hart, *The Oxford Companion to American Literature*, 5th ed. (New York: Oxford University Press, 1983), 537.

140. E. B. White, "The Cold," in *Writings from the New Yorker, 1927–1976*, ed. Rebecca M. Dale (New York: HarperCollins, 1990), 115.

141. Cited in Eric Pace, "William Shawn, 85, Is Dead: New Yorker's Gentle Despot," *New York Times*, December 9, 1992, B13.

142. Joseph Epstein, "Talk of the Town," *Times Literary Supplement*, September 4, 1992, 6.

143. A. J. Liebling wrote about boxing, dining, politics, and other matters for the *New Yorker*. His tribute to New York City is *Back Where I Came From* (1938; San Francisco: North Point Press, 1990). Joseph Mitchell wrote many finely observed essays for the *New Yorker* that celebrate New York City's eccentrics. Many of these are collected in *Up in the Old Hotel and Other Stories* (New York: Pantheon Books, 1992).

144. John Updike, "Remembering Mr. Shawn," *New Yorker*, December 28, 1992–January 4, 1993, 141.

145. White, "New York," in *Writings from the New Yorker*, 207–8.

146. E. B. White, "Here Is New York," in *Essays of E. B. White* (New York: Harper and Row, 1977), 118–33.

147. John Updike, *Self-Consciousness: Memoirs* (New York: Alfred A. Knopf, 1989), 222.

148. John Updike, "Spring Rain," in *Assorted Prose* (New York: Alfred A. Knopf, 1965), 104–5.

149. John Updike, "A Gift from the City," in *The Same Door* (1959; New York: Crest, 1964), 122–41.

150. John Updike, "New York City," *New Republic*, August 22 and 29, 1994, 44.

151. Cited in John Guare, introduction to Dawn Powell, *The Locusts Have No King* (1948; New York: Yarrow Press, 1990), ix.

152. Gore Vidal, introduction to Dawn Powell, *The Golden Spur* (1962; New York: Vintage Books, 1990), xvi.

153. Powell, *The Golden Spur*, 14.

154. Ibid., 51.

155. Dawn Powell, *Turn, Magic Wheel*, in *Dawn Powell at Her Best*, ed. Tim Page (South Royalton, Vermont: Steerforth Press, 1994), 195.

156. Cited in Tim Page, introduction to *Dawn Powell at Her Best*, xiv.

157. Truman Capote, "New York," in *A Capote Reader* (New York: Random House, 1987), 291.

158. Truman Capote, *Breakfast at Tiffany's* (1956; New York: Signet Books, 1980).

159. Cited in Clarke, *Capote*, 491.

160. Truman Capote, *Answered Prayers: The Unfinished Novel* (1987; New York: Plume, 1988), 6–7.

161. Cynthia Ozick, "Washington Square, 1946," *Metaphor and Memory: Essays* (New York: Vintage Books, 1991), 112–19.

162. Cited in Jacoby, *The Last Intellectuals*, 20.

163. Richard Poirier, "The Scenes of the Self," *New Republic*, August 2, 1993, 33–39; Brad Gooch, *City Poet: The Life and Times of Frank O'Hara* (New York: Alfred A. Knopf, 1993).

164. Joan Acocella, "Perfectly Frank," *New Yorker*, July 19, 1993, 71.

165. Frank O'Hara, "A Step Away from Them," in *The Harvard Book of Contemporary American Poetry*, ed. Helen Vendler (Cambridge: Belknap Press of Harvard University Press, 1985), 214.

166. Cited in Helen Vendler, *Part of Nature, Part of Us: Modern American Poets* (Cambridge: Harvard University Press, 1980), 189.

167. Ibid.

168. Frank O'Hara, "A True Account of Talking to the Sun at Fire Island," in Vendler, *The Harvard Book of Contemporary American Poetry*, 220.

169. John Ashbery, "Self-Portrait in a Convex Mirror," in ibid., 234.

170. John Ashbery, "The Friendly City," *New Yorker*, May 10, 1993, 60.

171. Geoff Ward, *Statutes of Liberty: The New York School of Poets* (London: Macmillan Publishers, 1993), 176.

172. Alfred Kazin, "Greenwich Village Writers," in Beard and Berlowitz, *Greenwich Village*, 301.

173. Dan Wakefield, *New York in the Fifties* (Boston: Houghton Mifflin, 1992).

174. Ibid., 6.

175. Malcolm Cowley, *The Dream of the Golden Mountains: Remembering the 1930s* (New York: Viking Press, 1980).

176. Dan Wakefield, "Writers and Readers Sharing the City of the Word," *New York Times*, September 18, 1992, C1–29.

177. Wakefield, *New York in the Fifties*, 20.

178. Joan Didion, "Goodbye to All That," *Slouching toward Bethlehem* (New York: Dell Publishing, 1968), 225–38.

179. Allen Ginsberg, "A Supermarket in California," in Vendler, *The Harvard Book of Contemporary American Poetry*, 153.

180. Allen Ginsberg, "Walking New York Part II," in *Collected Poems, 1947–1980* (New York: Harper and Row, 1984); *New York Observed: Artists and Writers Look at the City, 1650 to the Present*, ed. Barbara Cohen, Seymour Chwast, and Steven Heller (New York: Harry N. Abrams, 1987), 121.

181. Barry Miles, "The Beat Generation in the Village," in Beard and Berlowitz, *Greenwich Village*, 165–79.

182. Cited in Barry Miles, *Ginsberg: A Biography* (New York: Simon and Schuster, 1989), 10.

183. Allen Ginsberg, "Kaddish," in Vendler, *The Harvard Book of Contemporary American Poetry*, 159.

184. Allen Ginsberg, "Mugging," in ibid., 187–88.

185. Wakefield, *New York in the Fifties*, 176.

186. James Merrill, "An Urban Convalescence," in *Water Street* (New York: Atheneum, 1967), 3–6.

187. Elizabeth Bishop, "Letter to N.Y.," in *Elizabeth Bishop: The Complete Poems, 1927–1979* (New York: Noonday, 1980), 80.

188. Cited in David Kalstone, *Becoming a Poet: Elizabeth Bishop with Marianne Moore and Robert Lowell*, ed. Robert Hemenway (New York: Farrar, Straus, Giroux, 1989), 18.

189. Ibid., 18.

190. Elizabeth Bishop, "Love Lies Sleeping," in *Complete Poems*, 16–17.

191. Elizabeth Bishop, "The Man-Moth," in ibid., 14–15.

192. J. D. Salinger, *The Catcher in the Rye* (1951; New York: Signet Books, 1963), 58–60.

193. Ibid., 75.

194. Cited in Lois Ames, "Sylvia Plath: A Biographical Note," in Sylvia Plath, *The Bell Jar* (1971; New York: Bantam Books, 1988), 205.

195. Cited in Helen McNeil, "Sylvia Plath," in *Voices and Visions: The Poet in America*, ed. Helen Vendler (New York: Random House, 1987), 474. *Mademoiselle* experience discussed, 475.

196. Linda W. Wagner-Martin, *Sylvia Plath: A Biography* (New York: Simon and Schuster, 1987), 96–104.

197. Plath, *The Bell Jar*, 1.

198. Ibid., 2.

1. Calvin Trillin, "What Makes New Yorkers Tick," *Time*, September 17, 1990, 52. In a 1990 telephone poll conducted by *Time* (reported in the same issue), 75 percent of those who responded said "pushy" best describes people living in New York City; 64 percent chose "arrogant" and 60 percent chose "sophisticated."

2. A *New York Times* poll in November 1991 revealed that 58 percent of its residents interviewed predicted the City would be a worse place to live in in ten to fifteen years, and 60 percent said they would prefer to live elsewhere if they had a choice. Pessimism permeated all groups, measured by income level, age, and boroughs. "If the ability to believe in the future is what separates a growing from a dying civilization, then New York is in deep trouble," says Stephen Berger, former executive director of the Port Authority of New York and New Jersey (Sarah Bartlett, "Beyond Just Complaining: Self-Fulfilling Pessimism Is Said to Infect New York," *New York Times*, December 27, 1991, B1–2).

3. "From ancient time," says Joel Kotkin, author and senior fellow at the Center for the New West, "urban centers are unique for their ability to nurture what could be seen today as outsider groups—minorities, immigrants, women entrepreneurs, gays, young singles—who could have an extraordinarily difficult time thriving in the more conventional and homogeneous society in the hinterlands" (cited in Tom Redburn, "In Search of a Vision for the City of the '90s," *New York Times*, July 31, 1994, "The News of the Week in Review," 4).

4. For Jason Epstein, "New York City is at risk of becoming the fortified island of opulence within a sea of misery and violence that many of its patricians now fear as they, along with the majority of New Yorkers polled by the *Times*, contemplate their escape" ("The Tragical History of New York," *New York Review of Books*, April, 9, 1992, 45–52).

5. Lewis H. Lapham, "Fear of Freedom," *New York Times*, June 6, 1992, 23.

6. Herbert Muschamp, "A Highbrow Peep Show on 42nd Street," *New York Times*, August 1, 1993, sec. 2, 34.

7. David Rieff, *Los Angeles: Capital of the World* (New York: Simon and Schuster, 1991), 18–20.

8. Thomas Bender, *New York Intellect: A History of Intellectual Life in New York City, from 1750 to the Beginnings of Our Own Time* (New York: Alfred A. Knopf, 1987), 343.

9. Lewis Mumford, "What Is a City?" in *The Lewis Mumford Reader*, ed. Donald L. Miller (New York: Pantheon Books, 1986), 104; and *The Culture of Cities* (New York: Harcourt, Brace, 1938), 3–10.

10. "To Mr. Mumford, the ideal urban area was something like a small town writ large. He championed a nostalgic image of a rational, orderly moderate-density city nestled within broad swaths of greenery" (Redburn, "In Search of a Vision for the City," 4).

11. Lewis Mumford, "East Side, West Side," in *Mumford Reader*, 18–23; and *Sketches from Life: The Autobiography of Lewis Mumford, the Early Years* (New York: Dial Press, 1982), 3–10.

12. Lewis Mumford, "All Around the Town," in *Mumford Reader*, 28; and *Sketches from Life*, 13–24.

13. Elizabeth Hardwick, "Boston: The Lost Ideal," in *Contemporary American Essays*, ed. Maureen Howard (New York: Penguin Books, 1985), 253.

14. Elizabeth Hardwick, "New York City: Crash Course," in *The Best American Essays 1991*, ed. Joyce Carol Oates (New York: Ticknor and Fields, 1991), 96.

15. Susan Edmiston and Linda D. Cirino, *Literary New York: A History and Guide* (n.p.: Peregrine Smith Books, 1991), 241.

16. Louis Auchincloss, "The Landmark," in *Tales of Manhattan* (Boston: Houghton Mifflin, 1964); cited in Barbara Cohen, Seymour Chwast, and Steven Heller, eds., *New York Observed: Artists and Writers Look at the City, 1650 to the Present* (New York: Harry N. Abrams, 1987), 47.

17. James W. Tuttleton, *The Novel of Manners in America* (New York: W. W. Norton, 1972), 247.

18. "Auchincloss's New York is a closed world whose seemingly well-polished surface masks an overwhelming desire to win at any cost" (Leo Braudy, "Realists, Naturalists, and Novelists of Manners," in *Harvard Guide to Contemporary American Writing*, ed. Daniel Hoffman (Cambridge: Belknap Press of Harvard University Press, 1979), 137.

19. Louis Auchincloss, *Diary of a Yuppie* (1986; New York: St. Martin's Press, 1987), 3.

20. Adam Begley, "Case of the Brooklyn Symbolist," *New York Times Magazine*, August 30, 1992, 41.

21. Paul Auster, *City of Glass* (1985; New York: Penguin Books, 1987), 8.

22. Sven Birkerts, "Paul Auster," in *American Energies: Essays in Fiction* (New York: William Morrow, 1992), 340.

23. Ibid., 342.

24. Ivan Gold, *Sams in a Dry Season* (New York: Houghton Mifflin, 1990), 79.

25. Ibid., 3.

26. Ibid., 78.

27. Jaime Manrique, *Latin Moon in Manhattan* (New York: St. Martin's Press, 1992), 3.

28. Oscar Hijuelos, *The Mambo Kings Play Songs of Love* (New York: Harper and Row, 1989), 11.

29. Epstein, "Talk of the Town," 8.

30. Robert D. McFadden, "Eustace Tilley's on Vacation, and, My, What a Stand-In," *New York Times*, February 15, 1994, B3.

31. Tom Wolfe, "Stalking the Billion-Footed Beast: A Literary Manifesto for the New Social Novel," *Harper's*, November 1989, 45–56.

32. Ibid., 45.

33. Tom Wolfe, *The Bonfire of the Vanities* (New York: Farrar, Straus, Giroux, 1987), 56.

34. Ibid., 12.

35. Ibid., 65.

36. Ibid., 77.

37. Ibid., 82.

38. Ibid., 91.

39. Ibid., 564.

40. Ibid., 34.

41. Ibid., 39–42.

42. Ibid., 333.

43. Ibid., 356.

44. Ibid., 59.

45. George Plimpton, "Tom Wolfe: The Art of Fiction CXXIII," *Paris Review*, Spring 1991, 112–13.

46. Hugh Selby Jr., "Landsend," in *The Last Exit to Brooklyn* (New York: Grove Press, 1964), 303.

47. Richard Price, "The Fonzie of Literature," *New York Times Book Review*, October 25, 1981, 34.

48. Richard Price, *The Wanderers* (1974; New York: Penguin Books, 1975), 1.

49. Richard Price, *Bloodbrothers* (Boston: Houghton Mifflin, 1976).

50. Richard Price, *Clockers* (Boston: Houghton Mifflin, 1992), 198–99.

51. Ibid., 369.

52. Ibid., 456.

53. Cited in Roger Cohen, "Bret Easton Ellis Answers Critics of 'American Psycho,' " *New York Times*, March 6, 1991, C14.

54. Norman Mailer, "Children of the Pied Piper: Mailer on 'American Psycho,' " *Esquire*, March 1991, 154, 156.

55. Bret Easton Ellis, *American Psycho* (New York: Vintage Books, 1991), 4.

56. Jay McInerney, *Brightness Falls* (New York: Alfred A. Knopf, 1992), 412–13.

57. McInerney also chronicled the story of a young man who loses himself in the City of the early 1980s in *Bright Lights, Big City* (1984: New York: Vintage Books, 1987).

58. McInerney, *Brightness Falls*, 8.

59. Ibid., 41–42.

60. Ibid., 79.

61. Ibid., 104.

62. Ibid., 398.

63. Ibid., 66.

64. Ibid., 36.

65. Ibid., 389.

66. Ibid., 225.

67. Ibid., 416.

68. Simon Schama, "New York, Gaslight Necropolis," *New York Times Book Review*, June 19, 1994, 1.

69. Peter Quinn, "Remembering New York's Deadliest Riot," *New York Newsday*, July 12, 1994, 3.

70. Peter Quinn, *Banished Children of Eve* (New York: Viking Press, 1994), 42.

71. Walt Whitman, *Leaves of Grass*, cited in ibid., 612.

72. Francis X. Clines, "Old Rivalries Die Hard, or Not at All," *New York Times*, February 27, 1994, 29.

73. Cited in ibid., 29.

74. Schama, "New York, Gaslight Necropolis," 31.

75. E. L. Doctorow, *The Waterworks* (New York: Random House, 1994), 6–13.

76. Ibid., 59.

77. Laurel Graeber, "Left Out by Edith Wharton," *New York Times Book Review*, June 19, 1994, 31.

78. A point amplified by Ted Solotaroff in "Of Melville, Poe and Doctorow," *Nation*, June 6, 1994, 784–89.

79. Doctorow, *The Waterworks*, 163–64.

80. Ibid., 156.

81. Willie Morris, *New York Days* (Boston: Little, Brown, 1993), 3–4.

82. Ibid., 75.

83. Ibid., 142–43.

84. Ibid., 365.

85. Ibid., 134.

86. Sarah Schulman, *People in Trouble* (1990; New York: Plume, 1991), 1.

87. Ibid., 4.

88. Ibid., 14.

89. Ibid., 195.

90. Ibid., 28.

91. Ibid., 119.

92. Ibid., 208.

93. Ibid., 170.

94. Ibid., 180.

95. Ibid., 224.

96. John Steinbeck, "Autobiography: The Making of a New Yorker," *New York Times*, 1953, cited in Cohen, Chwast, and Heller, *New York Observed*, 123.

97. Jay McInerney, introduction to *New York: An Illustrated Anthology*, compiled by Michael Marqusee (London: Conran Octopus, 1988), 7.

98. Writers' Guild of America East, "Why I Write in New York," Program for the 44th Annual Awards, March 22, 1992, the Waldorf-Astoria, New York City.

99. Walt Whitman, cited in *Mumford Reader*, 13.

100. Allen Ginsberg, "I Love Old Whitman So," *Massachusetts Review* 33, no. 1 (Spring 1992), 77.

I N D E X

Aaron, Daniel, 147, 248

Abel, Colonel Rudolf, 235

Abel, Lionel, 255

Abie's Irish Rose (play), 215

Absalom, Absalom! (Faulkner), 191

Academy of Music, 77, 85

Acocella, Joan, 271

Adams, Franklin P., 158

Adams, Henry, 6–7, 50, 56

Adams, John, 5

Adams, William T., 88

Adrift in New York (Alger), 89–91

Advertisements for Myself (Mailer), 263, 264

African-Americans: black theater and musicals, 166, 176; emigrating, 86; feminism, 175–76; first black congregation, 13; free blacks in New York City, 9; "Great Northern Migration" of, 110, 171, 174; Harlem Renaissance, 84, 113–14, 123, 163–78, 232; Irish-Americans and, 300; lynchings of, 165; Negro national anthem, 111; "Negro plot" of 1741, 4; "New Negro" movement, 164; New York National Guard Fifteenth Infantry Regiment, 169–70; population of, 232; race riots, 165, 179, 195–96, 201; segregation, 110, 175; slavery, 13, 30; writers, 84, 110–14, 163–88, 189–205

Age of Innocence, The (Wharton), 35, 43, 71, 77–80, 85

AIDS (Acquired immune deficiency syndrome), 293, 297, 304–6

Ainslee's, 92

Albany, New York, 50

Alberti, Rafael, 210

Aleichem, Sholom, 95

Alfred A. Knopf publishers, 186

Alger, Horatio, literary presence in New York, 13, 83, 86, 87–91, 120, 225

Algonquin Indians, 3

Algonquin Round Table set, 123–24, 158–60

Allen, Oliver E., xiii–xiv, 85, 122, 232

Aller Retour New York (H. Miller), 219–20

Along the Way (J. W. Johnson), 111

Ambassadors, The (H. James), 43, 67

"America" (McKay), 114

American democracy: Cooper on, 18–19; Tocqueville on, 9–10; Whitman on, 31–32

American Democrat, The (Cooper), 18–19, 21, 140

American Dream, An (Mailer), 264–65, 296

American Earthquake, The (Wilson), 148

"American James, The" (Howells), 49

American Negro Theater, 187

American Notes (Dickens), 10, 11

American Psycho (Ellis), 293, 295, 296

American Scene, The (H. James), 49, 55, 56, 60–61, 63, 75

American Scholar (journal), 290

"American Scholar, The" (Emerson), 20

American Transcendentalism, 21

Amsterdam News, 187

Anabaptists, 4

Anderson, Sherwood, 135

Andrews, Esther, 138

Andrews, William L., 165

Anglican Church, 4

Anglo-Saxon Century and the Unification of the English-Speaking People, The (J. R. Dos Passos), 135

Another Country (J. Baldwin), 202–3

Answered Prayers: The Unfinished Novel (Capote), 268, 269

Apollo Theater, 183

Aquarium of the City of New York, 28

Arcturus, 21

Arendt, Hannah, 265

Armies of the Night, The (Mailer), 262

Armstrong, Louis, 166, 176, 194

Arrogant Beggar (Yezierska), 100

Asch, Sholem, 95

Ashbery, John, 271

Assistant, The (Malamud), 261–62

Astor, John Jacob, 108

Astor, Mrs. William, 63

Atlantic Monthly, 40, 48

A. T. Stewart's Marble Palace, 12

Auchincloss, Louis, 73, 285–86

Auden, W. H., 209–10, 270

Audubon Ballroom, 205

Auster, Paul, 286–87

"Author at Sixty, The" (Wilson), 149–50

"Autobiography of an American Jew, The" (Cahan), 98

Autobiography of an Ex-Colored Man, The (J. W. Johnson), 111–12, 113

Autobiography of Malcolm X, 204

Awake and Sing! (Odets), 216

Backward Glance, A (Wharton), 67, 70, 71–72

Baldwin, David, 199

Baldwin, George, 141

Baldwin, James: Harlem Renaissance and, 165; literary presence in New York, 193–94, 199–204, 234; on Mailer, 263; writings for the *New Yorker*, 265

Balzac, Honoré de, 64

Banana Bottom (McKay), 180

Banished Children of Eve, 300–301

Banjo (McKay), 180

Barbary Shore (Mailer), 262–63

Barbizon Hotel, 278

Barnes, Djuna, 144

"Barnum's Gallery of Wonders," 37

Barrett, William, 249, 252–53, 255

Barthelme, Donald, 265

"Bartleby, the Scrivener: A Story of Wall Street" (Melville), 24–25, 137

Baseball: Boston Red Sox, xi–xii; Brooklyn Dodgers, 161–62, 227, 232; "last golden age of baseball," 232; New York Giants, 232; New York Yankees, xii, 123, 227, 232; World Series, 232

Bashaw of Tripoli, 15

Bashevis, Isaac, 95

Battle of Brooklyn Heights, 5

"Beat Generation" movement, 274

Beautiful and Damned, The (F. S. Fitzgerald), 127–28, 147

Beginning of the Journey, The (D. Trilling), 245

Bell, Bernard W., 178

Bellevue Hospital, 183

Bell Jar, The (Plath), 276, 277, 278–79

Bellow, Saul, 233, 255, 256–60

Benchley, Robert, 124, 159

Bender, Thomas: on Irving, 15; on Melville and Whitman, 20; on New York's intellectual life, xiii, 6, 282–83

Bergstein, Eleanor, 308

Berlin, Irving, xii

Best of Times: An Informal Memoir, The (J. Dos Passos), 134–35, 138

Big Jim Europe's (band), 170

Big Money, The (J. Dos Passos), 137, 143

Big Sea, The (Hughes), 183

Billops, Camille, 170

Biltmore Hotel, 277

Birkerts, Sven, 287

Bishop, Elizabeth, 275–76

Bishop, John Peale, 144

Blacker the Berry, The (Thurman), 182, 183–84

Black Manhattan (J. W. Johnson), 111, 113–14, 166

Blair, Marie, 147

Blake, Eubie, 164

Blakes and Flanagans, The (M. A. Sadlier), 107

Bleak House (Dickens), 24

Bloodbrothers (Price), 294

"Bloodhounds of Broadway, The" (Runyon), 226

Bloom, Alexander, 249, 253

Boas, Franz, 176

Bode, Carl, 88

Bodenheim, Maxwell, 211

Bolero (Ravel), 152

Bone, Robert A., 169, 182–83

Bonfire of the Vanities, The (Wolfe), 219, 290–93

Book of American Negro Poetry, The, 113, 173

Book of Common Prayer, The, 68

Boston, Massachusetts, xi–xii, 6, 40, 43

"Boston: The Lost Ideal" (Hardwick), 284

Bostonians, The (H. James), 54–55, 64

Boston University, 253

Bowen, Elizabeth, 278

Bowery Boys (street gang), 7–8

Brace, Charles L., 88

Bracebridge Hall (Irving), 17

Braithwaite, William Stanley, 176

Brandeis University, 253

Bread Givers (Yezierska), 100–101

Breakfast at Tiffany's (Capote), 269

Breslin, Jimmy, 225, 233, 237–38

Brevoort, 138

Bridge, The (H. Crane), 141, 153, 154–55, 157–58, 161

Brightness Falls (McInerney), 293, 297–300

"Broadway Complex" (Runyon), 226

"Broadway Incident" (Runyon), 226

Bronx, New York: becomes part of the City of Greater New York, 86; Bronx River Parkway, 123; Co-op City, 294;

DeWitt Clinton High School, 181, 201, 247, 248; middle class growth in, 122; in Odets plays, 215; in Price novel, 293–94; Puerto Ricans of the South Bronx, 189; South Bronx, 189, 233; in Wolfe novel, 291, 292

Brooklyn Bridge, 85, 140–41, 153, 154–55, 156, 157–58

Brooklyn Eagle, 30, 211

Brooklyn Evening Star, 27–28

Brooklyn, New York: Battle of Brooklyn Heights, 5; becomes part of the City of Greater New York, 86; Brooklyn Dodgers, 161–62, 227, 232; Brooklyn Heights, 153, 155, 251, 285; "Brooklyn symbolist," 286; "Crossing Brooklyn Ferry" (Whitman), 29, 152, 155–56, 158; Front and Fulton Streets, 27; Gowanus Canal, 294; Greenwood Cemetery, 285; Halsey Street, 192–93; as an independent city, 28; Irish-American culture in, 236; Jewish immigrant communities in, 214, 261; *Last Exit to Brooklyn* (Selby), 294; *Leaving Brooklyn* (L. S. Schwartz), 234–36; in Mailer novel, 262; Moore's life in, 161–62; Park Slope section, 286, 301; street gangs, 28; *A Tree Grows in Brooklyn* (Betty Smith), 236; in Wolfe story, 218

Brooklyn Bridge, 85, 140–41, 153, 154–55, 156, 157–58

Brooklyn Eagle, 30, 211

Brooklyn Evening Star, 27–28

"Brooklyniana" (Whitman), 26, 27

Brooklyn Standard, 26

Brooks, Van Wyck, 5

Broom, 153

Brown, Charles Brockden, 13–14

Brown, Claude, 204, 205

Brown, Tina, 290

Brown Girl, Brownstones (Marshall), 189–90, 191

Bruccoli, Matthew J., 221

Bruce, Tammy, 296

Bryant, William Cullen, 18

"Bunner Sisters" (Wharton), 74–75

Burroughs, William, 274

Bury the Dead (Shaw), 244

Butterfield 8 (J. O'Hara), 221–22

Byrd, William, 4

Cafe Royal, 60

Cagney, James, 105, 106

Cahan, Abraham, 260; James Weldon Johnson and, 113; literary presence in New York, 83, 95–100, 120

"Call for Realism, A" (Howells), 43

Call it Sleep (Roth), 212–13

Cambridge, Massachusetts, 43, 48

Cane (Toomer), 176–77

"Cape Hatteras" (H. Crane), 156–57

Capote, Truman, 235, 265, 267–68, 269–70

Carnegie, Andrew, 98

Carnegie Hall, 85, 123

Carson, Rachel, 265

Castle Clinton, 7, 86

Castle Garden, 28

Catcher in the Rye, The (Salinger), 276–77

Cathedral of St. John the Divine, 203–4, 308

Catholicism: Catholic worship in New York City, 13; F. S. Fitzgerald's lost, 125; Irish Catholic Democrats, 108–10; Irish Catholicism, 106, 107, 239; Irish immigrants, 37; under the British, 4

Central Park, 123; beginnings of, 7, 9; in Cheever novel, 243; in Ellison novel, 197–98; F. S. Fitzgerald's recollection of, 133; in Jamesian novel, 54–55, 66;

Henry James' impression of, 62;
Olmsted-Calvert plan for, 37–38, 39;
Trollope's perception of, 13; zoo, xii,
104, 277
Century magazine, 173
Century's Ebb (J. Dos Passos), 138
Chambers, Whittaker, 138
Chametzky, Jules, 96, 98
Charles II, 4
Charles V, 3
Charles Scribner's Sons publishers, 64,
118, 124, 125
Chase Manhattan Building, 232
Cheever, John, 233, 240–43, 265
Chicago, Illinois, 257, 260
Children of Loneliness (Yezierska), 100
Children of the Poor, The (Riis), 101
Chinaberry Tree, The (Fauset), 172
Chosen Country (J. Dos Passos), 135
Christian, Barbara, 190–91
Christian socialism, 48
Christ in Concrete (di Donato), 208
Chrysler Building, 207
Church of the Ascension, 62
City College, 252, 261
City Hall, 7
"City in the Sea, The" (Poe), 154
"City of Dreadful Night, The" (O.
Henry), 93–94
City of Glass (Auster), 286–87
"City of Orgies" (Whitman), 33
"City of Refuge, The" (R. Fisher), 175
Civic Club, 172, 173, 204
Civic Repertory Theater, 215
Civil War, U.S.: Irish immigrants in the
Union Army, 25; Whitman's role in
the, 30, 32
Clark, Lewis Gaylord, 20
Clark, Willis Gaylord, 20
Clines, Francis X., 301

Clinton, DeWitt, 7, 13
Clockers (Price), 293, 294–95
Clurman, Harold, 215
Codman, Ogden, 69–70
Cohan, George M., 84, 105, 106, 126,
128
Cole, Bob, 111
Cole and the Johnson Brothers, 111
Color (Cullen), 181
Color of a Great City, The (Dreiser), 118
Color of the City, The (Dreiser), 115
Columbia College, 5
Columbia University, writers educated
at, 111, 248, 249, 254, 261, 272, 274,
286
Comédie humaine, La (Balzac), 64
Commentary, 246, 247, 248, 254
Communist Party: Dos Passos and the,
136, 138–39; Ellison's satire on the,
196, 197, 198; Michael Gold and the,
207, 213–14; Halper's pro-Communist
work, 214; McCarthy and the, 223,
225; New York intellectuals and the,
246, 247; Odets and the, 215; Roth and
the, 213; Wilson's study of Commu-
nism, 150
"Commuting" (Cullinan), 237
Company of Women, The (Gordon), 239
Company She Keeps, The (McCarthy), 222–
23, 224, 225
"Congo Love Song" (Cole and the John-
son Brothers), 111
Connelly, Marc, 159
Connolly, Cyril, 231
Conrad, Peter: on García Lorca, 210; on
O. Henry, 93; on Irving, 16, 17; on
Jamesian novel, 51; on tales of urban
life, 103; on Whitman, 17, 27
Conroy, Jack, 214
Continental Congress, 5

Cooke, Michael G., 178
Cooper, James Fenimore, 140; literary presence in New York, 2, 14, 18–19, 21
Cooperstown, New York, 18, 140
Copper Sun (Cullen), 181
Cornell University, 294
Corry, John, 304
Corso, Gregory, 274
Costello, Frank, 123
Cotton Club, 166
Cowley, Malcolm, 133, 308; Hart Crane and, 153–54; Michael Gold and, 214; on the Greenwich Village "idea," 123; McCarthy and, 223; Wakefield and, 272–73
"Crack-Up, The" (F. S. Fitzgerald), 209
Crane, Hart, 139, 141, 152–58, 210
Crane, Stephen, 155; literary presence in New York, 83, 95, 102–5, 118, 120
"Crapy Cornelia" (H. James), 64, 66
Crash of 1929, 132; Great Depression and the, 206–9, 227
Crèvecoeur, J. Hector St. John de, 8
Crime and violence: race riots, 165, 179, 195–96, 201; street gangs, 7–8, 28, 37, 294
Crisis, 164, 173, 185, 187, 188
Crocker, Richard, 109
"Crossing Brooklyn Ferry" (Whitman), 29, 152, 155–56, 158
Croton Reservoir, 10, 302
Crowninshield, Frank, 123
"Cruel and Barbarous Treatment" (McCarthy), 224
Crumb, Robert, 290
Crystal Palace Exposition of 1851, London, 8
Cullen, Countee, 114, 165, 181–82, 201
Cullinan, Elizabeth, 233, 236–37
Culture of Cities, The (Mumford), 283
Cummings, E. E., 138, 144

Cuomo, Mario, xiv–xv
"Curious Shifts of the Poor" (Dreiser), 117–18
Custom of the Country, The (Wharton), 71, 75–77

D. & J. Sadlier Company, 106
Daily Texan, 303
Daily Worker, 207
Dangling Man (Bellow), 257
Darwin, Charles, 102, 117
Dead Rabbits (street gang), 7–8, 28, 37
Dead Sea Scrolls, 150
Death and Life of Great American Cities, The (Jacobs), 254
Death of a Salesman (A. Miller), 216, 255–56, 261
Decoration of Houses, The (Wharton), 69–70
Decter, Midge, 304
Dell, Floyd, 136, 145
Delmonico's, 11, 12, 85
Democracy in America (Tocqueville), 9–10, 18
Democratic politics, 9–10, 18–19; Irish Catholic Democrats, 108–10; New York magazine wars and, 19–21; Tammany Hall, 108–9, 110, 123; Young America literary group and, 20–21
Democratic Review, 19, 30
Democratic Vistas (Whitman), 23, 31–32, 113, 137
"Desolate City, The" (McKay), 179
Dewey, John, 100
DeWitt Clinton High School (Bronx, NY), 181, 201, 247, 248
Dial, 21, 145, 161
Diary of a Yuppie (Auchincloss), 286
Dickens, Charles, 2, 9, 24; visit to New York City, 10–12
Dickstein, Morris, 245, 250, 255

Didion, Joan, 234, 273–74, 304
di Donato, Pietro, 208
DiMaggio, Dom, xii
DiMaggio, Joe, xii
Dissent, 248
"Di Yunge" (Young Ones) literary group, 95
"Dock Rats" (Moore), 161
Doctorow, E. L., 227–30, 300, 301–3
Donleavy, J. P., 240
Dos Passos, John, literary presence in New York, 134–44, 221
Dos Passos, John Randolph, 135
Dostoyevsky, Fyodor Mikhaylovich, 295
Douglass Pilot, 201
Draft Act, Irish immigrants against the, 25, 300–301
Dreiser, Theodore, 138, 221, 257; literary presence in New York, 84, 114–20
Dresser, Paul, 116, 117
Drum-Taps (Whitman), 30
Du Bois, W. E. B., 164, 165, 170, 173, 176, 185
"Duel, The" (O. Henry), 94
Dunbar, Paul Lawrence, 167–69, 187, 192–93
Duncan, Isadora, 138
Dunne, Finley Peter, 84, 106
Dust Tracks on a Road (Hurston), 176
Dutch East India Company, 3
Dutch Reformed Church, 4, 22
Dutch settlers, 3–4, 16, 26
Dutch West India Company, 3
Duyckinck, Evert A., 21

Eastman, Crystal, 178
Eastman, Max, 136, 138, 178, 214
"East-Side Ramble, An" (Howells), 47, 96
Ebbett's Field, 162
Ebony, 188

"Echoes of the Jazz Age" (F. S. Fitzgerald), 127
Edel, Leon, 145
Edinburgh Review, 14
Education of Henry Adams, The (H. Adams), 50
Egoist, 161
Egyptian pyramid, 67
Eliot, T. S., 129, 142, 145, 154, 155, 161
Ellington, Edward Kennedy "Duke," 166, 172
Ellis, Bret Easton, 293, 295–97
Ellis Island, 84, 100; Henry James's visit to, 59–60; opening of, 28, 85–86
Ellison, Ralph: Harlem Renaissance and, 165, 177; literary presence in New York, 193–99, 234
Emergency Quota Act of 1921, 122
Emerson, Ralph Waldo, 8, 161; "The American Scholar" lecture, 20; letter to Whitman, 27; visit to the James's home, 49
Emmet, Robert and Kitty, 50
Empire State Building, 63, 134, 149, 207, 220
Enemies, a Love Story (I. B. Singer), 261
"Enormous Radio, The" (Cheever), 242
Epstein, Joseph, 265, 290
Erie Canal, 7
Esquire, 160, 209
Evans, Walker, 206
Ev'ry Month magazine, 115, 117
"Exhibition of the Industry of All Nations," 8
Exile's Return (Cowley), 123, 133, 272
"Experiment in Misery, An" (S. Crane), 103

Fairy Tale of New York, A (Donleavy), 240
Faithfull, Starr, 221
"False Dawn" (Wharton), 80–81

Fanning, Charles, 107, 125, 237, 240
Farrell, James T., 208, 223, 257, 294
Faulker, William, 191
Fauset, Jessie, 172–73, 175, 185
Federal Writers' Project, 14
Fenway Park, xii
Ferber, Edna, 159
Ferries, 26, 207
Fields, James T., 40
"Fifth Avenue, Uptown: A Letter from Harlem" (J. Baldwin), 202
Fifty Years and Other Poems (J W. Johnson), 113
Fighting 69th, The (film), 105
Final Payments (Gordon), 238–39
Fire!!, 176, 183
Fireside Pentecostal Assembly, 199
Fisher, Philip, 133
Fisher, Rudolph, 175
Fitzgerald, F. Scott: Dos Passos and the Fitzgeralds, 134–35; Great Depression and, 209; Irving and, 16; Kazin on, 251; literary presence in New York, xiii, 121, 122, 124–34, 303; Long Island landscape and, 197; McInerney and, 297; Parker and death of, 160; Wilson and, 146–47
Fitzgerald, Zelda Sayre, 124, 125, 127, 128, 131, 132–33
"Five-Forty-Eight, The" (Cheever), 241
Five Pointers (street gang), 37
Flatiron Building, 59, 149
Fleischmann, Raoul, 158
Fleischmann's Yeast, 158
Fleisher, Von Humboldt, 257
"Folks from Dixie" (Dunbar), 168
Ford, John, 206
Forsaking All Others (Breslin), 238
Fortune, 249, 250
Foster, Stephen, 301
Four Million, The (O. Henry), 86, 91–92

Frady, Marshall, 304
Fragments of the Century (Harrington), 270
Frank, Waldo, 101
Frank's Campaign (Alger), 87–88
Frederick Douglass Junior High, 200–201
Free-Soil Party, 30
Frick Museum, 282
"Friendly City, The" (Ashbery), 271
Fromer, Harvey, 232
Fuchs, Daniel, 214
Fugitive Slave Law, 30
Fuller, Charles H., 308
Fuller Building, 59
Fulton Ferry, 26
Fussell, Paul, 77

García Lorca, Federico, 207, 210
Garland, Hamlin: Henry James and, 64, 65; review of Stephen Crane's *Maggie*, 104–5
Garretsville, Ohio, 153
Garrick Gaieties, 158
Garvey, Marcus, 164, 176
Gates, Henry Louis, Jr., 170
Gates, Robert A.: on Cheever, 241; on J. Dos Passos, 142; on New York City's middle class, 122; on West, 211; on Wolfe, 218
Geismar, Maxwell, 256
General Motors Building, New York World's Fair, 228
"Genius," The (Dreiser), 116
"Geoffrey Crayon Papers" (Irving), 20
George's Mother (S. Crane), 95, 102
George Washington Bridge, 123, 203
"Ghostly Father, I Confess" (McCarthy), 225
Ghosts (Auster), 286
"Gift from the City, A" (Updike), 267
Gilded Age, 34, 86, 120, 301
Gill, Brendan, 158, 160

"Gimpel the Fool" (I. B. Singer), 260
Gingertown (McKay), 180
Ginsberg, Allen, 234, 274–75, 308
"Girls in Their Summer Dresses, The"
    (Shaw), 244
Going to Meet the Man (J. Baldwin), 203
Gold, Ivan, 286, 287–88
Gold, Michael, 213–14; editorship of
    New Masses, 138, 143; editorship of the
    Liberator, 178; night in a Hooverville,
    207
Golden Spur, The (D. Powell), 268
Goldman, Emma, 138
Gomez, Esteban, 3
"Goodbye to All That" (Didion), 273
Goodman, Paul, 253
Gordin, Jacob, 60
Gordon, Mary, 233, 238–39, 279
*Gospel of Wealth and Other Timely Essays,
    The* (Carnegie), 98
Go Tell It on the Mountain (J. Baldwin), 200
Gottlieb, Robert, 289–90
Grace, William R., 108
Grafton, Massachusetts, 270
Grand Central Terminal, 85, 277
Granich, Irwin *see* Gold, Michael
Grapes of Wrath, The (Steinbeck), 206, 208
Great Barbecue, 34
Great Depression: Harlem and the, 114;
    New York in the mid 1930s, 123, 206–
    9, 226–30
Great Gatsby, The (F. S. Fitzgerald), 16,
    121, 128–31, 133–34, 146, 292, 297
Great Neck Estates, Long Island, 128
Great War (World War I), 63, 67, 77, 82,
    105, 136
Great World and Timothy Colt, The (Auchin-
    closs), 286
Greenberg, Clement, 246
Greenwich Village, 123–24; James Bald-
    win's move to, 202; Dos Passos's move

to, 138; Ginsberg's discovery of, 274,
    275; McCarthy's move to, 223; Moore's
    move to, 161; Ozick's move to, 270;
    Poets Corner in, 220; satire on, 143–
    44; Lionel Trilling's move to, 248; in
    Wakefield memoir, 272; Wakefield's
    move back to, 273; Wilson on, 144,
    145; writers attracted to, 234
"Greenwich Village in the Early Twen-
    ties" (Wilson), 147
Group, The (McCarthy), 223
Group Theater, 215
Growing Up Absurd (Goodman), 253
Guggenheim Museum, 233
Gurjieff, Georges I., 176
Guthrie, Woody, 206
Guy, Francis, 27
*Guys and Dolls: The Stories of Damon
    Runyon* (Runyon), 225, 226

Halberstam, David, 232, 304
Hale, John Parker, 30
Hall, Gilman, 92
Halper, Albert, 214
Hamilton, Alexander, 6
Hamlet (Shakespeare), 184
Hammett, Dashiell, 211
Hammill, Pete, 234
"Harbor Dawn, The" (H. Crane), 156
Hardwick, Elizabeth, 223, 255, 283,
    284–85
Harlem (journal), 183
"Harlem: Mecca of the New Negro"
    (Locke), 173
Harlem: Negro Metropolis (McKay), 180
Harlem (play), 183
"Harlem: The Cultural Capital" (J. W.
    Johnson), 178
Harlem Book of the Dead, The (Billops), 170
"Harlem Ghetto, The" (J. Baldwin), 202
Harlem Hospital, 199

Harlem Renaissance, 84, 113–14, 123, 163–78, 232

Harlem Renaissance (Huggins), 112–13

Harlem River, 203

"Harlem Runs Wild" (McKay), 179

Harlem Shadows (McKay), 177, 179

"Harlem—Then and Now" (J. Baldwin), 201

Harlequin Ballads (Fleisher), 257

Harper, J. Henry, 41–42

Harper and Brothers, Publishers, 41, 42, 57

Harper's Magazine, 282, 303–4, 305

Harper's Monthly, 41, 42

Harrington, Michael, 234, 270

Hart, Lorenz Milton, 158

Hart, Moss, 159

Harvard University, 262

Harvey, Colonel George, 57

Hawkins, Coleman, 192

Hawthorne, Nathaniel, 20, 21, 39, 95

"Hawthorne and His Mosses" (Melville), 23, 32–33

Haymarket riot, 45

Hazard of New Fortunes, A (Howells), 35, 42, 43–46, 96

Hecht, Ben, 159

Hellman, Lillian, 138

Hemenway, Robert E., 176

Henry, O., literary presence in New York, 83, 86, 91–94, 103, 120, 225

Heraclitus, 3

Here at the New Yorker (Gill), 158

"Here Is New York" (E. B. White), 266

"Heritage" (Cullen), 181

Heron, Liz, 144

Hersey, John, 265

Heyward, Dubose, 166

Hijuelos, Oscar, 289

Hillyer, Robert, 137

Hindenburg, 228

Hine, Lewis, 102

"Hiroshima" (Hersey), 265

History of New York from the Beginning of the World to the End of the Dutch Dynasty, A (Irving), 15–16, 17, 290

History of the United States during the First Administration of Thomas Jefferson (H. Adams), 6, 7

Hoboken, New Jersey, 56, 99

Holland Tunnel, 123

Homage to Blenholt (Fuchs), 214

Home as Found (Cooper), 19

Home to Harlem (McKay), 179, 180, 182

Homeward Bound (Cooper), 19

"Homosexual Villain, The" (Mailer), 263

Hone, Philip, diary of New York society, 36–39

Hone Club, 36

Hook, Sidney, 253–54, 255

Hoover, Herbert, 149

"Hoovervilles," 206

Hopkins, L. A., 116

Hotel Metropole, 116

House of Five Talents, The (Auchincloss), 285

House of Gold (Cullinan), 236

House of Mirth, The (Wharton), 71, 72–74

"House-Top, The" (H. Melville), 25

Howe, Irving, 95, 201; New York intellectuals and, 233, 246–47, 249, 253, 255

Howells, William Dean, 34–35, 64; Cahan and, 94–95, 96, 98; Stephen Crane and, 104, 105; Dreiser and, 115; literary presence in New York, 39–49, 81–82, 86

"How I Found America" (Yezierska), 101

Howl and Other Poems (Ginsberg), 274

How the Other Half Lives (Riis), 45, 101

"How to Live on $36,000 a Year" (F. S. Fitzgerald), 132

Hudson, Henry, 3

Huggins, Nathan, 112–13; on Harlem, 164, 170, 174, 186; on Thurman, 182

Hughes, Langston: James Baldwin and, 201; Ellison and, 195; Fauset and, 173; Harlem Renaissance and, 164, 165, 166, 167, 175, 176; James Weldon Johnson on, 114; literary presence in New York, 185–87; portrayal of Thurman, 183

Humboldt's Gift (Bellow), 257

Hungry Hearts (Yezierska), 100

Hurst, Fanny, 176

Hurston, Zora Neale, 164, 167, 175–76, 184, 186

"Hymn of the City" (Bryant), 18

Iceman Cometh, The (O'Neill), 211–12

"If We Must Die" (McKay), 179

"I Happen to Like New York" (C. Porter), 134

Immigrant processing, 28

Immigration acts, 122

"Impressions of a Cousin, The" (H. James), 53–54

Indian War of 1643–45, 3

"In Dreams Begin Responsibility" (D. Schwartz), 253

Infants of the Spring (Thurman), 182, 183, 184

Intellectual Memoirs: New York 1936–1938 (McCarthy), 223–24

In the Country of Last Things (Auster), 287

Invisible Man (Ellison), 177, 193, 194, 195–99

"In Zich" (Introspectives) literary group, 95

Irish-Americans, 84; patriotism of, 105; politics of, 108–10, 123; portrayal of Irish-American culture, 236–39; speech of, 105–6; writers, 105–10, 121, 122, 124–34, 138, 211–12, 236–40

Irish immigrants: against the Draft Act, 25, 300–301; blamed for Wall Street fire, 36–37; Catholicism, 37, 239; emigrating, 85, 86; in O. Henry story, 93–94; Howells visit to an Irish ghetto, 47

Irish Voice in America, The (Fanning), 107

Irvin, Rea, 290

Irving, Washington, 1–2, 290; literary presence in New York, 14–18, 20, 32, 92, 156; pseudonym, 17

Italian-American writers, 208

Italian immigrants, 60, 86

I Thought of Daisy (Wilson), 143–44, 150–51

Ivy, J. W., 188

Jacobs, Jane, 254

Jacoby, Russell, 254

James, Alice, 49

James, Caryn, 159

James, Catharine Barber, 50

James, Henry, 34–35, 146, 148, 223, 274; Auchincloss and, 285; James Baldwin and, 194; Bellow and, 260; Cahan and, 95, 98; English language and, 106; Howells and, 42–43, 47, 48, 49; literary presence in New York, 49–67, 81–82, 86, 270; Wharton and, 57, 70–71, 75

James, Henry, Sr., 49

James, William, 49, 57, 88

Jazz, black, 166, 175

Jazz (Morrison), 170–72

Jazz Age, 127, 132

"Jazz at Home" (Rogers), 175

"Jazzonia" (Hughes), 175
Jefferson, Thomas, 6
Jewish-Americans: Jewish intelligentsia, 233, 255–65; writers, 83–84, 95–102, 207, 212–14, 234–36, 246–47, 249–53
Jewish Daily Forward, 95, 260
Jewish ghettos, 47–48, 246, 255
Jewish immigrants: in Cahan's novels, 95, 96–100; depiction of Jewish women, 100–101; emigrating, 86; in Fuchs's novels, 214; Henry James's encounter with, 60–61; Jewish refugees from Germany, 122; population of, 95; in Riis's novels, 101–2; in Roth's novel, 212–13; in Yezierska's novels, 100–101
Jews Without Money (M. Gold), 213, 214
Jimmie Marshall's Hotel, 111
John Reed Club, 246
Johnson, Charles S., 165, 167, 172, 174, 175
Johnson, James Weldon: at dinner honoring Fauset, 173; on Harlem, 178; literary presence in New York, 84, 110–14, 120, 163, 165, 166, 167, 204
Johnson-Reed Immigration Act of 1924, 122
"Jolly Corner, The" (H. James), 64–66
Jones, Mrs. Cadwalader, 57
Jones, Edith Newbold *see* Wharton, Edith
Jones, Lucretia and Frederick, 69
Jones, William Alfred, 21
Josephson, Matthew, 34
Joyce, James, 66, 145, 148, 196, 236, 244; *Ulysses*, 142, 156, 213
J. Walter Thompson Agency, 153

"Kaddish" (Ginsberg), 275
Kalstone, David, 275
Kaltenborn, H. V., 227
Kansas State College, 178

Karl, Frederick R., 257, 261
Kaufman, George S., 159
Kazin, Alfred: xvi; on Bellow, 256, 257, 258; on F. S. Fitzgerald, 133, 134; New York intellectuals and, 233, 249–52, 255; on Roth, 213
Kelly, "Honest" John, 108
Kenmore Hotel, 210–11
Kerouac, Jack, 274
Kief, William, 3
King, Larry, 304
King's College, 5
Klein's (department store), 214
Knickerbocker Magazine, 11, 19, 20, 21
"Knickerbocker Writing," 14
Knight, Sarah Kemble, 4–5
Knopf *see* Alfred A. Knopf publishers
Koch, Kenneth, 271

La Farge, John, 62
La Favorita (Donizetti), 28
Lafayette Avenue Presbyterian Church, 161
Lafayette Theater, 200
La Guardia, Fiorello, 232
"Landmarker, The" (Auchincloss), 285
"Landsend" (Selby), 294
Lang, Dorothea, 206
Lapham, Lewis H., 282
Lardner, Ring, 128, 135
Larsen, Nella, 165, 176, 177–78
Last Exit to Brooklyn (Selby), 294
Last Intellectuals: American Culture in the Age of Academe, The (Jacoby), 254
Latin-American writers, 188–89, 288–89
Latin Moon in Manhattan (Manrique), 288–89
Law for the Lion, A (Auchincloss), 285–86
Lawrence, D. H., 29–30, 180
Lawson, John Howard, 137, 138

Lazarus, Emma, xv

Leatherstocking tales, Cooper's, 18

Leaves of Grass (Whitman), 21, 26, 27, 28, 29, 30, 32, 308

Leaving Brooklyn (L. S. Schwartz), 234–36

LeCorbusier, 233

"Legend of Sleepy Hollow, The" (Irving), 18

Lemmon, Jack, xii

Lenin, Vladimir Ilyich, 254

Leonard, John, 265

Letters from an American Farmer (Crève-coeur), 8

"Letters of an Altrurian Traveler" (Howells), 46–47

"Letter to N.Y." (E. Bishop), 275

Lever House, 232

Lewis, David Levering: on Cullen, 182; Harlem Renaissance and, 165, 166; on McKay, 179

Lewis, R. W. B., 75, 77

Lewis, Sinclair, 123, 142–43

Liberal Imagination, The (L. Trilling), 255

Liberator, 136, 145, 178, 214

Liebling, A. J., 2, 105, 265

Life of Damon Runyon, A (Breslin), 225

Life Studies (Lowell), 158

"Lift Every Voice and Sing" (J. W. Johnson), 111

Lincoln Center, 233

Lind, Jenny, 28

Linden Hills (Naylor), 190, 191

"Litany in Time of Plague, A" (Nashe), 297

"Litany of the Dark People, The" (Cullen), 181

Literary Friends and Acquaintance: A Personal Retrospect of American Authorship (Howells), 39

Literary World, 21

Little, Malcolm (Malcolm X), 163, 204–5

Locke, Alain, 185, 195; Harlem Renaissance and, 165, 173, 174–75, 176

Locked Room, The (Auster), 286

Loesser, Frank, 226

Long Day's Journey into Night (O'Neill), xii

Longfellow, Henry Wadsworth, 20

Long Island, New York: in Ellison novel, 197; Fire Island, 271; Great Neck Estates in, 128; Levittown, 232; Nassau County, 232; Suffolk County, 25–26; Whitman's name for, 29

Long Way from Home, A (McKay), 179

Los Angeles: Capital of the Third World (Rieff), 282

"Lost Decade, The" (F. S. Fitzgerald), 134

"Love Lies Sleeping" (E. Bishop), 275

Low Company (Fuchs), 214

Lowell, Robert, 158, 284

Luce, Henry, 123, 249, 250

Lyles, Aubry, 166

Lyrics of Lowly Life (Dunbar), 168

MacArthur, Charles, 159

Macbeth, Welles's production of, 200

McCaffrey, Lawrence J., 239

McCarthy, Mary, 208, 222–25, 255

McClure's Magazine, 98

Macdonald, Dwight, 223, 247, 249

McDougald, Elise Johnson, 175

McDowell, Deborah E., 172–73

McInerney, Jay, 293, 297–300, 307–8

McKay, Claude: Fauset and, 173; Harlem Renaissance and, 164, 165, 177; literary presence in New York, 114, 178–81

MacShane, Frank, 221

Mademoiselle, 273, 278, 279

Madison, John R. *see* Dos Passos, John

Madison, Lucy Addison, 135

Maggie: Girl of the Streets (S. Crane), 102–3, 104–5

Maggie-Now (Betty Smith), 236

Mailer, Norman: on Ellis's *American Psycho*, 296; literary presence in New York, 233, 255, 262–65; Mailer-Breslin mayoral campaign, 237; writings for *Harper's Magazine*, 304

Main Street (S. Lewis), 123

Majors and Minors (Dunbar), 168

Making It (Podhoretz), 254

Malamud, Bernard, 233, 255, 261–62

Malcolm X, 163, 204–5

Mambo Kings Play Songs of Love, The (Hijuelos), 289

Manchild in the Promised Land (Claude Brown), 204, 205

Manhattan '45 (J. Morris), 231–32

Manhattan Island: becomes part of the City of Greater New York, 86; "Black Manhattan," 110–11; Brooklyn vs., 26; discovery and establishment of, 3–4

"Manhattan" (Rodgers and Hart), 158

Manhattan Transfer (J. Dos Passos), 139–43, 221

"Man in the Brooks Brothers Shirt, The" (McCarthy), 224

"Man-Moth, The" (E. Bishop), 275–76

"Mannahatta" (Whitman), 29, 31

Manrique, Jaime, 288–89

Man Who Came to Dinner, The (Kaufman and Hart), 159

Margin of Hope (Howe), 247

Marshall, Paule, 189–90, 191–93

Martin, Judith (Miss Manners), 295

Martin Chuzzlewit (Dickens), 11

Marxism, 138, 247

"Masque of the Red Death, The" (Poe), 152, 219, 293

Masses, 136, 214

Mathews, Cornelius, 21

Maxwell, William, 237

"May Day" (F. S. Fitzgerald), 126–27

May Day riots, 132

Melting-Pot, The (Zangwill), 61, 97

Melville, Herman, 2, 8, 35, 90, 198; Bender on, 20; "inside narratives," 95; literary presence in New York, 21–25, 32–33

Memoirs of a Catholic Girlhood (McCarthy), 223

Memoirs of Hecate County (Wilson), 148, 150, 152

Mencken, H. L., 303

"Men in the Storm, The" (S. Crane), 103, 118

Mercy of a Rude Stream (Roth), 213

Merrill, James, 275

Messenger, 183

Methodist Episcopal Church, 13

Metropolitan Museum, 39, 62

Metropolitan Opera House, 77, 85, 233

Middle of the Journey, The (L. Trilling), 249

Millay, Edna St. Vincent, 123, 138, 144–45, 270

Miller, Arthur, 216, 233, 255–56, 261

Miller, Flournoy, 166

Miller, Henry, 219–20

Miller, Perry, 11, 19

Minsky's, 136

Minuit, Peter, 3

Miss Lonelyhearts (West), 211

Miss Manners (Judith Martin), 295

Mitchell, Joseph, 265

Moby-Dick (Melville), 21, 22, 23, 198

"Modern Poetry" (H. Crane), 154

"Modest Proposal, A" (Swift), 15

Monthly Magazine, 13

Moore, Marianne, 160–62, 270, 275, 278

Morris, Jan, 231–32

Morris, Willie, 300, 303–4

Morrison, Toni, 165, 167, 170–72

Moses, Robert, 233, 254

Most Likely to Succeed (Dos Passos), 139

Motherwell, Robert, 271

Mount Calvary of the Pentecostal Faith
　Church, 199

Moynihan, Daniel Patrick, 105

M'Robert, Patrick, 5

Mr. Sammler's Planet (Bellow), 259–60

"Mugging" (Ginsberg), 275

Mumford, Lewis, 2, 22, 282–83

Muschamp, Herbert, 282

Museum of Modern Art, 233, 271

Museum of Natural History, 116, 277

Mustapha Rubadub Keli Khan, 15

"My City" (J. W. Johnson), 111

"My Lost City" (F. S. Fitzgerald), 132

Nashe, Thomas, 297

Nation, 179

National Association for the Advance-
　ment of Colored People (NAACP),
　113, 164, 188

National Organization for Women, Los
　Angeles Chapter, 296

National Urban League, 164, 181

National Winter Garden, 146

Native Son (R. Wright), 187, 193

Naylor, Gloria, 188, 189, 190–91

"Negro Artist and the Racial Mountain,
　The" (Hughes), 186

"Negro in American Literature, The"
　(Braithwaite), 176

*Negro in Chicago: A Study of Race Relations
　and a Race Riot, The* (C. Johnson), 172

"Negro Speaks of Rivers, The"
　(Hughes), 185

Negro World, 164

New Amsterdam, failure as a commercial
　enterprise, 3–4

New Challenge, 195

"New Frontage on American Life, The"
　(C. Johnson), 175

Newhouse, S. I., Jr., 289

Newman, Paul, xii

New Masses, 138, 143, 214

New Negro, The (Locke), 174, 175, 176,
　178, 179, 185, 204

"New Negro" movement, 164

New Netherland, 3

New Playwrights' Theater, 138

Newport, Rhode Island, 69

New Republic, 145, 223, 248, 250

Newsboy's Lodging House, 88

"New York: World-Famous Impossibil-
　ity" (Bellow), 260

New York Academy of Fine Arts, 7

New York City: asylums, 10, 11; begin-
　nings as a commercial center, 2–8; dis-
　covery and establishment of Manhattan
　Island, 3–4; during Revolutionary War,
　5; economic reversals, 7; education in,
　5; the El (elevated trains), 54, 85; eleva-
　tors, 59; epidemics, 7; highway proj-
　ects, 123, 233; omnibuses, 13, 28, 40;
　population of, 5, 7, 9, 12, 85, 95, 110,
　232; prohibition in, 123, 166; race riots,
　165, 179; reminiscences of, xii-xiii; sky-
　scrapers, 40, 57–58, 85, 140, 146, 149,
　207, 232–33; street gangs, 7–8, 28, 37,
　294; suicides in, 117; water-supply sys-
　tem, 10, 67, 302

"New York City: Crash Course" (Hard-
　wick), 284

New York City Aquarium, 28

New York City Ballet, 233

New York City Board of Health, 47

New York City Sanitary Commission, 37

New York City streets and neighbor-
　hoods: the Bowery, 84–85; Broadway,
　7, 10, 84–85, 140, 225, 241, 261; Fifth
　Avenue, 67, 84, 85, 145, 146, 195, 199,

243, 302; Grammercy Park, 57; Halsey Street, 192–93; Harlem, 86, 110, 123, 163–64, 166–67, 177, 179, 199; Hell's Kitchen, 85; Henry Hudson Parkway, 123; Hester Street, 48, 86, 100, 101; highway projects, 123, 254; "Jewish Harlem," 213; Lenox Avenue, 185, 199; Little Italy, 86; Lower East Side, 86, 100, 101, 102, 213, 217, 246, 286, 299; Madison Avenue, 243; "Midtown," 249, 271; "Millionaire's Row," 84; Mulberry Street, 101, 102; Riverside Drive, 207; St. Luke's Place, 161; St. Nicholas Avenue, 195; Sugar Hill, 182, 199; Theater district, 111; Times Square, 123, 202, 207, 271; Tin Pan Alley, 111; Union Square, 214; Upper West Side, 260; Wall Street, 24, 36–37, 59, 122, 206, 295, 296, 298; Washington Square, 44, 57, 61, 270. *See also* Greenwich Village

New York Daily News, 194

New York Days (W. Morris), 300, 303–4

"New York Edition" (H. James), 63–64

New Yorker: Cheever and the, 242; Cullinan and the, 237; editorship of, 233, 265, 289–90; founding of the, 123, 158–59; on Howe, 247; Parker and the, 160; writers with the, 233–34, 265–67, 269, 279

New York Evening Post, 18, 109

New York Evening Sun, 145

New York Federal Writers' project, 180

New York Gazette, 4

New York Harbor, Statue of Liberty in, xv

New York Herald Tribune, 237

New York Historical Society, 7, 37

New York Hotel, 50

New York Intellect: A History of Intellectual Life in New York City, 282–83

New York intellectuals, 233, 245–55, 279; Jewish intelligentsia, 255–65

New York in the Fifties (Wakefield), xiii, 272

New York Jew (Kazin), 249, 250, 252

New York Journal American, 237

New York Morning Chronicle, 14

New York National Guard, Fifteenth Infantry Regiment, 169–70

New York Panorama, 207

New York Post, 196

New York Post-Dispatch, 211

New York Public Library, 10–11, 250, 275; Harlem branch, 177; Hudson Park branch, 161

New York Review of Books, 246

New York Saturday Review, 142

New York school of painters and poets, 271

New York Society Library, 5

New York Sunday World, 92, 93

New York Tablet, 106

New York Times, 159, 240, 273

New York Tribune, 101

New York Trilogy, The (Auster), 286–87

New York University, 61

New-York Weekly Journal, 4

New York World, 117, 158, 159

New York World's Fair (1939), 207, 227–30

Nichols, Beverley, 231

"Niggeratti," 184

Nigger Heaven (Van Vechten), 166, 180

Nin, Anaïs, 219

Nobody Knows My Name (J. Baldwin), 202

"Nobody Knows the Trouble I've Seen" (spiritual), 111

"No Door: A Story of Time and the Wanderer" (Wolfe), 218
"Noises in the City" (Shaw), 244
Nolan, Johnny, 88
North America (Trollope), 12
Norton, Charles Eliot, 48
Notebooks (H. James), 52
Notes from the Underground (Dostoyevsky), 295
Notes of a Native Son (J. Baldwin), 193, 201–2
Notions of the Americans (Cooper), 18

Oak and Ivy (Dunbar), 168
Observations (Moore), 161
"O City of Broken Dreams" (Cheever), 241–42
Odets, Clifford, 207, 215–16
O'Dwyer, William, 232
Of Time and the River: A Legend of Man's Hunger in His Youth (Wolfe), 217, 220
O'Hara, Frank, 234, 270–71
O'Hara, John, 207, 221–22
Old New York (Wharton), 80–81
Oliver, Joseph "King," 164
Olmsted, Frederick Law, plan for Central Park, 37–38
Olympic, 146
O'Neill, Eugene, 106, 138, 211–12
One Man's Initiation (J. Dos Passos), 136
One Way to Heaven (Cullen), 182
On Native Grounds (Kazin), 250, 255
"On Saturday, the Siren Sounds at Noon" (Petry), 187–88
"On the Banks of the Wabash" (Dresser), 117, 119–20
"On the State of American Literature" (C. B. Brown), 13–14
"Open Boat, The" (S. Crane), 103
Opportunity, 164, 167, 172, 181

O'Sullivan, John L., 20, 30
Other Side, The (Gordon), 238, 239
Other Voices, Other Rooms (Capote), 269
"Out of the Cradle Endlessly Rocking" (Whitman), 29
"Over There" (Cohan), 105
Oxford University, 303
Ozick, Cynthia, 270

Page, Geraldine, xii
Painters and poets, New York school of, 271
Parker, Dorothy, 124, 138, 159–60
Park Row Business Building, 85
Partisan Review: Bellow and the, 256, 257, 260; McCarthy and the, 223, 224; move to Rutgers University and Boston University, 253; New York intellectuals and the, 245, 246, 247–48, 249, 252, 253; proletarian literature and the, 214
Party at Jack's (Wolfe), 218–19
"Passing" (Hughes), 186
Passing (Larsen), 177–78
Pater, Walter, 136
Paul, Sherman, 146
Paulding, James Kirk, 14
Pennington, Anna, 147–48
People in Trouble (Schulman), 300, 304–6
People's Voice, 187
Perelman, S. J., 211
Perisphere, Trylon and the, 207, 227, 228
Petry, Ann, 165, 187–88, 190
Philadelphia, Pennsylvania, 3, 5, 6, 7
Phillips, William, 255; editorship of *Partisan Review*, 246, 248; leaves *Partisan Review*, 253
Pierce, Franklin, 30
Pierre; or, The Ambiguities (Melville), 22, 23–24, 25, 90

Pilgrim's Progress, 47

Plath, Sylvia, 234, 276, 277–79

Plaza Hotel, 85, 133, 134–35, 146

Plum Bun (Fauset), 172–73

Plunkitt, George Washington, 109–10

Podhoretz, Norman: on Alger, 88; on Bellow, 257; on New York intellectuals, 246, 248–49, 253; turn to conservatism, 254

Poe, Edgar Allan, 20, 137, 152, 154, 219, 293

"Poet, The" (Dunbar), 168

Poet in New York (García Lorca), 210

Poetry, 161

Poirier, Richard, 270

Politics, 247

Porgy (play), 166

Porter, Algernon Sidney, 92

Porter, Cole, 134

Porter, W. C., 92

Porter, William Sydney *see* Henry, O.

Port of New York (Rosenfeld), 121–22

Portrait in Brownstone (Auchincloss), 285

"Portrait of the Intellectual as a Yale Man" (McCarthy), 225

Powell, Adam Clayton, 196

Powell, Dawn, 138, 267–69

Praisesong for the Widow (Marshall), 191–93

Price, Richard, 293–95

"Pride of the Cities, The" (O. Henry), 91

Priestly, J. B., 233

"Princess with the Golden Hair, The" (Wilson), 148, 150, 151–52

"Prisoner of Sex" (Mailer), 304

Pritchard, William, 152, 157

Proletarian literature, 214

Prostitution, child, 38

"Providential Match, A" (Cahan), 96

P. T. Barnum's American Museum, 12

Public Enemy (film), 105

"Public Parks and the Enlargement of Towns" (Olmsted), 37–38

Pug Uglies (street gang), 28

Putnam's, 24

Quakers, 3, 4, 5

Queens, New York, 86, 122, 237, 238, 283

Queensboro Bridge, 130, 146

Quicksand (Larsen), 177

Quindlen, Anna, 233, 240

Quinn, Peter, 300–301

Radio City Music Hall, 207, 241, 276

Ragged Dick; or, Street Life in New York (Alger), 88–89

Ragtime (Doctorow), 227

Rahv, Philip: Bellow and, 256; editorship of the *Partisan Review*, 214, 246, 247, 248; leaves *Partisan Review*, 253; McCarthy and, 223

Rank, Otto, 219

Rapp, William Jourdan, 183

RCA Building, 207

"Recuerdo" (Millay), 145

Red Badge of Courage, The (S. Crane), 103, 104

Redburn (Melville), 22

Red Ribbon on a White Horse (Yezierska), 100, 101

Reed, John, 136, 138

"Returning Soldiers" (Du Bois), 170

Revere, Massachusetts, 87

Revolutionary War, U.S., 5

Reynolds, Quentin, 211

Rich, Frank, 225

Rieff, David, 282

Riis, Jacob, 44–45, 83, 95, 101–2, 120

Riordon, William L., 84, 109–10

"Rip Van Winkle" (Irving), 17–18, 156

Rise of David Levinsky, The (Cahan), 97–100

Rise of Silas Lapham, The (Howells), 41, 98

"River, The" (H. Crane), 156

Robber barons and politicos, 34

Robinson, Bill "Bojangles," 170

Rockefeller Center, 207, 250, 267, 277

Rodgers, Richard, 158

Rodriguez, Abraham, Jr., 188–89

Roebling, John Augustus, 155

Roebling, Washington, 155

Rogers, J. A., 175

Rolling Stone (O. Henry journal), 92

Romantic Egotist, The (F. S. Fitzgerald), 124

Roosevelt, Franklin D., 149, 235

Roosevelt, Theodore, 35, 101

Rosamond, J., 111

Rosenberg, Harold, 254

Rosenberg, Julius and Ethel, 253, 278

Rosenfeld, Paul, 121–22, 149

Ross, Harold, 123, 158–59, 265

Roth, Henry, 207, 212–13

"Rouge's Gallery" (McCarthy), 224

"Round of Visits, A" (H. James), 64, 66–67

Rum politics, 102

Runyon, Damon, 208, 225–26, 237

Russell, Lillian, 128

Russell, Pee Wee, xii

Rutgers University, 253

Rybezynski, Witold, xiv

Sacco-Vanzetti case, 138

Sadlier, James, 106

Sadlier, Mary Anne, 84, 106–7

"Sailing to Byzantium" (Yeats), 252

St. John's Chapel, 148

St. Lawrence (ship), 22

St. Patrick's Cathedral, 85, 105, 125, 267

Salinger, J. D., 234, 265, 276–77, 279

Salmagundi; or, The Whim-Whams and Opinions of Launcelot Langstaff, Esq. & Others (Irving), 14–15

Salome of the Tenements (Yezierska), 100

Sams in a Dry Season (I. Gold), 287–88

San Remo, 274

Sante, Luc, 84

Schama, Simon, 227

Schnellock, Emil, 219

Schulman, Sarah, 300, 304–6

Schultz, Arthur Flegenheimer "Dutch," 123

Schuyler, James, 271

Schwartz, Delmore, 249, 251, 252, 253, 257

Schwartz, Lynne Sharon, 233, 234–36, 279

Scott, Sir Walter, 17

Scott, Winfield, 30

Scribner's *see* Charles Scribner's Sons publishers

Scribner's Magazine, 69, 72, 218

Scully, Vincent, 58

"Search through the Streets of the City" (Shaw), 244–45

"Season of Divorce, The" (Cheever), 242–43

Secession, 153

Seize the Day (Bellow), 258–59

Selby, Hugh, Jr., 294

Self-Consciousness: Memoirs (Updike), 266–67

Seven Arts (McKay), 178

Shahn, Ben, 206

Shaw, Irwin, 233, 243–45

Shawn, William, editorship of *New Yorker*, 158, 233, 265, 289

Sherwood, Robert, 159

Shuffle Along (musical), 166, 178

Sick Friends (I. Gold), 287

Sinclair, Upton, 86

Singer, I. J., 95

Singer, Isaac Bashevis, 95, 233, 255, 260–61

Sister Carrie (Dreiser), 116, 117, 118–19, 128, 221

"Situation in American Writing, The" (symposium), 248

Sketch Book, The (Irving), 17

Sketches from Life (Mumford), 284

"Slaves on the Block" (Hughes), 186

Slesin, Aviva, 159

"Slob Murphy" (Sullivan), 107–8

Small Boy and Others, A (H. James), 49, 50

Smith, Alfred Emanuel, 108, 109, 149

Smith, Bessie, 164

Smith, Betty, 233, 236

Smith, Elihu Hubbard, 3

Smith, Marguerite and L. G., xiii

Smith, Sidney, 14

Smith College, 277–78

Snow Scene in Brooklyn (Guy), 27

Socialism, 48, 250

"Song of Myself" (Whitman), 27, 137

"Sonny's Blues" (J. Baldwin), 203

Sorel, Edward, 290

Southern Review, 224

Spanish writers, 207, 210; Latin-American writers, 188–89, 288–89

Specimen Days (Whitman), 26, 30

Spencer, Anne, 173

Spencer, Herbert, 108–9, 117

Spidertown (Rodriguez), 188–89

Sport of the Gods, The (Dunbar), 167–69, 187

"Spunk" (Hurston), 175

Stalin, Joseph, 223, 225, 254

Stamford, Connecticut, 146

Star Shines over Mt. Morris Park, A (Roth), 213

Starting Out in the Thirties (Kazin), 249

Staten Island, New York, 86

Staten Island Ferry, 207

Statue of Liberty, xv, 197

Steendam, Jacob, 3

"Steeple-Jack, The" (Moore), 161

Steinbeck, John, 206, 208, 307

Steinem, Gloria, 264

"Steps of the Pentagon" (Mailer), 304

Stewart, A. T., 108

Stewart, Donald Ogden, 159

Stieglitz, Alfred, 148

Stock market crash of 1929, 132; Great Depression and the, 206–9, 227

Stories (Cheever), 240–41

Stowe, Harriet Beecher, 168

Street, The (Petry), 187, 188, 190

Street gangs, 7–8, 28, 37, 294

Streets of Night (J. Dos Passos), 136

Strictly Business (O. Henry), 94

Strong, George Templeton, 8–9, 21; diary of New York society, 36–39

Student and Schoolmate, 88

Studies in Classic American Literature (Lawrence), 29–30

Studs Lonigan (Farrell), 294

Sturgis, Jonathan, 42–43

Stuyvesant, Peter, 3, 17

Styron, William, 304

Sullivan, James W., 84, 107–8

Summer in Williamsburg (Fuchs), 214

"Supermarket in California, A" (Ginsberg), 274

Survey Graphics, 173, 174

Sutton Hotel, 210–11

"Sweatshop school," 95

Sweet Bird of Youth (Williams), xii

Sweet's Catalogue Service, 153

Swift, Jonathan, 15

Synge, John Millington, 113

Table Money (Breslin), 238

Talese, Gay, 304

Tales of Manhattan (Auchincloss), 285

Talking Heads (musical group), 295

"Talk of the Town" section (*New Yorker* magazine), 265, 266, 290

Talleyrand-Périgord, Charles Maurice, 6

"Task of the Negro Womanhood, The" (McDougald), 175

Tate, Alan, 153

Taylor, Bayard, 40

Tenants, The (Malamud), 262

Tenement Tales of New York (Sullivan), 107–8

Terre Haute, Indiana, 115

Tetractys Club, 21

Textures of Irish America (McCaffrey), 239

Thayer, William Roscoe, 72–73

Their Eyes Were Watching God (Hurston), 175–76

Their Wedding Journey (Howells), 40–41, 43, 44

There Is Confusion (Fauset), 172

This Side of Paradise (F. S. Fitzgerald), 125–26, 132

Thoreau, Henry David, 24, 49

Three Soldiers (J. Dos Passos), 136

Through the Eye of the Needle (Howells), 47

Thurber, James, 158, 159

Thurman, Wallace, 165, 176, 182–84

Time, 123, 249, 250

Time-Life Building, 250, 251

"Time of Her Time, The" (Mailer), 264

Tocqueville, Alexis de, 2, 9–10, 13

Tomorrow Will Be Better (Betty Smith), 236

Toomer, Jean, 173, 176–77

To the Finland Station (Wilson), 150

Touchstone, The (Wharton), 71

Tower Building, 85

Town House (Cheever), 242

Trachtenberg, Alan, xiv, 36; on Alger hero, 88; on Central Park, 38; on Hart Crane, 157

Traveler from Altruria, A (Howells), 47, 95

Treaty of Paris, 5

Tree Grows in Brooklyn, A (Betty Smith), 236

Trillin, Calvin, 281

Trilling, Diana, 245, 255

Trilling, Lionel, 274; New York intellectuals and, 233, 245, 248–49, 255

Trinity Chapel, 69

Trinity Church, 58

Trollope, Anthony, 2, 9; visit to New York City, 12–13

"Tropics in New York, The" (McKay), 179

Trotsky, Leon, 223, 225, 246, 254

Truants, The (Barrett), 252

"True Account of Talking to the Sun at Fire Island, A" (F. O'Hara), 271

Trylon and the Perisphere, 207, 227, 228

"Tunnel, The" (H. Crane), 157

Turnbull, Andrew, 128

Turn, Magic Wheel (D. Powell), 268

Tuskegee Institute, 178, 194

Tweed, William W. "Boss," 108, 301

"Two Morning Monologues" (Bellow), 257

Typee (Melville), 22

Uhry, Alfred, 308

Ulysses (Joyce), 142, 156, 213

"Under the Bamboo Tree" (Cole and the Johnson Brothers), 111

Union Square (Halper), 214

United Nations, 231

United States in 1800, The (H. Adams), 6, 7

United States Magazine and Democratic Review (O'Sullivan), 20

Universal Negro Improvement Association, 164

University of Texas, 303

Unterecker, John, 153

Updike, John: on Wharton, 74; on Wilson, 152; writings for the *New Yorker*, 233, 265–66, 267

"Urban Convalescence, An" (Merrill), 275

Urban League, 164, 181

U.S.A. (J. Dos Passos), 137, 139, 143

Utopian fiction, 46–47

Valley of Decision, The (Wharton), 70

Vanderbilt, Cornelius, 85

Vanderbilt, Henry, 85

Vanderbilt, Kermit, 44

Van Doren, Carl, 173

Vanity Fair, 123, 144, 160, 186, 290

Van Vechten, Carl, 166, 180, 183, 186

"Van Winkle" (H. Crane), 156

Variety, 206

Veblen, Thorstein, 136

Vendler, Helen, 161, 271

Verrazano, Giovanni da, 3

Victim, The (Bellow), 257–58, 259

Vidal, Gore, 268

Village Voice essays, Mailer's, 263

Virginia, 7, 26

Vogue, 160, 273

Voyager: A Life of Hart Crane (Unterecker), 153

Wagner, Robert F., Jr., 232

Waiting for Lefty (Odets), 215–16

Wakefield, Dan, xiii, 234, 272–73, 279

Waldorf-Astoria Hotel, 63, 85, 99

Walker, James John "Jimmy," 108, 109, 149

Walker in the City, A (Kazin), 249, 252

"Walking New York Part II" (Ginsberg), 274

Waller, Thomas Wright "Fats," 164

Wall Street: fire, 36–37; Great Depression and the Wall Street Crash, 206–9, 227

Wanderers, The (Price), 294

Ward, Geoff, 271

Warren, Robert Penn, 224

Washington, Booker T., 168, 196

Washington, George, 5

Washington, Mary Helen, 187, 188, 190

Washington Square (H. James), 35, 51–53, 64

Washington Square College, 270

Washington Square Park, 254

Waste Land, The (Eliot), 129, 142, 154, 155, 161

Waterworks, The (Doctorow), 227, 300, 301–3

Ways of White Folks, The (Hughes), 186

Weary Blues, The (Hughes), 185, 186

Weatherby, W. J., 204

Web and the Rock, The (Wolfe), 218

Welles, Orson, 200

Wells, H. G., 122–23

West, Nathaniel, 207, 210–11

Wharton, Edith, 34–35, 43, 227; English language and, 106; Henry James and, 51, 57, 70–71; literary presence in New York, 67–82, 85, 86

Wharton, Edward, 69

Wheatley, Phillis, 181

Whistler, James McNeill, 43, 47

White, E. B., writings for the *New Yorker*, 159, 233, 265, 266

White, Morton and Lucia, 51

"White City, The" (McKay), 180–81

"White Negro, The" (Mailer), 263

Whitman, Walt, 2, 10; Bender on, 20; Conrad on, 17; Hart Crane and, 152–53, 157, 158; Dos Passos and, 137–38; Ginsberg and, 274; Hardwick and, 284; Howells and, 39–40; literary presence in New York, xv, 25–32, 103; Moore

and, 161; Frank O'Hara and, 270, 271;
Quinn and, 301; Strong and, 38; tribute
to, 308; Young America literary group
and, 21
Whitney Museum of American Art, 233
Whittier, John Greenleaf, 20
Wilbur, Richard, 278
Williams, Ted, xii
Williams, William Carlos, 271
Willy Burke; or, The Irish Orphan in America
(M. A. Sadlier), 107
Wilson, Edmund: Dos Passos and, 143;
on F. S. Fitzgerald, 125; on Greenwich
Village, 144; marriage to McCarthy,
223–24; Lionel Trilling and, 248; liter-
ary presence in New York, 145–52;
writings for the *New Yorker*, 265
Wilson, Woodrow, 165
Winthrop, John, 88
Wolcott, Alexander, 124
Wolfe, Thomas, literary presence in New
York, 207, 216–19, 220, 270, 290–93
Wolff, Cynthia Griffin, 69, 72, 79
Women: black women writers, 187–93;
depiction of African-American, 175–
76, 177–78; depiction of Jewish, 100–
101
Women of Brewster Place, The (Naylor),
190–91
Woolcott, Alexander, 158, 159
Wooley, Monty, 159

"Words for Hart Crane" (Lowell), 158
Wordsworth, William, 18
Works Progress Administration, 166
World of Chance, The (Howells), 40
World of Our Fathers (Howe), 95, 201, 247
World's Fair (Doctorow), 227–30
World War I (the Great War), 63, 67, 77,
82, 105, 136, 164
World War II, 207, 227, 231
World without End, Amen (Breslin), 237–38
Wright, Frank Lloyd, 233, 282
Wright, Orville and Wilbur, 156
Wright, Richard, 187, 193, 195
Writers' Guild of America, 308

Yankee Doodle Dandy (film), 105
Yankee Stadium, xii, 123
Yeats, William Butler, 209, 252
Yekl: A Tale of New York (Cahan), 95, 96–
97
Yezierska, Anzia, 83, 95, 100–101, 120
Yiddish poets, 95
Yiddish theater, 60–61, 95
You Can't Go Home Again (Wolfe), 218–19
Young America literary group, 20–21
"You're a Grand Old Flag" (Cohan), 105

Zabar's, xii
Zangwill, Israel, 61, 97
Zenger, Peter, 4
Zimmer, Don, 161–62